Ancient Peoples and Places

PERU

General Editor

DR GLYN DANIEL

DR GLYN DANIEL *Ancient Peoples and Places*

PERU

G. H. S. Bushnell
M.A., Ph.D.

71 PHOTOGRAPHS
11 LINE DRAWINGS
AND A MAP

London

THAMES AND HUDSON

THIS IS VOLUME ONE IN THE SERIES
ANCIENT PEOPLES AND PLACES

CONTENTS

ILLUSTRATIONS

IN THE DECADE following the end of the Second World War there has been a considerable and growing interest in archaeology, particularly in prehistoric and protohistoric archaeology, which deals with the ancient peoples and places of the world. There are now in English many books introducing the aims and methods of archaeology, and describing the broad general conclusions of prehistory, but there is a great need for small books which take a limited area or a single people and set forth the current state of knowledge about it in a way attractive to the non-specialist archaeologist as well as the ordinary interested reader. It is to fill this gap that we have designed this series: in each book we intend, with the aid of the written word and numerous illustrations, to bring to life a specific people or place in the ancient world.

This book on Peru, by Dr. Geoffrey Bushnell, the Curator of the Cambridge University Musuem of Archaeology and Ethnology, is the first volume in the series. It will be followed shortly by *The Scythians,* by Tamara Talbot Rice, which will contain much material hitherto unpublished in English. Books in active preparation range over the ancient countries and nations of the world; from the Celts and Phoenicians and the Vikings to Sicily, Wales and Wessex. We hope also to include sometimes books dealing with quite small areas of exceptional interest such as the great Boyne cemetery in Ireland which contains New Grange and Dowth, or the north Wessex area which has such important and remarkable monuments as Windmill Hill, Silbury Hill and Avebury.

It is not intended that these volumes should as a series comprehend all the ancient past in time and space—that would surely be impossible. Rather we hope that they should deal with peoples and places of general interest when experts are available ready and willing to embark on the difficult and often thankless task of being popular without being pompous or patronizing. Dr. Bushnell sounds the right note. He brings to his subject a wealth of learning and presents it in a clear and palatable form. In this way we hope to achieve our aim—to bring the ancient peoples and places of the world—or at least some of them—within the comprehension of everyone.

GLYN DANIEL

Foreword

OUR KNOWLEDGE of Ancient Peru has increased very rapidly in recent years, and most of this new information is set out in papers and handbooks published by universities, museums and scientific institutions in the United States, or privately circulated in Peru. Most of these publications are not available in this country, except in a few specialized libraries, and not all of them are even to be found there. P. A. Means published a general work called *Ancient Civilizations of the Andes* in the United States in 1931, but the latest book to be published in Great Britain was T. A. Joyce's admirable *South American Archaeology*, which appeared in 1912. Both contain much that is worth reading, but in the nature of things they are very much out of date. There is a most excellent general account of Peruvian archaeology in *Andean Culture History* by Bennett and Bird, to which I am greatly indebted, but it was published just before the first results of radiocarbon dating became available. Being a museum handbook, it has not a wide circulation, even in the United States. To all of these sources, to the study of museum collections in Great Britain, France and the United States, and to visits to Peru in 1938 and 1951, I owe the information presented in this book.

See *Bibliography*

Pottery and other objects from the middle and later parts of the archaeological succession are abundant in museums in Great Britain and elsewhere, and photographs for illustration are easily obtained, but material from the early cultures, which were unknown until a few years ago, is very rare outside Peru. For this reason, I am particularly grateful to my friend Señor Rafael Larco Hoyle, of Lima and the Hacienda Chiclin, near Trujillo, for the magnificent photographs of Cupisnique, Salinar, Virú (Gallinazo) and other pottery, which add distinction to our series of plates. The subjects come from his family's private museum at Chiclin, and not only their discovery but also our very knowledge of the cultures to which they belong are due largely to his own work. If it had not been for his kindness, it would not have been possible to illustrate the early periods in anything like an adequate way.

I am also grateful to the University Museum, Philadelphia, Pa. and the Musée de l'Homme, Paris, for permission to reproduce photographs taken from material or negatives in their possession. To Mr. Adrian Digby, Keeper of the Department of Ethnography, British Museum, I am much indebted for help in connexion with the photography of objects in the Department.

Dr. Irving Rouse of Yale University has kindly obtained permission for me to reproduce the Chavín carving shown in Figure 4, and Dr. J. H. Rowe of the University of California has been good enough to assure me that the drawing of Interlocking vessels forming Figure 10 may be reproduced.

I would like to express my gratitude to Mrs. Glyn Daniel for the personal interest she took in drawing many of the figures and the map.

My thanks are also due to Mr. L. P. Morley, the photographer of the Cambridge University Museum of Archaeology and Ethnology, for the skill and patience which he has expended on many subjects from that Museum.

It is fitting to end this introduction with a tribute to the memory of Wendell C. Bennett. He excavated in many different parts of Peru and Bolivia, and his knowledge, freely given to the world, was both wide and deep. His many friends will long remember a wise counsellor and a most kindly and cheerful companion.

G. H. S. B.

Chapter I

Introduction

W HAT WE MEAN by Ancient Peru is not quite the same geographically as the modern state of Peru, although the boundaries approximate to one another in some directions. Highland Bolivia is included in it, but the greater part of the lowland forest area east of the Andes, which now falls within its frontiers, is not. As so defined, Ancient Peru was a cultural area, the whole of which shared a common tradition of long duration, and it is often called by archaeologists the Central Andes.

There can be few regions in the world where a short journey brings the traveller into such variations in climate and topography as Peru. On the west is the coastal plain, one of the great deserts of the world, where there are miles of scorched rocks and crescent-shaped sand dunes. Life would be impossible here were it not for the river valleys which cross it from east to west, where the ancient peoples irrigated an area greater than their successors ever did until quite recent times. To the traveller who flies over the coast, these valleys appear as a succession of narrow green belts amid great stretches of yellow and brown; they vary greatly in size though the larger ones are generally in the north. A short distance inland rise the foothills of the Andes, range upon range, and far above, on a clear day, may be seen one or other of the snow-capped peaks of the Western Cordillera. Many of the valleys are household words in Peruvian archaeology, among them being Chicama, Moche and Virú in the north, Chancay in the centre, and Chincha, Ica and Nazca in the south. In some cases, the valleys are separated, not only by desert strips, but also by rocky spurs, and the result is that the culture of each developed to some extent in isolation, though as time went on some tribes were able to subjugate their neighbours and add valley to valley,

Plate 3

13

particularly in the north, where the larger size of the valleys allowed powerful units to develop. It is important to realize that the water supply of a valley all came from a single source, the river, and that this, of necessity, imposed a high degree of unity on the inhabitants as soon as the population increased beyond the smallest scatter. As irrigation developed, it became necessary to organize the people, not only to construct and maintain the ditches but also to see that the water was fairly distributed. The consequence was, in several instances, the emergence of a highly centralized type of state. Although the topographical contrast between mountains and coastal plain is very great, the difference presented, in many cases, less of an obstacle to cultural diffusion than the deserts and rocks of the coast, although the peoples themselves must generally have retained their permanent domicile near the altitude at which they were born.

The mountain region, which forms the backbone of the area, is highly diversified. Below the high ranges, with their snow-capped peaks, are passes, high plains or *punas,* basins, and numerous river valleys, most of them steep and narrow. Small numbers of people can live in many places in the valleys, but there are only six areas which could support large groups in ancient times. These are, from north to south, the Cajamarca Basin, the Callejón de Huaylas, which is the basin that feeds the Santa River Valley, parts of the Mantaro River Valley, the Cuzco Basin and adjacent valleys, the high plains to the north-west of Lake Titicaca and the Bolivian Plateau to the south-east of it. The punas are generally covered with grass, and although they lie at such a height that, when the sun is off them, the cold chills the marrow of anyone accustomed to a lower level, they form ideal grazing grounds for the herds of llamas and alpacas which are such a valuable asset to the inhabitants.

The water supply presents a contrast to that of the coast. There are regular rains and multiple sources of supply are

Plate 2

14

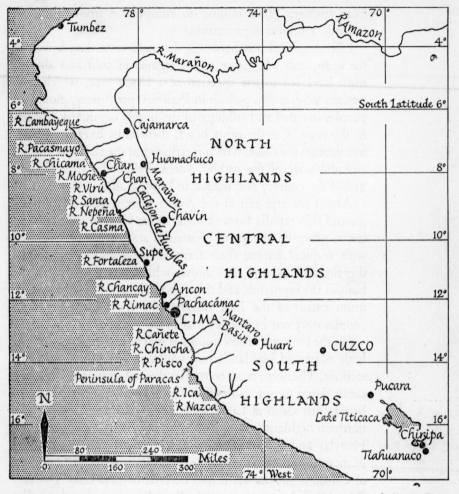

Fig. 1. Map of Ancient Peru.

available in each area. There is no exclusive dependence on
irrigation, although some of the terraces, which were formed on
the steep hillsides in order to extend the limited area available
for cultivation, were watered by stone-lined channels leading

Plate 71

15

from springs. There is thus no compulsion from this cause towards a unified organization.

Life in general was harder in the mountains than it was on the coast, and adaptation to the rigours of cold and altitude must have led to the selection of a hardy race, which may explain why, at two periods in Peruvian pre-history, mountain peoples invaded and subjugated the highly organized dwellers in the coast. On the other hand, there must have been more free time on the coast, which is reflected in the elaborate burials and the scale of the public works, before the Inca Empire united the country and tended to bring it all to one level.

About the area east of the Andes there is little to say. The ground falls rapidly from altitudes of the order of ten thousand feet to generally less than a thousand, and the earth is covered with tropical forests; these form an insuperable bar to the digging-stick type of agriculture, which was the basis of life both in the highlands and the coastal plain. Even at the maximum extent of the Inca Empire, the writ of the highland peoples only ran in a small part of the area.

For the purposes of description, it will be convenient to divide both coast and highlands into northern, central and southern sections. The north coast comprises the valleys from the extreme north down to just south of the Casma Valley, the centre from here to just south of Lima, and the south the remainder. The northern highlands cover the Cajamarca Basin, the Callejón de Huaylas and the intervening area, the centre comprises the Mantaro Basin, and the south extends from the neighbourhood of Cuzco south-eastwards into Bolivia, beyond Lake Titicaca. Parts of all these areas are virtually unknown archaeologically, but perhaps the worst gaps are in the central highlands and the extreme north, both highlands and coast. The most complete succession so far known is in the central part of the north coast, where the Virú Valley has been studied in detail, and a great deal of work has been done in the neighbouring Valley of Chicama.

It is well known that the Spaniards, after their arrival in the New World, found two areas which stood out from the others, namely Mexico and Peru. The difference between these areas and those which surrounded them was mainly political, since the peoples of Central America, Colombia and Ecuador were at much the same technological level as those of Mexico and Peru. Wherever natural conditions permitted, they depended on digging-stick agriculture, they wove, they made pottery, and they knew the same metallurgical processes. It is probable that the Peruvians surpassed all others in the excellence of their weaving, but the metal work of the tribes of parts of Ecuador, Colombia and the Isthmus of Panamá was as good or better than that of their more powerful neighbours. On the other hand, the peoples outside Mexico and Peru consisted mainly of small independent tribes, as for example, the peoples of the Coclé district in Panamá, who were divided into a number of tribes, each under a despotic chief. The chief exception is found in the highland basins round Bogotá in Colombia, where a number of related tribes, the Chibcha, controlled a large area at the time of the Spanish Conquest, but they seem to have fought among themselves a great deal, and in any case it is unlikely that they could have extended their dominion far outside their own highland area even if their progress had not been interrupted by the Europeans. The Valley of Mexico was occupied, in the last few centuries before the arrival of the Spaniards, by a number of related tribes. One of these, the Tenochcas, generally called the Aztecs, of Tenochtitlan on the site of Mexico City, had achieved what must have been a rather uneasy domination over the remainder when the Spaniards arrived, and had subjugated a considerably wider area to the extent of exacting tribute from the inhabitants. The Aztec Empire, as it is sometimes called, did not approach that of the

B

Incas of Peru, in size, cohesion, or thoroughness of organization. The latter, as we shall see, was a true empire with a
pyramidal organization culminating in an absolute hereditary
ruler, the Supreme or Unique Inca, to give him one of his
honorific titles, whereas the Mexican Montezuma, whom the
Spaniards regarded as the Emperor, was one of two almost
equal high chiefs, who were chosen by the tribal council, in
which the ultimate authority rested. The Aztec state was,
nevertheless, highly organized, their society showed a high
degree of specialization, and in Tenochtitlan, their capital,
they had an urban centre of great splendour.

Such in brief outline was the picture in the sixteenth century,
but, if we look back at earlier times, the same areas were always
in advance of their neighbours. The civilized area of Mexico
comprised, it is true, much more than the Valley of Mexico,
since it included pretty well the whole of the south and south-
east of the country and much of Guatemala and Honduras.
Both of the nuclear areas, as Peru and Mexico are sometimes
called, have, indeed, been more fully explored than the neighbouring ones, but this is largely due to the fact that they
attracted exploration because their archaeological remains were
more spectacular than those of other areas. It cannot be claimed
that much of America south of the Rio Grande has yet been
explored as fully as it deserves, nevertheless it is clear that future
discoveries can never challenge the pre-eminence of Mexico
and Peru.

THE HISTORY OF EXPLORATION IN PERU

Much of what we know about the Incas and the tribes under
them is derived from written sources, since some Spanish
writers and some like the Inca Garcilazo de la Vega, who were

of mixed Inca and Spanish blood, knew their civilization either at first hand or from their parents. The study of these writings, attempts to reconcile contradictions between them, and observation of the spectacular architectural remains of Inca times at Cuzco and elsewhere, have provided material for many publications, including Prescott's *History of the Conquest of Peru* and Sir Clements Markham's *Incas of Peru,* both of which are full of valuable information though deceptive in some respects.

It is not the object of this work to give a full account of Inca civilization, for which reference can be made to other sources, particularly J. H. Rowe's account in the *Handbook of the South American Indians (see* Bibliography, p.141).

Something has long been known of pre-Inca cultures from the numerous pots, pieces of fine textiles, and objects of gold, copper, wood and stone, which have been looted from the coastal graves and found their way into museums, but in view of the lack of written records of these earlier periods, the building up of any sort of chronology had to await the beginning of serious archaeology. This started when Max Uhle, the German archaeologist and anthropologist, began work in the nineties of the last century, and carried on a series of excavations during the next twenty years, first for the University of Pennsylvania, then, under the patronage of Mrs. Phoebe Hearst, for the University of California, and finally for the Peruvian Government. Much of his work was never published by him, but with the aid of his collections and notes at the University of California, A. L. Kroeber and others produced a masterly series of publications on his collections from various sites. Kroeber himself followed this up by an expedition to Peru in 1925 and 1926, under the auspices of what was then the Field Museum at Chicago, which resulted in several additions to our knowledge of various parts of the coast, and at the same time the Ecuadorian archaeologist, Jacinto Jijón y Caamaño, worked in the neighbourhood of Lima. S. K. Lothrop, whose special contribution to Peruvian archaeology is in the field of metallurgy, was also working there in 1925.

By this time, largely owing to Uhle's work, we knew that in all parts of the coast there were comparatively old cultures, particularly Proto-Chimú, now called Mochica, in the north and Nazca in the south, which were obliterated by the spread of a highland culture with its centre apparently at Tiahuanaco, on the Bolivian side of Lake Titicaca. Later, local cultures emerged again on the coast, the Chimú in the north having some features in common with its Mochica predecessor but the others distinct from those which went before. These were soon submerged in their turn by the spread of the Incas. Of the earlier part of the succession, all that was known was the existence of shell middens near Ancón, in the central coast, which Uhle believed to be the dwellings of primitive cannibalistic fisher folk, but which have since been recognized to belong to the Chavín horizon. At this time it was also realized that wide areas were united by the art styles, shown chiefly in pottery and textiles, of Tiahuanaco and the Incas, and they were called Horizon Styles.

Beginning as early as 1913, Julio C. Tello, the doyen of Peruvian archaeologists, ranged far and wide over Peru, exploring the most inaccessible places and making large collections. This work he continued until his death in 1947, but although he published several general schemes of development of the Peruvian Cultures, he never gave the detailed evidence on which they were based to the world, and it is to be feared that much information died with him. Perhaps his chief contribution to archaeology, and it is a very great one, is his recognition of the importance and early date of the Chavín Culture, of which the type site is a great temple at Chavín in the northern highlands. For some years he and Uhle engaged in a controversy about the origin of the Peruvian Cultures, Uhle maintaining that all the main ones came from Central America by sea, while Tello was of the opinion that they all took their origin in the Peruvian Andes. The final answer has yet to be determined, but recent work has revealed surprisingly close relationships between Chavín and Central America, though many of Uhle's contentions will not bear critical examination.

In 1934 began a period of great activity with Wendell C. Bennett's expedition to Tiahuanaco, the first of a most fruitful series covering much of Peru and highland Bolivia. His work continued at intervals until shortly before his premature death in 1953, at about the time when the results of his last expedition to Huari in the Mantaro Basin were ready to go to press. In 1940 and 1941 a Columbia University expedition under Duncan Strong, one of Kroeber's associates in his earlier work, worked in the Central Coast, and among other sites investigated the great ruins at Pachacámac, where Uhle had worked before. After Strong had returned home, Gordon R. Willey continued the work of the expedition with excavations on Uhle's 'primitive' sites at Ancón and Supe, thereby increasing our knowledge of the Chavín horizon on the Central Coast.

In the meantime, Rafael Larco Hoyle and his family were working quietly in and around their estates in the Chicama Valley in the north coast. Among his discoveries in this and the neighbouring valleys is a representative of the Chavín horizon, besides two subsequent pre-Mochica periods, and he distinguished five successive stages in the Mochica itself. A number of useful publications bear witness to these and other discoveries, and not least among the family's contributions to knowledge are their magnificent collections housed in the Museo Rafael Larco Herrera on their hacienda at Chiclín, where many archaeologists and interested visitors have enjoyed their generous hospitality.

Immediately after the war of 1939 to 1945, a number of United States institutions, with the collaboration of the

Peruvian Instituto de Estudios Etnológicos under Dr. Luis E. Valcárcel and Dr. Jorge C. Muelle, launched the Virú Valley project, in which it was planned to survey the archaeology, human geography and ethnology of a self-contained area of manageable dimensions from the earliest time to the present day. The scheme was successfully carried through and most of the results have been published by the institutions concerned, with the consequence that we now have a complete, well attested sequence in one area, although we yet have much to learn about the total development of the cultures represented. Among those who took part were Bennett, Willey and Strong, whose earlier work has already been mentioned, Junius Bird, Clifford Evans, Donald Collier, and James A. Ford. At much the same time, John Rowe, of California, spent some years in Cuzco, where he investigated the chronology of the Inca period both in the library and in the field, besides excavating the first pre-Inca remains to be found in the region. More recent work includes another Columbia expedition under Strong, this time to the south coast, which has produced some important data, of which only a summary has yet been published, and an investigation by Henri Reichlen, of Paris, and his wife, of the region round Cajamarca in the northern Andes.

In spite of all that has been done, the general picture of Peruvian archaeology is still full of gaps, large areas have barely been touched, and there is still plenty of work to do.

DATING AND CHRONOLOGY

As a result of the Virú Valley work and that which went before it, it has become possible to formulate a series of developmental stages which, as a working hypothesis, have been applied to the whole Central Andean area, enabling us to

See *Bibliography*, Bennett, 1948

think of it as a unit and greatly clarifying description. This scheme was first put forward at a conference held at the Larcos' museum at Chiclín in 1946, and further defined at one held in New York in the following year. An outline of the scheme will be given at this point, in order to clarify what follows, and further details will accompany later chapters.

The earliest inhabitants of Peru were a hunting people, generally called the Early Hunters. They were succeeded by the Early Farmers, a sedentary people whose dwelling sites are so far known only on the coast, where they lived by fishing, gathering of wild plants, and small-scale agriculture. After this began the Formative Period, divided into two stages, the first a theocratic stage to which the name Cultist is sometimes given, and the second characterized by diversity of development in different areas and by the introduction of new technical processes, called the Experimenter Period. According to our present knowledge, the Cultist Period is synonymous with the Chavín horizon, a name which will recur constantly in the following pages. After the Formative comes the Classic Period, characterized by the complete mastery of practically all the pre-Columbian crafts and technological processes, and the existence of some flourishing states, whence it is sometimes called the Mastercraftsman or Florescent Period. The Mochica and Nazca cultures, already mentioned, are among those assigned to this stage. The term Classic was first applied in the New World to a similar stage in Middle America, but its exact equivalence in time and in character to the Peruvian Classic is in some doubt. The post-Classic follows; it is a time when there were few technological developments, but a good deal of political evolution. It has three divisions; in the first, the highland culture associated with the name of Tiahuanaco spread over most of the coast, a movement probably accompanied by military force, and for this reason it is called the Expansionist Period. Then came the City Builder Period, associated, at any

DATE	TITLE OF PERIOD		Coast		
			NORTH	CENTRAL	SOUTH
1500	POST CLASSIC	Imperialist	Inca	Inca	Inca
1000		City Builder	Chimu	Cuismancu	Chincha
		Expansionist	Coast Tiahuanaco	Coast Tiahuanaco	Coast Tiahuanaco
500					
	CLASSIC	Mastercraftsman or Florescent	Mochica	Interlocking	Nazca
A.D.					
B.C.		Experimenter	Gallinazo or Virú	Negative	Necropolis
500	FORMATIVE	Salinar or Puerto Moorin		White-on-Red	Cavernas
		Cultist	Cupisnique	Coast Chavín	
1000					
1500					
	EARLY FARMERS		Early Farmers		Early Farmers
2000					
2500					
3000	EARLY HUNTERS ? Between 3000 and 7000 B.C.				
7000					

24

Fig. 2. Chronological Ch

Highlands

FAR NORTH	NORTH	CENTRAL	SOUTH (Cuzco)	(Titicaca)	
Inca	Inca	Inca	Inca	Inca	1500
Huamachuco			Early Inca	Local cultures. Chullpa	
Tiahuanacoid (Cajamarca)	Local Tiahuanaco		Local Pottery Styles	Decadent Tiahuanaco	1000
		Huari	Tiahuanaco		500
Cursive (Cajamarca)	Recuay			Classic Tiahuanaco. Pucara	
					A.D.
				Early Tiahuanaco	B.C.
Chavinoid (Cajamarca)	White-on-Red		Chanapata	Chiripa	500
	Chavín				1000
					1500
					2000
					2500
					3000

Peruvian Cultures.

rate in the coast, with the building of great urban centres, many of them associated with the Chimú Culture, already men- tioned. Finally came the Imperialist Period, the time of the spread of the great Inca Empire.

Until a few years ago, the only dates available for Peruvian archaeology were some for the Inca Period, derived from study of writings at the time of the Spanish Conquest. For the earlier periods there was nothing but intelligent guesswork. The next step was taken by Junius Bird who, in the course of his work on the Virú Valley project, made some estimates of the rate of accumulation of middens and natural deposits, which gave dates of about 3000 B.C. for the beginnings of agriculture and over 1000 B.C. for the introduction of pottery. Subsequent developments have shown that these are of the right order of magnitude. For the later periods, James A. Ford made esti- mates based on the relative thicknesses of deposit in the Virú Valley, but these suggest the telescoping of the latter part of the succession to what many archaeologists consider an un- reasonable extent. An attempt has also been made to date some Mochica artifacts found buried in the guano on various islands off the coast in the last century, using estimates of the rate of accumulation of the guano and the depths at which the objects were found, but the figures were based on nineteenth century records since the guano was long since quarried away, so there is some doubt about the reliability of the evidence. A date in the ninth century A.D. was indicated for certain Mochica artifacts.

After this came radiocarbon dating, which has put the earlier part of the sequence on a much firmer footing. At the XXIX International Congress of Americanists in New York in 1949, Dr. W. F. Libby of Chicago announced the first date to be measured for the American continent, namely, about 800 B.C. for the beginning of the Chavín Period on the coast. Dates which have since been obtained are a good series for the

See *Bibliography*, Johnson, 1951

26

Early Farmer deposits in the Chicama Valley, with a few for the Mochica and earlier periods in the same region, and a very few for the south coast. No post-Mochica dates have been measured. At the other end of the scale, Rowe's studies of post-Conquest records strongly support the date of A.D. 1438 for the beginning of the Inca expansion.

In sum, the early part of the succession, the Early Farmers and the beginning of the Chavín Period, is soundly dated and the dates are generally accepted. The same is true of the Inca expansion. The situation for the intermediate periods is not so satisfactory, since the radiocarbon dates are few and surprisingly early, so that their acceptance makes it necessary to spread the latter part of the succession over an unexpectedly long time. They conflict seriously with Ford's estimates for the Virú Valley. This is best illustrated by the Mochica Period; radiocarbon indicates that it is unlikely to have ended in the Virú Valley after about A.D. 300, or 500 at the latest, whereas Ford puts it as late as A.D. 1150. Some archaeologists find both these extremes difficult to accept and compromises have been suggested, but pending further measurements, I propose to accept the radiocarbon dates with due reservations, and place the Mochica Period vaguely in the first half of the first millenium A.D., though it may have begun up to three centuries earlier. The great need at present is for more measurements, not more guesses. Most of our dates so far come from the north coast, where we also have the most complete succession, but other areas can be correlated with it with the aid of horizon styles and general development.

Before going on to deal in detail with the growth of the Central Andean civilizations, a few words must be said about their nature and the characteristics which are shared by the whole area during a long period of time. The essential pattern took shape in the Formative Period, but its full flowering came later.

In the first place all were based on intensive agriculture, with no more elaborate tools than the digging-stick, clod-breaker and hoe. Many plants were cultivated, the chief being maize, which gives good crops up to a height of about 12,000 feet, but only ripens in a few places above. At greater altitudes its place is taken by another grain called quinoa, which is hardier. The potato is a native of the area, and assumed a great impor-tance throughout the highlands. Irrigation was an essential feature, and it was accompanied in the highlands by terracing, which extended the cultivable area and resisted erosion. Fer-tilizers were used, namely bird guano and small fish heads in the coast, and llama or human dung in the highlands. Food was preserved by drying or freezing, a well-known example being the dehydration of potatoes by repeated exposure to frost and sun, sometimes followed by pressing, which produces an insipid substance called chuño; this is still much eaten at the higher altitudes. Dried meat, called charqui, whence the name 'jerked' meat, was prepared by a similar process. The narcotic coca, which was grown in the valleys on the eastern slope of the Andes, was chewed with lime everywhere in the area, and its use on the coast is one of the factors which proves the existence of trading contacts with the highlands at an early date.

Plates 2, 58, 63, 70

In the highlands, the herding of llamas and alpacas, the domesticated American cousins of the camel, was second only to agriculture in importance, but they do not live permanently on the coast, although they were often taken there and their skeletons are commonly found in archaeological deposits. The alpacas were prized particularly for their wool, and the llamas were used as pack animals (although they will carry little more than 100 lb), their meat was eaten, and their hair was sometimes used for coarse textiles. The dog and the cavy, or guineapig, were the only other domestic animals, the latter being the chief source of meat in Inca times. Hunting was always subsidiary, and organized hunts became an upperclass occupation in later times, but there is evidence for the hunting of deer, pumas and foxes, and the wild representatives of the llama family, the guanacos and vicuñas.

The basic social unit was a village group consisting of a number of related families under a headman, owning their lands in common, to which the Quechua name of *ayllu* was applied when the Inca conquest spread that language outside the Cuzco area. On this were superimposed complex types of society, with marked distinctions of class and function.

An important characteristic of all Central Andean peoples was great manual skill associated with very simple apparatus, a feature which they shared with other South and Middle American peoples. Their weaving was unsurpassed and is particularly characteristic of the area; they applied most of the known techniques, using both cotton and wool, with great dexterity on a simple backstrap loom. Pottery was skilfully modelled and painted, producing vessels of great artistic merit, but the potter's wheel was unknown. Gold, silver, copper and their alloys were worked by a variety of processes, and the production and working of bronze were finally mastered. Among the useful metals, the most obvious absentee was iron, which was unknown anywhere in America, except for rare instances derived from meteors. Many other materials such as wood, basketry and stone were skilfully worked, and were used, where appropriate, on a large scale for massive building as well as for the smallest ornaments. As an example, it is only

Plates 1, 69–71 necessary to cite the fine masonry of the Incas, with stones between which a knife blade cannot be inserted. It appears that everyday products, such as domestic pottery and textiles, were made by the members of each family, but that the finer ceremonial goods, which, so far as our evidence goes, were generally made to be buried with the dead, were the work of specialists.

The later cultures of Peru, those of the Incas and their immediate predecessors, possessed most of the features that are regarded as the hallmarks of a civilized community in the Old World, particularly fully efficient food production, urban centres, a formal political state, public works, and classes and hierarchies. The advanced cultures of the Mastercraftsman Period possessed most of these features, with the apparent exception of urban centres, though recent work in the Nazca area seems to have revealed a considerable city. On the other hand, all the New World cultures lacked certain features which accompanied the growth of civilization in the Old. Iron and the potter's wheel have already been mentioned, and to these are to be added any sort of draught animal and wheeled transport. Above all, Peru lacked written records, even the picturewriting of Middle America, and although there must have been strong oral traditions, supplemented by mnemonic devices, such as the system of knotted strings called the *quipu* and perhaps others, the catastrophe of the Spanish Conquest must have been a great blow to these traditions. The result is that our knowledge of the intangible features of Inca civilization, literature, laws and so on, is very imperfect, and we are cut off almost completely from those of preInca ones.

Great interest has been aroused in recent years by Heyerdahl's voyage across the Pacific on the KonTiki raft, and by his theory that Peru played a major role in populating Polynesia. It is unquestionable that wooden rafts were in use in ancient Plate 50 times on the Peruvian coast, since centreboards and steering sweeps like those used on the modern balsa rafts of Ecuador and on the Kon-Tiki are found in graves, particularly on the southern part of the coast. It is not known whether the rafts themselves were built of the light balsa wood now used, and it may not have been available before the Incas conquered part of what is now Ecuador. The prevailing opinion is that they were used for coastwise traffic, as the Spaniards observed when they arrived in the region, although Heyerdahl's discovery of potsherds of Peruvian north coastal types on the Galápagos Islands shows that they could travel a considerable distance from the coast. This, however, is a very different matter from colonizing Polynesia, and the theory that the Peruvians did so does not commend itself to the majority of serious students either of Oceania or of Peru.

At no time and in no place has archaeology escaped the attentions of cranks, and Peru is no exception. The idea of Perry that the civilization of ancient Egypt was transplanted lock and stock, with the possible loss of the barrel, to Peru has been largely forgotten in the light of increased knowledge, but the ruins of Tiahuanaco, in the Bolivian highlands, were still provoking the wildest speculations less than a decade ago. This site dates from some time in the first millenium A.D., and can certainly not be appreciably older, but by considering it in isolation from the general development of Peruvian culture, invoking irrelevant considerations of astronomy, and ignoring the most elementary facts of geology, a writer has seriously claimed that it is a quarter of a million years old and that it was overwhelmed by an ocean tide some 14,000 feet high!

Chapter II

The Early Hunters

LITTLE IS KNOWN of the earliest men who lived in Peru, but some light can be thrown on them by giving an outline of early man elsewhere in the American Continent. The first men to arrive in the New World must have come from Asia across the Bering Straits, at a time when all men lived by hunting and gathering wild plants. There were times during the Ice Age when this route was blocked by ice, but there were others when it was clear, although the ice elsewhere still locked up so much water that sea-level was low and the straits either narrower than they are now or quite dry. Large mammals, like mammoth, mastodon and an extinct species of bison, found their way across and down into America, making tracks through the grass-lands which provided them with food. Man in search of meat followed them, and evidence of his presence in the shape of pressure-flaked stone projectile points and other stone tools is found in many parts of the United States, especially the Great Plains, in Mexico and elsewhere. An early type of point called the Folsom has been dated in the United States at about 8000 B.C., but it is known that other types are older, since they have been found in deposits underlying Folsom ones and separated from them by signs of an advance of the ice. One such advance has been dated to a period just before Folsom, but its duration is uncertain, and all that can be said at present is that the pre-Folsom men must have been in America by at least 10,000 B.C. and probably earlier.

Excavations by Junius Bird at the opposite end of the continent, in Southern Patagonia, have shown that man was hunting sloth, horse and guanaco in that region by between 6000 and 7000 B.C., so he must have been in Peru before that. His route into South America could only have been across the

Isthmus of Panamá, whence he could have followed the Cauca or the Magdalena Valley into the Colombian Andes. From here, his most reasonable way southward into Peru was to follow the highlands, since tropical forests on either side in Colombia and Ecuador would be a bar both to him and to the animals which he hunted. In Peru, there are rock shelters near Huancayo in the central highlands, which may belong to this period. They contain flaked stone points and tools such as scrapers and blades, and they lack pottery in a region where it is abundant, so it is reasonable to regard them as pre-ceramic rather than merely as a non-ceramic survival of later date. In the desert north coast, Rafael Larco and Junius Bird have found workshop sites where pressure-flaked points and other implements were made, at La Pampa de los Fósiles and other sites between the Chicama Valley and that of Pacasmayo to the north of it. The points generally have a short stem, and may be long and lanceolate, but are more commonly more or less triangular. Some were made in a rather unusual way from a thin layer of tabular chert of the thickness of the implement, so all that was necessary was to trim the edges into shape. Roughly made side scrapers and blades are also found. Although there are no stratigraphical indications of age, the presence of pressure flaking in a region where it does not occur at a later date makes it virtually certain that these sites are to be ascribed to bands of these early migrants, who left the bleak highlands for the warmer climate of the coast, at a time when the climate was doubtless wetter than it is now. Although it is likely that other early hunter sites will be found, they are bound to be sparsely distributed, since the population at this time, consisting as it did of nomadic bands, must have been extremely small.

Recent work by Duncan Strong in the south coastal area, which has only been published in brief outline, has shown the presence of sand-blasted stone tools, including flaked projectile points, obsidian scrapers and knives, and many obsidian flakes,

C

in low shell heaps in the Bay of San Nicolas, just south of
Nazca. They are accompanied by shellfish, and bones of fish
and sea-lions, and seem to point to a stage when the hunting
peoples realized the possibilities of food obtained from the sea,
and could therefore settle down without practising any form of
cultivation.

CHAPTER III

The Early Farmers

ALONG THE PERUVIAN COAST are several sites which were the dwelling-places of a people very different from the early hunters. We do not know where they came from, but we do know that they are the first link in a chain of development which went right up to the time of the Spanish Conquest in the sixteenth century. The earliest signs of their presence can be dated at about 2500 B.C. and we do not yet know anything about what went on in Peru between the first appearance of the early hunters and this time. The sites are middens, mounds formed by the accumulation of debris round the dwellings, and in at least one of them the dry climate and the lack of ground water has allowed all the perishables to be preserved, so that we have a complete cross-section of the belongings of the people. There is one site near Pacasmayo, two in the Chicama Valley, one in the Virú Valley, and some, about which little has yet been published, just south of Lima and in the neighbourhood of Nazca.

One of those in the Chicama Valley, the Huaca Prieta, has been carefully excavated by Junius Bird, whose work in Patagonia and elsewhere has already been mentioned, and this has given us most of the information we have about the period. It lies at the mouth of the valley, on the right bank of the river, and is about 40 feet high. The valley must have looked rather different from what it does now; there was no irrigation, the vegetation must have been confined to naturally wet areas along the meandering river, and there may well have been swamps and lagoons along the lower reaches. The Quechua word Huaca, belonging properly to certain classes of objects of worship, is applied nowadays to any ancient mound or ruin or even to pottery vessels from graves, and the designation Huaca

Prieta, or Dark Huaca, refers to its unusual dark colour, which
is due to the organic debris consequent on its being a midden
and not an artificial pyramid like so many of the huacas along
this coast. It had a bad name among the local 'huaqueros' or
grave-robbers, who came to leave it severely alone because it
never yielded any of the pots which they sought, but when Bird
was looking for possible pre-ceramic sites, Rafael Larco called
his attention to it, with remarkable results.

The midden is some 12 metres or 40 feet thick and it has
given a consistent series of radiocarbon dates from carefully
collected samples, perhaps the most reliable application of the
method yet carried out. The dates range from about 2500 to
1200 B.C., giving an accumulation rate of rather under a metre
a century. The people lived mainly on the harvest of the sea;
they collected shellfish, and since these include deep-water
mussels they were probably good swimmers, and they caught
fish in seine nets, which had floats made of bottle-gourds and
sinkers made from cobble-stones with a hole pecked through.
Similar nets are still used in the district by men who wade into
the sea at low tide, so their use does not necessarily imply the
presence of boats. The bones of a few marine mammals,
namely sea-lions and porpoises, are found, but no land animals,
and there are no hunting weapons. The other source of food
was plants; wild plants were gathered, and a few were cultivated, including squash, gourds, beans, chile peppers, and
various tubers and roots, but maize, the great staple of later
times, was quite unknown. Cotton was extensively used, and
is presumed to have been cultivated. It has given rise to a good
deal of speculation, since some geneticists believe that American
domestic cotton contains an Asiatic component which, they
say, must have been introduced by men crossing the Pacific in
boats.Whatever views about trans-Pacific voyages we may hold,
2500 B.C. is an excessively early date for them to have occurred.
The bottle-gourd is likewise believed by some to be of Old

World origin, but it may be suggested that enough attention has not been paid to the possibility that both plants were distributed naturally to the New World, under suitable climatic conditions in Tertiary times.

Fabrics, bags and fishing nets were made from cotton and a bast fibre derived from a species of milkweed. The fibres were spun by hand and are extremely irregular in thickness; no regular spindles and no spindle whorls have been found. The heddle was unknown and fabrics were made by hand, twining being the predominant process in about three-quarters of the fragments examined. In a small proportion, the wefts were darned in to produce a warp faced cloth similar to those made with a heddle, but this process is nearly always used in combination with twining, and the two may even appear in a single pick of weft. Bone needles, which may have been used in the darning, are among the finds on the site. Ornament was produced almost entirely by warp manipulation, sometimes combined with a limited use of colour, namely, the natural white and brown shades of cotton, plus a blue dye and sometimes a red pigment rubbed either into the threads or the finished product, though this is very fugitive. The effects include warp stripes and occasional warp float patterns, mostly very fragmentary, in the woven pieces, and transpositions of warp, to produce zigzag effects, most commonly in the twined pieces. The latter can be used in combination with colour, since the transpositions can be done in such a way as to bring alternate warps diagonally across their neighbours, so that one only of each pair is seen on the surface; if the warps alternate in colour, it is then possible to produce patches of a single colour on the surface, while the others are hidden behind. This technique, in combination with twining, is quite characteristic of the period and is never found again throughout the long tradition of Peruvian weaving. None but rectangular fragments have been found, some as small as five inches square, and some up to five

feet by four feet, but none can definitely be identified as garments, although some could possibly have been used as shawls.
Rush mats were similarly made by twining, and so were
baskets, but coiled basketry was not made. Among single
thread techniques, figure-eight looping was used to make nets
and bags. For knotted nets, the knot used was the cow-hitch,
which continued to be used in later times and is still widespread in South America. It is worth observing that it is not
found in Polynesia, though it should occur there if the islands
had been populated by people coming on Kon-Tiki rafts from
South America. Bark cloth occurs in small quantities, which
is a curious feature since it is a material associated rather with
the tropical forest than with this coast, where there are no trees
with suitable bark.

As has already been indicated, the inhabitants of the Huaca
Prieta and similar sites had no pottery. They seem to have
cooked by roasting on hot stones, or by boiling water in gourd
containers by throwing hot stones (pot boilers) into them. The
only stone implements are crude, percussion-flaked scrapers and
blades, in no way resembling the pressure-flaked points of the
early hunters. If the exceptionally dry climate had not preserved the perishable materials, few artifacts apart from these
tools and the net sinkers would have been preserved in the
lower part of this deposit, and we should have had a totally
false idea of the culture of the people.

Subterranean houses, consisting of single rooms of various
shapes, generally oval, lined with cobble-stones, and roofed
over at ground level with wooden or whalebone beams covered
with stones and mud, were found in the upper part of the
midden. Similar ones, lined with rectangular mud bricks,
called in Peru *adobes*, are found on the Virú Valley site, where
stones are not available in the immediate neighbourhood. The
earlier graves at the Huaca Prieta were simple pits, but the later
ones were similar to the rooms. There were few grave goods—

perhaps a cord bag containing a few leaves and dried flowers, and in one case a chewed quid, which is suggestive because in modern times a chewed quid of coca is reckoned to be a cure for some ills such as kidney trouble and toothache. At any rate the germ of the idea that the dead could carry something out of this world, which was expressed so dramatically in the elaborate burials of later times, was already present.

I have referred to these people as the Early Farmers, but

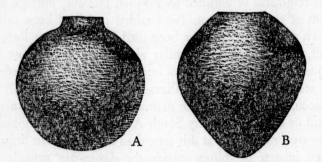

Fig. 3. Domestic pottery of the earliest type from the north coast, belonging to the Early Farmer stage after 1200 B.C. and the Chavín Period. Plain red or black ware. The height of such jars is from about 1 foot to 1 ft. 8 in.

perhaps a better name would be the Early Gardeners. Their agriculture can only have been on an extremely small scale, and there is no evidence for domestic animals, though doubtless they had the almost universal dog.

About 1200 B.C., some additions to the equipment of the people were made, without altering materially their way of life, and for this reason I prefer to class these people still with the Early Farmers rather than with the subsequent stage, as some writers have done. The most important new feature was pottery, but one of its chief advantages, namely, its use for cooking, was not at first grasped by all the inhabitants and pot boilers

Fig. 3

continued to be used for a time. The pots were simple jars, with an ovate profile, and the only ornament consisted of applied fillets of clay, which were either notched or pinched into a wavy form. The colour ranged from dull red, through dark brown to black, and its variability indicates that oxygen control in firing was very imperfect. Other pottery artifacts were stamps, either flat or of the roller type, probably for making designs in paint on the body, and fragments of figurines. There were fragments of polished jet plaques, probably mirrors, and beads of shell and bone. Bone tablets and bird bone tubes, which are believed to have been used in taking some form of snuff, were also found; similar objects for this purpose are frequently found in deposits of later periods, and snuff made of the seeds of a tree called Piptadenia, or less commonly of tobacco, as an intoxicant for shamans, or merely as a stimulant, is still in use among many South American tribes. Altogether there were more signs at this time than there had been hitherto of an interest in things outside the day-to-day struggle for existence. There were also developments in building methods and houses were built above ground of adobes of various forms. The earliest of these were cylinders set vertically, some of them solid and some built up from thin discs, with the interstices filled in with clay, but later walls were built from conical ones, laid on their sides in two rows, with the points interlocking.

For all this information about the Early Farmers, we are

See *Bibliography*, Bennett, 1948; Strong and Evans, 1952

indebted to Bird's excavations in the Chicama Valley, supplemented by those of Strong and Evans in Virú, but more should soon be learnt from the sites recently discovered by Strong on the coast near the Nazca Valley in the south. So far, we only know that they are deep shell middens of early date, and that the lower levels appear to lack pottery and to contain textiles and plants similar to those found in the Chicama Valley.

Chapter IV

The Formative Period

T HE NAME Formative was originally coined to describe the early stages of civilization in Middle America, but it has been adopted in Peru to cover cultures on much the same level. In both cases, they were the first steps in the development of the full flowering of the ancient American civilizations, differing from them in degree rather than in kind. The process began earlier in Middle America than it did in Peru, since agricultural peoples, settled in villages and making good pottery, were already established in Mexico by about 1500 B.C., and they grew maize, a plant which gives such good returns for the labour spent on it that there is much free time available for activities outside the production of food. The importance of maize in the high civilizations of America can scarcely be exaggerated, since it has been calculated that a Maya Indian in Yucatan can grow enough of it to support himself and his family, without domestic animals, by working for 48 days in the year. This figure must vary in different places, and there cannot have been so much surplus time in the early days of agriculture, but it gives an idea of the potentialities of the plant.

THE EARLY FORMATIVE OR CULTIST PERIOD

Maize had appeared in Peru, together with an elaborate form of pottery for ceremonial use and a religious cult which required imposing buildings, by about the ninth century B.C. and it probably arrived somewhat earlier, say 1000 B.C. All the known sites of this period belong to some form of the Chavín Culture, of which the north coastal aspect is sometimes called

Fig. 3, A, B

Cupisnique. There is reason to believe that the new features were introduced by an immigrant people. The older inhabitants continued to live on and near some of their original sites, where their presence is shown by the persistence of the old types of utilitarian pottery, but the newcomers imposed their religious system on them. Food obtained from the sea was still important at this time, and some settlements, which have left large middens, were still on the sea-shore. Others were inland along the margins of the river valleys, but the central parts of the valleys, which later became so important, were still unoccupied, probably because the farmers were still unable to cope with the scrub and marshes which bordered the rivers themselves. Middens at Ancón and Supe, in the central coast not far north of Lima, are a considerable way from any cultivable land, and in the case of Ancón the distance amounts to 10 kilometres, but the proximity of the sea must have outweighed this disadvantage. Modern Peruvian Indians make light of long distances on foot, and their predecessors probably felt the same.

See Bibliography, Willey, 1953

In the Virú Valley, the only area where settlement patterns have been seriously studied, the population was small and the sites few. Little is left of the houses except the rough stone foundations, set in mud, of some small groups of rectangular or irregularly shaped rooms scattered at random. A pot in the form of a house shows a rectangular, gabled building, with thin walls but thicker foundations, and a thatched roof. The walls of these buildings were probably of adobe or cane. Subterranean houses, similar to those of the earlier period, but lined with adobes instead of cobbles, were still constructed in the Huaca Prieta in the Chicama Valley.

It is unlikely that irrigation had developed to any extent even by the end of the period, and cultivation must have been done in small clearings in exceptionally favourable spots, not necessarily very near the habitation sites. In addition to maize, the new plants included peanuts, alligator pears, warty squash and manioc. The people possessed dogs, since the desiccated remains of a small brown one were found in the cemetery at Supe. They also had llamas, which were almost certainly domesticated, since their bones were found at Supe and the remains of sacrificed animals were found on a ceremonial site in the Virú Valley. Their presence proves communication with the highlands, since they do not live permanently on the coast, and the evidence is supported by the occasional use of their wool in textiles in the later part of the period.

Relatively few textiles of this time have been preserved, and most of them are of cotton. The overwhelming majority are rectangular pieces of some kind of plain weave, with variations made by crossing single warps with a pair of wefts and vice versa, or by crossing pairs of warps with pairs of wefts. The commonest patterns are coloured warp stripes, which mostly seem to be based on the natural browns and whites of the cotton, and there are also weft stripes and tartan-like combinations of both. Angular patterns, such as interlocking steps, frets, and hollow rectangles, were produced by brocading or by building up patches of different colours after the manner of tapestry, although true tapestry, in which the wefts hide the warps, is rare. The patches of colour were joined by interlocking the adjacent wefts or by passing them round a common warp, or were separated by kelim slits, features which were all common in later tapestries. At Supe were found a few remarkable designs in the shape of a head combining condor and feline characteristics in typical Chavín style, and carried out in true tapestry technique. It is rather surprising to find tapestry with cotton wefts, since it is difficult to cover the warps with them, and it was much commoner for wool to be used in the later periods. Another type of textile was gauze, but examples are very rare. Loom weaving was clearly the normal process at this time, and twining appears to have gone entirely out of fashion, although it was by far the commonest way of making

basketry. Unlike those of the Early Farmers the threads used
were evenly spun, and pottery spindle whorls were used.

What little evidence we have suggests that clothing was
scanty. The textiles found in graves are merely rectangular
shrouds, and no clothing has been identified under them. One
pot found by Larco in a north coast cemetery depicts a man

*Fig. 4. The Feline God, with snake head appendages.
Incised design from stone frieze slab at Chavín. Length about
3 ft. 3 in. (After Bennett.)*

Plate 4

wearing a breech clout and a close-fitting headgear, and
another which represented a nursing mother is not altogether
clear but it shows that the upper part of the body was bare
except for a veil-like head-dress falling down the back. There
is some indication of body painting, in the shape of stamps
made of pottery, found in graves.

We must go on to consider the ceremonial centres, the
religion they existed to serve, and the art which adorned them.
The principal object of worship was a feline god, of which the
prototype must have been either the puma or the jaguar, or

Fig. 4

44

perhaps both. The jaguar lives only in the tropical forests, but the puma is found all over South America in both highlands and lowlands, so on the whole it is the more likely of the two to have impressed itself on the imagination of the highland and coastal peoples.

By comparison with the ordinary settlements, some at least of the religious buildings were large and imposing, but there were no large concentrations of population round them. It has been suggested that the actual building of the temples was done by a comparatively small number of skilled masons, and that they were assisted in the collection and preparation of the materials by large numbers of people who gathered from time to time for religious festivals. Andean Indians have always been very much addicted to making pilgrimages of this kind in historic times, the shrine at Copacabana in Bolivia being a well-known instance, and it is reasonable to believe that this habit has persisted from early times.

The most notable of the centres was that at Chavín de Huántar, which has given its name to the Chavín Culture. It lies on a tributary of the Marañon River, just east of the watershed bordering the Callejón de Huaylas in the north highlands, and consists of massive rectangular platform-like buildings, ranged round a central court and faced with alternate courses of thick and thin dressed stone blocks, into which are tenoned massive human heads, many of which have feline tusks. The buildings are honeycombed with galleries and chambers on two or three levels, connected by stairways and ramps.

Many stone carvings come from this site, all of them being distinguished by feline features in some form, chiefly fangs and claws. One group consists of slabs with incised designs, mainly from a fallen frieze which formerly encircled the buildings, and besides complete felines, conflations of felines with other animals in the shape of condors and snakes with feline fangs,

Fig. 4

claws or markings are found on them. A most remarkable example of rather a different type is the tall stele known as the Raimondi stone, now in the National Museum at La Magdalena Vieja, near Lima, which bears a standing figure with a feline face, holding an elaborate staff in each claw-like hand, while from the head projects a monstrous appendage facing upwards and consisting of a series of fantastic snouts with feline fangs and snakes projecting on either side. Within one of the galleries of the building, Tello discovered a standing stone shaped more or less like a prism tapering downwards, and carved with a tusked feline face and other features.

Pottery has been found on this site, and it generally takes rather simple forms, of which the most typical is the open, flat-bottomed bowl, though bowls of other forms and narrow-mouthed jars or bottles are also quite common. More elaborate forms, like the stirrup spout, which will be described in connexion with north coastal sites, are rare. The ware is monochrome, red, brown or black in colour, and it may be decorated by incision, finger-nail impressions, a series of fine punctuations produced by rocker stamping, brushing, or applied strips. The designs produced by these processes are commonly geometrical, such as solid triangles and rectangles, or curvilinear, in which case they may be parts of life forms which cannot be recognized on fragments. The ubiquitous dot and circle design is also found. These designs may be emphasized by shading, cross-hatching or rocker stamping. The variability in colour is due to lack of uniformity in the oxygen supply in firing, but the vessels are nevertheless hard and well fired.

Isolated finds of stone sculpture related to the Chavín style are found in various parts of the north highlands, but the most important site in that region outside Chavín itself is Kuntur Wasi in the upper part of the basin of the Jequetepeque River. Adequate reports of it are not available, but it is known that it is a triple-terraced pyramid crowning a hill-top, and that it

Plates 7, 8

Plate 5

formerly supported some form of temple. Some of the carvings found near it are related to those of Chavín, and Chavín type pottery is also reported. Gold ornaments with hammered repoussé decorations and turquoise have been found in graves there, but it is not clear whether they are contemporary with the Chavín material. Potsherds of generalized Chavínoid character have been found in small quantities in the lowest levels of stratigraphical tests in the Cajamarca Basin, just over the watershed to the east of the Jequetepeque drainage, but they are decorated by red and white painting as well as by incision and it is therefore very probable that they belong to a slightly later development.

The most extensive discoveries of the Chavín horizon in the north coast are those made by Rafael Larco in the Chicama and neighbouring valleys, to which he gave the name Cupisnique, after the small valley which yielded his first finds. Most of his material comes from cemeteries which he has excavated, and its richness indicates that many of the graves were those of important people. The graves were pits of various shapes, rarely lined with rough stones, and the bodies were generally buried in a flexed position, lying on the back or on one side. They were accompanied by grave goods, particularly stirrup-spouted jars, a form which is rare on Chavín sites elsewhere, *Plates 4, 7, 8* and which may well have been made specially for burial. The stirrup spout has a long history in the north coastal area, and, apart from two interruptions, is found there right up to the time of the Spanish Conquest; it is accompanied by the flat base, and the presence of these two features distinguishes this area from the southern part of the coast throughout the archaeological sequence. Cupisnique stirrup spouts are distinguished from those of later periods by their massive character. The jars themselves are very variable in shape, ranging from spheroidal forms which may bear incised designs, sometimes including *Plate 8. See* feline fangs and eyes, to elaborately modelled representations of *also Plate 5.*

human beings, animals, fruits and other objects, some of which were made in moulds. Plate 6, which presumably represents the face of an old woman, is a vivid illustration of the strength of the modelling.

Other grave finds in this region include stone plates and bowls, jet mirrors, shell and turquoise pendants and beads, and bone spatulae and rings, most of them adorned by carving which represents feline faces or fangs, thus testifying to the strength of the cult. Many of the graves contain little bags full of red paint composed of clay with traces of mercury and lead compounds, and when the flesh decayed this coloured the bones red, which at first led to the erroneous belief that the burials were secondary. Secondary burial, in which the bones are placed in their final resting place after the decay and removal of the flesh, is quite exceptional in Peru at any time, in fact our present knowledge suggests that it was not practised at all, although it occurs quite frequently on the Ecuadorian coast, and is one of the many features which differentiate the archaeo-logy of the two regions.

No Chavín buildings have been excavated in the Chicama Valley, but some foundations are believed to belong to cere-monial buildings of the period. In the neighbouring Virú Valley, the lower parts of the rough stone walls of a simple rectangular temple containing two low platforms, with a stair-way leading up to one of them, were found. This was chiefly interesting for the burials of four llamas which were found in or near it. All except one either had the remains of rope harness in place, or had their legs tied together with it, and there is little doubt that they had been sacrificed.

Farther south, in the Nepeña Valley, there are remains of more imposing buildings at Cerro Blanco and Punkurí. The first has stone walls bearing relief decoration in clay, painted brick-red and greenish-yellow, representing eyes and feline fangs of Chavín type, and is associated with incised and polished black pottery. That at Punkurí is a terraced platform with a wide stairway, on which stands a feline head and paws, modelled in the round from stone and mud, and painted. At its feet is the burial of a woman who is believed to have been sacrificed. Higher up are clay-plastered walls made of conical adobes, bearing incised designs of Chavín character.

The next valley to the south, that of Casma, has remains of rather similar character. At Moxeke and Pallca are terraced, stone-faced pyramids with stone stairways. Moxeke has niches containing clay-plastered reliefs made of mud, stone and conical adobes, showing felines, snakes and human beings of Cha-vínoid character, painted in white, yellow, black and red. Pallca is associated with dark-coloured monochrome pottery, and a bone spatula carved with a Chavín-type snake head with feline features has been found there.

In the same valley, at Cerro Sechín, is a rectangular building consisting of a series of superimposed platforms with a central stairway, on either side of which, at the bottom level, stands a row of unshaped flat stelae alternating with smaller stones, which are more or less square in form, and which were set in pairs or threes on top of one another. All bear remarkable incised or low relief designs. Most of those on the stelae are standing men, wearing loin-cloths and truncated conical hats and carrying staves or clubs, but a few lack the hats and weapons and have a limp or depressed appearance (one may be meant to be cut in half) as though they had been vanquished by the other type. Those on the smaller stones are severed human heads in profile, like head-hunters' trophies, the earliest example of a feature common in Peruvian art. One of the stelae bears a double column of such heads, seen full face. Some Chavín pottery has been found on the site, and although the carvings have no feline features and are not similar to Chavín types, small objects from various parts of the coast bear designs which link the two styles, and Sechín must be of similar age.

Plate 9

Plate 10

The sites in both Nepeña and Casma are very imperfectly studied, and the succession is not sufficiently well known for it to be possible to say where Sechín belongs in the Chavín Period, but the opinion of most archaeologists is that it is earlier in date than Moxeke and Pallca. Some writers have conjectured that there may be some connexion between the carvings of Sechín and a row of stones bearing low relief figures called Los Danzantes at Monte Albán, in the Mexican state of Oaxaca. In view of other evidence, there may well be a contact between Mexico and Peru at this time, but it cannot be said that there is any close resemblance between the carving of these two sets of figures.

To the south of Casma, no unquestioned ceremonial sites have been found, but there are remains of dwelling sites in the shape of shell and refuse mounds at intervals on the coast as far south as the neighbourhood of Pachacámac, south of Lima. Of these, the only ones which have been studied in any detail are those at Ancón and Supe, which have already been mentioned. An important cemetery has recently been found by Peruvian archaeologists near Ancón, and this has yielded many artifacts of wood, bone and stone, as well as baskets, pottery and cotton textiles. The pottery is similar to that of Chavín itself, consisting mainly of bowls and flasks, whereas the stirrup spouts so characteristic of Cupisnique are very rare. The stone objects include pestles, cylindrical mortars with engraved designs, and tetrapod plates; among those of wood are bowls, rectangular dishes and boxes, and there are bone awls and spatulae. Many of these are carved with feline designs of Chavín character.

With one possible exception, no metal is found at this period except gold. A thin crumpled fragment of hammered sheet gold comes from Supe, and a little simple hammered gold work is reported from Virú, but away to the north, at Chongoyape in the Lambayeque Valley, some more elaborate objects have been found. There are head-bands, cuffs, ear spools, tweezers, rings and other things, with elaborate repoussé Chavínoid designs; welding and soldering were employed in their manufacture. There are also a few objects of silver. It is believed that the Chavín religion and art style survived in this area to a later date than it did farther south, and that this is the explanation of the relative complexity of the metal-work. Some support is given to this theory by the association of pottery of Chavín character with later types in graves at Pacatnamú in the Jequetepeque Valley.

Two reasons have been given for the local variations in the expressions of the Chavín Culture. The first is that there was local specialization, with emphasis on stone-carving at Chavín de Huántar, elaborate pottery in the Chicama area, metallurgy in the far north, and so on. The other is that the variations are largely due to differences in time. The duration of the period is unknown, but evidence of increasing elaboration within it has been found in the Virú excavations. As has been already said, the peculiar site at Sechín is probably earlier than Moxeke and Pallca in the same valley, where the polychrome painting of the reliefs may well indicate an approach in time to the later Mochica Culture, of which polychrome frescoes are a known feature. Kuntur Wasi also is believed to be later than the type site of Chavín de Huántar. Both causes probably played their part in producing the differences, but it will not be possible to do more than speculate on the extent of their influence until detailed studies, like those carried out in Virú, are made in many more areas.

There is, then, evidence of the Chavín Culture spread over a wide area in the northern highlands and the north and central coast, but so far it has not been found elsewhere in Peru. It is united by the presence of similar pottery types, and by evidence of a religion of animal worship, in which the cult of a feline god held the foremost place. There are a number of ceremonial centres which show a considerable variety in detail, and each seems to have been the nucleus of a group of scattered settle/ ments, but there is no indication that the centres were united by any sort of political organization. Weapons are not common; flanged and spiked stone mace/heads and polished stone lance/ heads occur in the graves of the Chicama region, the spear/ thrower was in use, and a single long palm/wood bow was found at Ancón, but some at least of these must have been used for hunting. Fortifications are unknown, so fighting can hardly have amounted to more than small/scale local raiding, and the carvings at Sechín indicate that head/hunting may have played some part in this. With a small population in a few scattered settlements, there cannot have been any of the competition for land which so often provokes wars.

An important question which remains is, where did the bearers of maize, ceremonial pottery, and feline cult come from? Tello upheld the view that the Chavín Culture came to the coast from the highlands, with its ultimate origin in the Amazonian forests, but recent work has shown that it is most unlikely that any high culture ever developed or survived for any length of time in these forests. Others have suggested that the art style at any rate developed on the coast, but Bird's demonstration that Chavín pottery appeared abruptly with maize in the Chicama Valley has given strong indications that the whole complex was probably imported from a source farther afield.

Clues to where its origin may be have recently been found far away from Peru. At Tlatilco, near Mexico City, is a site belonging to the Formative Period, which shows many specific resemblances to Chavín, particularly in the pottery. It has been stated that some sherds from the two areas are so alike in ware and decoration that it would be hard to distinguish them, and those highly distinctive features, the stirrup spout and zigzag rocker stamping are found in both. The practice of fronto/ occipital head deformation in both areas may be more than a coincidence, and the representation of felines was a characteristic feature of the Olmec Culture of Mexico, which had a great influence on the art of the Tlatilco site. The site has not been very precisely dated, but it is believed to belong somewhere in the middle of the Formative Period of Mexico, and to be approximately of the same age as the beginning of the Chavín Culture. It must not be thought that the cultures of the two areas are identical, and attention must be drawn to two main differences. As far as our present imperfect knowledge goes, there were no buildings in Mexico which were comparable in elaboration with those of the Chavín Culture at the time when Tlatilco flourished, and certainly none at Tlatilco itself. In common with other Mexican Formative sites, Tlatilco is distinguished by an abundance of pottery figurines, whereas these are virtually lacking in the Formative of Peru.

South of Tlatilco, there are large gaps, but some evidence to link the two areas is beginning to appear. In Honduras, at the Playa de los Muertos in the Ulua Valley, there is a site whose pottery resembles that of Tlatilco very closely. This also is a long way from Peru, but a very recent discovery on the Babahoyo River on the coastal plain of Ecuador gives promise of further links. On this site a deep cut by Dr. Clifford Evans and his wife, and Señor Emilio Estrada, has yielded pottery with many of the features common to both the Mexican and Peruvian areas.

THE LATER FORMATIVE, OR EXPERIMENTER PERIOD

The Later Formative Period was one of technological innovation and variety in expression in different areas. The overwhelming preponderance of feline motifs in art had disappeared, which suggests that the widespread feline cult had suffered a setback, though examples of a modified form are found in the south coast. There is also evidence for the persistence or revival of the cult in both north and south coasts in later times, though it no longer had a virtual monopoly. Ceremonial structures in the form of pyramids occur in Virú, but nothing comparable in elaboration to Sechín, Punkurí and the rest has yet been found. A modelled jar from the Chicama Valley, in the form of a circular building, with a flat roof supported by walls consisting of stepped pillars surmounted by a decorated pierced frieze, probably represents an adobe temple or shrine.

The definition of the limits of the period is bound to be somewhat arbitrary, and as knowledge increases some cultures may be shifted into the succeeding Classic stage, just as it has already been suggested that some Chavín manifestations may have persisted after the Cultist Period, but in general it seems to be a valid division. There is insufficient dating evidence at present, and it cannot be said with certainty that all the Experimenter Cultures, which are more widely distributed than those of the preceding period, are contemporary. Although there is great diversity in different areas, the north and central coast from Chicama to near Lima, and the Callejón de Huaylas in the north highlands, are linked by two styles of pottery painting, which are regarded as marking two horizons, an older White-on-Red horizon and a younger Negative one. The following are the developments ascribed to the Experimenter Period:

The Salinar Culture, belonging to the White-on-Red horizon in the Chicama Valley.

The equivalent of Salinar, called Puerto Moorín, in the Virú Valley, where it is followed by the Virú or Gallinazo Culture, of the Negative horizon, most of which is placed in this period.

A White-on-Red horizon in the Callejón de Huaylas. This is followed by the Recuay Culture, with negatively painted pottery, which is generally placed in the succeeding Classic Period.

Representatives of both horizons in the central coast.

The Paracas Cavernas and Paracas Necropolis Cultures in the south coast.

The Chiripa and perhaps the Early Tiahuanaco Culture in the south highlands, near Lake Titicaca.

The Chanapata Culture, near Cuzco, in the south highlands.

In addition, some little-known painted pottery styles found in the Cajamarca Basin in the northern highlands probably belong to this stage.

There was an improvement in agricultural methods at this time, and evidence from the Virú Valley shows that irrigation developed rapidly in the later part of the period, although it is doubtful if it was practised at the beginning. In the highlands there are indications of stone-faced terraces, perhaps the fore-runners of the irrigated terraces which are such a striking feature of the landscape in some of the narrow Andean valleys, and which greatly extend the cultivable area. It seems also that a number of new plants were cultivated. Among these, a grain called quinoa, which is of great importance in modern times at altitudes too great for maize to ripen, was found by Bennett in a stone bin at the south highland site of Chiripa. Coca, the leaves of which are still chewed by Andean Indians as a nar-cotic, has been found in a south coastal grave, and other new-comers are a variety of bean and a sterile hybrid like a cucumber, which can only be propagated by means of cuttings.

For evidence about houses and villages in the coast we are mainly dependent, as before, on the work which has been done in the Virú Valley. In the Puerto Moorín Period, the founda-tions, of rough stone or conical adobe, of two main types of settlement have been found; one consists of scattered irregularly

See *Bibliography*, Willey, 1953

shaped rooms, and the other of haphazard clusters of rooms, which tend to be more or less rectangular because they touch their neighbours. An open-fronted house, with a sloping roof supported on beams with a central post, is represented on a Salinar pot. There are also a few hill-top redoubts, containing houses and a pyramid within a stone wall, which suggest that there was at times a necessity for look-outs or defences, although there is no evidence for warfare on any considerable scale.

In the Gallinazo Period, sometimes called Virú, because its main development is in the Virú Valley, there were great developments. The dwelling sites were what are described as agglutinated villages, that is to say large groups of adjacent rooms, with successive stages piled one on another like a Near Eastern tell, and they may be built initially on a platform mound. Some of these are associated with pyramids, and were therefore religious and probably administrative centres also. They were built of adobes which varied in form, the conical ones of earlier times having given place first to balls and then to rectangular ones, while the material was sometimes used in the massive form called tapia. The main irrigation canals seem to have developed in this period, and some cultivation plots con-nected by narrow, looped channels can still be seen. The number and distribution of the sites suggest a great increase of population, made possible by irrigation, which in its turn imposed the necessity for a closely integrated society, since an elaborate system of canals can only be maintained and the water shared out by strict control. In the final stage of the Gallinazo Period, both population and irrigation system seem to have reached the maximum, and imposing strong points, containing adobe pyramids and dwellings defended by walls, a develop-ment of the older redoubts, were perched in commanding positions on peaks overlooking the valley. This last stage was contemporary with part of the Classic Period in the Chicama Valley, and is properly placed in that period.

The utilitarian pottery in the Virú Valley gives us further information about the population. From its earliest appearance it developed gradually in type, without sudden changes, right through the Formative Period, and this indicates that the same people remained there, although they increased in number. The simple jar with rounded base, ovate profile, and plain *Fig. 3B* constricted mouth, continued, and the other main type in Puerto Moorín times was very similar, with a wider mouth and

A   B

Fig. 5. A, B. Domestic jars of the Experimenter Period, in the Virú Valley. A. Puerto Moorín stage. B. Gallinazo stage. The size of these and similar types of the same age is very variable. They range from about 2 ft. down to about 8 in. in height, but most appear to exceed a foot.

low, everted lip. The chief changes which occurred were better *Fig. 5A* mixing of the paste and more uniform oxidation in firing, producing thin, even-textured ware of a uniform brown or red colour. In Gallinazo times, the gradual change continued; for example, the jars developed a more globular outline, and some had a high flaring collar. These were the pots which were in *Fig. 5B* domestic use, but there were other types to which brief reference has already been made, which were designed for religious or ceremonial purposes and are found almost exclusively in the graves. The decorated wares of the Chavín Period, outstanding among which are the Cupisnique types, belonged to this class and those of the Upper Formative in the same region are related to them but show considerable change.

Some details must now be given of the various Experimenter cultures. Salinar, in the Chicama Valley, is known chiefly from funerary pottery belonging to the White-on-Red horizon, which resembles the plain pottery only in the paste and the oxidized firing. Like those of Cupisnique before them, the vessels are elaborately modelled and take many forms, including
Plate 11   the old stirrup spout, as well as jars with a narrow, tube-like neck and a strap handle, and globular jars with a symmetrical arrangement of a sloping spout balanced by a modelled figure, the two being connected by a flat, bridge handle. The first whistling jars belong to the latter type, and the figure holds a spherical whistle, which sounds if air is drawn through it by pouring water out of the jar. In later times, the whistle is gener-ally hidden within the figure, or a head which takes its place.
Plate 12   Human figures, birds or animals are frequently shown on Salinar vessels, and more often than not they are perched on the top rather than forming the body of the jar, but the modelling is not so naturalistic as in Cupisnique. The human figures are lively little caricatures, with little or no clothing, sometimes shown in erotic attitudes, which are, unlike most of those depicted on vases of the Classic Period, invariably natural. Simple white lines, or triangles, sometimes filled with dots, are painted direct on the red surface of some Salinar jars. The burials with which these pots are found are generally in an ex-tended position, in a simple grave, which may be covered with slabs or poles, and in some cases they had a round or oval gold plaque in the mouth, an interesting custom which is found also in later times. Salinar is the same as the Puerto Moorín Culture of the Virú Valley, of which various features have already been described.

Little can be said about the White-on-Red horizon in the Callejón de Huaylas and the central coast, in both of which it is only known from trial excavations. The highland sites, near Chavín and Huaráz, have yielded grave pottery which is mostly in the form of bowls with slightly rounded bases and flaring sides, painted with simple designs such as triangles covered with dots or groups of parallel zigzag lines. The exca⁄vations in the Chancay Valley in the central coast produced huddled burials, protected by parts of large storage jars, which had been wrapped in textiles and in one case had a metal mask. This mummy bundle type of burial belongs to a south coast

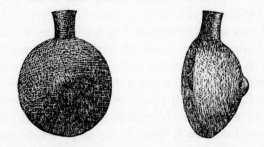

Fig. 6. Mammiform jar. The type is characteristic of the Central Coast in the Experimenter and Classic Periods. Height varies from about 6 in. to 2 ft.

and south highland tradition, which does not spread to the north until later times. The commonest pottery types are in⁄curved bowls with a pair of loop handles, and mammiform jars with a collar, carelessly painted with white dots, dotted triangles or broad white zones on red, or in some cases one half white and the other red. The general simplicity of the forms links this area with the north highlands and distinguishes it from the Chicama region, as in Chavín times.

Fig. 6

The Negative horizon is represented in the Virú and Santa valleys by the Gallinazo or Virú Culture, which is found so sparsely in the Moche and Chicama valleys that Larco believes that the graves there must belong to migrant groups from Virú.

Although its later stages must be regarded as Classic, it is convenient to speak of it here. Something has already been said of the buildings, irrigation canals and plain pottery, and a word must be added about the funerary pottery. Stirrup spouts and Plates 13, 14, 17 other modelled vessels are frequent, particularly a spout and bridge type with a tapering spout. Most of these vessels are red in colour and some are decorated with negative designs in black, produced by painting a pattern in wax before firing and covering the whole with black, so that when the pot is fired the wax comes off and the design stands out in red on a black See Plates 26–8 ground. Negative painting is widespread in Peru and only in a limited area can it be regarded as marking an horizon. It is uncertain where it was invented, but the oldest examples are probably in the south coast, and in the north it is most likely that it spread from Virú up into the highlands, whence it may have moved northwards into Ecuador and Colombia. Little can be said about its occurrence in the central coast, since it is only known from sherds found in the deeper refuse levels at the important ceremonial centre of Pachacámac, south of Lima. The Virú vase shown in Plate 14 is one of the few feline representations in this period, and that in Plate 17 represents a warrior holding club and shield sitting in a small raft made Plate 18 of a bundle of reeds, such as fishermen still use on the Peruvian coast. It illustrates the emergence of militarism and the warrior class, and raises the question of the use of the sea for transport. Balsa wood rafts were used for long voyages in Inca times and sailing rafts were in use on the south coast at an earlier date, but the roads from valley to valley were the controlling factor in coastal communications until the arrival of the Spaniards, who depended on the sea and neglected the roads. In aboriginal times, the domination of one valley by another depended on the existence of a road, and the variety in the coastal cultures during the Experimenter Period shows that few of the valleys were connected in this way.

In the south coast, the main developments so far known are in the Nazca and Ica valleys and the Paracas Peninsula, but we can only have a one-sided view of them until Professor Duncan Strong's work is fully published. Up to the present the cultures of this area have been chiefly known from the rich burials found by Tello on the arid peninsula of Paracas, whither the dead must have been carried from the valleys where they had lived. There are two main types called Paracas Cavernas and Paracas Necropolis.

The Cavernas type of cemetery consists of deep dome-shaped rock-cut chambers, which may be up to 25 feet below the surface, approached by a narrow, vertical shaft with steps cut in the walls, above which is a wider, cylindrical antechamber lined with stones. They contain many mummy bundles, in one case 55, in which the body sits with the knees up to the chest, wrapped in many layers of cloth. These are mostly of plain weave or gauze, with little colour except two-colour stripes. The skulls are generally flattened artificially, and frequently trepanned, extensively and sometimes repeatedly. The reason for this is unknown, but it has been suggested that it was a consequence of fighting with the stone-headed clubs which are found in many of the graves; this suggestion does not carry much conviction, since clubs are by no means confined to this time and place, whereas the practice of trepanation is more frequent and extensive here than anywhere else, and some religious explanation is more probable. Whatever the reason, the victims survived the operation, and not once only. Among the rich grave goods are highly characteristic pottery types, including heavy open bowls with simple negative designs in orange and dark brown, plain or incised black bowls or jars, and bowls and jars painted after firing in black and rich red, yellow and green resinous colours separated by incised lines. The jars take many forms, which include the double spout and bridge, and the variety in which one spout is replaced by a head, and

Plate 15
Plate 16

the designs include feline faces, which is one of the chief reasons why some writers have argued that Cavernas belongs to the Chavín horizon, although the style is distinct. All, both bowls and jars, have the rounded base which is characteristic

Plate 21

of the south coast. Very rare are strange figurines, similarly decorated but in pale colours. A cemetery at Ocucaje in the Ica Valley has yielded similar pottery from shallow, rectangular graves, also human skulls cut vertically in half, the front half retaining the hair and skin. Houses and other structures of adobe and wattle and daub have also been found at Ocucaje.

The other Paracas type, Necropolis, consists of rectangular pits of various sizes, unroofed and filled with mummy bundles and sand, from which over 400 bundles have been taken. These contain a body sitting with the knees up, often in a basket, and wrapped in many layers of superb textiles, many of which are covered with intricate embroidery in vivid colours, reds, blues, yellows, greens, browns and others, representing grotesque figures, monsters, birds, animals and other designs, arranged with great artistry. They take the form of mantles, shirts, loin-cloths, turbans and other garments, and a single bundle may contain many examples of each, which are quite unworn and were presumably made specially for burial. They are distinguished by the use of embroidery for ornament, in contrast to the weaving techniques like tapestry and brocade which were common in other Peruvian cultures. There are

Plate 19

fragments in many museums which give a good idea of the colouring and the nature of the designs, but the figures dressed in complete garments in the National Museum in Lima make a sight not easily forgotten. The skulls of these mummies are highly deformed in a manner different from those of Cavernas, with the result that they are long and narrow, but trepanation is

Plate 20

relatively rare. The pottery includes shapes similar to the Cavernas ones, but it is generally lighter in construction and cream or brown in colour.

The burials were those of honoured and important people, and the preparation of their graves and all that were in them must have occupied much time and effort. We know little about the living on whom this burden lay, although Strong's excavations have shown that some of them lived in the Nazca and Ica valleys, where he has found remains of wattle and daub houses, and evidence of three stages of development. The correlation of Cavernas and Necropolis with these is not simple, but it appears that the earliest stage has negatively painted pottery and other Cavernas features, and that the second has elements of both cultures. As far as it goes, this supports the usual view that Cavernas precedes Necropolis, but this order is not universally accepted.

See *Bibliography*, Bird and Bellinger, 1954

The Formative cultures of the south coast are in a tradition distinct from those of the north, since they have different pottery shapes, polychrome painting of pottery, advanced development of textiles, full clothing in breech clout, shirt and mantle, and different burial customs. Even the feline motifs are in a different style. The origin of this tradition is obscure, and so are its relations with Chavín and the subsequent northern cultures, but the development of clothing perhaps points to an immediate source in the cold highlands.

The Experimenter Period in the south highlands is represented by Chiripa, a site excavated by Bennett on the Bolivian shore of Lake Titicaca. This was a village of fourteen rectangular houses standing round a circular court. They were built of rectangular adobes on a foundation of stones packed in clay, and were thatched with grass. The cold was resisted by two features, namely, double walls with storage bins between the two thicknesses, and vertical slots for the reception of sliding wooden doors. The most usual pottery vessel is a thick bowl with flat base and vertical sides, painted with simple geometrical designs, like steps, in broad yellow strokes on a red slip, which, like the white-on-red of the coast, suggests the tentative beginnings of painted decoration. It is probable that the early stage at the famous site of Tiahuanaco in the same neighbourhood should also be classed as Experimenter, but it will be convenient to discuss the site as a whole under the heading of the Classic Period. (*Note:* Bennett originally regarded Chiripa as later than the Tiahuanaco Classic Period, but in his later publications he abandoned this opinion, having become dissatisfied with the evidence.)

At Chanapata, on the outskirts of Cuzco, J. H. Rowe did some trial excavations on a site where a road section revealed rough stone-walling and potsherds of non-Inca types. He found a semi-subterranean room, bounded by retaining walls, and some huddled burials in circular or oval pits, with no grave goods. Abundant potsherds were found in the excavation, and the same types can still be collected on the site. They are hard and mostly brown, dull red or black, either plain or decorated by incision, stabbing or appliqué ornament, or by partial burnishing. There are collared jars, flat plates and bowls of various shapes, including flat based ones, with vertical or flaring sides. Some finer, painted wares are present, but they are in two colours only, as in other cultures of this period. The designs are very simple, and include circles and stepped forms in white on red, or red on buff.

There were few advances in metallurgy during the Experimenter Period, but a gold-copper alloy is known from Salinar and the central coast, and pure copper is found at Cavernas and Chiripa.

CHAPTER V

The Classic Period

THE CLASSIC PERIOD in Peru is marked, not only by the full development of technical processes, which has suggested Bennett's alternative name of Mastercraftsmen, and by flourishing art styles, but by the establishment of highly organized and aggressive states. This feature, which is not characteristic of the Classic of Middle America, may well have been due to the topography of the coast, where dependence on irrigation imposed a strict organization on the inhabitants of the valleys. This does not account for similar social developments in the southern and central highlands, because highland basins, in contrast to the coastal valleys, generally had more than one source of water, so there was not the same compulsion towards unity. There is as yet no satisfactory explanation for what happened in this highland region, unless it was due to copying of the coast, but the centre of development is still not absolutely certain, so it is perhaps premature to seek an explanation for it. The chief expressions of the Classic Period are to be found in the north and south coast, and in the south and central highlands, and subsidiary ones are known from the north highlands and the central coast. The extreme north of both coast and highlands, and much of the central highlands, are still little known.

Agriculture was fully developed, with elaborate irrigation patterns filling some but not all the coastal valleys, and it is probable that the terraces of the highland valleys were greatly extended. The full range of pre-Columbian plants was known and cultivated, and grave finds and representations on pottery suggest that many of them were added during this period, including such well-known vegetables and fruits as the potato, the sweet potato, the papaya and the pineapple.

Practically all the aboriginal techniques of weaving were known, and both cotton and the wool of the llama and the alpaca were extensively used. Textiles are better preserved in the south coast than they are in the north, but it appears also that elaborate weaving was a speciality of the south coast at all times, and part of the south coast tradition. Tapestry, brocade, double cloth, gauze, warp stripes and weft stripes are all common, and twill was known, but the embroidery so characteristic of Paracas Necropolis was out of fashion. No textiles of this time have been preserved in the wet climate of the highlands, but spindle whorls and statues representing clothed figures give indirect evidence of their manufacture. A simple type of belt loom was used for many of the processes and its use is proved by the painting on a remarkable pottery vessel of this period from the north coast, which shows a number of women working under the direction of a formidable-looking matron. Actual examples of later periods are known from coastal graves. Elaborations of this sort of loom must also have been in use. The twills which have been found indicate the use of three heddles instead of one, and modern analogies suggest a similar arrangement for making double cloth. The width which can be woven by a single weaver on such a loom does not exceed about 2 ft 6 in., and the discovery of fabrics up to 17 feet wide was a puzzle, until some modern Peruvian weavers provided the clue by remembering that their mothers used to work wide looms of the same type in teams, sitting side by side.

Mechanical aids, however, meant little to the old Peruvians, and manual dexterity was all-important. Many processes like braiding were carried out entirely by hand, and others like the making of triple cloth and tapestry depended little on normal loom processes, a fact which is particularly apparent in the case of a rare piece of tapestry from Nazca, in which beads are strung on some of the warps. Another hand process consisted in building up patches of warp of different colours on scaffold

wefts on a frame. The threads of adjacent patches are interlocked with one another, and each patch has wefts of the same
colour darned in, and in their turn interlocked with one
another at their edges. The scaffold wefts can then be removed,
and if an unfinished piece had not been found it would have
been difficult to guess how it had been made. The whole
process calls for the greatest skill and care in the maintenance
of constant tension, otherwise the fabric would become hope-
lessly distorted.

The fine quality of many of the fabrics depends on the
selection and spinning of the fibres, at which the Peruvians
were adept. A measure of this is given by the fact that a tapestry,
of post-Classic date it is true, has as many as 500 two-ply wool
wefts to the inch in some places, whereas the best that Medieval
Europe attempted was about 100. Dyeing was another important factor, and it is surprising to realize that the great range of
colours found at Paracas was produced by combinations of
only three vegetable dyes, indigo, red and yellow to orange-
brown, with the natural colours of cotton and alpaca wool,
using where necessary an alum mordant. Needlework involved
the use of many varieties of stitch, and although knitting was
unknown an identical effect was produced with a single needle
in making borders of three-dimensional birds and flowers at
Nazca and Paracas. Most garments were made by joining
rectangular pieces, and tailoring was unknown, but some were
woven to shape. Thus it was possible to widen the shoulders
of a shirt or the ends of a loin-cloth by spreading the warps at
the appropriate place, and inserting extra ones between them
where there was room. The end beams of a loom could be set
farther apart at one side than at the other, and extra wefts carried
across part only of the web, which would produce a fabric
longer at one side than at the other. Two forms of tie-dyeing
were in use in Ancient Peru, but, so far as we know, they date
from post-Classic times, so they will be described later. Many

Plate 40

of the work-boxes used by Peruvian women have been preserved; they are mostly of wood covered with twilled basketry and contain, among other objects, balls of wool and cotton, and numerous thin, pointed spindles, some of them wound with thread, with small, delicately decorated whorls of wood or pottery. These were suitable for spinning with one end resting in a bowl, which was the ancient custom, rather than falling free according to modern practice in the Andean region.

In metallurgy, it is believed that all the pre-Columbian processes and alloys were in use, with the exception of the making and fashioning of bronze. Metals were used chiefly for making ornaments, such as collars, ear spools, nose ornaments and false faces for mummy bundles, but in the Mochica Culture of the north coast, which seems to have specialized in metallurgy just as the southern area did in textiles, useful objects such as blades for digging-sticks, mace-heads and lance-points, were made of copper. Gold, silver and copper, and alloys of gold and copper and silver and copper were all worked. It is believed that gold was obtained mainly from placer deposits, but there is no evidence about the sources of silver and copper. There is some reason to believe that both were smelted from ores in post-Classic times; in the case of copper this could be done fairly easily, and the corpse of a miner, with his basket full of a powdery copper ore, which was found in a collapsed shaft in North Chile, is one of the most popular exhibits in the American Museum of Natural History. On the other hand, both metals occur in a native state, and it is reasonable to believe that this was their source in the early days of their use.

Plate 45

In working the metals, gold was hammered and embossed as in the past, and the same processes, in combination with annealing, to soften them when hammering had made them hard and brittle, seem to have been applied to the other metals.

See Plates 47-9

Casting was employed, and it is probable that the *cire-perdue* process was known. Gilding seems to have been done by the application of gold leaf, but the details of the process are not known. It may also have been done to gold-copper alloys by leaching out the copper on the surface with organic acids, hammering and burnishing, but this method was commoner in Ecuador and Colombia. Gilding by the use of mercury was not known. Pieces of metal were joined by welding, that is by heating and hammering, and by soldering, which was probably done by covering the junction with powdered copper salt mixed with gum; on slow heating, the gum would char and reduce the salt to metal, producing a local patch of gold-copper or silver-copper alloy of lower melting point than the metal which was being joined. Objects made partly of gold and partly of silver are known, and it has been suggested that they were made in two stages by the *cire-perdue* method.

Although each area in Peru had reached a similar techno-logical level, and each had imposing buildings and public works, the art styles differed radically from one another, and at least in the north and south coast they continued the older traditions. This is sufficiently exemplified by the ceremonial pottery, which in the north coast was distinguished by natural-istic modelling, stirrup spouts, flat bases, and few colours, and in the south coast by round bases, double-spouted jars and polychrome painting, with figure modelling far less frequent and far more stylized than in the north.

Plates 22-5

Plates 30, 32

The Mochica Culture of the Pacasmayo, Moche and Chi-cama valleys represents the Classic Period over much of the north coast. It was in part contemporary with the Gallinazo Culture of the Virú Valley, and late in their history the Mochica people invaded Virú and subjugated it, extending their conquests beyond it to the Santa, Nepeña and Casma valleys. The name Mochica is taken from the language which was spoken by the Chimú people in the same area, and these their predecessors may or may not have spoken it. It is a con-venient name, and has superseded the old terms Proto-Chimú

NORTH COAST
Mochica Culture

and Early Chimú, because these tended to cause confusion by obscuring the fact that there was a break between Mochica and Chimú. The name is preserved in the modern valley and village of Moche.

Like other peoples at this time, the Mochica depended largely on agriculture for their living, but fishing naturally con-tinued to play its part, as it always did on the coast. Fish were caught with barbless hooks and nets, both from the shore and from the reed boats already mentioned. Judging by represent-ations on pots, hunting was rather an upper-class sport than a general means of supplementing the food supply, since richly attired men are shown throwing darts from spear-throwers at deer surrounded by nets into which they had been driven. Men are also depicted shooting birds with a blow-gun, but this must have been an individual occupation.

The Mochica occupation of the Virú Valley resulted in some changes in the distribution of sites, but dwellings, temples and strong points do not seem to have altered very much in type. Plain rectangular adobes were the usual material. The vast adobe pyramids called the Huaca del Sol and the Huaca de la Luna in the Moche Valley date from this period, and so do many pyramids and other works in Chicama. Among these is a great earthern aqueduct at Ascope, which is about 50 feet high and carries a canal for nearly a mile across the mouth of a dry valley. It was intact until it was accidentally breached during the abnormal rainy season of 1925, and it remains an extremely impressive sight, which gives some idea of what the Mochica were capable of. A canal in Chicama, 75 miles long, which still irrigates some fields near Chan Chan, the Chimú capital, is believed to date from this period.

While the existence of these great works and the extensive irrigation patterns implies closely-knit organization, we know little about its details, apart from what can be gleaned from scenes and people represented on the ceremonial pottery. Gorgeously attired individuals, sitting on thrones or carried in litters, must in some cases be important chiefs, and others, who may wear masks, doubtless represent gods or priests impersonating gods. An important burial from the Virú Valley, which will be described later, seems to be both warrior and priest attired and equipped to represent a god. Combinations of this sort, and numerous representations of warriors and weapons, show that the organization was not exclusively theocratic, as it seems to have been in the Early Formative Period, but that there was a strong secular side to it also. Varieties in type and elaboration of costume, and the advanced condition of the crafts, point to a specialized as well as a stratified society. Women are depicted plainly clad in a kind of long shirt with a cloth covering the head, and they do not appear in the elaborate ceremonies painted on some of the pots, so they are generally believed to have had a subordinate place, but there must have been exceptions, since one burial in Virú had grave goods of considerable importance.

Plate 24

The domestic pottery continued to change gradually, and the most popular type in Mochica times was a wide-mouthed red jar or deep bowl of globular outline, while collared jars decreased in popularity. Grey wares, fired under reducing conditions, are present in increasing quantities. As before, the ceremonial pottery differed in a marked degree from the utilitarian wares, and took the form of the well-known red and white modelled type to which reference has already been made. This is a thin, well-fired ware, red in colour, to which is added a slip, either white or partly white and partly red. Details are then picked out in red on the white, or less commonly in white on the red. Late in Mochica times a third colour, black, was sometimes added to a small extent. The vessels are of many shapes, of which the most frequent is some form of stirrup spout and others include bell-shaped bowls with ring bases and flasks with flaring collars, which may be either globular or elaborately moulded. More or less hemispherical bowls, double vessels, and a peculiar flattened bowl, known as a dipper, with a constricted mouth and a conical handle projecting from the side like that of a frying pan, are also found. The plain forms are decorated either with pressed relief or with painted designs, which may take the form of elaborate scenes; some of the best of these are found on the bell-shaped bowls, where they generally occupy a broad zone on the inside, adjacent to the margin. Some vessels show a combination of these techniques, which may also be combined with moulding.

Larco has established five successive stages in the development of Mochica pottery, and it will suffice to say here that they are distinguished by such features as the form of the stirrup and the nature of the decoration; for example, Plate 25 shows an early form of stirrup, which has something in common with its Cupisnique ancestors, and an early form of pressed relief, and Figure 7 shows a late form of stirrup and a late type of painted decoration. In general, elaborately painted scenes and carelessly executed painting are signs of a late date, and so is black paint.

Most of the vessels were made in two-piece pottery moulds, such details as stirrup spouts being added afterwards. The moulds themselves were made from a solid or thick-walled model, and, being porous, they absorbed moisture from the castings which therefore shrank away from them and could easily be removed when dry. This method results in the production of near duplicates, but they are seldom exact since minor differences in decoration and even in form were introduced while finishing the vessel.

The naturalistic modelling and the elaboration of the painting makes these vessels singularly informative sources of evidence about the life of the people. Some head jars are so expressive and so carefully modelled as to be clearly portraits, and the faces would not look strange among the inhabitants of the remoter coastal villages at the present time. Others could well be caricatures. Several varieties of male dresses are shown, a usual type being a square-cut shirt, like a modern poncho sewn up at the sides, under which the breech clout can just be seen. In other cases there seems to have been rather a longer

Fig. 7. Late Mochica stirrup-spouted jar with geometrical painting. Height 10 in.

under-shirt with a skirt reaching to the knees, sometimes girded with a sash, with a short poncho-like shirt with short sleeves over it. Another variety is a mantle worn over a shirt. Some of these garments display elaborate geometrical borders and other decorations, sometimes heraldic in effect; on one jar there is a warrior with a tabard-like shirt gyronny red and white, along-side one with his shirt divided bendwise into red and white

Fig. 8

halves, the white one sprinkled with red dots. No shoes or sandals are shown, but the legs may be painted to resemble socks. Most men are shown wearing ear ornaments, which generally take the form of spools which may have large circular ends. Examples are known of gold, silver, copper, wood and bone, with inlays of shell, turquoise and other materials. There was great variety in head-dresses, which in some cases were simple skull-caps, but were often of great elaboration and included reconstructions of birds and animals, semi-lunar copper blades, bushes of feathers, and many other features, as varied as the crests on any medieval roll of arms. The warrior with the gyronny shirt has a conical helmet with a kind of mantling, both similarly adorned, surmounted by a copper blade. All head-dresses were secured by a band under the chin. The nature of the head-dress must have been related to the rank and function of the wearer, though it is only possible to suggest what a few of them represent. One group, who are believed to be messengers, wear only a breech clout and a head-dress which includes an animal head and a long appendage trailing behind, and they are seen speeding along and carrying a bag which may contain beans. Beans bearing dots, lines and other designs are, indeed, shown on these and other scenes, and Larco, who has found actual beans with incised designs in graves, regards the markings as ideographic writing, but, if they are, nothing is known of their meaning. In some cases messengers are shown with wings and wearing humming-bird masks; in fact masks of various types as well as face paint are common.

Prisoners are shown naked, generally with a rope round the neck, but class distinctions are maintained even here and they were made to carry their captive chiefs in litters, stripped like themselves of everything except in some cases their head-dresses. Sometimes they were executed by being thrown down a precipice, and since a tusked god is often the executioner, this was probably a sacrifice to the god. Very frequent is a more or

Fig. 8

Plate 23

less human figure, with feline tusks to represent a god, who is
probably the successor of the feline god of Chavín times, and
he appears so often and in so many guises that he must have
had a dominant place, though he no longer held the monopoly.

Plate 22

*Fig. 8. Two Mochica warriors fighting. Painting from a vase.
Both hold maces with pointed staves. The victor, who has
knocked off his opponent's helmet, holds him by the hair. He
wears shirt and helmet decorated with a design like a medieval
'gyronny' coat of arms. The device on the left is a trophy
of arms, which includes two maces, two darts and a square
shield. Humming-birds hover above. (Redrawn from Larco.)*

There are other gods in the form of fish, bats, birds and other
animals with partly human forms or merely human limbs, also
completely grotesque demons which may emerge from great
conch shells.

Warriors carry small square or round shields and maces with

Plate 24 *Fig. 8*

75

Fig. 8 ·

pear-shaped heads, sometimes flanged, with the staff pointed at the other end to serve as a spear, and when fighting they grasp the hair of an opponent in the moment of victory. They may fight with a copper axe, with convex blade, held in the hand. Copper-tipped lances and spear-throwers are found in the graves, and both may have been used in war, but the spear-thrower is more often depicted in hunting scenes on the pottery. Weapons are sometimes shown alone on pots, in which case they may be personified by being given some human features, and the remains of a polychrome fresco on one of the great pyramids at Moche appear to represent them in revolt against their human masters. Music and dancing have their place on some vases. Panpipes are very frequently represented, and are played by gods, men, or even skeletons in a sort of dance of death. There are actual pottery trumpets, both straight and looped, and conch shells with the end removed were used for the same purpose, as indeed they still are on the Peruvian and Ecuadorian coasts. Pottery whistles were in use, particularly the spherical ones built into whistling jars, and so were notched flutes of bone and pottery, of a type still used in Peru under the name of quena, and actual examples are common in addition to representations on pots. Rattles were made of pottery, metal or strings of large seeds, and, again, they are depicted on pots, as are drums and tambourines.

Human beings suffering from various diseases are vividly shown on some of the pots, and others appear to have been deliberately mutilated by the amputation of limbs, lips or nose, perhaps as a punishment. There are some few vases, which have the form of a potato with painted or modelled 'eyes', surmounted by a human head with the mouth mutilated to resemble the eye of the potato, and it has been suggested that this was a form of magic to stimulate the fertility of the plant. Amputations may have been done also for medical reasons, and circumcision was practised. There are representations of medicine men performing cures by sucking the affected part to remove a foreign body, which is still a well-known shamanistic practice. Ghastly figures, naked and with the face flayed, are depicted tied to a frame and exposed to birds of prey, and it is believed that this was the mode of execution of persons guilty of serious crimes. Some modelled vessels show scenes of sexual activity, and it is noteworthy that most, if not all, are perversions of some sort, in contrast with the natural ones on the earlier Salinar vessels. They are far from common and form but a small proportion of the very large collections of Mochica pottery which exist, so when it is considered that a vessel of this kind is bound to attract attention it is clear that they do not necessarily indicate that these practices were particularly prevalent. Larco states that they are confined to the latest stages of the Mochica Culture.

Representations on pottery are not confined to the supernatural, the spectacular and the abnormal, and almost anything may be shown. There is even an instance of a man washing his hair! The animal and vegetable worlds are well shown. There are deer, fish, foxes, frogs, monkeys, snakes and other animals, but birds in particular are beautifully modelled or painted, and the species can sometimes be identified. Owls are particular favourites, and human figures with owl faces, wings and tails are often found. The naturalistic jaguar shown attacking a prisoner on Plate 23 is a rare type. Among vegetables there are maize, potatoes, squash and gourds. Gourds were also sometimes used as containers, and they may be decorated with incised designs.

Plate 25

The Mochica buried their dead lying on the back in an extended position in a rectangular grave, which may be lined with courses of stones, or with rectangular adobes in which niches are contrived for the reception of offerings. The bodies are often wrapped in cloth, which is rarely well preserved, and sometimes enclosed in bundles of canes or in cane coffins, or in rare instances they may be protected by large jars or parts of them. A piece of metal wrapped in cloth, gold, silver or copper according to the degree of the dead, was commonly placed in the mouth, and instances occur of cane tubes extending to the surface of the ground, which Larco interprets as vehicles for offerings of food or drink, although they could possibly be for the passage of the spirit.

A striking instance of the burials in canes was excavated by Professor Strong at the Huaca de la Cruz in the Virú Valley. In a rectangular pit about 11 feet deep, which appeared to have been hastily dug, he found the remains of a man wrapped in fine cotton cloth inside a bundle of canes with a copper plate in his mouth, accompanied by several Mochica jars. On removing this, a rectangular cane coffin with the remains of a coarse covering of twill was seen, and with it were two headless sacrificed llamas. The crouched remains of two sacrificed women were found outside the coffin at two opposite corners. The coffin was opened and inside was a rich array of grave goods, including 27 jars of late Mochica type, gourd bowls, three boxes made of wooden slats wrapped with coloured thread, and the decayed remains of feather fans and ornaments and elaborate head-dresses. In their midst were three wooden staves, which were old when buried and had been repaired. One was a war club with a pear-shaped head carved with an elaborate fighting scene, and a socketed copper point. The second had a carved owl sitting on the top, and the third was a copper-shod ceremonial digging-stick on the top of which was carved the figure of a god in human form with feline tusks, wearing a loin-cloth and a semi-circular head-dress with a feline face in front and a cushion-like protuberance at the back. The staring red and yellow eyes, the tusks and other features were marked by shell inlay, some of which was missing. At the god's right hand stood a small boy with a large mouth, which may formerly have had feline tusks, holding some lumps

See *Bibliography*, Strong and Evans, 1952

Fig. 9

of turquoise. There can be no doubt that the pair were meant to represent the feline god and an attendant, in the character of the patron of agriculture, and that the turquoise grains were maize which the boy would plant while the god dug, just as the women still plant the seed while their husbands dig with the taccla or digging-stick.

When most of these things had been removed, the skeleton of a small boy was found on the left side of the coffin. He had

Fig. 9. Tusked god and boy from the head of a ceremonial digging-stick in the burial of a Mochica Warrior-Priest, Huaca de la Cruz, Virú Valley. Height about 6 in. (Redrawn from Strong.)

a deformed skull and a heavy jaw, he was wrapped in cloth and some gilt copper plates were sewn to it round his waist. Beneath him was a horizontal cane partition which occupied most of the coffin, and under this was the body of an old, old man wrapped in cloth, with the remains of a head-dress like that on the god on the staff, a gilt copper mask inlaid with turquoise over his mouth and a simple copper mask over his face. He and the boy clearly represented the two figures on the digging-stick, but the war club and the owl staff show that the old man had other functions as well, and Strong has justly called him the Warrior-Priest. The significance of the owl staff is not known, but it doubtless betokened some kind of authority, and the whole assemblage indicates the dual character, religious and secular, of the Mochica rulers. Why was he buried hastily with his venerable insignia? The pottery belongs to the very last stages of the Mochica Culture, when the art was showing signs of weariness and disintegration, and the Mochica domination was soon to be eclipsed by the arrival of invaders bringing new ideas from the south. It may be that the death of the old man brought a dynasty to an end, and perhaps the enemy was already at the gate.

NORTH
HIGHLANDS

In the northern highlands, there are two very different aspects of the culture of the Classic Period, neither of them known in great detail. The more northerly, in the Cajamarca Basin, was entirely independent of outside influences from any Peruvian area yet studied, between the modified Chavín Period already mentioned and the end of the Classic. During this time there arose a pottery style known as Cursive, from its lightly painted

Plate 29

running designs which vaguely recall writing, in brownish-black, sometimes also in red, on a white or cream ground. Highly stylized animals or animal heads are sometimes included in the painting. Most of the vessels are open bowls of various forms on ring bases. Large plain cooking pots on tall tripod feet appear here in the Classic Period, a feature which suggests very strongly that there were contacts with the Ecuadorian Andes, although there is no sign of the Cursive style there.

Plates 26-8

In the Callejón de Huaylas is the remarkable pottery style of Recuay. This consists of vessels decorated with black negative designs over white and red, one of the most characteristic being a highly stylized feline in profile with an elongated comb projecting from the head. There is a great deal of lively modelling different in character from the Mochica and inferior to it. A

very typical feature is a broad, nearly horizontal flange surrounding the mouth of a jar. Highly stylized and rather crude
stone statues representing warriors and women are linked to
Recuay by some of the incised designs which adorn them, and
it is believed that some rather elaborate stone buildings of two-
or three storeys, roofed with stone slabs, may belong to it.
Recuay graves are stone-lined, and may be a simple box or a
gallery. In general, this area demonstrates the highland prefer-
ence for stone over adobe as a building material, which is a

*Fig. 10. Two bowls, painted in black, white and red. Inter-
locking style, Classic Period, Central Coast. Approximate
height 7 in. (After Kroeber.)*

reflection not only of its availability but of the wet climate with
its regular rains.

The central coast is an area of minor importance in the central coast
Classic Period, and it has not yet been possible to learn much
about the nature of the buildings or the distribution of the
population. A polychrome pottery style called the Interlocking
links a number of valleys, and gets its name from the small,
angular interlocking units, some apparently purely geometrical *Fig. 10*
and some derived from animals and fish, or their heads, which
may cover the surface after the manner of some of the textiles.

F

The interlocking designs may occupy a limited area such as a border, or be replaced by scattered ones of the same character. It is known that the important ceremonial site of Pachacámac, a short distance south of Lima, was occupied at this period, and most of the ruins in the lower Rimac Valley, in which Lima lies, appear to belong to it. Among these is a notable group of rectangular adobe pyramids variously called Aramburú and Maranga, where Professor Kroeber excavated a number of extended burials, mostly wrapped in cloth and lashed to a litter made of canes, generally face downwards and accompanied by a single pot or nothing at all.

SOUTH COAST
Nazca Culture

In the south coast, the Classic Period is represented by the Nazca Culture. Until the recent work of Strong, this was chiefly known from the polychrome funerary pottery, which is extensively represented in museums all over the world. Practically nothing was known about any dwellings or ceremonial centres. Strong's work is very recent and only a brief summary is available, but he found what he describes as a great capital at Cahuachi in the Nazca Basin, though it is not clear whether it can properly be described as an urban centre. It includes wattle and daub rooms, walls built of conical adobes, platforms and pyramids.

The Nazca Culture was confined to three comparatively small valleys, those of Nazca, Pisco and Ica, and it differs from the Mochica in not providing any evidence for expansion or aggressive tendencies. In view of the smaller area and smaller population, the irrigation canals did not need to be on such a large scale, and no fortifications have been discovered. The pottery does not provide the same sort of evidence about the structure of society as that of the Mochica, but, such as it is, it indicates an interest rather in the supernatural than in the rank and occupations of men. The burial tradition of the south continued, and huddled, cloth-wrapped mummies were buried in circular chambers, approached from the surface by a shaft. The textiles were not as rich or abundant as those of Paracas, but their production doubtless absorbed a great deal of the time and energy of many workers, to a degree which the grave offerings of the north coast, which consisted predominantly of mould-made pottery, could not have done.

The pottery was thin, well fired, and, in contrast with the Mochica, was painted in many colours. The ware is buff or red, and it is painted in up to eight colours, the most usual being shades of red, yellow, brown, grey and violet, together with black and white, the designs being outlined with black in some cases. Several chronological stages were distinguished on typological grounds by Kroeber many years ago, the chief being an early one, Nazca A, and a late one, Nazca B, with a mainly post-Classic Nazca Y. Strong's stratigraphical work has con-firmed this, but he has added an early stage before Nazca A, of which details are not yet available. Most Nazca A pots have rather a sombre red background to the designs, and white back-grounds are usual in B. Bowls and beakers of various types are the commonest forms, but double spout and head and spout jars are very characteristic. Modelling plays a very minor part and seldom goes beyond the head on a jar; the one man band belongs to Nazca Y, when modelling is more frequent. The painted designs fall into two main groups, the first consisting of recognizable but stylized life forms, such as birds, fish or fruits, and the second of religious and mythological themes, such as complex demons; for example, a centipede with a feline face, which may wear a mouth-mask like the metal ones that are found on some mummies. Some of these demons carry human heads, which are also a very common feature by them-selves, generally forming part of the painted decoration on a vessel but sometimes a whole pot. The frequency of this motif shows that the head cult, to which attention has already been drawn, was very strong at this time. The treatment of the human face in Nazca art is highly characteristic and is not confined to the pottery. There is a strong likeness between the

Plate 30

Plate 31

Plate 32

Plate 34

Nazca pottery demons and those on the Paracas Necropolis textiles, which implies that there cannot be any very great difference in age between them.

When the traveller by air looks down on the desolate pampas round Nazca, he sees a multitude of long, straight lines, geo‑

Plate 35

metrical figures and other markings on the ground, a pheno‑ menon which has not been observed elsewhere in Peru except on a small scale in the Virú Valley. They were formed by removing the dark brown crust, rich in iron oxide, which covers the yellow sandy surface in this neighbourhood, and piling it up round the exposed areas. The lines may radiate from a point in almost any direction, form parallel groups, or be distributed irregularly, and they vary from half a kilometre to more than 8 kilometres in length. They are associated with elongated, solid areas of more or less rectangular, trapezoidal or triangular form, one of the largest being 1700 metres long with a mean width of 50 metres. Spirals and zigzag lines are frequent, and there are irregular forms besides occasional birds and fish. Lines frequently intersect and figures may be superimposed on one another, but examples of the various types are associated in a way which suggests that no great time difference is involved. Their actual age is a mystery, but a clue is that some animal forms have appendages which recall in a vague way those of some monsters on Nazca Y or even possibly Nazca B pots. Their object has not been satisfactorily explained; the best sug‑ gestion so far is that the lines were for making astronomical observations for calendrical purposes, and that the elongated geometrical figures were the result of adjusting a line as the position of the first appearance of a star above the horizon varied over a period of years. This does not explain the zigzag lines and curvilinear forms. Whatever the explanation, the setting out and execution of these perfectly straight lines and other figures must have required a great deal of skill and not a little disciplined labour.

The remaining area where cultures ascribed to the Classic Period are known is the southern highlands, with its two important sites at Tiahuanaco and Pucara. Of these, Tia-huanaco is by far the better known, and in view of its wide-spread influence on subsequent developments, its importance is very great. The ruins, with their imposing stonework, attracted attention long ago, and not only have they suffered greatly from the plundering of the stones for building, but they have been the victims of a great deal of unsound speculation, which has ascribed an absurdly great age to them on ridiculous grounds. Tiahuanaco is believed to have been a ceremonial centre under strong religious control, and it was perhaps built with the aid of pilgrims, as has been suggested for some of the Formative sites. The art is stiff, formal and impersonal. The neighbourhood lies at a great height and is cold and bleak, but it supports a fairly large scattered population and may have done so in the past. It is suitable for the herding of llamas and alpacas, and the growing of potatoes and grains like quinoa. The ruins consist of a number of units, each of regular construction, but their relation to one another is haphazard. There is a stone-faced stepped pyramid, more or less triangular in plan, made by improving a natural hillock, and on the top are foundations of buildings and a reservoir. Near by is a rectangular enclosure measuring 130 metres by 135 metres, formerly slightly raised, with the remains of a dressed stone retaining wall consisting of upright stones alternating with a filling of smaller rectangular blocks, most of which have disappeared. Within it, at one end, is a smaller enclosure, approached from the outside by a wide stairway of six great monolithic steps between a pair of massive uprights, which form part of the wall common to the outer and inner enclosures at that end.

Some stone statues have been found in these enclosures, and a most striking feature, standing in one corner of the outer enclosure, is a great monolithic gateway, cut from a block of

Plate 36

85

Fig. 11

lava 12 feet 6 inches by 10 feet, bearing a central carved figure at the top, dominating a frieze of three rows of attendants, below which is a border of frets enclosing faces like that of the central figure and ending in condor heads. The central figure stands facing the front and holding a staff vertically in either hand. The hands lack the little finger. The staves have condor heads at the lower end, and that in the right hand, which is probably a spear‑thrower, has a condor at the upper end to represent the hook, while that in the left hand is bifurcated and terminates in two condor heads at the top. It may be intended to represent a quiver containing two darts. The trapezoidal head of the figure is surrounded by a halo of appendages, which include six puma heads on long necks, each with a ring balanced on the end of the snout like a lump of sugar, and the face has round, staring eyes from which fall bands bearing circles, sug‑gesting tears. Condor and puma heads are repeated on the body of the figure, and from his belt hangs a row of faces, perhaps trophy heads. He is generally said, without any certain evidence, to represent a great creator god of Peruvian mythology, who in much later times was recorded by the Spanish chroniclers under various names, the best known being Viracocha. The attendants, who run in towards him, have faces like his own, but in profile, or condor faces, and are dressed in winged cloaks bearing numerous condor head appendages. They carry staves similar to his. The weeping eyes, the running figures, and above all the condor and the puma, represented so differently from the felines of northern Peru, are features which recur constantly wherever the influence of Tiahuanaco is felt.

There are other units, of which the chief are a rectangular enclosure, and a platform or pyramid, much destroyed, which was built of very large stone blocks, some of which weigh over 100 tons. Associated with this are many remarkable carved blocks, including some with recessed geometrical decorations, such as squares with stepped sides, and some very large ones containing niches and doorways, which may have been parts of chambers with monolithic walls. The stones composing this and other Tiahuanaco masonry may be fitted and held in

Fig. 11. Central figure from monolithic gateway at Tiahuanaco. Height about 2 ft. (After Joyce.)

place by means of accurately cut notches or by copper cramps, straight or T-shaped at either end, set in grooves.

A number of massive monolithic statues have been found in and around Tiahuanaco, the largest being 24 feet in total height. They resemble pillars bearing relief designs rather than true sculptures in the round; clothing is indicated by lightly incised designs, and the figures may carry beakers or unidenti' fied objects. Other carvings include slabs with relief designs, and heads tenoned for insertion into walls. It is natural to suppose that the incised designs on the statues are derived from textile patterns, but the same may probably be said of the carvings on the monolithic gateway, and although no highland Tiahuanaco textiles have been preserved, very similar designs appear on coastal ones which were subject to Tiahuanaco in' fluence. Classic Tiahuanaco pottery lacks some designs found on the stonework, such as the full'face standing figure, which appear on coastal pottery and textiles, and there is no stonework on the coast, so it is most likely that textiles were the main vehicle for the passage of Tiahuanaco designs from highlands to coast.

The only stratigraphical excavation at Tiahuanaco was done by Bennett in 1932, and he was permitted to work only on a very limited scale. He established a succession of periods marked by pottery styles, comprising a Classic which is believed to correspond to the major building works, preceded by an Early Period, and succeeded by a Decadent one. The typical decorated Classic pottery is a fine, polished polychrome, which most commonly has a red slip and designs painted in yellow, grey or brown, black and white, or some of these colours. The colours, originally bright, may weather rather faint and indistinct. Pumas and condors in profile, with eyes divided vertically into black and white halves, are common designs, and so are geometrical figures such as steps, triangles and the com' bination expressively called the step fret. Like all Tiahuanaco art, the designs are stiff and formal. The shapes include a tall, graceful, hollow'sided beaker, the kero, and various types of bottle and flaring'sided bowl, including modelled puma vessels. The Early Tiahuanaco polychrome vessels are decorated in

Fig. 12
Plates 39, 42

shiny black, white, red, orange and brown, direct on the micaceous buff clay or on a slip of the same colour. There are characteristic interlocking geometrical designs, and curious animal forms, with divided eyes, which look more like broken-down, stylized developments than primitive ones, although they are quite different from the Decadent Tiahuanaco designs. A very typical Early Tiahuanaco shape, the 'spittoon', is illustrated in Plate 38. The post-Classic Decadent stage shows greater frequency of geometrical designs, the breakdown of animal forms, with repetition of eyes or heads instead of whole figures, and a general degeneration in execution. Colours become duller, and lack the polish of the Classic Period. Among vessel shapes, the beaker or kero becomes less graceful and may have a disproportionately small base. Decadent Tia-huanaco may have continued in the home area in Bolivia for a long period, until shortly before the Inca Conquest in the fifteenth century.

Fig. 12. 'Kero' or beaker. Classic Tiahuanaco. (To show the form, not the decoration.) Height about 6 in.

The Classic Tiahuanaco Culture in its pure form has a limited distribution, although a few sites with its masonry, its pottery or both have been found in the neighbourhood of the type site. The area has not been very fully explored, but it is most unlikely that any centres of the period comparable in importance with Tiahuanaco have escaped notice. On the other hand, clear signs of Tiahuanaco influence in the shape of characteristic designs without some features of the total culture, for example the stonework, are widespread. Derived Tia-huanaco, as Bennett calls it, in one form or another, is found in the Eastern Cordillera in Bolivia, at Huari in the central high-lands, and in many parts of the coast, but its developments in the two latter areas belong to the next chapter.

Pucara lies some distance north-west of Lake Titicaca on the side opposite to Tiahuanaco, near a station on the Juliaca to Cuzco railway. This is well known to travellers as a flourish-ing pottery-making centre at the present time, and well-made

Pucara

bulls and other objects are laid out for sale beside the line. The excavations there have not been fully described, but it is known that the site includes rough, probably domestic, buildings of undressed stone, and a well-built sanctuary. This consists, at ground level, of a series of horse-shoe-shaped walls of red sand-stone, made up of straight sectors, which enclose a slightly sunk terrace bounded by white sandstone slabs, and containing a sunk court, some fifty feet square and seven feet below the terrace, also bounded by tall white sandstone slabs and entered by a stair. The outer horse-shoe wall includes in its thickness a series of small chambers, entered from the inner side, each containing one or two altar-like slabs. The central court has a stone-lined grave chamber containing several burials, in the centre of each side. The original height of the walls is unknown, and there is no evidence that the structure as a whole was roofed. There are surface indications that there were other similar structures on the site. The masonry is not so well fitted as that of Tiahuanaco, and chinks may be filled with adobe or pieces of stone.

Apart from the walls, the stonework consists chiefly of statues and standing slabs or stelae. The statues are mostly rather less pillar-like than those of Tiahuanaco, and generally represent a man wearing nothing but a breech clout with curious square side flaps and some form of cap. He may hold a trophy head and possibly a knife. The stelae frequently have a step cut out of one side at the top, and are carved with fine champlevé or incised designs which generally take the form of a lizard-like creature with a ring above the head, or of complex geometrical figures, mostly made up of elements like checkers, stepped crosses, jagged zigzags, diamonds and chevrons, suggestive of textile patterns.

Among a variety of plain red and brown mica-tempered pottery wares is a highly characteristic polychrome. This is made of a reddish-buff micaceous paste very similar to that used in Early Tiahuanaco, and designs are either painted direct in red and black on the natural colour, or in black and rather fugitive yellow over a red slip. A highly characteristic feature is that the outlines of the colour patches are incised. No whole vessels have been found, so our knowledge of designs and shapes is imperfect, but there are puma or cat figures in profile with the head shown full face in low relief, human and condor heads in profile, concentric circles in black and red, and geometrical figures such as stepped lines. Eyes are divided vertically like those of Tiahuanaco animals, but the natural buff of the clay may take the place of the white. Another feature which the two cultures have in common is the ring balanced on the nose of a cat. As far as can be deduced from sherds, the commonest forms are a flat-bottomed bowl with flaring sides, and a bowl with a low ring base.

Plate 37

Pucara pottery and sculpture have demonstrated the distribution of the culture over the area between the type site and the north-west end of the Lake, but it has not been found elsewhere. Its relation to Tiahuanaco is uncertain, they have features in common but there are many differences. No chronological stages have been distinguished, but on the whole it gives the impression of being rather older than Classic Tiahuanaco.

CHAPTER VI

The Expansionist Period

THE CLASSIC PERIOD was succeeded by the Expansionist Period, the first stage of the post-Classic, which has
been given this name owing to the wide and rapid spread of
features associated with Tiahuanaco. It has been conjectured
that the stage was set for this expansion by the development of
a general state of unrest, the chief outward expression of which
was the Mochica conquest of the valleys to the south of their
original home. Elsewhere, the isolation of the north highland
culture of Cajamarca began to be broken down, and there are
signs that the influence of Recuay was making itself felt on the
coast.

The appearance of Tiahuanaco elements on the coast was
sudden and catastrophic. The chief signs of the change are the
introduction of a new art style in most of the coast and part of
the highlands, and the appearance of new types of settlement
and southern burial customs in the north coast. Although there
is clear evidence for the influence of Tiahuanaco in all this, it
is not a simple case of an invasion of the coast by Tiahuanaco
people. There are features in common between the two areas but
many differences—there is a Bolivian Tiahuanaco tradition and
a distinct Peruvian one. Peruvian Tiahuanaco has many variations,which emerge more strongly as local traditions in the coast
make themselves felt, but, at the beginning, the style which is
called Coast Tiahuanaco A indicates a considerable degree of
unity over the whole area, and it is expressed chiefly in the
pottery and textiles over the whole coast from Nazca to Moche.

The stone carving and building which is so characteristic
of Bolivian Tiahuanaco is altogether absent from the coast.
Several features which belong to it and which curiously enough
do not occur on Bolivian Tiahuanaco pottery, are constantly

found on the coastal pottery and textiles, where they are associated with divided eyes and other features shared by highland pottery. Among these Classic stone-carved designs are the full-face standing figure from the great gateway, its face alone, and the running winged figures which accompany it; details may be modified or simplified, for instance, puma heads may replace condor ones in some positions, and the 'tears' on the face of the central figure may be elaborated into trophy heads or simplified into wavy lines, but it is clear that it is intended to show the same personages. It has already been suggested that these designs may have been transferred to the coast from the highlands largely by means of textiles, but this may not be the complete explanation because the colour scheme of the pottery in both areas is similar, whereas that of the textiles, preserved only in the coast, is always somewhat different and may be totally distinct. Both highland and coastal pottery are well made and polished, the ground is generally red and the designs are painted in black, white, yellow and grey though the colours normally remain more vivid on the coastal pots. Although many of the shapes in the two areas differ, there are two in common, the beaker or kero, and a cup of squatter proportions, but there is a tendency for the sides to be straight instead of concave on the coastal examples. Some textiles have a red ground, with designs worked in yellow, white, brown and blue, and in these cases the scheme is not very unlike that of the pottery, since blue has taken the place of grey and brown that of black, but in a large group most of the area is occupied by yellows and oranges or light browns, with details in a number of colours, including blue, green, red, pink, black and white. Too much must not be made of the differences, since we do not know enough about the exact chronology, or the availability of different dyes, to be able to assess the importance of these factors.

Plate 41

Some consideration may now be given to the general result

of these changes, and to the way in which they came about. In the south coast, highland designs began to appear on vessels of Nazca shapes in the late stage which has been called Nazca Y. The next step was the obliteration of the Nazca Culture, which never reappeared, and the same applies to the Interlocking pottery style of the central coast. In the north, in the valleys of Virú, Moche and Chicama, the Mochica Culture was sub-merged or driven out, but its relative strength is shown by the fact that elements of it, particularly the modelling tradition in pottery, reappeared later, when local cultures developed again, although much was changed.

Huari

See *Bibliography*, Bennett, 1953

There is an intermediate site between Tiahuanaco and the coast, which has made the relations between them somewhat clearer, namely, Huari (or Wari) in the Mantaro Basin in the central highlands, which was the subject of Bennett's last work. This was a great habitation site with a good deal of rough walling. It also contains some stone statues and a little dressed stonework of a ceremonial nature, in the form of subterranean chambers on one, two or three levels, which may be a link with the stonework of Tiahuanaco, although it is less elaborate and lacks copper bonding cramps. The pottery includes a poly-chrome which is in the coastal or Peruvian tradition, with such features as the standing figure with his staves, skulls, rows of chevrons, profile puma and condor heads but not whole animals, and so on. There are other, non-Tiahuanaco, pottery styles at Huari, which Bennett regards as representing a local development, although some types may show influence from Nazca, and others, such as a local cursive style, are almost certainly due to influences from the north, since there are also some cursive sherds in distinctively Cajamarca style, which must have been carried from there.

A great deal remains to be done in the Mantaro Basin, and the predecessors of the Huari Culture have yet to be found and its own distribution traced, but Bennett considers that the best

explanation of the facts as we know them is that the introduction of the distinctively Tiahuanaco designs on pottery, and
perhaps the stonework, was due to an invasion of an established
culture by alien elements from Tiahuanaco. He shows reason to
believe that the Huari Culture at the type site was rather later in
date than Classic Tiahuanaco. The total Huari Culture was
not carried on to the coast, any more than the total Tiahuanaco
Culture was carried to Huari; it was the religious symbols
which travelled, the standing figure with his attendants, the
trophy heads which he carries, and the cat and condor heads
with which he is adorned, and they seem to have been carried
on mortuary textiles and to a lesser extent on ceremonial pottery
in a form which had developed at Huari. The conclusion is
inescapable that the expansion was basically religious in
character, but its catastrophic effects show that it must have
been backed by military force.

More can now be said about the special features of Coast
Tiahuanaco. Apart from the Virú Valley, most of our knowledge is derived from grave goods in cemeteries and we have
little information about the buildings. At Pacheco, in the
Nazca Valley, is a cemetery that is known for its polychrome
pottery, which takes three rather special forms. There are large,
thick, U-shaped urns with flattened bases, decorated with some
of the best coastal examples of the full-face standing figure,
which may have been made to contain mummy bundles.
There are also fragments of large, boldly painted human heads,
and large vessels in the form of a llama, with a collar-opening
set in the back.

In the central coast, the best-known cemeteries are at Ancón
and Pachacámac, and these contain many mummy bundles
with finely woven wrappings, buried in conical or cylindrical
chambers, with a covering of wood, stone, cane or mats. The
best and most usual of the textiles at this period are of tapestry,
but all the older techniques continued in use. Two processes,

SOUTH AND
CENTRAL
COAST

95

which if known before had rarely been used, now became common, namely, knotted pile cloth, used chiefly for making square caps, and a method of tie dyeing in which pieces of the cloth are gathered up and whipped round with waxed thread before dipping, to resist the dye, leaving rows of diamond-shaped outlines in the colour of the undyed cloth. By an ingenious application of this method, a patchwork of squares of different colours, bearing contrasting diamonds, was built up, and large pieces were sometimes used to wrap mummies.

The ikat method of tie dyeing is believed to have been introduced towards the end of the period. This process, in which the warps are dyed before weaving, the pattern being produced by wrapping those portions which are not to be dyed with waxed thread before dipping, is fairly common in modern times in western South America. It was extremely rare in Ancient Peru. Only four examples have been reported, belonging either to this period or the subsequent one, from the north and central coast. The rare occurrence of such a highly specialized technique suggests introduction from outside Peru, and it is tempting to look to Indonesia, but, until something is known of its age there, speculation will be profitless.

Tapestry designs include not only close copies of the Tiahuanaco figures already mentioned, but also various degrees of stylization, of which the most extreme are abstractions in which little can be recognized except the divided eyes. Apart from the beakers and cups which have already been mentioned, highly characteristic Central Coast A forms are the double-spout-and-bridge jar, with rather long, tapering spouts, and jars with a modelled face on the collar. As time went on, the Tiahuanaco symbolism began to break down, and rather an ill-defined Coastal Tiahuanaco B stage was reached. Signs of this are seen in what Uhle long ago called the Epigonal style, which may still retain recognizable Tiahuanaco characteristics like the divided eyes on the head cup from Huacho, though in general

Plate 33

Plate 41

Plate 43

the designs show evident signs of degeneration, with a tendency to break up into geometrical patterns. The stylized tapestries mentioned above are evidently a product of the same trend. The full development of Coastal Tiahuanaco B is reached in the black-white-red pottery style with purely geometrical decoration. In company with the painted pottery styles of later Coastal Tiahuanaco stages are found red and black wares with pressed relief decoration, prominent among which is coarse stippling, which may form the background to human or animal figures or scrolls.

Plate 54

Besides pottery and textiles, many objects of various kinds have been found in Coast Tiahuanaco graves, and they show that wood, shell, metals, bone and stone were worked with equal skill. Among the most interesting are the carved wooden paddles and centre boards with which rafts like the Kon-Tiki were steered. The examples illustrated are from Ica, in the south, and their ornamental carving shows that they were probably made for burial in the graves in which they were found, but plain ones exist. Those illustrated may possibly belong to the subsequent period, but Coast Tiahuanaco examples exist, and they show that coastwise travel on rafts was already possible at this time, although it was never the main means of communication.

Plate 50

In the north, the Virú Valley survey has told us what little we know about the effect of what may be called the Tiahuanaco-Huari crusade on mundane things such as domestic pottery and buildings, as well as on the temples and forts. To deal with the latter first, both the large pyramids and the Gallinazo-Mochica strong points went out of use, and the main type of structure which can be regarded as a public building is a large high-walled rectangular compound without interior divisions, of which three examples were found in the lower part of the valley. The walls were of adobe, in the massive cast form known as tapia, and some of them survive to a height of ten

NORTH COAST

G

97

See *Bibliography*, Willey, 1953

feet. Their function is uncertain, but the discoverer, Professor Willey, considers that they may be some sort of religious or political meeting place. Groups of dwellings or small villages, enclosed within more or less rectangular compound walls of smaller size than the previous type, also came into vogue. A typical example of medium size measures 60 feet by 40 feet. The walls have foundations of stone in the upper part of the valley, and of tapia in the lower part, surmounted in each case by plain rectangular adobe bricks. The interior is divided into rooms, with courts and corridors, and in some cases there is a low pyramid or platform, perhaps a kind of domestic shrine. The introduction of this type of dwelling did not mean that the older ones all went out of use; a considerable number of the unenclosed clusters of houses were still in-habited, and it is only natural that much of the original population should continue to live in their old homes. The introduction of the enclosed type of village is believed to mark the beginning of the trend towards the urbanization which was characteristic of the following period, and outside Virú there

Plates 51-3

is evidence that Chan-Chan, near Trujillo, the greatest urban site of the Chimú in later times, was already occupied, though nothing is known of the scale of the occupation.

There is little published evidence about the burials of this period in the north, but from a statement that graves were a yard or less in diameter in the Virú cemetery we may infer that the custom of burying the dead sitting in a crouched position was introduced from the south at this time. This has recently been confirmed by Collier's work. Cloth-wrapped mummies of this form were common in the north in the subsequent City Builder Period.

See *Bibliography*, Collier, 1955

The pottery in Virú showed marked changes with the fall of the Mochica. Grey and black wares became predominant on the domestic sites, showing the mastery of the reducing flame in firing, and the old distinction between domestic and funerary wares became less marked, so that decorated pottery is found in some quantity in the household rubbish and plain wares are occasionally found in graves. The black and grey decorated forms are extremely varied in form, and include such types as double vessels, double-spout-and-bridge jars, and canteen-shaped bottles. Their decoration is in pressed relief, and takes the form of geometrical designs such as angular step-frets or curvilinear scrolls. Some have slightly sunken areas bearing pictorial designs such as men holding staves, moons, or cats, in low relief against a stippled background. These wares are closely related to those already mentioned from the central coast. Plain black or grey jars with an applied face on the collar are also common. In earlier times, the changes in domestic wares from period to period were so gradual as to suggest that they developed locally, but at this time there is a strong indica-tion of the import of wares of a different tradition from outside. The source of these black and grey wares is believed to be the far north of the coast, the Lambayeque and neighbouring valleys, and it has been suggested that their arrival in Virú may be due to a forcible removal of part of the population by the highland invaders, a foretaste of Inca practice. The obvious difficulty about this very interesting suggestion is that there is little evidence of Tiahuanaco-Huari intrusion north of the Chicama Valley. Further study of the far north is needed to clarify the matter.

It is not possible to say exactly where the relatively pure Coast Tiahuanaco A stage and the decadent B stage fall in the Virú Tiahuanacoid sequence, since the characteristic painted pottery types are funerary and are insufficiently represented on the living sites which have been studied; but the typical A polychrome and the black-white-red geometrical B ware are both present. The B stage is also represented by a special type of face-collar jar with pressed relief pictorial designs on the body, painted in subdued black, white and red over a buff ground. The two stages are similarly represented in the valleys of Moche and Chicama.

Plate 44

The Tiahuanaco expansion in the north did not stop short on the coast, but affected the north highland basin of the Callejón de Huaylas also. Its influence here is shown in a painted pottery style which is closely related to Coast Tiahuanaco A of the central and south coasts, found associated with local wares including a negative black-on-red or -orange, and others apparently related to the north coast. This assemblage was excavated by Bennett in domestic rubbish as well as in stone-lined graves, some of them eight feet deep. Other Tiahuanaco-influenced wares are found in local collections, but their associations are uncertain.

The effect of the Tiahuanaco contact does not seem to have been very profound, since the pottery is associated with a great deal of stone building, which is rather rough but which in a general way continues the local tradition of Chavín and Recuay. Besides the tombs, there are houses built of rough stone, with one or two floors, containing from one to four rooms, roofed with stone slabs with earth piled on the top. There are also a few examples of a more elaborate type of building of similar construction, which Bennett has called temples. He has described one of these called Wilkawain, with three storeys each containing seven rooms with ventilating shafts, which is built of split but undressed stone, laid in alternate rows of thick and thin stones, with the interstices chinked with small stones. The alternation in thickness provides a faint reminiscence of the fine masonry of Chavín. The temple has a projecting course of stones at the top, with a recessed one beneath it, and below this was a row of cat heads tenoned in, but all of them have now been lost. This work has nothing in common with the stone masonry of Classic Tiahuanaco, and it is clear that the Tiahuanaco influences reached this area by way of the coast and not along the highlands.

Farther north, in the highland area to the east of the Chicama Valley, are a number of sites of the Expansionist Period, which

are altogether free from Tiahuanaco influence. Chief among
these is the great fortified hilltop of Marca Huamachuco, containing many buildings whose walls survive to a considerable
height, grouped about a circular citadel and enclosed within a
great outer wall. The walls are skilfully built of irregular stones,
a type of masonry which is called pirca in Peru, and some
buildings had two or even three storeys. It may be that these
fortifications were a reaction, which proved successful, to the
menace of the Tiahuanaco-Huari expansion. Ornamental
stone-carving is found here, and it includes stylized feline heads
with zigzag crests and tenons for insertion into walls, besides
small slabs carved with step frets. Among the pottery, some
types seem to be local, and there is a cursive style which seems
to be derived from Cajamarca, which is not far away, but what
stage in the Cajamarca succession it belongs to is not known.

In the Cajamarca Basin itself, the influence of the expansion *Cajamarca*
was felt, and pottery of various Tiahuanacoid styles has been
found there. The Reichlens, who have studied the region, have See *Bibliography,*
claimed that these include not only coastal types, but also Reichlen, 1949
Huari and Decadent Tiahuanaco sherds from the highlands.
If this is so, they must have by-passed part of the intervening
area, including the Callejón de Huaylas, in their travels, but
this is quite possible, since pure Cajamarca cursive-style sherds
were found, it will be remembered, at Huari. The Tiahuanaco
influence made itself felt gradually, and was not strong enough
to oust all the local characteristics, since cursive designs at first
continued in use on a reduced scale, subsequently giving place
to felines and heads of felines painted in a cursive manner, after
which these in their turn broke up into symbolic designs. All
this decoration was painted in black and red or black and
orange on the local white or cream paste, on small tripod and
ringed-based bowls, which were local forms.

Cajamarca in its turn influenced the coast. Open bowls on
ring bases or tripod feet, decorated in pure cursive style, are

found occasionally in the coastal valleys between the Lam-bayeque region and Moche, in Coast Tiahuanaco contexts, but they are almost certainly trade pieces from the type area. Later on, probably through their agency, appeared a coastal style called Cursive Modelled, which is believed to belong to the earliest stage of the Chimú Culture of the subsequent City Builder Period. It belongs in the same northern region but its range extends south to the Santa Valley. It is found on spout-and-bridge whistling jars, which are surmounted in most cases by modelled figures, and have long, tapering spouts. The ware is buff or reddish buff, and the typical painted decoration con-sists of red stripes, between which are black patterns such as zigzag lines, running scrolls, and scale patterns. It is the manner of execution of these rather than the patterns themselves which suggest derivation from the Cursive style.

CUZCO   The evidence for the sudden beginning and gradual fading of the great expansion in the various areas of the Central Andes has now been reviewed, but a conspicuous gap remains. No mention has been made of the Cuzco region, and in spite of its proximity to Tiahuanaco no conspicuous remains of the period have been identified there, although a Tiahuanacoid pottery horizon has recently been identified, followed by local pre-Inca styles. It was suggested at one time that the early Incas were already settled at Cuzco and were able to resist outside pressure, but this is ruled out by the new discoveries.

The most recent estimates of the duration of the Expansionist Period do not allow it more than 300 years, and place its beginning at about A.D. 1000; no radiocarbon dates for the period have been determined, but if any reliance can be placed on those available for the Classic Period, it probably began several centuries earlier.

CHAPTER VII

The City Builder Period

THE EXPANSIONIST PERIOD was brought to an end by the emergence of three states on the coast, one of which, the Chimú in the north, was large and powerful enough to be described as an empire. In all three, great urban centres were built, whence the name City Builder, which has been applied to the period of independence of these states, before they fell to the conquering Incas. It has already been suggested that the idea of the planned centre of population, within a compound wall, was brought from the south in the Expansionist Period, since structures of this kind on a small scale were already in use in Virú at that time. Huari itself is unlikely to have been the source of the idea, since the plan of the greater part of that site is not sufficiently regular and most of the surviving walls do not appear to belong to houses. Perhaps the origin is to be sought in the south coast, where Strong has found what he calls, in his preliminary account, a city of the Classic Period at Cahuachi in the Nazca Valley. The building of the cities and the con‚ centration of large numbers of people there is an index of the nature of the period, which was one of social and political development with little technological advance. The people had been organized in Classic times, but the process was intensified now, and the city plans, where they have been studied, appear to have been developed with a view to imposing strict control.

Two types of urban site have been distinguished in the Chimú area, and we may for convenience describe them as cities and towns. Both include rectangular units, containing planned groups of dwellings enclosed in massive walls, but some at least of those in the cities are more elaborate, and contain in addition terraced buildings with large rooms. These have walls richly decorated with textile‚like designs modelled in

Plate 51

Plates 52, 53

relief in mud plaster, as well as courts and mounds, and are believed to have been the dwellings of the ruling class and the cult centres. The towns seem to have served two purposes. Some are built in strategic positions, particularly at the places where valleys open out from the foothills on to the coastal plains, since it is here that the main irrigation canals are taken off; these would have accommodated garrisons. The others are situated in large irrigated areas, and would have been the homes of the labourers who worked them.

Although there were no notable advances in techniques at this time, with the possible exception of the invention or at any rate the limited spread of bronze, there are changes of emphasis, and in pottery and textiles there are signs of a tendency to mass-production. In metalwork the casting of copper was employed on a larger scale than before in the production of ornaments, useful objects like the blades of digging-sticks, or weapons such as mace-heads. Gold, silver, copper and their alloys were used abundantly in making vessels and articles of personal adorn-ment and use, such as crowns, ear ornaments, collars, armlets, lime spoons and thin sheet ornaments for sewing to garments. In pottery there was a tendency to standardization and reduc-tion in the number of colours. The modelling tradition revived in the north, but it was dull and lifeless by comparison with that of Mochica times. Elsewhere, entirely new styles evolved. Textiles are similar over the whole coast, and to distinguish between those of the different areas is a specialized task. Cloths of many types, predominantly of cotton, were made in abun-dance, but perhaps the most characteristic are garments adorned with regular rows, horizontal or diagonal, of conventionalized birds, animals or fish. These are generally brocaded, or worked in double cloth, in which case the field may be divided into squares of two alternating colours, each charged with a device of the opposite colour. Tapestry is normally confined to borders and other small areas, and embroidery is limited similarly.

Plate 47

Plate 45

Plates 46, 49

Feather-work is frequently found, feathers of various colours being sewn to a cotton cloth to build up a design, such as the stylized owls on the poncho figured in Plate 57. Feather head-dresses are often associated with such garments, and in the example illustrated a rectangular flap bearing owls like those on the poncho hangs down behind.

The best examples of textiles and feather-work, together with baskets, decorated gourds, and objects of wood, bone, shell and other materials, come from the graves. Throughout the coast, the normal form of burial is the mummy bundle, in which the crouched body is wrapped in textiles and the bundle provided with a false face usually of wood or metal, although pottery masks may be used. Neither at this nor at any other time was any process of embalming employed; the entrails were some-times removed and the cavity stuffed with grass, but this was by no means the rule and, in general, preservation is due entirely to the dry climate. Most bodies are quite dried up, but the slowness of decomposition in some cases is illustrated by a Chimú mummy found by Strong in Virú, which emitted such a foul smell that it was most unpleasant to work around, in spite of the lapse of at least 500 years. The grave goods differ greatly in elaboration according to the status of the deceased, and the graves themselves vary from a simple pit marked at the surface by an upright stick or paddle, to a square chamber roofed with canes or mats supported on beams, sometimes con-taining two mummies accompanied by pots, weaving instru-ments, beads and other grave goods.

In the Virú Valley, there was a great reduction in the number of sites, and most of the surviving ones were in the neighbour-hood of the shore. It may be that they depended for cultivation chiefly on plots of ground called pukíos, excavated down to the water table, which can only be reached in that way near the coast, and that the irrigation canals which had served most of the valley were in decay. Both of the main types of settlement,

NORTH COAST
See *Bibliography*,
Willey, 1953

the enclosed compounds and the irregular clusters of rooms, were still present, but the trend towards the first type continued. The population of the valley had clearly been drastically reduced, and very likely large numbers of people had been moved away, perhaps to Chan-Chan in the Moche Valley to the north. Virú had become a backwater and no great town or city was built or occupied there, although those rectangular compounds which contain mounds are like the characteristic city enclosures in miniature, and one has been found with some remains of mud plaster relief decoration on the entrance jambs.

Chimu
The date of foundation of the Chimú kingdom in the Moche Valley is uncertain, but the latest estimate is by John Rowe, based on post-Conquest writings, which puts it in the first half of the fourteenth century, though it can hardly be as late as this if the radiocarbon dating of the earlier periods can be relied on. Like the Mochica in the same region, it spread over the adjacent valleys, Virú being an early victim, and by the time it fell in its turn to the Incas in the middle of the fifteenth century, the Chimú dominion stretched from Tumbez in the far north nearly to Lima. It was a despotic state, and Rowe suggests that the Incas learnt many of the characteristic features of their civilization from it, including the rectangular city plan and mass production of goods.

Plates 51-3
The Chimú capital was Chan-Chan, and this is the outstanding example of the type of city referred to above. It covers an area of about eleven square miles, and contains ten or more large, walled, rectangular enclosures, oriented more or less in one direction but not in direct relation to one another. Each of these could have been the dwelling, or at least the headquarters, of some such division of the nation as a clan. In the spaces between them, there are irrigated areas, reservoirs and cemeteries, and on the outskirts is a great irrigated area with small compounds, and stone buildings which appear to guard canals

and roads, as well as large cemeteries. There are also numerous sunken pukíos, now full of reeds.

The enclosures average about 1300 feet by 650 feet, but some are larger, and the walls, which may be double or triple, stand up to a height of as much as 40 feet in places. The most usual building materials are rectangular adobe bricks, set in mud mortar, and often disguised by a coat of mud plaster, which makes them look like tapia, the puddled variety of adobe. The latter is used also, and so is a sort of clay concrete, mixed with stone and shell. The compounds vary in plan, but most of them contain a palace-like building with its decorated walls, inner compounds containing small rooms, perhaps for retainers, a stone-lined reservoir, irrigated plots, a pyramid, generally of modest dimensions, and rows of cells, sometimes described as prisons but which could equally well have been storerooms. The walls have no parapets, no means of access to the tops, and few entrances, and they seem to have been disciplinary rather than defensive.

The development of great cities of this type is believed to have been dependent on the combination of the irrigation schemes of more than one valley, and in the case of Chan-Chan water was derived from Chicama as well as Moche. The towns which were built to defend and work this system illustrate both the types mentioned above. One of defensive character is in the narrow part of the Moche Valley, up which it straggles for five miles, occupying terraced hillsides and small side valleys, and it includes regular compounds of both stone and adobe. It commands three of the main canals. The other, which consists mainly of scattered compounds, lies in Chicama in the midst of an area, formerly irrigated, alongside the great canal which led to Chan-Chan. Examples of all three types of settlement are found in the valleys farther north, and the diversion of water from one valley to another is illustrated by the existence of two great cities in small valleys adjacent to the large one of Lambayeque, from which water had to be taken in order to support them. The many buildings and the irrigation systems must have required a great deal of organized labour for their construction and maintenance, but an even greater problem must have been posed by the constant supply of food to cities like Chan-Chan. There was of course no wheeled transport, and although llamas were used they can carry very little even in their own mountain home, so the bulk of the food must have been carried on men's backs. As far as is known, there was no medium of exchange, so the distribution of food must have been a function of authority.

Although the roads of Ancient Peru are generally thought of in connection with the Incas and spoken of as Inca roads, inter-valley roads were always necessary to the coast states, and quite vital to the Chimú Empire, with its great extent along the coast. The Incas made use of them also, but they were more concerned with communications along the highlands, and between the highlands and the coast, so the principal coastal roads must date from pre-Inca times; the Incas may have modi-fied them in some sections. It is even possible that the Chimú had something to teach the Incas in this matter as in others. There are almost continuous traces of a road from the Motupe Valley just north of Lambayeque to the Chao Valley just south of Virú, with remains even farther south in Santa, Nepeña and Casma, which ran the greater part of the length of the Chimú Empire and must have existed at the time of its greatest extent. The remains differ in elaboration, and like our own roads they tend to be wider and more imposing near the great centres of population. In the deserts between valleys they were tracks between very low walls, or even marked by posts only, but in valleys the simplest type is a levelled surface 15 to 25 feet wide, enclosed between walls of stone or adobe about 3 feet high, though one of this type widens out to 80 feet as it approaches Chan-Chan. In some places the surface of the road is raised, and it may be flanked by canals. Some have an outer pair of walls 80 to 160 feet away from the road, enclosing cultivated fields.

Not much in the way of frontier defences has been observed in the Chimú area, which may be partly due to insufficient search, but it is probable that any work of this kind was concentrated on places where a threat was believed to exist. Much of the area was of course bounded on the east by uninhabited, barren hills. Paramonga, in the Fortaleza Valley, is a great terraced structure built of rectangular adobes, which is believed to be a fortress. It crowns a spur overlooking the valley, which is near the southern limit of the Chimú Empire, and it may have served to overawe a recently conquered people.

Plate 56

The Chimú Culture is familiar to many through its pottery, which is abundant in many museums. The most usual type is polished black ware, and the commonest shape is the stirrup-spouted jar, revived from former times in a somewhat modified form, with the spout generally squared in section and a small modelled animal or projection applied where the arch joins the upright. Other common types are the jar with a spout connected to a modelled figure by a flat bridge, and the double whistling jar with modelled figures standing on it, both of which are of southern origin; both may have been made in this sort of ware before the end of the previous period, but they are much more frequent in Chimú times. Decoration is chiefly by modelling in the round, normally in moulds, application, and pressed relief, the llama head illustrated being of better quality than the general run of modelled figures, which are far inferior to most Mochica work. Similar work is done in polished red ware, but it is not nearly so common, although a good deal of undecorated domestic red ware has been found at Chan-Chan. Painting is rare, but occasional modelled vessels decorated in black or black and red on a reddish-buff ground are found, including the cursive modelled type already described.

Plate 55

Plate 58

South of the Chimú was a much smaller state, which occupied the Chancay, Ancón and Rimac valleys in the central coast. The chroniclers give it the name of Cuismancu. Urban centres are found in this area also, and the chief of these is Cajamarquilla in the Rimac Valley above Lima; no plan of it has been published but it probably belonged to the city type. As in other parts of the coast, adobe was the main building material, but there was a greater use of tapia here than in the north. The chief archaeological evidence for this state is the existence of a single late pottery style in these valleys. The ware is thin, dull red or cream in colour, with a creamy-white slip, decorated with textile patterns in black. The chief shapes are an egg-shaped jar with a flaring collar and a pair of small loop handles, a similar jar with a modelled human face on the collar and skimpy limbs in low relief, and bowls of various types which may have a ring base. Both form and decoration are derived from the local expression of the black-white-red style of late Expansionist times, and the dropping of the red colour, as well as the poverty of the modelling, gives an impression of degeneracy.

Plate 59

cf. Plate 54

SOUTH COAST
Chincha

On the south coast was another state, the Chincha, which occupied the valleys of Chincha, Pisco, Ica and Nazca, to which may perhaps be added Cañete, at its northern margin, on the strength of the presence of the Ica pottery style. The chroniclers describe Chincha as a powerful state, which made incursions eastwards into and beyond the mountains, and they say that it was only conquered by the Incas after fierce battles, but the archaeological evidence does not suggest that it was organized to the same degree as the Chimú. There are some imposing ruins in the Chincha and Ica valleys, but true urban sites are rare. The ruins are much damaged, but although the plans are generally rectilinear in character, most of them give the impression of being grouped about a ceremonial nucleus, with terraces and pyramids. There are rooms and courts, but

they are believed to be either ceremonial or the houses of important people, and do not point to large concentrations of
population. This may be a reflection of the smaller size of the
valleys of the south. Tapia is a common building material, but
hard rectangular adobes are also used, and they are so much
better in quality than modern ones that Dr. Uhle observed that
they fetched ten times as much when sold for building houses,
a fact which has resulted in much destruction.

The Ica pottery style, which provides the archaeological
evidence for a political unit in this area, is found in all the
valleys enumerated above. It grew out of the Tiahuanacoid
Epigonal style, and passed smoothly through various stages,
which differ only in minor details; after a time, Inca features
appeared on some of the local forms, and then Inca influence
increased until the arrival of actual Cuzco types, which apparently marked the subjugation of the state by the Incas. The
vessels are made of hard, well-burnished, buff or dull red
ware, covered with painted decoration in black, white and red,   Plates 60-1
in the form of textile-derived patterns, which are chiefly geometrical but include small birds and fish. The commonest
forms are globular or ovoid jars with constricted necks and
flaring collars, and bowls with angular outlines and solid,
chamfered rims. Other bowls have a gently convex base which
meets the sides at a sharp angle; the sides slope slightly inwards
and may be shallow and almost straight, or deep and concave.
A variant of this form, with a blunt junction at the base and
a more pronounced outward curve at the top, is shown in
Plate 60.

The highland basins, with their broken topography and   HIGHLANDS
multiple sources of water supply, are not so suitable for large
concentrations of population as the flat coastal valleys, and
urban sites of this period have not been recognized within the
highland basins. There are developments east of the Cajamarca
Basin, in the Valley of the Marañon in the Department of

Amazonas, which will for convenience be mentioned here, although their age has not been determined. Full publication of these is not available, but M. Reichlen has reported that he has discovered great walled towns near a place called Kuélape. These have mummies built into the walls. In the same neigh-bourhood are mummies with an outer casing and a false head made of stone and mud plaster, set up in groups on ledges on cliffs. There are also curious little gabled stone houses up to three storeys in height, built against cliffs in fairly inaccessible positions, to contain burials. They are painted red and white, and have ornamental T-shaped niches or openings in the out-side walls. All the burials found had been disturbed, so their original form is unknown.

It is not known whether these three types are contemporary or not, but all suggest a comparatively late date. The large towns may belong to this period, but they may also be related to the fortified site of Marca Huamachuco, belonging to the Expansionist Period. The mummy bundle type of burial belongs to one of these two periods elsewhere in the north, and the local variety with an outer casing may be an adaptation to the wetter conditions of the Marañon Valley. The nearest parallel to the three-storey burial houses is in the stone temples like Wilkawain, in the Callejón de Huaylas, also belonging to the Expansionist Period. It is probable that all these develop-ments would have reached this remote spot later than their appearance in the main centres of civilization, so they are probably of the City Builder Period. No Inca influence has been reported.

In the south highlands, the Tiahuanaco Culture passed through a period of decadence of unknown duration, of which the tangible evidence is the Decadent Tiahuanaco pottery style. It is believed to have ended before Inca influence reached the area in the fifteenth century. After its disappearance, a large number of stone burial towers called chullpas were built in the

Plate 62

area. They may be round or square, built of fine, dressed masonry or rough stones. Most have the burial chamber inside them, but some of the rough ones are solid, and the chamber is then excavated in the ground beneath them. It is not certain to what extent the differences are due to chronology, but the solid type with an underground chamber is believed to antedate Inca influence in the area, and the others to be later than its arrival. The final Inca conquest of the district took place about 1470, but they fought there earlier and their influence may have been felt as early as 1430. The chullpas are associated with various pottery styles, chief of which are either plain, or black on red. One of the latter types has been found stratified between Classic Pucara and Inca remains at Pucara, which serves to confirm its relative age. No decadent Pucara, corresponding with Deca-dent Tiahuanaco, has been found, and it is probable that the site and its sphere of influence were eclipsed in their prime by Tiahuanaco itself.

While these developments were taking place in the high plains round Lake Titicaca, and the coastal states were build-ing their cities, there was still nothing very spectacular in the Cuzco Valley. There was rather a lowly early Inca culture there, and the evidence for it will be described in the next chapter.

H

CHAPTER VIII

The Imperialist Period

THE INCA EMPIRE, after which this period is named, spread from small beginnings to its utmost limits in about 90 years, and in so doing it overflowed the limits of the Peru, vian area to cover much of Ecuador in the north and Chile in the south. It was a true empire, a term which cannot properly be applied to any other ancient American state except the Chimú, but it must still be emphasized that the features which went to make up the Inca Culture and Empire were the result of the gradual growth of Peruvian civilization, which we have traced from its beginnings, and not of the import of anything from outside.

The name Inca is used in various ways, as will be seen later, but in its origin it belonged to a group of tribes which were living in the neighbourhood of Cuzco before the fifteenth century, and spoke the Quechua language. Inca pottery and other material remains are greatly different from any of those which preceded them at Cuzco, showing that they must have come there from elsewhere. This is supported by the legend, which has been published many times, concerning their origin, the substance of which is that four brothers and four sisters, with their followers, emerged from caves some eighteen miles south, east of Cuzco, and started on a leisurely journey in search of good farm,lands, where they could settle. They carried a golden staff with which they tested the depth of soil. Three of the brothers were disposed of in various ways, and eventually the remaining one, Manco Capac, with his three sisters, chose the site of Cuzco, and after expelling the inhabitants, founded the city there. Although the story is legendary, the first Inca ruler of Cuzco whose name is known with any degree of reliability was called Manco Capac.

The place where the Inca actually came from is not known, but there is no reason to suppose that they travelled very far, and their origin is most likely to have been in the same highland zone where they settled down, and not, as one theory has claimed, in the coast, since in this region of great contrasts in height people are at their best at the altitude in which they have always lived. Various versions of their list of rulers were recorded by the chroniclers of the sixteenth and seventeenth centuries, and Rowe has sifted these and reached the conclusion that a list of thirteen names, beginning with Manco Capac and ending with Huayna Capac and his two sons Huascar and Atahuallpa, can be relied on. Using this list he has estimated that the Inca dynasty at Cuzco began about 1200.

During the course of his archaeological excavations there Rowe has found remains of the Early Inca Period, which is defined as the time between their first settlement and the beginning of their great conquests in the fifteenth century. He has discovered wall foundations of rough stone, burials, and accumulations of domestic rubbish. The cooking pottery consists of buff ware, some of it very rough, and there are painted wares with a buff paste, decorated in black, or black and red, either directly or over a white slip. Designs are entirely geometrical, and not unlike those on late Inca wares, but are not so finely executed. The shapes also are generally similar to the later ones. It is not a very remarkable series of wares, and its importance lies in the fact that it is clearly ancestral to the typical late Inca ones. Little metal has been found, but there were ground slate knives and bone tools. Burials were of the seated, flexed type, wrapped in cloth or mats, like the mummy bundles of the coast, and they owe their preservation to their position in beehive-shaped stone tombs built in cracks in the cliffs, which kept them dry.

Like most Peruvian highland Indians, the Inca were rather short and stocky, averaging about 5 ft 3 in. in height, with broad shoulders, and the deep chests associated with a people who live in the rarefied atmosphere of the high Andes. They had a brown skin, straight hair, rather a broad face with a prominent nose, straight or slightly hooked, and little facial hair. The coastal peoples were very similar in appearance, but generally rather slighter in build.

For the first two centuries after their settlement in Cuzco, the Inca seem to have been involved from time to time in plundering raids and minor wars with neighbouring tribes, but there were no permanent conquests. Other tribes were similarly engaged, and by the beginning of the fifteenth century the more prominent among them were the Lupaca and the Colla in the Titicaca Basin, the Quechua who adjoined the Inca on the northwest and the Chanca beyond them. The Quechua probably shared a common language with the Inca and were friendly with them. The Lupaca and the Colla were at enmity with one another, and Viracocha, the eighth in the line of Inca rulers, allied himself with the Lupaca; this probably marked the beginning of Inca influence in the Titicaca region. Meanwhile the Chanca defeated the Quechua, and prepared to attack the Inca when Viracocha was old and feeble. He and his son and heir designate, Urcon, left Cuzco for a more defensible spot, but another son, afterwards the Emperor Pachacuti, refused to leave and led a desperate resistance. The Chanca were repulsed and afterwards soundly beaten, leaving the Inca in a position of power. Pachacuti was crowned, in 1438 it is believed, and the great Inca conquests began.

Unlike the previous wars in the district, the Inca campaigns were not mere raids, and the conquests were consolidated and made permanent. Being a highland people, the Inca naturally made their first conquests in their own environment, and Pachacuti spread his empire over the highlands from near Lake Titicaca in the southeast to Lake Junin in the northwest, by about 1460. His son Topa Inca, a man of equal ability, was by then old enough to be associated with him, and together they greatly enlarged and consolidated the Empire. Topa Inca fought his way north to near Quito, whence he invaded the central part of the Ecuadorian coast near Manta, where there was a sanctuary of some renown. From there he is said to have made a voyage to some islands on a raft made of balsa logs, a craft particularly characteristic of Ecuador to this day, since the tree grows there in abundance. The story may well refer to an island called La Plata, which can be seen from the neighbourhood of Manta, since Inca remains have been found there, or with less likelihood to the Galápagos Islands where Peruvian coastal potsherds, probably from the Chimú area and culture, have been found. After this, Topa Inca attacked the Chimú Empire from the north, the direction whence trouble was least expected, and subdued it without serious difficulty, continuing southwards to Pachacámac.

Although some tribes, like the Cañari of Ecuador, put up a bitter resistance to the Inca, their conquests did not always involve fighting, and diplomacy, in the shape of a combination of threats and promises, backed by the approach of an organized army, often sufficed to bring about the submission of an enemy. Of the Chimú, Professor Willey writes: '. . .the great valley irrigation systems were highly specialized means of sustaining life, and because of this specialization they were vulnerable to attack and disruption. With the urbantype life of the later periods, the dense population centers imprisoned in narrow valley oases would have appeared as overripe plums to the more mobile highlanders.' When the Chimú had submitted, it seems that they were allowed to go on living much as they did before; in fact, recent writers have suggested that Chimú Culture influenced the Inca much more than the Inca affected the Chimú, so that many features of the later Inca Empire were derived from the coastal state. Even after its absorption in the Inca Empire, the Chimú black ware pottery style, blended with

See *Bibliography*, Willey, 1953

Inca forms, continued to spread southwards on the coast, and it is found in increasing quantities in Inca times in the southern valleys of Chincha and Ica. As Kroeber said many years ago, neither the native Cuzco nor the native Chimú ware spread at all widely; but a blend of the two, with a heavy proportion of black ware, flooded Peru shortly before Pizarro.

While Topa Inca was engaged on these campaigns, Pachacuti concerned himself mainly with the organization of the Empire, and the rebuilding of Cuzco and the shrines and buildings in the neighbourhood, until he resigned his Empire to his son in his old age in or about 1471. At about the same time, Topa Inca undertook a new expedition against the south coast of Peru, and after he became Emperor he invaded the lowlands to the east of Cuzco, but soon had to turn back and suppress a rebellion of the Aymara tribes in the Titicaca region, led by the Colla and Lu-paca, now allies. He then pushed on and conquered highland Bolivia and north-west Argentina, after which he descended into Chile, where he fixed the southern boundary of the Empire on the Maule River, about 35 degrees south latitude.

Topa Inca died about 1493 and was succeeded by Huayna Capac his son, the last undisputed ruler of the Empire. He spent much of his time in administration and in quelling minor revolts, but also conquered the Ecuadorian highlands north of Quito after a bitter struggle, on the shores of a lake still called in the Quechua tongue Yaguar-cocha, the Lake of Blood. He extended his dominion in the coastal plain of Ecuador also, and conquered the island of Puná in the Gulf of Guayaquil, but parts of the coast between there and Manta were never subdued. When he died of a pestilence in 1527, he had heard of the arrival at Tumbez of the first Spanish expedition. The remainder of the story is well known—the succession of Huas-car as Emperor and the successful revolt of his half-brother Atahuallpa, who was seized by Pizarro and his handful of followers in the moment of victory.

Wherever the Inca spread, there is tangible evidence of their presence. Many of their buildings have disappeared, but examples are still found at widely separated points. A constant feature is the trapezoidal opening, doorway, niche or window, and buildings containing them are generally made of adobe on the coast and stone in the highlands. Coastal examples which may be mentioned are the 'palace' at La Centinela in the Chincha Valley, where there may also have been a temple, and the great 'sun temple', with its attendant buildings, which was put up to overshadow the ancient sanctuary at Pachacámac. In the hills, Inca ruins are found at least as far north as Inga-pirca in the Province of Cañar in southern Ecuador.

Plates 1, 71

In its homeland round Cuzco, Inca masonry takes several forms, and at one time it was believed that they indicated differences of age, but it is now known that all date from the great period in the fifteenth century. The differences are primarily ones of function. There are two main types, one composed of polygonal blocks, generally of large size, and the other of regular courses of rather small rectangular blocks with sunk joints. The polygonal type is used chiefly for massive enclosure walls, and for the main retaining walls of terraces, and the best example, the three ramparts of the great fortress of Saccsai-huaman, which dominates Cuzco, contain stones up to twenty feet in height. The rectangular type is generally used for buildings, and the finest of all, which is flat, without the sunk joints, is derived from it and is used for special buildings. An example of the latter is the famous curved wall, which lay beneath the sanctuary wall of the Dominican church in Cuzco until the earthquake of 1950 relieved it of that load, and another seen on the right of Plate 1, belongs to what must have been an important shrine in the remote city of Machu Picchu. A modification of the polygonal type of masonry is built of much smaller polygonal stones, and is sometimes described as cellular; it also is used both in buildings and in terraces. More

Plate 70

Plate 69

than one type may be seen in a single wall, for instance, rectangular masonry may be used for convenience on either side of a doorway in an otherwise cellular wall. This fine stone walling, of whatever type, was used mainly for public buildings, such as the palaces of the Incas, temples and the houses of the Chosen Women, generally called the Virgins of the Sun. The average dwelling was probably of irregular field stones set in mud, of turves set in courses, or of adobe, and Rowe has suggested that the polygonal masonry was an elaboration of the irregular stonewalling, while the rectangular type with sunk joints was inspired by the turf construction.

Plate 69

In all the fine masonry, the stones fit perfectly together at the surface of the wall, in spite of the fact that the softest stone used in the Cuzco district is comparable in hardness with the Carboniferous Limestone of Yorkshire, and a good deal of it is of igneous rocks which are much harder. They are believed to have been worked roughly into shape with stone mauls, and finally ground in with blocks of sandstone, but whatever the method, the story that not even a knife blade can be inserted between them is no exaggeration. Many of the stones must have been brought from considerable distances, and the very impressive remains which are incorporated in the Spanish buildings of Cuzco, or stand deserted elsewhere in the same district, bear witness to the abundance of regimented labour which the Incas had at their disposal. The buildings depend for their effect on their massiveness and fine finish, and the exteriors have little in the way of ornament, although it is known that the thatched roofs were finely worked into patterns. Even the trapezoidal niches are mostly found inside the buildings, and representational carving on buildings is extremely rare, since there are practically no examples beyond a few very small snakes and pumas on some buildings in Cuzco.

On the other hand, portable objects may be carved with some elaboration. Flatbottomed stone dishes are highly characteristic Inca objects, and many of them bear snakes on the outer wall or have lugs in the form of animals instead of handles. The example figured is exceptional in its elaborate low relief figure carving, but it is of particular interest by reason of the woman spinning with a falling spindle as she walks, just as modern highland women do throughout the Central Andes. It is possible but unlikely that this dish is just post-Conquest, and this way of spinning was almost certainly in use in the highlands by Inca times, although the lighter spindle, supported in a bowl, was always popular on the coast. The carving on this dish is stiff and rather crude, but some examples of another type of object are real works of art, namely, small stone figures of alpacas with a cylindrical hole in the back which are found buried in the fields. Crude pottery models of alpacas are still used for fertility ceremonies near Cuzco and are subsequently buried in the yards where the animals are kept, so it is inferred that the stone ones were used for the same purpose.

Plate 64

Plate 63

In its homeland around Cuzco, Inca pottery is of excellent quality, and is made of a few standard wares in a few standard shapes. Cooking pots, namely, a pedestalled bowl with a broad loop handle and a cover, and two forms of tripod, one a bowl and the other a peculiar vessel opening at the side, were made of hard plain brown ware, but it is the painted wares that are most characteristic. These are highly polished, and are normally polychrome, the usual colours being red, white, black and yellow, but orange may be found also, particularly in a provincial variety made near Lake Titicaca. There are a number of varieties, but they can be grouped together under the generic name of Cuzco Polychrome. Some attractive vessels are decorated with rows or a scatter of little painted stylized animals, birds or insects, but these are not the most common, and the usual designs are geometrical, for example, diamonds, checkers, parallel stripes, cross-hatching and saltires.

There is also a very frequent design like the backbone of a fish, consisting of a central rib and a row of parallel lines, each ending in a knob, on either side, which may be a conventionalized plant.

Plate 67

Of the shapes, the most typical is the jar to which the name of aryballus has been given, with a conical base and tall, flaring neck. In origin it was a large jar for carrying water and perhaps chicha, a maize beer which is still largely used in the Andes, and it was designed to be carried on the back, with the aid of a rope which passed through the two vertical strap handles and over the nubbin below the neck; the nubbin is generally modelled in the shape of an animal head. A great many were made in smaller sizes, down to miniatures a mere six inches

Plate 65

high. Another very typical form is a shallow saucer, with a handle in the form of a bird's head or less usually a loop on one side, and a pair of minute projections opposite to it. Jugs and

Plate 66

bottles with flatstrap handles are common also, and so are straightsided keros or beakers, a form which was also made in wood and decorated with inlaid scenes and figures in coloured lacquer. Wherever the writ of the Incas ran, these forms are found, but they were made, generally in a modified form, of the local wares. Thus it is quite common to find a shortnecked aryballus, with no nubbin, made in the Chimú black ware and decorated with pressed relief. In Chile, both aryballus and saucer were made in local polychrome. Local shapes were also modified by the introduction of Inca details; for instance, a tall neck with flaring mouth, derived from the aryballus, is often found on double whistling jars in the Chimú region, and the form persisted into postConquest times, because examples with a European green glaze are sometimes found. Reference has already been made to the wide distribution of a blended ChimúInca style.

In the use of metals, the chief innovation associated with the Inca was the spread of bronze throughout the Empire, even to such remote parts as Ecuador. Tools and weapons were cast in both copper and bronze, and forms particularly associated with the Inca are a flat, trapezoidal axe-blade with ears to assist in binding it to the haft, and the tumi or knife, with handle projecting at right angles to the blade. These metals were also used for making decorative and ceremonial objects, such as pins and figurines. They were the only metals available to commoners, gold and silver being reserved to the Emperor, to privileged nobles, and to the use of religion. Most of the surviving objects are of thin sheet metal, hammered into shape, but accounts given by the chroniclers suggest that they were sometimes made solid. Characteristically Inca objects of these metals are little figurines representing men, women, llamas and alpacas.

Plate 48

The Empire expanded, as has been shown, with great rapidity, and as it grew its organization was built up. The Emperor at its head was an absolute monarch, and in the great period he was a son, though not necessarily the eldest son, of his predecessor. Although the name Inca is often applied to his office without qualification, he was properly called Sapa Inca, meaning Unique Inca, and he had other titles, including Intip Cori, Son of the Sun, in reference to his supposed direct descent from the sun, by virtue of which he was worshipped as a god during his lifetime, as well as after death. His despotism was a benevolent one, and he cared for the material welfare of his people, because he knew that this was necessary for the prosperity of the State and his own well-being. He had a chief wife, the Qoya, who from the time of Topa Inca was his full sister, but he had many secondary wives also, by whom he had many children.

The male descendants of each Emperor formed what was called a royal ayllu, and these formed the original aristocracy, the Incas by blood. The word ayllu denotes the groups into which most Andean tribes were divided; the ayllu appears to have been a kin group, an enlarged family or group of families, with descent in the male line, and marriages took place within the group. It has sometimes been called a clan, but it was not one in the strict sense, since clans have descent in the female line and marry outside the group. The Inca made use of the ayllus of conquered tribes, but regrouped them if necessary to make village units of convenient though variable size, so that they sometimes became groups of unrelated families. Each ayllu held lands which were divided into three portions, one for the Emperor, one for the Sun, and one for the ayllu itself; the cultivation of the first two was the normal form of taxation, and the products were used for the maintenance of government and religion. The ayllus were grouped into provinces, and within each province the ayllus were classified in two, or in large provinces three, moieties, analagous to the Upper or Hanan, and the Lower or Horin, divisions of the original Inca tribes. The provinces in their turn were grouped in the famous four quarters of the Empire, Chinchasuyo in the north-west, Cuntisuyu in the south-west, Antisuyu in the north-east, and Collasuyu, including the Titicaca area, in the south-east, which met in Cuzco along lines running approximately north and south, and east and west.

The administration of these and smaller divisions required a multitude of officials, and by the time of the Spanish Conquest a twofold noble class had been evolved, the Incas who held the higher posts, and the Curacas, who were less important. The original Incas by blood, the royal ayllus, numerous though their members had become, were insufficient to fill all the higher posts, and Pachacuti created a new class of Incas by privilege, derived from other Quechua-speaking tribes. All were distinguished by special headbands and large ear-plugs, whence the name Orejones, or Big-ears, given them by the Spaniards. The curacas included some of the chiefs of conquered tribes who had submitted without opposition, and they had charge of administrative units of a hundred taxpayers and upwards. Both classes were hereditary and exempt from taxation.

The four quarters and the provinces were ruled by Inca nobles, and within the provinces the ayllus were grouped and divided into units of approximately 10,000, 5000, 1000, 500 and 100 taxpayers or heads of families, each under its curaca of appropriate grade. Under them were non-hereditary officials in charge of 50 and 10 taxpayers. The people were further divided into twelve age groups, each with its defined duties and exemptions. It has been stated already that the normal form of taxation was agricultural work, but there was also a special labour levy, the mit'a, for the army, the roads and other public works, and the mines. Specialists of various kinds paid their tribute in the employment of their skills or abilities; thus, there were the runners who were posted along the roads to carry messages by relay, the metal-workers and the tapestry-weavers. Specialists were supported out of public stores, but those who were away from home temporarily on the mit'a tasks had their lands tilled and their families supported by their ayllu. So efficient was the system that it is said that the Incas called out the mit'a to perform unnecessary tasks in order to keep the people from idleness and mischief.

Women were not free from organization and control. An Inca official visited the villages at regular intervals to inspect any girls who had reached an age of about ten. He divided them into two classes; those of special beauty or promise were sent away to be educated in special institutions by the State, or reserved for sacrifice on special occasions or in emergencies, such as the accession or serious illness of an Emperor, and the remainder were left behind, to be married in due course to the boys of the village by the curaca, who picked their mates for them. Those who were taken away were placed in convents called Accla Huasi, the Houses of the Chosen Women, in the

Plate 69

provincial capitals or in Cuzco, and here they learnt such things as spinning, weaving, and cooking. Those destined for sacrifice were regarded as fortunate, since they were assured of a life of ease and comfort in the world to come. The others were divided into those who would be given as wives to nobles or successful warriors by grace of the Emperor, and the Mama-conas, some of whom would be secondary wives or servants to the Emperor, and some dedicated in perpetual chastity to the service of the temples and shrines. Those who served the Emperor included specially skilled weavers, who made fine clothing for him.

Fig. 13

The numbering of the people and their produce required a special class of accountant, the quipucamayoc, who were skilled in recording the figures on the quipu, an arrangement of knotted strings of various thicknesses and colours, on which different numbers were recorded with knots of various sizes. It is unlikely that they could have been used for recording any-thing except numbers, and records of a particular commodity—quantities of maize or chicha for example—were probably decipherable by different quipucamayoc from those who could read the census records. The same accountants are now believed to have used an abacus, and in both it is likely that a decimal system was employed, unlike the arithmetic of the Maya, which was vigesimal. A form of quipu is still used by Andean herds-men to keep count of their flocks, but the surviving ancient examples are from coastal graves. Most of these are believed to date from the Inca Period, but the idea may be as old as the Mochica since quipu-like objects are painted on some of their pots. There is no record of any system of weights among the Inca or other Peruvian peoples, and the way in which quan-tities were measured is uncertain. Small balances with beams of the order of six inches long, made of richly carved bone or wood, or of metal, belonging to various periods, are found on the coast, but they can only have been used for very small

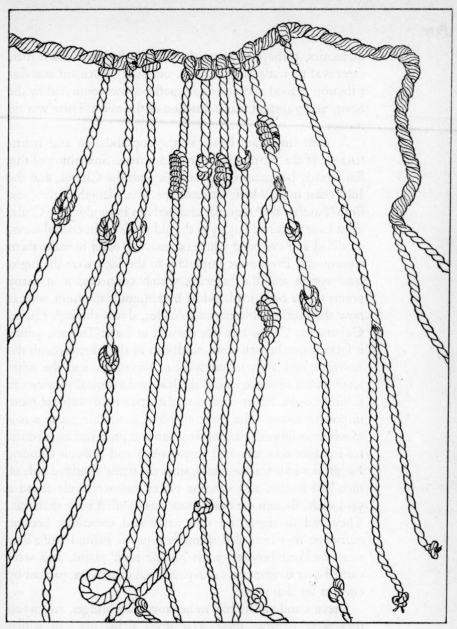

Fig. 13. Portion of a 'quipu', the Inca counting device.

quantities, perhaps of precious material. Beyond local barter, there was no trade in Inca times, since the movement and distribution of food and other commodities was controlled by the State, and transport was a function of the mit'a. There was no money.

A most important factor in the consolidation and maintenance of the Empire was the road system. Something of this has already been said in connection with the Chimú, and the Inca coast road, which traversed the whole length of the coast from Tumbez to Arequipa, and perhaps beyond it into Chile, must have consisted largely of the old roads of the coastal states, modified and extended where necessary in order to make them continuous. Even more important to the Inca were the highland system and the branches which connected it at many points to the coast road. At its maximum it ran from what is now the northern frontier of Ecuador, down through Quito, Cajamarca, Cuzco and other towns to Lake Titicaca, where it forked; one branch went north-east of the lake, through the Bolivian highlands to north-west Argentina, and the other went on the opposite side of the lake and eventually down the Chilean coast. Spurs connected the main road with the more important towns. The construction of mountain roads was a much more formidable problem than was presented by the coast roads, since they traversed very broken and difficult country. No great width was necessary, since the traffic consisted only of men and llamas, and in some places they were only about a yard wide, though the main route was doutless more than this. They had to zigzag up mountains and sometimes became stairways; they tunnelled through spurs or behind cliffs; they were enclosed between walls on the high plains, and were carried over swamps on stone-paved turf causeways, pierced by culverts for drainage.

Streams and valleys had to be crossed by bridges, and when they were narrow, these were stone slabs, some of which survived in Cuzco until a few years ago, or simple wooden constructions consisting of a pair of beams supporting cross-pieces. The wider valleys were crossed by suspension bridges, of which there was a famous example over the gorge of the River Apurimac, north-west of Cuzco, which was a formid-able obstacle to the Inca expansion until it was crossed in this way. Such bridges consisted of five great cables of vegetable fibre, sometimes obtained from an aloe called maguey, three supporting the floor and two serving as rails. They passed over four stone towers, two at each end, on a foundation platform, in which were embedded beams to which they were attached. The bridge was maintained by people who lived nearby, so paying their labour tax, and they had to renew the cables every year or two, a great undertaking with bridges which might be as much as 200 feet long. They swayed disconcertingly in the wind, and to cross them was a disagreeable experience; never-theless, the Spaniards could devise nothing better, and the Apurimac bridge was maintained until the latter part of the nineteenth century.

Rest houses, called tampo (Hispanicized into tambo), some-times accompanied by government storehouses, were built at intervals of four to eight miles along the roads for the use of official travellers—no others were allowed—and posts for the relay runners already mentioned were placed at intervals of a mile and a half, perhaps less. The posts consisted of a hut on either side of the road, each to house a pair of runners, called chasqui, who are said to have been capable of carrying a message 150 miles a day. When the Emperor, his family, and some few of the nobles travelled, they were carried in a canopied litter by four bearers, who were specialists at the task and worked in relays, but this was a privilege reserved for the highest in the land.

Several other features of Inca policy helped to weld the Empire into a coherent whole, although the process was not

I

complete when it was brought to an end. A well-known procedure, not unknown in the Old World, was to move
potentially unruly sections of the population from a newly-
conquered area into a settled one, replacing them by loyal
colonists. People so moved were called mitimaes. It was
suggested in a previous chapter that this may have been done in
the Expansionist Period, but even if this were not so, it is one of
the features which the Inca may well have learnt from the
Chimú. The wisdom of the Inca is shown by the fact that they
realized the effect of altitude on health, and mostly sent the
mitimaes to a place on the same level as their home-land.
Another factor which helped the coherence of the Empire was
the spread of the Quechua language. To what extent this was
deliberate policy is uncertain, but the Inca administrators spoke
it, and it doubtless spread down through the minor officials to
the commoners, partly from necessity and partly as a matter of
prestige. The process was far from complete when the Spaniards
arrived, and it was greatly extended by the Christian mission-
aries.

When conquered chiefs were retained in office as curacas,
some of their sons were taken away to be educated like the
nobles at Cuzco. Objects of worship belonging to conquered
tribes were in some cases carried there also, with their attendant
priests. In this way they both served as hostages and gave the
provinces a feeling of community with Cuzco.

It is not possible to understand the nature of the Inca Empire
without having some idea of the religion on which its whole
life was based, and of which the ruler was an integral part.
At the head of the supernatural hierarchy was a creator god,
who had made not only earthly things but the other gods. He
had various titles, but is generally known by the Hispanicized
version of one of them, Viracocha, meaning Lord. He was
rather remote from everyday things, and although he was
represented by idols in human form in some of the temples,

more attention was paid to the inferior gods, all in a sense his deputies. Pachacámac, the god of the great coastal sanctuary of the same name, had a great importance in the coast, and when the Inca absorbed him into their religious system, they fostered the impression that he was the same creator god, without ever calling him Viracocha. Below Viracocha came heavenly bodies, the sun, the moon, some of the stars and Venus, also the earth and the sea. The sun had a particular importance to the highlanders, partly because of its necessity for ripening the grain and of the chill which descends on the rarefied atmosphere of the Andes when it is obscured, and partly because it was the personal god and ancestor of the Emperor and his family.

In spite of this, the famous temple at Cuzco, of which the remains are still to be seen in the Dominican friary there, was not primarily a sun temple, as it is generally called, since Viracocha held the chief place and the sun shared the remainder with the moon, the thunder, the stars and others. Judging by the existing remains, the buildings consisted of a number of rectangular rooms set round a court within an enclosure wall, and although it was built of the finest masonry and adorned with gold plates, the plan was that of the normal house compound, and it has rightly been described as a house of the gods made in the likeness of the houses of men. Such temples were truly the houses of the gods and their attendants, since their golden images were kept there, and were taken outside into the squares of the cities for the great public ceremonies.

Below the chief gods were a large number of local shrines and objects of veneration, called huacas from a Quechua word meaning shrine, although the varied objects to which it is applied are perhaps better described as holy things. They were extremely diverse in character, and included springs, rocks, hills, caves, tombs and the mummies of the dead. The mummies of previous Emperors had special honour. They were cared for, each by the royal ayllu composed of his descendants, and the later ones were kept in the palaces they had used during life, and treated as far as possible as if they were still alive. They were brought out into the squares of Cuzco to take part in the great festivals, like the images of the greater gods. There is a striking example of a holy rock at Kenko, near Cuzco, where a massive pointed limestone outcrop, twenty feet high, has its base encased in a rectangular masonry platform, and forms the focal point of an elliptical amphitheatre, which is enclosed by a low wall of Inca masonry. Mountain passes and difficult points on roads were and still are venerated by praying and adding a stone or a quid of coca to a pile of stones by the roadside, called apacita. There was also a wide variety of portable amulets, like the stone figures of alpacas already mentioned, and they included images of maize cobs or potatoes, crystals, and curiously shaped natural stones.

Temples and shrines were cared for by priests of various grades, at the head of whom was a high priest who was generally a near relative of the Emperor, and their duties included divination, sacrifice and curing, as well as the care of the shrines. The public expression of religion consisted of festivals, of which there was one associated with each of the twelve months, in addition to special ones held in times of emergency, such as drought or pestilence. The months were lunar, but twelve lunar months are about eleven days short of a solar year and it is not known how the two were reconciled. Preparation for a festival included fasting from certain foods and sexual intercourse, and the ceremonies themselves chiefly took the form of processions, sacrifices and dances. Llamas were the most common sacrificial victims, but guinea-pigs and commodities such as maize beer, called chicha, were also sacrificed. Human sacrifice was practised, but only in serious crises and on very special occasions, the victims being either children or those who had been reserved from among the Chosen Women.

Plate 68

Plate 63

There can be little doubt that this provides the explanation of a find made by Uhle when he was excavating the Inca cemetery at Pachacámac, namely, the mummies of a number of richly-dressed young women, who had been strangled and yet buried with every appearance of honour. It is known that they had a convent which helped to serve the 'Sun Temple' at this important site.

Apart from the public ceremonies of religion, private practices included purification and divination. Sin against their moral code was regarded as provoking the anger of the gods, disqualifying the offender from taking part in ceremonies, and perhaps causing bodily harm to himself and illness to the Emperor. It was purged by confession of sins of word and deed to a priest, followed by penance and washing in running water. Divination took many forms, ranging from the solemn consultation by the Emperor of one of the great official oracles in his temple before undertaking a campaign, to the counting of a pile of maize kernels by a humble villager to determine, according to whether the number was odd or even, if the day was propitious for him to begin his planting or not.

The motives which impelled the Incas to undertake their great conquests and the reasons for their success now require consideration. They used much the same weapons and tactics as their opponents, so the reason cannot be sought in superior armaments. Slings and the bolas were used for distant fighting, and they adopted the use of the spear-thrower from their coastal subjects. They did not themselves use the bow, but they had some soldiers from the margins of the eastern forests who did. At close quarters they used star-headed maces of stone or copper on wooden handles, sword-clubs of hardwood, stone or copper battle-axes of various forms, and lances. They protected themselves with quilted cotton armour, helmets of quilted cotton or plaited cane, and small round or square wooden shields covered with skin or cloth.

Plate 70

Plate 1, 71

Towns and villages were not fortified, and defensive works consisted of hill-top forts, called in Quechua pucara, to which the inhabitants fled when attacked. These forts are exemplified, on the grandest scale, by Saccsaihuaman, with its three great ramparts on one side and a precipice on the other, crowning the hill above Cuzco, which was built in its present form by Pachacuti more for show than from necessity. The city of Machu Picchu, down the Urubamba Valley near the frontiers of the highland dominion, may appear to be an exception by reason of its very strong and inaccessible position on a saddle bordered by two precipices, but this is a consequence of the topography and it has no defensive walls.

Once the Inca conquests had begun, the fundamental factor in their continued success was their sustained offensive spirit, which contrasted with the raiding pattern general in highland warfare. This was combined with superior transport and supply facilities, afforded by their roads and stores of food, so that they were able to place an overwhelming force in a given place when they wished. Apart from the Emperor's picked bodyguard of nobles, there was no standing army, but there was an organization which ensured that sufficient trained men were available when required. All able-bodied men were trained to arms, and the main body of any force consisted of mit'a levies, organized according to the provinces they came from in squadrons, which were subdivided in the same decimal system as the population at large, under officers of similar grades. These levies were marched about under strict discipline, but the actual mode of fighting was similar to that of other Andean tribes; it started at a distance with showers of sling stones, bolas and darts, and when the opponents came to close quarters each man fought individually. One successful tactical modification introduced by the Incas was to divide their forces, one part engaging the enemy while the other was held in reserve and thrown in at a critical moment.

The motives for the sustained aggressiveness of the Inca are another question. The first conquests of neighbouring tribes could have been undertaken from motives of vengeance and a desire to consolidate their position, but the personality of Pachacuti must also be taken into account. As power and wealth increased, there seems to have developed a thirst for more, and each new conquest enriched the State and added to the glory of the Emperor. The royal ayllus and the Incas by privilege grew up into an hereditary aristocracy, exempt from the labour tax, and being polygamous, they increased rapidly. They were educated in the arts of war, and the fighting spirit was encouraged. Wars not only employed and restrained seditious tendencies, which are known to have existed, but provided posts of responsibility in the administration of the conquered provinces. The structure of the ruling classes was thus in an unbalanced condition, which required expansion in order to maintain stability, and developments designed to rectify this might well have taken place if the Empire had lasted longer.

The Empire was, indeed, still in course of evolution, when the end came. It had two great weaknesses. One was that there was no fixed method by which the Emperor designated his successor, and any of his sons by his chief wife could be chosen. When Huayna Capac died suddenly without naming his successor, this led to the strife between Huascar and Atahuallpa each supported by a powerful faction, which left the Empire in a weakened state when the Spaniards arrived. It was unlucky for the Inca that they came at that time, since Atahuallpa would doubtless have been universally recognized within a few years. The other weakness was excessive centralization in the Emperor. Every official was responsible to the one above him and so up to the Emperor, but there was little or no cohesion between those of the same grade. It was a pyramid, but it was built of disconnected rods, and when struck at the apex it fell to pieces. Before the coming of the Spaniards this mattered little; it was unthinkable that any outside enemy should lay hands on the divine Emperor, but the Europeans saw him as a misguided heathen and they had no scruples. After the fall of Atahuallpa in 1532, resistance was maintained in isolated places for forty years more. Pizarro set up Manco, a grandson of Huayna Capac, as a puppet ruler, but he rebelled and gathered a considerable following, laying siege to Cuzco and Lima. This rising was a serious threat to the Spaniards, but it was dispersed, and Manco fled down the Urubamba Valley, eventually taking refuge at an inaccessible place called Vitcos, where he, and after his death his sons, maintained a precarious rule until 1572. After his flight, the issue was never in doubt. The Spaniards gained rapidly in strength and the old civilizations of the Central Andes had gone for ever.

AFTER THE CONQUEST

See *Bibliography, Handbook of South American Indians*

While resistance was maintained by the few in the Urubamba Valley, the bulk of the population fell under the Spanish yoke, and Rowe has aptly said that the Indians exchanged a despotism of predictable demands and justice for another of limitless demands and justice reserved to their oppressors. In the first years of the colony, roads were neglected, much irrigated land fell into disuse, and the population of the occupied provinces was drastically reduced. Recent studies indicate that the reduction was mainly due to the flight of Indians to the remoter districts, especially to the lowlands east of the Andes, but forced labour, in the shape of the old mit'a intensified, particularly in the mines and at unaccustomed altitudes, doubtless took its toll in deaths. Much information about conditions at this time, the life of the Indians under the Incas and afterwards, their customs, and the good and bad sides of

Spanish rule, is given by the numerous line-drawings in a work by Felipe Guaman Poma de Ayala, dating from the end of the sixteenth century. See *Bibliography*, Guaman Poma de Ayala, 1936

Apart from mass baptisms without instruction, which had little effect, the conversion of the Indians to Christianity was slow at first, and it was not until late in the sixteenth century that much progress was made. Even then, a great many of the old beliefs survived, the worship of the heavenly bodies and the huacas continued, and it was not until about the middle of the seventeenth century, after an intensive campaign for 'the extirpation of idolatry', that true Christian doctrines were generally understood and held. Some of the old practices, including fertility ceremonies, continued after this time—in fact they still do—but they had degenerated into mere superstitions, and were tolerated because they were no longer regarded as 'idolatry'. The state of affairs in the intermediate period is illustrated by the case of a huddled mummy bundle found on the coast, which bore the appearance of a normal late pre-Conquest burial. When it was unwrapped, a printed indulgence bearing the date 1580 was found next to the body.

Material features of the old culture also survived in places. The art of weaving remained at a high level, and fine ponchos and other textiles, bearing a combination of European and indigenous features, have survived in some numbers. The wooden kero, or waisted beaker, continued to be made, and there are many fine examples, with elaborate designs inlaid in polychrome lacquer, whose post-Conquest origin is shown by representations of stringed musical instruments and European dress. Pottery also was made in hybrid forms, particularly in the area of the old Chimú state. There are examples of black ware jars with a bearded Spanish face on the neck, and there are double whistling jars of characteristically Chimú-Inca forms, made, not in the customary black ware, but in a buff-coloured ware covered with a European green glaze.

Most of the Indians at first continued to live on their village lands under their curacas, but as time went on an increasing number left the land and became servants in Spanish households. This class, called yananconas, earned certain advantages including exemption from the mit'a, and they tended to increase and to become a landless urban proletariat, until eventually, late in the sixteenth century, their numbers had to be checked by legislation.

By no means all of the old Inca nobility were killed or followed Manco to his refuge at Vitcos, and many of them came to terms with the conquerors, some of whom took wives from among them. The Inca Garcilaso de la Vega, well known for his writings about the Incas, was the son of such a union, and he spent most of his days in Spain. The Incas, the curacas and the yananconas, all tended towards integration with Spanish society, and those of higher degree appeared on occasion in Spanish dress. Many of the curacas, indeed, proved themselves worse oppressors of their brethren than their Spanish overlords; for example, one of them was deposed for 'extorsions, violence, and tyrannies . . . to the point of committing the cruel act of branding them on the buttocks like mules'.

Descendants of the Inca nobility were still recognized in the eighteenth century, when some of them held important offices and lived in considerable state. There seems to have been a kind of romantic revival of interest in the past, since portraits of the period depict them richly dressed in Inca style, with some European details, with their Spanish coats of arms beside them. When increasing oppression provoked rebellions of the Indians in the eighteenth century, nobles of this sort provided the leadership. It is worthy of note that most of these risings, including the final great revolt of 1780 under José Gabriel Tupac Amaru, were directed against the local administration while remaining loyal to Church and Crown, both of which were regarded as in some degree the protectors of the Indians at that time. The

Inca nobles have long since disappeared, and now under the
Republic the distinction between the Indians and those of
mixed blood, the mestizos, is somewhat blurred, but there are
still many distinctively Indian communities, which reflect the
tradition of the ancient ayllus, the base of the pyramid of Inca
society.

Bibliography

BENNETT, WENDELL, C., "Excavations at Wari, Ayacucho", *Yale University Publications in Anthropology*, No. 49, 1953.
Ancient Arts of the Andes, Museum of Modern Art, New York, 1954.
"A Reappraisal of Peruvian Archaeology," (Editor), *American Antiquity*, Vol. XIII, No. 4, Part 2. April, 1948.

BENNETT, WENDELL C. AND J. B. BIRD, *Andean Culture History*, American Museum of Natural History, Handbook Series, No. 15, New York, 1949.

BIRD, J. AND L. BELLINGER, *Paracas Fabrics and Nazca Needlework*, The Textile Museum, Washington, D.C., 1954.

BUSHNELL, G. H. S. AND A. DIGBY, *Ancient American Pottery*,* Faber and Faber, London, 1955.

COLLIER, DONALD, "Cultural Chronology and Change as reflected in the Ceramics of the Virú Valley, Peru," *Fieldiana: Anthropology*, Vol. XLIII. Chicago Natural History Museum, 1955.

DOERING, H. U., *The Art of Ancient Peru*,* Zwemmer, London, 1952.

GUAMAN, POMA DE AYALA, FELIPE, "Nueva corónica y buen gobierno," *Institut d'Ethnologie Fravaux Mémoires*, Vol. XXIII. Paris, 1936.

HANDBOOK OF SOUTH AMERICAN INDIANS, Volume 2, Smithsonian Institution, Bureau of American Ethnology, Bulletin, 143. Especially articles by Bennett, Larco Hoyle, Kubler, Rowe and Valcárcel.

JOHNSON, FREDERICK, "Radiocarbon Dating," (Editor), *American Antiquity*, Vol. XVII, No. 1, Part 2, July, 1951. (Article by J. Bird on S. America.)

Bibliography

KUBLER, G., *Cuzco*, UNESCO Museums and Monuments—III, H.M. Stationery Office.

LEHMANN, W. AND H. U. DOERING, *The Art of Old Peru*,* Benn, London, 1924.

REICHLEN, H. AND P., "Recherches Archéologiques dans les Andes de Cajamarca," *Journal de la Société des Américanistes*, Nouvelle Série t. XXXVIII, 1949, p. 137, Paris.

STRONG, W. D. AND C. EVANS, JR., *Cultural Stratigraphy in the Virú Valley*, Columbia University, New York, 1952.

WILLEY, GORDON R., *Prehistoric Settlements in the Virú Valley*, Smithsonian Institution, Bureau of American Ethnology, Bulletin 155, 1953.

In this list, *Andean Culture History*, the *Handbook of South American Indians*, and *Prehistoric Settlement Patterns in the Virú Valley* contain especially full bibliographies. References given in them are not repeated here unless there is strong reason for doing so. Publications which are virtually unobtainable are omitted. Those marked with an asterisk are included because they contain useful illustrations.

SOURCES OF ILLUSTRATIONS

Original photographs for the plates were supplied by the Author, 69; Rafael Larco Hoyle, 4–8, 11–15, 17, 29; American Geographical Society, 51; Cambridge University Museum of Archaeology and Ethnology, 19, 21–5, 30–2, 37–8, 40–1, 43–4, 46–9, 54–5, 57–61, 63, 65–7; A. Costa, 36; John R. Freeman, 33–4, 45, 50, 64; Hans Mann, 1–3, 9, 10, 18, 35, 52–3, 56, 62, 71; Musée de l'Homme, 26–8, 39, 42; Peabody Museum, Harvard University, 20; Philadelphia University Museum, 16; Nicholas Young, 68, 70.

Figures 1, 3, 5–9, 12, 13 were drawn by Mrs. G. E. Daniel, Fig. 11 is reproduced by courtesy of the Medici Society and was originally published in T. Joyce, 'South American Archaeology'.

THE PLATES

4

6

7

8

9

11

13

14

15

16

17

19

20

22

23

24

25

26

27   2

31

32

33

34

35

36

37

38

39

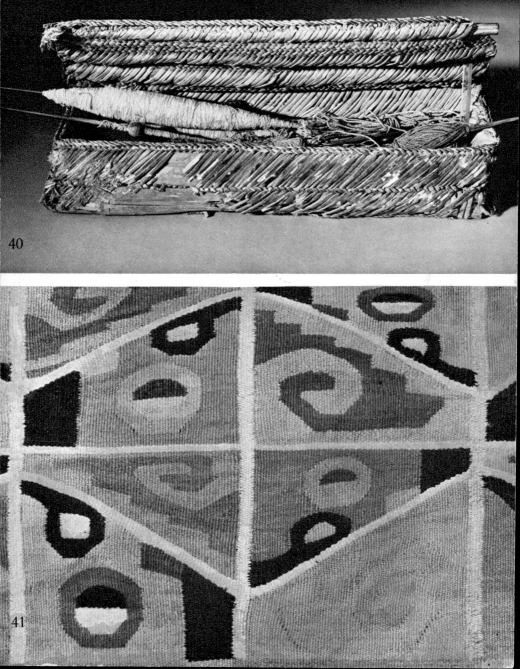

40

41

42

43

44

45

46

47

48

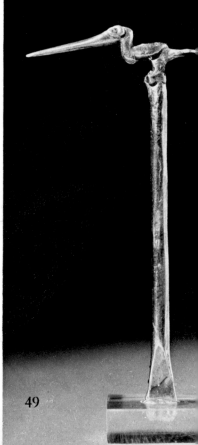

49

50

51

52

54

55

56

58

5

60

61

63

64

65

66

67

NOTES ON THE PLATES

Notes on the Plates

1 View from the late Inca city of Machu Picchu up the Urubamba Gorge. Inca masonry of the finest type, forming part of a shrine, on the right.

2 The high plateau (*puna*) in the Titicaca region, showing llamas.

3 Quebrada de Pescadores, Southern Peru. Small valley, showing the marked contrast between the irrigated valley bottom and the surrounding barren hills.

4 Stirrup-spouted jar representing woman suckling child. Cupisnique Culture, Chicama Valley. Rafael Larco Hoyle Collection.

5 Bottle, showing highly stylized incised designs, probably feline eyes and claws, surrounded by rocker stamping. Cupisnique Culture, Chicama Valley. Rafael Larco Hoyle Collection.

6 Vase representing aged woman's face. Cupisnique Culture, Chicama Valley. Rafael Larco Hoyle Collection.

7 Stirrup-spouted jar with applied knobs and highly roughened surface. Cupisnique Culture, Chicama Valley. Rafael Larco Hoyle Collection.

8 Stirrup-spouted jar with incised designs, probably feline motifs. Cupisnique Culture. Chicama Valley. Rafael Larco Hoyle Collection.

9 Row of engraved stones. Temple at Cerro Sechín, Casma Valley. Coastal Chavín Culture.

10 Engraved stones representing man cut in half, and trophy head. Temple at Cerro Sechín, Casma Valley. Coastal Chavín Culture.

11 Stirrup-spouted jar with engraved and partly painted concentric circles. Salinar Culture. Rafael Larco Hoyle Collection.

12 Stirrup-spouted jar representing a monkey standing on a circular vessel, which is actually annular since it is formed around a central opening. Salinar Culture, Chicama Valley. Rafael Larco Hoyle Collection.

13 Spout and bridge jar representing a monkey. Gallinazo or Virú Culture. Rafael Larco Hoyle Collection.

14 Spout and bridge jar, representing feline. Gallinazo or Virú Culture. Rafael Larco Hoyle Collection.

15 Double spout and bridge jar, with engraved design. Paracas Cavernas. Rafael Larco Hoyle Collection.

16 Polychrome bowl decorated with resinous colours outlined by incisions, applied after firing. The designs represent snake heads. Paracas Cavernas. Height $4\frac{1}{2}$ in. University Museum, Philadelphia.

17 Spout and bridge jar decorated negatively in black on a red ground. Represents a warrior riding on a small reed *balsa* raft (*caballito*). Gallinazo or Virú Culture. Rafael Larco Hoyle Collection.

18 Boy on *balsa* raft (*caballito*). Peruvian Coast.

19 Embroidered polychrome textile borders, in rose red, dark blue, green, yellow-brown and other colours. The upper one shows a pair of interlacing snakes enclosing naturalistic animals, and the lower one feline monsters. Width of upper piece, $5\frac{1}{2}$ in. Paracas Necropolis. C.M.A.E.

20 Double spout and bridge jar, painted white with the tips of the spouts red. Diameter, 8 in. Paracas Necropolis. Peabody Museum, Harvard University.

21 Rare figurine of pinkish-white pottery with details picked out in red and buff, and outlined by incised lines. Height, $3\frac{1}{2}$ in. Paracas Cavernas. C.M.A.E.

22 Red and white jar, representing feline god holding copper hand axe and severed human head. Height, $15\frac{1}{2}$ in. Mochica Culture. C.M.A.E.

23 Red and white jar, stirrup spout broken, representing naturalistic jaguar attacking man. A rare type. Height of jaguar, 8 in. Mochica Culture. C.M.A.E.

24 Red and white stirrup-spouted jar, depicting warrior holding club, standing on globular vessel decorated with stylized rays in low relief. Height, $11\frac{1}{2}$ in. Mochica Culture. C.M.A.E.

25 Red and white stirrup-spouted jar, decorated in relief with demon catching fish. Height, 9 in. Mochica Culture. C.M.A.E.

26-8 Modelled vessels with negative decoration in black over white and red. Recuay Culture.

29 Interior of bowl painted in brown on white in cursive style. Rafael Larco Hoyle Collection.

30 Double spout and bridge jar, painted with humming birds in two shades of red, black, white, yellow, purple and grey. Height, 5 in. Nazca Culture. C.M.A.E.

31 'One man band', a spout and bridge polychrome jar. Height, $6\frac{1}{2}$ in. Late Nazca (Nazca Y) Culture. C.M.A.E.

32 Double spout and bridge jar, representing a trophy head, the lips fixed together with wooden pins or thorns. Height, 5 in. Nazca Culture. C.M.A.E.

33 Cap made of pile cloth. Probably Coast Tiahuanaco Period. Height, $3\frac{1}{2}$ in. British Museum.

34   Shell inlaid with a face and surrounding mosaic of multi-coloured shell fragments. Width 4½ in. Nazca Culture. British Museum.

35   Geometrical markings as seen from the air. Nazca Valley.

36   The monolithic gateway of Tiahuanaco, with wall footings and other carved stones.

37   Sherd painted in black and red, outlined by incision, on a reddish buff ground. The feline face is about 2 in. wide. Pucara. C.M.A.E.

38   Spittoon-shaped vessel, painted in black, white, red and orange, on a reddish buff ground. Height, 4½ in. Early Tiahuanaco. C.M.A.E.

39   Polychrome bowl decorated with a puma and geometrical designs. Classic Tiahuanaco.

40   Work basket, containing spools wound with spun thread and other weaving materials. Length, 14 in. C.M.A.E.

41   Piece of tapestry in at least two shades of yellow or brown, with black, white and rose pink. Coast Tiahuanaco. C.M.A.E.

42   Puma-headed polychrome bowl. Classic Tiahuanaco.

43   Head-vase painted in black, white and red. Height, 5½ in. Coast Tiahuanaco B, or Epigonal. From Huacho, Central Coast. C.M.A.E.

44   Bottle, decorated with designs in pressed relief and painted with sub-dued colours, black, white, orange and grey, over a red slip. Height, 7½ in. North Coast Tiahuanaco B. (Variant of the more usual black, white, red over buff). C.M.A.E.

45   Silver beaker of type common in post-Classic times in many parts of the Coast. Height, 8 in.
     Gold wrist ornament. Nazca. Both, British Museum.

46 Gold mask for sewing to a garment. Height, 7 in. From Ica, South Coast. Probably City Builder Period. C.M.A.E.

47 Copper staff head, bearing macaws, parrots and other birds. Height, 6 in. Chimú. C.M.A.E.

48 Gold male figurine and silver female one. Height, 2½ in. Inca. C.M.A.E.

49 Gold lime spoon. The lime was chewed with coca leaves. Height, 3 in. C.M.A.E.

50 Wooden centre-board and two steering sweeps for raft. Height of centre-board, 52 in. Probably from Ica. British Museum.

51 Air view of part of Chan Chan, the Chimú capital.

52 Wall with mud-plaster reliefs. Chimú Period. Chan Chan.

53 Detail of mud-plaster relief. Chan Chan.

54 Black-white-red jar. Height, 12 in. Late Coast Tiahuanaco (B) style. Central Coast. C.M.A.E.

55 Stirrup-spouted blackware jar with pressed relief design. Height, 9½ in. Chimú. C.M.A.E.

56 Air view of Chimú frontier fortress of Paramonga.

57 Feather shirt *(poncho)* and head-dress, decorated with stylized owls. Chimú. C.M.A.E.

58 Llama-head blackware bowl. Height, 5½ in. Chimú. C.M.A.E.

59 Black-on-white bowl. Height, 6½ in. City Builder Period. From Chancay Valley, Central Coast. C.M.A.E.

60 Polychrome bowl. Height, 3½ in. Ica style, City Builder Period, South Coast. C.M.A.E.

61 Polychrome bowl painted with blurred textile designs. Height, 3½ in. Ica style, City Builder Period, South Coast. C.M.A.E.

62 Ruined circular burial chamber (*chullpa*). Lake Titicaca region.

63 Alpaca made of banded agate. Length, 5½ in. Inca. C.M.A.E.

64 Stone dish with figure designs including llama and woman spinning. Inca. Diameter, 20 in. British Museum.

65 Cuzco Polychrome saucer. Diameter, 3½ in. Inca. C.M.A.E.

66 Cuzco Polychrome bottle. Height, 4 in. Inca. C.M.A.E.

67 Cuzco Polychrome aryballus. Height, 14 in. Inca. C.M.A.E.

68 Sacred rock at Kenko, near Cuzco. Inca.

69 Street scene, Cuzco, showing late Inca masonry of finest type. Reputed palace of Huayna Capac on left, and substructure of convent of Santa Catalina, formerly the Accla Huasi or house of the Chosen Women, on right.

70 Late Inca masonry facing of lowest rampart of fortress of Saccsaihuaman, dominating Cuzco.

71 Late Inca city of Machu Picchu.

Index

204

Music, musical instruments, 76
Mutilation, 76

Nazca Culture, 20, 23, 67, 82–4, 94, 110
Nazca Valley, 61, 63, 95, 103
Needles, 37
Needlework, 67
Negative horizon, 54, 59, 60
Negative painting, *see* pottery
Nepeña Valley, 48, 50
Nets, 36, 38
North Coast (area defined), 16
North Coast tradition, 69
North Highlands (area defined), 16

Ocucaje, cemetery, 62
Olmec Culture, 53

Pacatnamú (site), 51
Pachacámac (site), 60, 82, 117, 119, 131, 133
Pachacuti, 116, 118, 124, 134, 135
Pacheco (site), 95
Paint, red, 48
Painting, *see* body painting, pottery, wall painting
Pallca (site), 49–51
Pampa de los Fósiles (site), 33
Papaya, 65
Paracas Cavernas Culture, 55, 61–3
Paracas Necropolis Culture, 55, 62, 63, 67, 84
Paracas Peninsula, 61
Paramonga (fortress), 109
Patagonia, 32
Peanuts, 42
Physical type, 115, 116

Pile cloth, 96
Pilgrimages, 44, 85
Pineapple, 65
Pisco Valley, 82, 110
Pizarro, Francisco, 118, 136
Playa de los Muertos (site), 53
Population, removal of, 99. *See also* mitimaes
Post classic period, 23
Potato, 28, 65, 76, 77, 85
Potato, sweet, 65
Pottery, 29
  black, white, red style, 97, 99
  cursive style, 80, 94, 101
  cursive modelled style, 102
  dipper, 72
  double jars, 99, 109, 122
  double spout and bridge, 69, 96, 99, 102
  glaze, 122, 137
  mammiform jars, 59
  moulds, 72, 169
  negative painting, 54, 60, 80, 100
  portrait jars, 72
  pressed relief, 72, 97, 99, 109
  rocker stamping, 52
  spout-and-bridge jars, 58, 60, 109
  stirrup-spouted jars, 47, 58, 60, 69, 71, 72, 109
  tripods, 80, 101
  whistling jars, 58, 102, 109, 122
  Early Farmer, 39, 40
  Formative, 45, 46, 57, 60, 61, 63, 64
  Classic, 71, 83, 88–90
  Expansionist, 93, 94, 95, 98–100
  City Builder, 104, 109–11
  Imperialist, 115, 117, 118, 121, 122
Prescott, W. H., 19

THE RESTLESS WIND

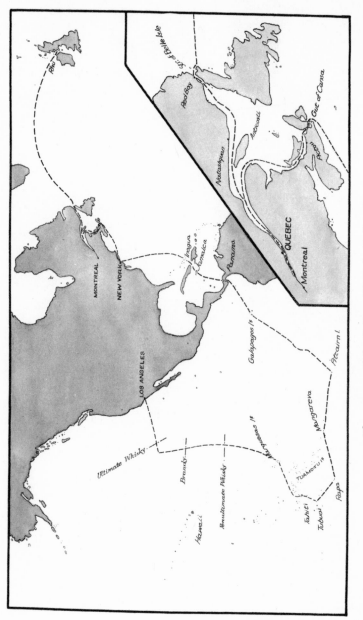

The voyage of the *Salmo*. (C. J. de C. Scott)

THE RESTLESS WIND

by

PETER HAMILTON

ST MARTIN'S PRESS

NEW YORK

First published in the United States of America 1963
Copyright © A. G. Hamilton 1961
Library of Congress Catalog Card Number: 63-9416
Manufactured in the United States of America
Published in Great Britain by William Blackwood & Sons Ltd. 1961

FOREWORD

EVERYWHERE we went during our cruise in *Salmo* people were kind to us : astonishingly kind. Conversely, it is one of the sad features of cruising that one makes so many friends and then loses track of them again.

Once I read a book written by someone I had met whilst he was cruising and I was living ashore. I had grown very friendly with him, and then our ways parted ; he went one way and I another. My first action, when I bought his book, I am rather ashamed of, because I turned to the chapter which covered his stay at the place where I was (it was Singapore) and read it through. ' I wonder if he mentions ME at all ' was what I was thinking.

With this in mind I re-read the manuscript of this book and was horrified to think of all the people who might do just what I did, and be disappointed ; for though I have introduced a few of the people whom we met, there are many, many more who have been left out. It is to those people particularly that I would now like to say " Thank you." It is not really the sailing bits of a trip such as ours which are the most pleasurable (though of course they form a part of the fascination), it is the constant friendliness with which one is received that is so heart-warming. Our visitors' book contains twenty-one pages of people who came on board or were good to us in one way or another. Obviously I cannot give each one an individual word, but I hope that each will realise just how grateful we were for all they did to help our voyage along.

CONTENTS

ILLUSTRATIONS

THE RESTLESS WIND

CHAPTER ONE

IN THE BEGINNING

It is very difficult to say exactly where a voyage begins. First of course there must be a dream, a longing for out-of-the-way places. Next must come a period of study, and then, most difficult of all, a decision. That's the really difficult bit—when the time comes, to say to yourself, " I WILL go on this voyage." After that it's easier and the preparations become concrete instead of abstract. Deeds not dreams.

So the story of the voyage that we made in *Salmo* really began 'way back, four or five years before I first set eyes on her, and all of that part must be taken for granted. . . .

It was a dark, blustery, November evening and the rain hurled itself against the wind-screen as I drove towards Hayling Island. It was hard to be enthusiastic about searching for a yacht on a day like that, and I remember that my chief feeling was a longing to have done with the whole business and to get away to seas where the sun shone. I had decided to spend a week's leave from the Navy in looking for a boat ; this was the eleventh one I'd been to see in five days, and there was no reason to suppose that it would be better than its ten predecessors.

The road stretched on and on, black and glistening, winding between hedges and ditches that ran with water, until at last a dilapidated notice-board appeared among a group of elms. On it was written in faded black letters : ' Hayling Island Yacht Station. No Admittance Except on Business.' So I turned off the road and sloshed the car through puddles for a couple of hundred yards towards a dimly seen group of corrugated-iron buildings. ' Bet the place'll be closed,' I reflected as I dived towards a lighted doorway marked ' Office.'

It wasn't, and a hot blast of fish-laden air hit me in the face as I burst in out of the rain. There was a man inside in a blue blazer, feeding cats. He looked startled at my advent but asked what he could do for me. I explained that I'd heard there was a Vertue-class yacht called (I consulted a piece of paper) *Salmo* for sale in his yard. Could I go and see her, please ?

" The BLOODY man," replied the manager, flinging down yet another saucer of fish, this time for a big brindled tomcat, " Aren't people just the ruddy limit ! So he's put her on the market, has he ? Who's the agent ? Laurent Giles, I suppose. Yes. Go on. Go and see her if you want. She's in that shed over there. Turn the lights out when you've finished and put the key back in here through the letterbox. . . . I'm going home. It fairly makes you sick," he added, almost to himself, " I could have sold that boat for him tomorrow, and now you say Giles has got it ? "

I hadn't said it, but the point seemed to be immaterial, and I was glad to escape from the cats and go into the boat-shed. Once I'd found the light switches *Salmo* was easily seen, for she was the only Vertue in there. I borrowed a ladder and climbed on board, first into the cockpit and then down into the cabin, which looked all bare and lonely with the floorboards up, the bunk cushions removed and everything with the forlorn air that laid-up yachts always have.

Forlorn or not, it was only a matter of moments before I realised that here, at last, I'd struck a honey. Workmanship and materials alike were excellent, and I think I'd decided to buy her within five minutes' acquaintance.

To be sure, there would be a few alterations to make before I could take her to sea. The cockpit would have to be made self-draining, and I'd probably have to remove both the anchor winch and the engine to save weight and space for water and stores, but apart from that she'd do.

I sank down on one of the bunks and began to dream anew ; for this the eleventh boat of my search was undoubtedly the one I was looking for. I would retire from the Navy and sail round the world for two years or maybe three. I'd do it now, while I was young enough to enjoy it, unattached and beholden to no one in particular. First would come Hudson Bay—but perhaps I'd call in at Angmansalik, in Greenland, first—and then I'd put the boat onto a railway-truck and send her to Vancouver ; and in front of Vancouver lay the whole Pacific. Surely for a start that was enough ! The dreams I dreamed that afternoon were splendid ones, even if they didn't work out, but the bunk where I sat to dream them wasn't. The mattress had been put into store and the bedspring thus left uncovered cut me to lozenges and recalled me to the present and to the fact that *Salmo* wasn't yet mine.

Already I loved her so deeply that I dared not leave her on the market one moment longer than I had to, so I turned off the lights, pushed the key of the shed through the office letterbox and, regardless of union hours, went to ring up Laurent Giles, who was indeed the agent.

I was, it appeared, the first on the scene, and within three days I found myself confronted with an awesome document to be signed and sealed in the presence of witnesses, stating that I was the owner of ' sixty-four sixty-fourth shares of the aforesaid vessel, her boats, arms, artillery and accoutrements,' which was all very satisfactory. My feelings of glory and importance were still further strengthened when I received a polite chit from Lloyds requesting me to furnish them with details of my titles, decorations, yacht clubs and racing flags so that they could be included

in the forthcoming edition of their Register of British
yachts. A footnote added that on payment of a fee of
three guineas I would receive (post free) a copy of this
volume bound in green Morocco and with my name embossed in gold on the front cover. For a leather binding
(also embossed) it would be a guinea extra.

Exalted, no doubt, by these unaccustomed attentions, I
took the bull by the horns and, with much heart-searching,
wrote a letter to Their Lordships requesting that my name
should be placed upon the retired list. I had butterflies
in the tummy as I wrote, and everyone to whom I mentioned the idea at once assured me that I was crazy.
" But you've only another five years to serve until you
get a pension," they'd say, or else, " Look, Old Boy "—
and I hate being called ' Old Boy '—" can't you see ?
They'll be putting up the pay this year, and besides what
do you WANT to leave the service for ? You've one of
the best jobs going (I was commanding a frigate at the
time) and if you go outside now you'll just become a
bum . . . an unemployable."

There was a nasty ring of truth about all this and it
was difficult to explain the other side of the question :
that too much security rotted all the fun out of life ; that
though I might visit port after port in H.M. ships, each
one always seemed just the same as the last ; I met only
the ' right ' people and did only the ' right ' things ; but
all the time I felt that there was a lot missing.

Once the letter was written and posted I felt better.
I knew I was right to have done it. The screwing up of
courage and the attempted balancing of pro and con had
been miserable, but with the letter in the post the world
became a brighter place.

The letter was followed by explanations to senior officers,
visits to London and further letters, but finally both the
Admiralty and myself became convinced that I was in
earnest, and in February 1956, for the first time in my

adult life, I found myself a civilian. Some friends offered me hospitality and the use of their workshop-garage, and I flung myself into the job of fitting out *Salmo* with gusto.

Then, one day, as I was leaving the house bound for the workshop with a packet of sandwiches, my hostess said, " We've a guest coming down from London for the week-end. Will you meet her at the station on your way home tonight ? The train's due at six-thirty."

I hate meeting trains, particularly trains containing unknown female guests of other people's, but I couldn't think of any excuse quickly enough to be convincing, so I said that I would, and went fuming on my way to Hayling Island. The day's programme was to prise out the engine (I'd found a buyer for it) and it turned out to be a long, cold, and incredibly oily job. The only tap in the yard was frozen, so I couldn't even wash afterwards : ' But at least,' I comforted myself, ' I'll be in time to meet this darned train.'

I was. I was ten minutes early, in fact, and the station looked cold and inhospitable. The platform was deserted, except for an old sheet of newspaper being whirled across it by an icy blast of wind. My stoicism melted away. This was too much. I hadn't a coat and I most certainly wasn't going to stand and freeze in the open when just across the road stood the ' Station Arms.' After the briefest of conscience-pleasing pauses therefore, I hurried over and found a glorious fire, and a big crowd of taxidrivers, also (I presumed) waiting for the London train to come in. One of them was holding the floor : " Now I saw that match," he said, " and it was the biggest scandal I ever DID see. That last goal now. Milligan was offside by a mile and, what's more, the ref 'e saw 'e was, but 'e didn't do nothing."

" Aw, nuts," said a very little man with a drooping grey moustache and two overcoats, and at once a colossal row began. Everyone present, including the barman, had apparently seen the match, known the referee since childhood or possessed strong views upon the offside rule. The noise was stupendous. I stood fascinated in the background and before I hardly knew it, found myself ordering another whisky.

The gale of laughter which ended the dispute made me look guiltily up at the clock. Oh, my gosh! Quarter to seven.

As I scuttled back across the road to the station I fervently hoped that the train might have had the good grace to arrive a bit late, but of course it hadn't, and there, huddled miserably by the ticket-barrier, stood a solitary female figure with a suitcase at her feet. Her teeth as I introduced myself were chattering, and I, warmed by the 'Station Arms'' fire and whisky, felt a most unutterable rat. My face and hands were still black with oil and my jacket had unaccountably split right across the back, but the waiting figure took it all in her stride, for it was Jill, my future wife and mate of *Salmo*.

The weekend passed quickly, and at the end of it I dreamed up some important business to be attended to in London so that I could drive Jill back to Windsor, where she stage-managed the Theatre Royal. Bearing in mind the maxim of the great Duke of Wellington, never to miss an opportunity, I extracted a promise from her, en route, to come for a sail in *Salmo* some day in the dim and distant future.

Just how dim and distant the day was to be I didn't foresee, which was probably as well, for delay followed delay, and every other yacht in the yard slipped away into the water while *Salmo* still lay where first I'd seen her, waiting for her cockpit to be finished.

But at long last her turn came and I decided that it would be a glorious opportunity to christen the new and incredibly expensive ciné-camera that I'd bought. The idea was that with its help I should make an epic film which producers in every continent would snap up as soon as I'd completed it. This, like most of my dreams, tended towards undue optimism, but it took me nearly three years to find that out.

'Arry, the yard's senior shipwright, shackled a wire onto *Salmo's* cradle and I expended a few feet of film on him as he did so, and then a bit more upon his bosom companion William, who drove the winch (and did everything else) with a Popeye-like pipe jammed into a corner of his mouth. Jerking along in fits and starts, *Salmo* began to inch her way out of the shed towards the top of the launching ramp, and I earnestly followed her every movement with each of the camera's three lenses in turn, flitting from vantage point to vantage point in a flurry of exposure-meters, camera-cases and tripods.

At last came the crucial moment when she was transferred to the trolley and stood poised on the brink, ready for the final whoosh that would take her down into the water with—for photographic purposes I hoped—a fine splash.

At the cry of " Let 'er go, 'Arry," I pressed the button and the camera whirred away, but, as seen through the viewfinder, nothing very much seemed to be happening. No whoosh, no splash.

The trolley had stuck. 'Arry put his shoulder to it and George and William came to help him. Still she refused to budge, so I laid down the camera and joined them. The weight of our combined shove just got her moving ; a final heave and she gathered momentum, and I leaped once more for the camera.

Historic first launches come, after all, but once and then are gone forever. I managed to get a fleeting one-and-a-half-second shot of the first flurry of the splash, but after that the camera stopped, unwound after all the film I'd wasted on 'Arry's first unsuccessful attempts at pushing. I began to see that the epic film idea wasn't going to be quite so straightforward as I supposed.

However, filmed or not, *Salmo* was at least waterborne, and as I was proposing to spend the night in her I strolled on board to park a few oddments before the mast was stepped. Horror of horrors . . . there was water over the top of the floorboards. I frantically wondered whether I'd absentmindedly left any holes open after removing the engine—water inlets, for example, or propellor-shaft tubes. I was fairly sure I hadn't, but the point was immaterial at the moment. Action was what was wanted and quick action at that. We either had to get her out of the water again or else pump with a vengeance. The yard kept a large motor-pump handy for just such emergencies, and miraculously it started the first time William cranked it. I cast the end of the suction hose down into the cabin, now nearly knee-deep, and prayed. The pump won. The water went back below the floors again and the hose made rude sucking noises in the bilges. The trouble, I saw at once, was not an unremembered hole, it was just honest to goodness leaking. Every joint spurted—spurted, not trickled—all along its length, gay little silver fountains joining one another to make a regular stream which flowed aft, rippling over the timbers, with the slope of the keel. Never before or since have I seen a boat leak so badly, and I had the gravest doubts whether she'd ever ' take up.' It was one of the gloomiest mornings I've ever spent, and quite soon I became convinced that I'd bought a chronic leaker which I'd never dare to take to sea.

There was nothing whatsoever to be done, however, but to wait and see. " After all," I told myself savagely, " I suppose there's always SOME chance that she'll cure herself. At least the bilges didn't look as though they'd been perpetually full of water."

A harrowing twenty-four hours ensued. Every half-hour, day and night, I had to start the pump before the water could reach bunk level and I found myself absolutely dead beat. But there were signs that the rate of flow was slackening. The pumping interval lengthened, first to one hour and then to two. During the second night I even had some sleep, and by the morning after that I found that I could keep pace with the hand-pump.

Meanwhile events were rapidly overtaking me. I had invited a friend, a prominent physician from a Midland hospital, to come and spend ten days holiday with me and take *Salmo* to Scotland. Leak or no leak, his holiday couldn't be put off and I'd agreed to meet him at Lymington, so off I had to go.

There was a terrific thrill in setting the sails for the first time and my morale soon returned. All the world seemed suddenly to be cheerful : the sun shone, the breeze blew and beneath my feet *Salmo* thrilled with life as we swept down the Solent. Even pumping seemed to be less distasteful than usual.

John was awaiting our arrival with a suitcase at the end of the yacht club jetty. " What in heaven's name is that thing ? " were his first words as he stepped on board.

" That," I replied proudly, " is the Prout canvas collapsible dinghy and I've got a red one so that it will show up well in coloured photographs."

" Oh that's what it is," said John. " Does it usually float ? "

" Of course it floats," I said. " At least I expect it does. It's widely advertised as the ideal tender for small yachts. It takes up very little room on board. As a matter of fact I haven't actually tried it out yet."

We decided to sail down towards the mouth of the river and pick up an unoccupied mooring and spend a quiet evening. I felt that I needed one. The tide was ebbing, so we swept towards our goal in fine style and John went forward to pick up the buoy. " It'll be on the port bow," I shouted, " I'm just going to round up to it now. . . . Hullo ! We seem to have stuck. I thought the channel was wider than this."

Long experience has made me a specialist in groundings, and I saw at a glance that if we didn't get unstuck within the next few minutes we'd spend an extremely uncomfortable, not to say undignified, night lying flat on our side on the mud. Experience also told me that that particular stretch of mud was very smelly, so we decided to haul ourselves off as quickly as may be.

" We'll just run a line out to the buoy," I said, " and pull. We're nearly bound to come clear. We're right on the edge of the channel."

The Prout was still partially wrapped in brown cardboard, so we tore this rapidly off and cast it over the side. Among the brown pieces that floated away seaward I caught a flash of white : " I say, John, there go the instructions on how this thing works."

" But don't you KNOW how it works ? " said John.

The next few minutes were painful. I felt the keel settling more and more firmly into the ooze and we found, in quick succession, several ways that the Prout didn't work.

" This jointed bit of stick thing," said John at length, " is obviously to stretch it out with. And this clip thing here is to keep it straight with once its stretched—but I still don't see just exactly how."

We finally had to descend to the undignified expedient of holding the sides out with our knees and paddling like Red Indians, but we did get the line out in the end and, what's more, come unstuck. To give the thing its due, that was the last trouble we ever did have with the Prout, which later became a great favourite and fully lived up to its advertising.

John had brought with him, besides his suitcase, a letter for me. It was from Jill. She was free the following Sunday, she said, and could she come for the promised sail, please.

I had planned to go north immediately, but very soon found myself explaining to John that the following Monday would be far more suitable. We'd spend the intervening five days, I suggested, sailing round the Solent, taking life easily and enjoying ourselves.

Apart from the fact that it cured the leak, this programme wasn't a great success and we both grew extremely bored. " She must be a hell of a nice girl, this," said John on the Saturday night, " if you're willing to waste all this time just to give her a half-day's sail."

" Oh well, you know," I replied rather feebly, " long standing engagement. Don't want to let her down."

Sunday dawned fine with a splendid breeze from the west, and a brainwave struck me as we had breakfast. Jill, I felt, couldn't possibly mind combining a day's sail with us going to Scotland. With the wind as it was we'd go eastabout and land her at Brighton or Newhaven or somewhere before going up the East Coast. There weren't any charts on board except a couple for the West Coast ; but there was an A.A. handbook with maps at the back of it, and I thought that would probably do.

John was doubtful. " Even if she's willing to do it," he remonstrated, " I still think we ought to have some charts. But I doubt if she will be. It all sounds too much like ' Once Aboard The Lugger ' sort of stuff."

Finally we decided to give it a trial. Jill was coming down to Portsmouth by train, so while waiting for it to come in I sailed past a frigate whose captain was a friend of mine and asked if they had any spare charts they could lend us. The Sub-Lieutenant who was officer of the day seemed taken aback by this request but went off to see what he could do, leaving us to tack back and forth beside the quarter-deck. After a long wait we saw him coming back on deck again with an apologetic air and a rather crumpled looking sheet of off-white paper. It looked as though it had been used to keep dirty footmarks off the chart-room deck. " Well, this is all I could

find," he began. " You see, sir, the navigator's ashore
as it's Sunday morning and he's got the charthouse keys
with him. This is an old chart that they've been using
for teaching sub-lieutenants with. But it is of the Thames
Estuary so it might be some help."

Close inspection suggested that it had been Piglet, Roo
and Tigger who had been learning navigation rather than
sub-lieutenants, but as had been surmised, we supposed
it might be of some help.

Jill's train arrived and I was in something of a tizz-
wazz as I prepared to go inshore in the Prout to fetch
her. " Be sure," I said to John, " and watch for the Isle
of Wight ferry going in and out. And don't come in too
close over this way because it's shallow. And mind the
moorings on the coal-hulk. And when we come back
again just bring her up into the wind so she stops. But
don't do it if a ship's coming out because we'd be in the
way and. . . ."

" Yes," said John, " and no where apposite. Don't
forget that we need some bread if we're really going to
Scotland."

Jill, it appeared, didn't mind in the least where we
landed her so long as she could get back to Windsor by
Monday morning, so we bought three loaves from a café
and Prouted back to John. There was a scramble, a
passing of loaves, introductions, and a collapsing of Prout
and then we were off. The wind was fresher than ever
and we fairly flew on our way with a rainbow of spindrift
arching off to leeward as the bows cut through the water.
" Oh, isn't this SPLENDID ! " said Jill. " Oh, I am glad
I came."

The weather, after a promising start, grew worse and
worse. So did John. " I hate this damned boat," he
said ; " I'm going to bed " ; and so with a mixture of
tact and seasickness he left Jill and me to take *Salmo*
on her headlong way. We both wore oilskins and every

now and then a splatter of spray would come flying aft
to sting our faces as we talked ; the tiller felt alive beneath
our hands and altogether it was a wonderful day to get
acquainted. We ate our sandwiches, we talked, made
coffee on the Primus and in no time at all, so it seemed,
Brighton lay abeam. The wind had backed and a fair
sea had built up by this time and the idea of Prouting
onto the end of the pier appealed to neither of us. Besides,
if we stopped we would have to wake John up and that,
we told each other, would hardly be fair. Better to go
on to Newhaven.

The cliffs reared higher and higher. We pointed out
Roedean, Rottingdean and Peacehaven to each other and
then ahead we could see the Seven Sisters and Beachy
Head. It was raining by now, hissing into the sea, splatter-
ing on deck and seeping down through the necks of our
oilskins, but somehow it all seemed rather fun and all
too soon we were flying between the breakwaters that
shield the Newhaven harbour entrance. " Hey, John ! "
we shouted down at his recumbent figure, " wake up.
We've arrived."

Newhaven looked bleak, rainswept and thoroughly Sunday afternoonish, but our entry felt triumphal ; it was
as if we were making our first landfall after crossing an
ocean rather than finishing off an afternoon's sail. A figure
ashore in streaming oilskins waved us to a berth, down
came the sails and we drifted peacefully to a halt. At
once the enchantment was broken. All the pleasure and
adventure went out of the day, to be succeeded by humdrum practicalities. " Where's the station ? " " What
time's the last train ? " " What shall we have for supper?"

The harbourmaster fidgeted on board to find out our
details : where to ; where from ; how long would we
stay ? and then told us a gale was forecast. He also said
there was a train to London at nine-fifteen. Fortunately
Jill has an untrusting nature, particularly with regard to

trains, and went to the station to check up on this while I cooked supper. It was to have been curry, because I fancy myself as a cooker of curries and wanted to impress Jill ; but it was not to be. She came flying back on board, grabbed her oilskin and looked round frantically for her bag. " Where is it ? Have you seen it ? Oh dear ! I KNOW I brought it on board with me. Oh ! we've only another five minutes now to the train. Oh, where is the thing ? " (how often since has this pantomime been repeated). And as soon as we found it, behind a cushion, inevitably, we flew off together to the station. The train was already there and we said goodbye to each other politely and rather awkwardly. " Well, thanks very much. It was a lovely day." " No, not at all. Thanks very much for coming."

The drizzle seeped down, dripping onto the roof of the train, sizzling as it hit the engine, and we both wished the guard would hurry up and wave his flag. There was so much we both wanted to say, but somehow couldn't manage to. ' In two more months,' I kept thinking, ' I'll be off for Canada and won't be back again for another two or three years.' The prospect suddenly felt flat and rather pointless. How much more fun it would all be if Jill was there to share it !

The train chugged off into the rain. We gave a last perfunctory wave to one another and I returned to *Salmo* in a vile temper. ' Why on earth,' I thought, ' couldn't I have met her a year ago. Everything would have been so much easier.'

The curry supper might just as well have been ashes for all the pleasure that either John or I had from it. I was lovesick : he was seasick.

CHAPTER TWO

CREW TROUBLE

THE maps at the back of our A.A. handbook proved to be invaluable. All the way from Newhaven to the Clyde they were in constant use, and took us safely up the East Coast to the Moray Firth, through the Caledonian Canal and finally round the Mull of Kintyre and back to my home anchorage at Rhu.

Ashamed though I am to admit it, the journey lasted a month. After all my hard work refitting I felt I needed a holiday and jolly well had one. John left at Blyth and I had a spell of single-handedness, but the final stages were made in luxury. My host and hostess of the fitting-out period, both keen sailors, took the boat over and I was able to relax, simply doing a bit of cooking from time to time to justify my presence on board.

Joan was terribly tactful, but at the same time deeply interested in all my doings, or such of them as she considered to be within her province. Women have one-track minds.

" I hear you took Jill out one day and sailed in pouring rain all the way from Portsmouth to Newhaven," she started off.

" Well," I replied, non-committally, " it only rained part of the time."

" And is it true that she's going to spend her summer holiday sailing round the Western Isles with you ? "

' Damn it,' I thought, ' how on earth do people GET all their information ; anyone would think the B.B.C. had decided that sailing and New Crew just didn't agree with each other, so we returned to the mainland and wearily tugged *Salmo* through the Crinan Canal against the wind on a long towline.   It was New Crew's last job, and he left on the early morning bus next day to spend a weekend with friends . . . still lying low.

Jill and I, after ten days of best behaviour, found ourselves alone on board and suddenly I began to feel embarrassed.   ". . . Er . . . er . . . now, look, Jill, I can perfectly well manage to get the boat back to Rhu from here by myself.   I mean, you mustn't feel that you have to stay on board as long as you were going to originally. Er, that's to say, if you feel you oughtn't to stay now that it's just the two of us, then of course, don't."

" But don't you WANT me to stay ? " she replied.

' Want you to,' I thought ; ' Good gracious, can't you see it's worse than that ? '

Perhaps she could ; for half an hour later, waiting only until we were clear of Tarbert harbour entrance and safely out into the usual gale conditions of Loch Fyne in July, we became officially engaged.   Jill, feeling that this was a moment either for celebration or restoratives, dived down into the cabin to get some.   There was a crash and a penetrating howl of, " Oh, my coccyx," and she arrived in a heap on the cabin deck, first bounce from the top of the ladder.   It was ten days before she could again sit down in any degree of comfort.

The rain rained and the gale galed, but we floated along in a sort of pink haze with the general intention of having a proper celebration at Colintraive and telling our respective families the news :   " My goodness won't they all be surprised ! " we told each other.

" Oh, and I think we ought to tell Joan and Bill too," I added ; " after all it was they that introduced us."

" Oh, yes.   What a good idea ! " said Jill.   " They will be surprised."

On arrival I rang up my brother and sister-in-law while supper was being prepared. It was my sister-in-law who answered the phone. " Oh hullo, Kay. Look, you know this girl that came out in the boat with me ? Well, we're engaged."

" Oh, you mean Jill ? " said Kay. " How splendid ! Yes, I thought you probably would be by now. Congratulations."

" Well," said Jill, when I rejoined her at the table, " was she VERY surprised ? "

" No, not very. As a matter of fact she seemed to have guessed already."

" But how on earth could she ? " Jill asked suspiciously. " What had you been telling them ? "

" I haven't been telling them anything. It's all very odd. I can't understand it."

Jill in her turn went to telephone.

" You know," she said when she got back, " it really IS funny. Joan and Bill weren't a bit surprised either."

We got back to Rhu the next day, having planned our campaign. It was a Sunday and I was due to sail on the Monday eight days later. Monday, Tuesday and Wednesday were set aside for a lightning round of ' In-lawing ' in the South of England ; Thursday, Friday and Saturday I would spend in victualling *Salmo* and generally getting her ready for sea ; Sunday would be free and then on Monday off I'd go.

" But what about a crew ? " Jill said. In the general flummox into which we'd thrown ourselves, this point had somehow been overlooked.

" Oh," I said, " yes, I'd forgotten that. Well, never mind, something will probably turn up."

The remarkable thing is that it did. There was a letter waiting for me when we got to my brother's farm later that night which read : " Dear Commander Hamilton, I have heard that you are intending to sail across to Port

Churchill in Manitoba in the very near future. I know that your boat is small and that you will certainly have arranged your crew already, but wonder whether there is a possibility of your being willing to take me along too. I am seventeen and have done a lot of sailing in my father's boat. I wish to settle in Canada and on arrival shall be quite able to look after myself. If you would be willing to take me along I should be eternally grateful and would of course undertake any duties which you wanted on the way over."

We had a glorious evening on the strength of all our good fortune and I arranged to interview this latest prospect as soon as I returned from England. His father agreed to come as well and everything seemed halfway settled.

Jill and I left by train for the South next morning, busily discussing wedding dates and all sorts of other things, and *Salmo* lay rolling at her moorings, alone and unprepared for ocean-crossing.

By the time I returned to Scotland several important items had been agreed. These were (1) that we should be married at Jill's home at Sutton on the 3rd November ; (2) That I should take *Salmo* as far west as I was able to before this time, but that if I dared return late for the wedding just because I was playing in the boat she'd never speak to me again ; (3) That immediately after we were married we'd both return to *Salmo* and continue the voyage more or less as planned. (4) That I'd have to get hold of a top hat from Moss Bros. so I couldn't just expect to get back on the morning of the third of November —I'd got to give myself LOTS OF TIME.

The latest applicant for crew membership turned out to be a very pleasant boy. His mother and father both came and we had a long afternoon discussing what clothes he should have with him as well as everything else. The only snag was, the father said as he finally left, that the immigration permit hadn't come through yet. Owing to Andrew's age, unexpected difficulties were cropping up. " Oh," I said. This sounded ominous.

Back at the farm my long-suffering sister Audrey spent the day in front of a gigantic pile of tins ripping the labels off and painting rather smudgy hieroglyphics onto them with a stick because no one could find a paint-brush. " This is a P,' she said, when I went to join her at it, " but it's run a bit because I had to thin the paint down and it means Peas.''

" Well, what are peaches then ? '' I asked.

" Well, as a matter of fact they're P.s too, but they're in green instead of red. All the fruit is green and everything else is red. You didn't have any other colours,'' she said rather plaintively.

I went away, murmuring to myself, " Now I MUST remember : Green P.s aren't Green Peas, they're peaches, green peas are red P.s.''

A friend in Ireland sent me an enormous ham wrapped in sacking, especially strongly cured, he told me. " But how on earth do I cook the thing ? '' I lamented. " There isn't a pot on board big enough to hold it. And besides does it keep better cooked or uncooked ? ''

We looked up the answer to these conundrums in a cookery book, found that ham kept better uncooked, so we rapidly cooked half of it and re-wrapped the rest in sacking until it should be needed.

I dashed off to the poultry farm next door and asked them for ten dozen eggs ; I wanted to be sure to have fresh ones, because I remembered the pain and grief I'd had in the past throwing egg after egg overboard after a mere week or so on board. I value my breakfasts highly.

Most of Friday was spent in haymaking, but in the evening my brother Jock came down to *Salmo* with me in the farm van, piled high with tins and boxes, the battery newly charged, chronometer, sextant, cameras, clothes and

a great many other things. On arrival we looked at the
Prout and we looked at each other and unanimously
decided to bring *Salmo* alongside to be loaded : a bit of
paint rubbed off, we felt, was a cheap price to pay for
not having to make an estimated ten trips in the Prout.
Slowly the mound on the end of the pier where we had
unloaded the van grew lower and lower, and *Salmo's* waterline sank farther and farther below the surface. By eleven
o'clock we were finished and sat down to have a beer.
Beneath the bunks on which we sat were all the tins.
With their labels off and with Audrey's hieroglyphics to
mark their identity, it didn't really matter if bilge-water
did slosh round them occasionally. The table between
the bunks was a home-made one and cunningly gimballed
with a big concrete weight at its foot to keep it upright
when the boat heeled. In harbour it folded out to give
a large flat surface, but at sea the flaps were turned inwards and had fine deep fiddle-boards round their edges
to stop things from sliding off. Water, forty-five gallons
of it, lived aft where the engine had been, and on top
of the tanks was a big cupboard running right across the
boat where I had stowed all the bulk foods like sugar,
flour, rice and so on. It was difficult to reach this cupboard without unshipping the ladder which led to the
cockpit, so for everyday use I kept smaller tins and jars
of all these things ranged behind the stove in the galley,
while all the crockery lived in a large rack over the top of it.
    Jock, who was seeing all these arrangements for the
first time (for there is a vast difference in a boat that is
fully stored for a two-month cruise and the same boat
in her ordinary state) was most complimentary. " You
know," he said, " I never dreamed we'd be able to get
all that mass of stuff on board even. And yet now it's
all stowed, you hardly notice it. And everything's so
get-at-able. No, these Vertues are certainly remarkable
little boats."

My peaceful last day at home was ruined at supper-time by the telephone. It was Andrew's father. " I'm really terribly sorry," he said ; " I've been on at the Immigration people all day, and they've been in touch with Ottawa. But Andrew won't be allowed to go. He's too young and would have to have a Canadian sponsor. We might be able to arrange one eventually, but as it is he can't go."

" Oh, what a pity," I said, and there was rather an awkward pause, so I had to go on, " Well, tell Andrew not to worry about it. These sort of things can't be helped. I hope he manages to get across all right later on when you can fix a sponsor."

" But what'll you do ? " said the father.

" Well, I'll just go alone, I think."

As soon as the words were out of my mouth it all seemed perfectly simple and straightforward ; the only point I couldn't quite make my mind up about was where to go to. Now that I was committed to single-handery, a route that would take me up the St Lawrence and through the Great Lakes seemed as though it might be more practicable than the Hudson Bay one. My objective, after all, was Vancouver ; how I got there didn't really matter much.

When I rang Jill up to tell her of the change of plan, I was still arguing with myself about the pros and cons of Hudson Bay versus St Lawrence. In answer to her query of " Well, what are you going to do ? " I replied " Well, the first part of the trip will be exactly as it was going to be. I'll go to a point about a hundred and fifty miles south of Cape Farewell in Greenland and see how things look. I'll probably branch off south there and make for the Belle Isle straits, north of Newfoundland, and go on up the St Lawrence, but if it looks pretty free from fog and ice then perhaps I'll just carry on through the Hudson Straits. You see. . . ."

But at this point Jill interrupted, " No you BLODDY well won't," she said. " It's all quite absurd. You told me yourself that it would be crazy to go messing about in the Hudson Straits by yourself. Now PROMISE that you'll go to Belle Isle."

" Oh, very well," I said, " you're probably quite right. Belle Isle then be it."

And that's how it was settled.

Next morning it was raining, real depression weather, but there seemed to be nothing to be gained by waiting, so I drove off to Rhu, having arranged with my sister Audrey to come and collect the car from the pier later on.

It was a strange feeling rowing out to *Salmo* in the Prout all by myself and knowing that that was how things would be henceforward for a month or so. I clambered on board, hauled the Prout up after me and collapsed it, lashing it securely against the guard-rails on the fo'c'sle. There were several other odd jobs to be done : shore-going clothes to be stowed ; hatchcovers to be secured ; sails to be bent on ; anchor-chain to be stowed away.

By myself it all took far longer than I had thought it would, and somehow the boat felt very empty. I kept glancing at the two bunks and thinking, ' Well at any rate I can take my choice of them now ' ; and then again, that with food for two embarked, I could take as long as I wanted over making the crossing, without going hungry. More space for stowing clothes in too. . . . I reeled off all the advantages I could think of, one after the other, because at the same time the unconscious, worrying half of my brain kept asking silly questions to which there was no answer. . . . ' What happens if you fall down and break a leg when you're half-way over ? ' ' What happens if you do meet ice even going the way you are, by the Belle Isle strait ? ' ' Do you REALLY think you'll be able to cope with all the sail-handling in gale conditions ? '

There was a bump alongside and Jock came on board loaded with parcels. He'd already offered to come with me, and it had taken an immense amount of persuasion to convince him that he would have been mad to do so . . . one can't just drop family, business, everything, for a couple of months without warning.

" Here are some mutton pies," he said ; " you probably won't feel like cooking much for lunch today, and they'll save you from getting too ravenous. And this is one of those big torches, the sort that you can hang up and use as a lantern or else use the other half to give a beam ; they are always handy things to have around, and there's a spare battery along with it. The pubs aren't open so I couldn't get a bottle of whisky, but here are a couple of books. You're bound to run short of reading matter sooner or later."

All his presents proved themselves to be quite invaluable, and except for the mutton pies, stayed on board for the next two years.

Audrey came out and Kay and all their children, and then quite suddenly I found that everything was ready and all that remained to do was to let go the mooring. The sails filled and off I went through the drizzle, zigzagging through the hundreds of other yachts moored near the pier.

CHAPTER THREE

ALONE

THE yachts dropped astern into the drizzle and the only
sound on board *Salmo* was the gurgle of the bow-wave.
Determined to be thoroughly matter-of-fact I went below
and fetched the cine camera. There was nothing worth-
while to photograph, but I felt that I should make some
attempt to capture the atmosphere of this rather bleak
departure, because my epic film had not yet progressed
very far. I fiddled with the exposure meter, made my
settings and pressed the button, counting the seconds
aloud to get the length of shot which I felt that the situation warranted. It all seemed strange and rather silly,
and I had the feeling that I must look uncommonly odd
as I stood in dripping oilskins taking photographs of dim
grey shapes astern : there wasn't even an ensign in the
foreground to give a dash of colour to the scene ; it had
seemed a pity to get it wet.

The rest of the morning crawled by. I soon had *Salmo*
sailing herself, because I felt that that is what a real
dyed-in-the-wool single-hander would do, so that he could
turn his attention to matters of real importance . . . to
making ' baggywrinkle ' perhaps, or recording immortal
thoughts in his diary ; but in my own case I really
couldn't think of anything to do. I was far too much
in a fidget to read or write and I didn't feel hungry ;
I just wanted to sit at the tiller and steer as being the
line of least resistance. ' But no,' I told myself, ' real
single-handers NEVER steer ' ; so I went down to the cabin

and made a cup of coffee that I didn't want and ate two
mutton pies. When this little meal was over I came on
deck again to see if we were still all right, and we were,
so I went below and washed the cup with great thoroughness and hung it up (real single-handers always keep the
boat in spotless order).

By tea-time the drizzle had eased and we (I could never
think in the singular ; it was always ' *Salmo* and me ')
were well down river past the Cloch lighthouse, I had
settled down sufficiently to read a book. But there was
enough traffic passing up and down the river to keep me
darting up to the cockpit every quarter of an hour or so
to see that I was clear of the fairway. On one of these
visits I noticed, a long way astern, a motor-boat, but I
thought nothing of it beyond supposing it to be a
fisherman.

The boat came closer and closer until it was obvious
that he was chasing me, so I went on deck to see who
it was and what he wanted, half wondering if I had left
anything vital behind that the family might think I ought
to have with me. It turned out to be the Press—a reporter
and a photographer in the local chandler's motor-boat.
The chandler was a friend of mine and was obviously
enjoying himself hugely. And well he might, I thought,
with a two pound an hour charter on his hands. It would
take them at least another two hours to get home again
and goodness knows how long they'd been chasing me
already.

" May I come aboard ? " shouted the reporter, and then
quickly did so before I had a chance to answer. He took
charge of the proceedings at once. " Now, we'll have a
few photographs first, please, Roger," he shouted down
to the photographer, who was a round little man in a
business suit and shiny shoes. " Off you go. Two or
three close-ups and a general shot . . . what's that ? Oh
yes, sure. I'll duck down out of the way ; wouldn't do

to have two people pictured in a single-handed crew, would it ? What's that you say ? A hat ? O.K., I'll ask him." He turned for the first time to where I stood in the cockpit, trying to look both nonchalant and seamanlike at the same time. " Now, Commander, will you wear a hat for this one ? Any hat'll do, yachting cap, anything."

" I haven't got a hat," I said.

" Well, a sou'wester then. Anything'll do."

" I haven't got a sou'wester. And besides it isn't raining."

This took him aback, but eventually the photographer was persuaded to take a picture which included my bald head, though it obviously outraged all his professional instincts. The two of them kept on muttering to themselves throughout the interview. . . . " Extraordinary. Quite extraordinary. Off to Canada and not a hat on the boat."

As soon as they'd had their fill of photographs I ushered them into the cabin with the idea of showing off the boat and pointing out my intended route on the nice new chart of the Atlantic that I had bought for the crossing ; but on the way down they caught sight of Jill's photograph, which I'd stuck up with cellotape beside the shaving-mirror. It fascinated them to the exclusion of all else.

" Who's that ? " they asked. " How old is she ? " (I didn't know the answer to that one, I had forgotten to ask her.) " Where does she live ? " " When are you going to get married ? " I felt very deflated. I knew that brides always stole the show at weddings, but here was Jill doing it two weeks after getting engaged.

They didn't stay long ; either the charter fee or else an office deadline was occupying their attention and they kept glancing at their watches. Quite soon they went back on board their motor-boat, circled once and disappeared astern. Their final good wishes were obviously genuine, and it made a pleasant and unusual last contact with the shore. It was to be exactly four weeks to the day before I had my next one.

The wind died as darkness fell and left us wallowing idle on a smooth grey sheet of water. The drizzle had set in once more and there seemed to be no point in staying awake any longer. I burrowed in the fo'c'sle for my guaranteed stormproof lantern, went through the messy ritual of filling it with paraffin, and left it dangling on the forestay, where it made the night seem even bigger and darker than it was before, and *Salmo* even smaller by comparison. I climbed gratefully into my bunk and was asleep in a matter of moments.

Three times during the night it sounded as though ships were passing uncomfortably close, but I could tell from the motion that there still wasn't a breath of wind, so I contented myself with cursing them for being mutton-headed so-and-sos and did nothing more about it. It was only when I went on deck in the cold grey light of early morning that I realised that my beautiful riding-light was one of the kind that refused to stay alight under any circumstances for more than a few minutes on end ; the least whiffle of wind or splash of drizzle snuffed it out completely. In a rage I flung it overboard, feeling that in the future I'd much prefer to sleep in main shipping channels knowing that I was unlit rather than just imagine I was.

The calm was succeeded by a gale which built up slowly throughout the day while I struggled towards the Mull of Kintyre. A perfectly horrible sea was running there, whipped up by the spring tides. Progress was painfully slow and I made less than twenty miles all day.

In retrospect, one night at sea is very like another, but this particular evening was so vile that I remember every detail of it. To start with I was feeling seasick, and then when I tried to comfort myself by doodling with a pair of dividers, doing little sums on the margin of the chart,

I found that if I maintained the present rate of progress I could expect to make a landfall in Canada in a hundred and three days, twelve days after my proposed wedding.

Overhead the wind whined dismally, and when I ventured into the cockpit the rocky coastline of the Mull of Kintyre to starboard looked menacing and hungry. The flash of the lighthouse brooding on its cliff seemed to stab at me like an accusing finger. " You foolish little man, you. Why are you doing this ? Why, why, why ? "

Foolish fancies, but very real ones, swing into the mind uninvited on occasions like these.

A heavier wave than ever bashed against poor *Salmo's* bow and surged aft, slopping and splashing over cleats, and then finally poured overboard again as we lurched in a new direction. She was badly overpressed, for I wanted to force her out to open water as soon as I could. There is a limit however to the extent one can force a boat and I knew that this had been reached, so I staggered forward to the mast and let go the fore-halyard. The sail was the smallest I had on board, the Number Three staysail ; it came down easily enough and I lashed it in a sodden bundle to the base of the pulpit. Relieved of its driving force *Salmo* immediately quietened. It was one of my favourite ways of heaving to. Back aft I staggered and then gratefully tumbled down into the cabin where I peeled off the dripping oilskins and hung them from their hook. There was nothing further that I could do for *Salmo* so I decided to look after myself.

Kay had given me a parting gift of lentil soup which, goodness knows how, she had put into a Bulmer's Cider bottle for safe keeping. In my cold seasick state, this seemed as though it would make an ideal supper. I hauled it from its stowage and with infinite care lit the Primus, going on deck twice in the process for a breath of air and to commune with nature.

On my return from the second visit, feeling very sorry for myself, I tried to tip the soup into a saucepan, but it had congealed into a glutinous mass and wouldn't move. Holding the bottle upside down and shaking it had no effect whatsoever, nor could I work it out by prodding with my finger. All I got was a tantalising lick. Spoon-handles wouldn't go down the neck, but I became determined not to admit defeat. The soup became a sort of symbol. I'd break the neck off the bottle and spoon the stuff out.

I gave the neck a sedate tap on the brass strip on top of the ladder ; then a harder one, and finally a full-blooded crack. The only result of this was to dent the ladder. A sort of frenzy possessed me. By gosh I WOULD break the beast. Whirling the bottle round my head I brought it down with a splintering crash and the entire thing burst to pieces like a bomb, depositing the soup with a dull ' flump ' onto the deck among a mass of splinters. Slightly sobered I regarded this for a moment and then a more violent lurch than usual flung me off balance and I put my foot into it, cutting my heel and adding blood to the mess. ' I WILL eat it,' I muttered to myself, and spoonful by spoonful cleaned the broken glass away and filled up the saucepan.

Fortunately it was very good soup and I gradually returned to sanity.

Sloshing slowly between Rathlin Island and the Mull (for even when hove-to we made a certain amount of way through the water) is a sobering experience and I went to bed murmuring ' I MUST wake up in five hours' time.' Sailing single-handed is easy enough when there's lots of sea-room, it's in restricted waters that the dangers arise, yet I had long ago decided that perhaps the greatest of any of these dangers was exhaustion. I therefore preferred to go to sleep and trust myself to wake up again rather than spend long hours unnecessarily on watch.

It blew great guns from the northward all next day, but because it was more free than it had been I decided to press on and get clear away from land.

We flew through the Rathlin sound and thereafter I edged away from the Irish coast. Half of me was shouting aloud ' Go on in to Londonderry. You've had a rough two days. Go in and have a rest,' but I was frightened to do so. I'd set out to sail from the Clyde to Canada and from the Clyde to Canada I jolly well would sail. To put in anywhere would be a weakness ; an admission of defeat very nearly. If I did go and have a rest I might even give up the idea of crossing altogether and be haunted ever afterwards with a fear of putting to sea. Unconsciously, almost, I altered course still farther to the northward. I didn't even want to be able to recognise the Lough Foyle entrance.

The northerly wind held for nearly two days, and by the end of it I had settled into a routine and was beginning to enjoy myself. *Salmo* sailed beautifully with very little attention, an inch or two on the sheets or a slight adjustment to the tiller-line was all that was necessary. And besides I wasn't at all particular about what course we made good so long as it was in the general direction of north-west. I planned to go fairly close to Rockall and on beyond that still to the north-westward until I hit the fifty-eighth parallel, where I'd level off and go west until Cape Farewell in Greenland was almost abeam. Then and only then would I slant south for Belle Isle. This was the summer route of the westbound windjammers and gave the best chance of meeting favourable winds. Farther south, westerlies and south-westerlies prevail.

It wasn't long before I discovered that such prayers for favourable wind as I might venture upon had to be very carefully thought out. Close-hauled we went slowly, but I never needed to go near the cockpit. Reaching or running we went faster but I dared not sleep ; beam

winds were the best of any, but I didn't want the Lord
to think me too choosey. What happened in practice
when the wind was free was that after supper (which I'd
cook with one eye cocked at the compass and the tiller-
line secured beside me at the galley), I'd clamber into
oilskins and go and sit in the cockpit to steer and make
a resolution that I'd keep on going until two o'clock in
the morning. Later on I would usually amend this to
one o'clock (or even a quarter to one) for one of the
beauties of being alone is that there's no one else about
to despise you for being weak-minded. When bedtime
came I would snug the boat down for the night and either
accept a not-very-satisfactory course and full sail, or else
take the mainsail off, when I could usually juggle things
so that the correct course was followed.

Occasionally, accidents occurred. Twice I was fooled
by the wind jumping very suddenly from south, when I
went to bed, to north when I woke up. In each case
I found to my annoyance that we were aiming in the
general direction of Ireland instead of Canada. But one
grows philosophic about things like that : what on earth
does it matter, after all, if one spends an extra day on
passage ?

As the days went by I grew lazier and lazier, and soon
found it intolerable to leave my bunk at intervals during
the night to see if the course was being held. Instead,
I devised a cunning arrangement whereby, by placing the
spare compass on the deck beside me, I could lean out
and glance at it in comfort. It wasn't altogether a fool-
proof method, because the cabin deck seemed to be badly
infected by magnetism (from the table-support) so I had
to make terrific mental allowances and remember on wak-
ing up that North ten East by the tell-tale compass meant
North thirty West by the steering compass. Again sometimes I'd get woozled in my calculations and either leap
from my bunk with an angry shout to find we were well

on course, or else remain passive while we went off at a tangent. But in general the system worked.

Sail changing and handling, particularly when the big sails, the mainsail and the Genoa, were involved, I found to be quite an undertaking at first, and used to sit and steel myself to do it for a long time before finally deciding that now I really MUST get onto it. But after a few days it grew easier. It's largely a matter of confidence. Just as soon as I realised that nothing terrible happened when I left the cockpit to work on the foredeck, even though the sails did shake and flap a bit, then I began to take all sail-handling as a matter of course, even in the roughest weather. The chief concession that I made to funk was that I always reefed earlier and more heavily when alone than I otherwise might have. After all, I felt, there was no point in making things more difficult by holding onto sail for too long.

The nastiest fright I had over sail-handling came when we had been at sea for ten or twelve days. Overnight I had left her running with just the Genoa set, and as I was taking a bleary look round before breakfast, some twinge of lunacy suggested that the spinnaker would make us go faster. It was blowing moderately hard—an ugly grey morning with the air filled with a mixture of rain and spray—and the deck was slippery and hard to stand on. I already had my spinnaker boom lashed in place across the pulpit (it was a patent method of my own) so I simply scrambled forward with the sail, rove the sheets and shackled on the halyard. The trick about setting a spinnaker, rigged as I have it, is to make sure that it goes up with the wind from dead aft ; so as soon as I had stowed away the Genoa, I moved aft to the cockpit. With no sail set the boat likes to lie beam on to the wind, but I steered her round until she was pointing as I wanted her to, and then leapt forward and hoisted away as hard as I could. Half-way up, the sail filled with a bang and flew out on the starboard side. The shock of it nearly lifted me off my feet, but I managed to catch a couple of turns round a cleat with the halyard before it did so. Being on such a long scope the sail went completely berserk and behaved like a seagull caught on a trout-rod ; flying up and down, backwards and forwards, trying to shake itself free. The mast was bending like a bow and it was obviously only a matter of moments before something parted. I leaped aft and steered downwind hoping that that would calm things down ; but it didn't, we just went tearing through the water at a dreadful rate like some demented speedboat.

' All right, all right. I'll douse the thing and start again,' I decided, and let go one of the sheets that held the foot of the sail tethered. ' Now,' I thought, ' held only at two corners instead of three it will behave like a flag and all the strain will be off the halyard. I'll just pull it in quickly.'

Some of the strain had certainly gone, but it was still a far heavier pull than it should have been. The sail flew out over the starboard side, six feet out of reach, and once more started flapping savagely. With a final effort I jammed myself against the single thin strand of wire that formed the guard-rail and exerted every atom of my strength ; pulling, clutching ; and inch by inch I heaved the sail towards me. At last I could lay a hand on the corner of it. I thought the battle was won ; a few more feet and I'd be able to smother it. I could feel the guard-rail biting into my waist, twanging with strain, and I tried to imagine what would happen if it broke : I'd just be flicked overboard like a shot from a catapult and *Salmo* would go racing off without me. I prayed that it wouldn't break, and went on pulling. Suddenly a new gust hit us and tore the sail out of my hand and back it went to its original position. Inch by inch the whole agonising procedure had to be gone through again, but this time there were no mistakes and I got it under control.

For a few minutes I was absolutely dead beat, partly

from physical strain, but mostly from a mixture of fright
and anger. ' Of all the damned fools,' I kept saying ;
' to try to set the sail like that on a day like this. You
don't DESERVE to have got it back.' In a very bad
temper I reset the Genoa and went below to make
breakfast.

For a single-hander the North Atlantic is the most soci-
able of all the oceans, for there are always birds to look at.
In the other oceans this is not so ; they are seldom seen
once one is well offshore, except occasionally albatrosses.
Here things were different and my bird book was in constant
use. I soon learned to recognise long-tailed pomarines,
Arctic skuas, great skuas and several sorts of tern. Two
common gulls even followed me the whole way over, though
what they got out of it (except the benefit of my somewhat
doubtful navigation) I don't know. They never ate such
few scraps as I threw overboard, but I grew quite fond
of them and used to miss them if they weren't lounging
overhead when I went on deck.

While in England I had stumbled on the existence of
a very remarkable and erudite body of men called the
Institute of Oceanography, and had gone one day to their
fastness near Godalming to ask if there was anything I
could do for them on my travels. Apparently there was,
and I was introduced in turn to their Discoloured-Water
man, their Whale man and their Squid man. Each lived
in a little world of his own, and to judge from the enthusiasm with which they greeted me, they must have
been lonely little worlds. "You know," said the Discoloured-Water man, "so few people know anything about
discoloured water. I've been studying this problem for
six years now, but there's so little to go on. The captain
of a ship sends in a report which is forwarded to us that
he passed through an area of discoloured water in position
such and such. He doesn't stop to take samples of it,
he doesn't even " (and here his voice sank a tone or two,

dramatically) " take the sea temperature. Nothing. Just sends in his report and we are expected to know what caused it." He had compiled a list he told me of nineteen possible causes of discolouration in deep water, but what he wanted was proof, proof, proof. He had devised, he said, a little bit of equipment to help him in his search and he proudly produced it for inspection. It was a wooden box like a schoolboy's tuck-box filled with screw-top lemonade bottles. There was also a thermometer with a long bit of string attached. All that the captain of a ship had to do, he said, was to take a water sample whenever he met any discolouration, neutralise it with formalin and take the sea temperature. Would I, he went on, almost shyly, care to take one of the boxes with me. It held eighty bottles, which should be quite adequate. I felt a beast when I refused it ; I could barely lift the thing and it would have been a menace in *Salmo*, overcrowded as she already was. The little man must have been used to disappointments ; he just sighed deeply and said, " Ah no. No, I feared you might find it a trifle . . . ah . . . cumbrous."

The Whale man was easy, he merely gave me forms to fill in, but the Squid man frightened the daylights out of me. He wanted, he said, samples of squid from all parts of the world. They had only had disappointingly few so far. " How," I had enquired, " do I catch them ? "

" Oh, it's quite easy," he assured me ; " you just need a good bright light and a jigger. You shine the light into the water on any calm night and jiggle the jigger up and down and sometimes you can get some really remarkable specimens."

" What do you call remarkable ? " I asked ; " I mean about how big ? "

" Well, myself," he admitted sadly, " I've never caught one bigger than nine feet, but I'm quite sure that you could get them up to about twenty. They fly too, you know," he went on dreamily, " like flying saucers, whirl themselves round the same way as jet engines do."

I at once made a resolve NEVER to shine a light bright or otherwise over the side on a calm night. Desperate battles between myself and even an eight-foot squid had no appeal at all.

I must, nevertheless, have hidden my terror fairly well, because on the Saturday before my departure a railway lorry deposited a large crate addressed to me and marked encouragingly POISON in red letters. I had opened this and found it contained a huge polythene jar of formalin. On the Monday morning's post there came an untidy brown paper parcel and a letter from the Squid man which said : ' Dear Commander, Just in case you should manage to get any specimens I have sent you a little formalin. You should neutralise it with hexamine which I enclose in this parcel. The specimens should be placed in any suitable tank or other container with a ten per cent solution of formalin, and shipped back to the laboratory AS SOON AS POSSIBLE. Best of luck.'

Warned by my callous refusal of the Discoloured-Water man's box of lemonade bottles, the Squid man had been cunning and sent his offering at the last moment when I had no time to send it back to him. I counted myself lucky he hadn't seen fit to send any tanks for twenty-foot squid as well.

Soon after the spinnaker incident I had to go into the foc'sle to get the uncooked half of the Irish ham. The stink in there was appalling. I thought at first a rat had died, but soon found it was the wretched formalin container which had a leaky top, so I decided to neutralise it. I didn't know the meaning of the word ' neutralise,' but it sounded as if it might be a way of reducing the potency. The instructions had seemed simple enough and on shore probably would have been, but in a greatly overcrowded forepeak things were different. I had to crouch over the jar like a witch with her cauldron, and spoon little driblets of hexamine (which is a sort of salty stuff) into it. As there were a good couple of pounds to be spooned this took more than half an hour, and by the end of that time I was choking and spluttering in agony. The stink was as bad as ever, so I wrapped insulating tape round the cork and swore I'd never go near the stuff again. Fortunately I never had cause to. No squid came our way.

I never really expected to see any other ships until I got close to Belle Isle ; for I was north of all but one of the shipping routes marked on my chart. This lone exception bore the intriguing legend ' Ivigtut to Inishtrahull (Occasional),' and conjured up romantic pictures in my mind of the inhabitants of Ivigtut (wherever that might be) eagerly awaiting the annual visit of the Inishtrahull whisky ship ; but I never went so far as to hope that I'd see one myself. Great was my excitement therefore when, on the day that I crossed this line, I saw smoke on the horizon. I snatched up the marathon letter to Jill which I had started the day after leaving Scotland and dashed off another couple of rather grubby pages and stuffed the whole thing into a cocoa-tin, hoping I could lure my Ivigtut friend close enough to let me throw the tin on board. Alas ! for false hopes—I never saw more of him than his smoke, and the letter remained unposted.

A boat at sea is very much of a living thing, and I found that in order to keep her sailing properly and safely I had to become very closely attuned to all her moods and murmurings. Because I spent so little time on deck I relied mostly on my ears to know that all was well. The mainsail, for instance, would make a slap, slap, slapping sound if we sailed too close to the wind, whereas if we bore away too much I would be warned by a strange little clicking tinkle which I traced to the jib-sheet shackle. There were a thousand and one noises, and though I could never recognise them all, any new one would always mean :

' Something funny happening. Go and see what it is.'
Lying warmly in bed it was difficult advice to follow, and
as I dragged myself out and into oilskins, preparatory to
an exploration trip on deck, I'd often be overcome with
loathing for boats and for the sea. But once on deck, I
rarely repented having gone.

One occasion I remember vividly. We had been bash-
ing our way against strong, nearly gale-force head-winds
for four days, and I had gone to bed wondering how on
earth Jill would get on in conditions like that when her
turn came. The boat was very noisy, with heavy crashes
coming every few moments as we slammed into the waves,
and there was a constant sound of water running aft over
the decks ; the wind whined in the rigging, and a thousand
little clicks came from bucket-handles, tins, and bottles
in the cabin as the lurches made them strain against their
lashings. It was a bang that woke me, but not a particularly loud one and it wasn't repeated. The motion
remained unchanged and I nearly decided that this extra
noise, half heard in sleep, was imagination. Reluctantly
however I dragged on my oilskin smock and trousers, pulled
the hood over my head and adjusted the rubber-edged
facepiece to make a watertight joint round my cheeks.
Then I went on deck. From the cockpit nothing unusual
could be seen, so I went forward carefully, handhold by
handhold, to the foredeck, and at once found that the
Prout dinghy had been washed away from its lashings.
By the mercy of Providence one single lashing still held
it trailing along the side, and it was the work of a moment
to heave to and recover it. I was much relieved ; I'd
grown very fond of the Prout and should have hated to
lose it.

It was the morning after this that the weather moderated
and I had an easy day's sailing which allowed me to go
over all the gear and check it for signs of wear. It was
as well that I did this, for I found that the length of

stainless steel wire which formed the tail of one of my
runners had stranded and was on the point of parting.
Had it done so it would have endangered the mast, so
as soon as I had replaced it I decided to replace its opposite
number on the other runner as well. Wire splicing in a
heaving cockpit is a lengthy business and requires considerable concentration, and my lookout suffered in consequence. It was only as I replaced the second runner
that I had a look round, and there, not two miles away,
was a ship heading straight for me.

It was a terrific thrill, and I darted into the cabin for
Jill's letter in its cocoa-tin. The visitor, however, proved
to be a nervous creature and refused to come within half
a mile. It was obvious that I was proving a major attraction, for the rails were crowded with waving figures, and
I soon saw he was trying to tell me something through
his loud hailer. Since however he had it trained directly
away from me I could hear nothing but a distant booming.
It was most irritating.

" You chuckle-headed ape," I shouted at him, " either
come a little closer or else train that damn thing so I
can hear it," and I shook my fist at him wrathfully. This
clearly delighted him, I could almost hear the conversation
on the bridge : ." Ah look ; he's seen us ; he's waving.
Give him a couple of toots on the siren and we'll get
going again." And get going they did, their parting toots
ringing like mockery in my ears.

(I wrote to the captain on arrival to ask him what it
was he'd been trying to tell me, and he replied that it
had been ' Do you realise that you are lying directly in
the track of Hurricane Betsy ? ' It's just as well that
he wasn't able to give me this gloomy warning or I should
have been thoroughly depressed by it. As it was, I just
thought that the weather looked like becoming pretty foul
and went below to cook supper.)

I quote from my diary for the next day : ' *August 22,*

Breakfast time. Three full weeks at sea since leaving Rhu : five hundred and fifty miles left to go to the Belle Isle Strait and we've now crossed the line marked on my chart " Normal limit of Drifting Ice (August)."

' Also to be recorded is the fact that it's blowing like nothing on earth. Having pottered disconsolately up top no less than five times last night to reduce sail, I'm now down to a tiny corner of mainsail and nothing else ; even that seems a bit much. I'll probably take it off very soon. About the only place on board where I can stay put is jammed in the bunk. As always *Salmo* is behaving splendidly, but it's very rough indeed. Let's hope it doesn't last too long.

' 11 *o'clock*. Yet ANOTHER ship. A Paraguayan this time, oddly enough. He had the good sense to come up very slowly towards me from leeward to see if I was all right, I suppose. It's far too rough to think of trying to go close to him and I didn't want to wave in case he thought it meant " Help, Help," so I tried to take a cine of him instead and look like a proper tourist. I don't suppose it will come out, because we were standing on our heads half the time. So was he, incidentally. Goodness knows what he thinks of me ; I turned in last night without any trousers on (I got them wet while reefing). I saw him first through one of the scuttles so went on deck at once, then saw he carried women on board so had to hurry down again and put a towel on. The glass, having been fairly high up to now, is dropping like a stone. It all looks most unpleasant.

' 1800. It's blowing even harder than ever and I've long ago taken all sail off. I don't want to turn tail on to the sea unless I have to, we'd lose too much distance. We seem to be fairly all right as we are, though there's spindrift everywhere and the wind is fairly shrieking in the mast. There are now a few patches of blue about and the barometer has steadied up after a very sharp fall.

I'd love to take some photographs of this, but it's out of the question, I'd just ruin the camera. The sea has built up enormously and is really most impressive, not to say frightening, and the motion's simply frantic. Goodness knows if I can manage to cook anything, I'm just going to try it now. I'm tired of my bunk.'

The cooking of that supper turned out to be quite entertaining, though I totally failed to see the joke at the time. I started with soup and that went all right, using a huge saucepan with very little soup in it. The spring curtain-rod that goes over the stove was an absolute boon on occasions like this, I just put it over the top of the saucepan and it never moved. The omelette which followed was far more difficult. I achieved the mixture all right, in a large mug secured on the cold half of the stove, breaking the eggs one-handed and being very careful to put away the salt, the butter and the milk as soon as I had used them and before turning to the next ingredient. It was when I reached the frying-pan stage that the real bother came. It was nearly dark and the battery-operated light was so low that I could hardly see what I was doing. I needed one hand to stop myself falling into the stove and the other to operate the fish-slice, so I had to fix the frying-pan to the stove. The gymbals weren't quite up to coping with the motion, so as soon as I poured in the egg mixture, it went careering round the pan like a wall-of-death rider while I rather futilely attempted to follow and damp the wave with the scraper. By the end it didn't look as symmetrical as the omelette one meets in restaurants, but it tasted excellent.

The gale died down after one more day and I resumed my course. It was growing far colder now and foggier. The farther west we went the greyer and bleaker it became. All the colour seemed to have been washed out of the world. The sea became grey, the sky became grey and even the boat seemed grey. In self protection I wore the violent red jersey that Joan, my erstwhile hostess, had knitted for me. Not only was the boat grey but it was damp as well. The whole hull seemed to perspire, and when I rummaged through the clothes locker, pretty well everything was mildewed. I decided that the time had come to do some drying out.

The boat was sailing herself and the sea was calm, so I opened the fore-hatch and threw half the sails out on deck to air and to give myself a bit of room in which to work down below. Then I turned my attention to the paraffin heater, which was one of the pressure variety. The sea was calm but not quite as calm as I had imagined, and in my attempts to fill the heater without a funnel a good large dose of paraffin found its way onto the deck. I didn't pay much attention and carried on priming the thing with methylated spirits, but a slight draught from the open hatch took much of the heat away from where it was needed to vaporise the paraffin. The result of this, naturally enough, was that when I tried to light the jet, it burst into sheets of flame and smoke as Primuses always do when they're not hot enough. ' I'll fix it,' I thought, and released the pressure from the tank. Unaccountably (probably I'd overfilled it) it wasn't pressure that came out of the release valve, it was a fountain of paraffin, which promptly burst into flame and arched down to the deck, which caught fire in sympathy. And there I was dancing about among the flames. Having perpetrated this sort of stupidity in the past in a boat without a fire extinguisher, I had taken the trouble to bring one with me this time, and I skipped aft to get it from the galley. ' Turn T handle to the right and operate like a pump,' said the instructions. I managed to do the turning part, but as for pumping, not a hope of it. I nearly burst myself trying to pull out the plunger, jammed solid by rust and neglect, but it was no use at all. The fire meanwhile was spreading rapidly and I became thoroughly frightened. My only bucket lived forward of the flames, so with a kangaroo-like bound, I went through them, found the bucket and arrived on the upper deck through the fore-hatch all in one movement, so to speak. Vigorous bailing soon brought the flames under control ; but what a mess ! The forepeak was all black, and bits of it were charred and the whole thing was very considerably wetter than it had been at the beginning of the operation.

As fires go, it hadn't really been a bad one, but imagination builds even the most insignificant into a veritable inferno when one is alone. It was a long, long time before I forgot the visions which had conjured themselves up during the few minutes of battle : of myself rowing sadly into the sunset in the Prout Canvas Collapsible Dinghy while *Salmo* smouldered in the background. I think my mind must have been influenced by early memories of the finales to Charlie Chaplin films.

In the prevailing fog, navigation grew increasingly difficult just as I began to be interested in knowing where I was. It is only at the edges of oceans that you need to know where you are. In the middle it doesn't matter.

Grey misty day succeeded grey misty day and I used to spend hours on end in the cockpit with a sextant in my hand waiting for a flash of sun. For six days I wasn't able to get so much as a blink, and a sense of claustrophobia began to haunt me ; it was far too easy to imagine the fog to be filled with icebergs. To take my mind off things I decided to make a gingerbread. I'd never made one before and had to follow the instructions in my cookery book line by line. At last the wonderful moment arrived when I took it from the little portable oven, all spongy, warm and brown, and smelling ambrosial. I wondered how soon, with any decency, I could eat it. Should I wait until it grew cold perhaps ? At that moment my eye was caught by that of the very forbidding and efficient looking female who had written my cookery book and

whose picture graced its back. She seemed to be chiding
me. I turned to her instructions and sure enough she
was. ' Gingerbread, Number 973,' she wrote ; ' Gingerbread MUST BE KEPT AT LEAST TWO DAYS before cutting.'
' Then to hell with you,' I thought ; I could bear her
rectitude no longer, and defiantly cut and ate four slices
in succession. It was wonderful.

In due course I got my sun sight and discovered that
if the chronometer had kept its rate I had another hundred
miles to go ; one day's sailing time if all went well.

The fog rolled back again, wet and cold. The sun disappeared and very soon I could see no farther than two
hundred yards. A pulpwood log floated past ; the peeled
bark showed up white in the water and gave me a fright
when first I saw it. My mind ran on icebergs. We were
right in the main path of them, though in August there
shouldn't have been many about.

My mood alternated between elation and depression
throughout the day. The passage was nearly over, but
the difficult part was only just beginning. It is much
easier to be bold and confident about making a landfall
in fog when one is planning a voyage than it actually is
when one comes to do it.

Suppertime. Fifty miles to go and still the fog swirled
all round about. Salmo was sailing fast with the wind
on the beam, but I was growing more and more worried.
Such elation as I had felt earlier had worn off completely
and had been replaced by a cold nagging worry. Foolishly,
I peered and peered into the moving grey blanket, seeking to shift it with the intensity of my gaze. We had
been a month at sea, and if the chronometer had been
gaining just two seconds a day for each of those days
my calculations could be as much as fifty miles out ; we
might even now be charging into the coast of Labrador
or Newfoundland. Should I have brought a wireless with
me after all, I wondered. I hate the things ; but at

least if I'd had one I'd know where I was. Now I only
THOUGHT I knew. In saner moments I preferred this state
of affairs, but after all the fog I'd had, this wasn't among
my saner moments.

'Oh, I wish it would clear,' I thought.

Another pulpwood log floated past. It was the fourth
I'd seen and obviously we were getting fairly close to
shore.

Should I heave to and wait till it cleared ? It would
mean wasting a wonderful breeze if I did, and wonderful
breezes are there to be used and not wasted. Fifty miles
was surely a safe enough margin. Or wasn't it ?

I made onion soup and beef stew for supper from some
of the salt beef that I'd made and kept in brine. It
cheered me greatly and I decided to carry on until I
reckoned there were still twenty miles to go. That would
be at midnight.

Promptly at twelve I hove to and breathed deep sighs
of relief when I had done so. At any rate we hadn't
hit rocks as yet. And we were thirty miles closer to the
shore than we would have been if I'd hove to when I
first wanted to at suppertime.

The weather had grown worse. The fog had turned to
rain and the wind was much stronger. It whined and
moaned in the rigging, but lying warmly in my bunk
there was a certain satisfaction in listening to its music.

'Perhaps,' I thought, as I dropped off to sleep, 'when
I wake up I shall be able to see land.'

CHAPTER FOUR

THE morning was glorious ; the sky was blue, the decks shone with dampness and the horizon stretched unbroken all round. I looked at my watch. Half-past six.

' Get the boat sailing. Have a cup of coffee and then take a sight while the going is good.'

The moon hung low in the sky to port and the sun was astern so I took a sun-moon sight and put it on the chart. Thirty miles left to go to Cape Bauld, the northern tip of Newfoundland and southern limit of the Belle Isle Straits. Fog had made me over cautious, but on a morning like this it didn't matter. Nothing mattered. I had two eggs for breakfast and lots of coffee and Huntley & Palmer's Breakfast-biscuits drenched in marmalade.

The wind had veered overnight and *Salmo* was close hauled, so I left her to look after herself and very assiduously DIDN'T look for land ; for once I start that game it becomes an obsession and very soon maddens me when I can't find any. The sea was calm and we surged along in glorious style, the tinkle of the bow-wave making a pleasant accompaniment to the job of cleaning the cabin. I folded the blankets neatly, brushed up all the fluff from the deck and scrubbed the stove until it looked enamel-coloured again instead of black and undulating. When I lit it, it didn't even give off its familiar blue smoke and the sweet-sour smell of burnt fat. It seemed almost a pity to use it any more.

In the late afternoon, after a long sleep, I went on deck and saw the blue outline of hills on the port bow. I felt very small and very grateful. The often recurring miracle of making a landfall never loses its impact ; the delight of seeing all one's meaningless calculations and criss-crossed lines on the chart translated into something tangible—blue hills breaking the horizon, has to be felt to be appreciated truly. Seamen have always known that their own private joys and sensations can't be shared. Flecker, quoting his Spanish Legend, sums it up in the conversation between a shellback helmsman and the inquisitive Count Arnaldos: " Wouldst thou, so the helmsman answered, learn the secrets of the sea ? Only those who brave its dangers comprehend its mystery." I like Flecker. He's a splendid author for livening up the night watches, his full-blooded meaty phrases sound terrific when declaimed into the darkness.

Cape Bauld has a lighthouse on it which I hoped to see by bed-time but didn't. It looked like being a busy night, so I decided to sleep until half-past twelve by which time Cape Bauld should be five miles away. *Salmo* would just have to find her own way inshore meanwhile.

The first thing I realised on getting up was that she hadn't made a very good job of it. We were inshore all right, within two miles in fact, but there wasn't a sniff of a lighthouse anywhere, only three rather mysterious white lights in a row on a hillside that weren't any help at all. I consulted the chart with the aid of a torch, but because it was the only chart of Canada that I had (I had dozens of the Hudson Straits and Greenland) it was covered with gloomy hydrographic warnings ' The principal lights and features ONLY are marked on this chart. For further detail reference should be made to . . .' and it gave a list of all the charts that it seemed to think I should have been carrying. This bit of coast didn't seem to interest it at all, indeed it gave the impression that it was uninhabited.

I knew we must be south of Cape Bauld, but had no

idea how far south, nor what inshore dangers there might be intervening. Visibility had closed down again slightly, and I was left with the choice of sailing blindly northward, or of waiting until daylight to get a clearer picture of what was happening. I have a fear of unknown coastlines, particularly when, as in this case, they are indented and have off-lying rocks, so I decided to waste a bit more time yet and remain hove to until dawn.

It was one of the most sensible decisions I have ever made ; for the first thing I saw next morning when I went on deck was an iceberg, a darned great big one, lying directly between me and Cape Bauld, which was now plainly in view about eight miles to the northward. It must have been mistier than I had realised during the night.

The iceberg seemed to be a real de luxe model, and though it was a mile away it gave me a heck of a fright. I'd never seen one before, so I decided to go up close and have a look at it. Goodness knows why—I certainly wasn't expecting it to bark at me—but the thing that impressed me most was its silence. There it was, this huge brute of a thing, half a mile long perhaps, white and very stately and utterly silent. Even the waves breaking round its skirts, and hollowing out caves and patterns, didn't interfere with the essential quiet of its presence. When I was close beside it, taking photographs, the sun broke through the overcast for a few minutes and the rays picked out all the shadows and buttresses, making them shine in shades of white and silver in glorious contrast to the darkness of the sky beyond. It must have been an old berg ; it had rolled over several times since it started its southward journey, and I could see the slanting weals down its sides where the waves had bitten into it in the past. The gash round its present waterline seemed to me to be just about as big as those I could see exposed, so it seemed prudent not to go too close.

It is an experience I shall be quite happy to forgo, that of being close to a million tons of somersaulting ice.

Just as I took my last photograph to show them back at home that I really had visited cold water, a great green pinnacle tumbled away from the berg, the base cut through by the waves, and it crashed into the water with a roar. It must have been fifty feet high and half as broad— nothing big when compared with its parent, but quite big enough to wreck a boat of *Salmo's* size. We passed five other calvings before I reached Cape Bauld, and I began to realise just what uncomfortable companions icebergs are to share a sea with, particularly a foggy sea.

My attention was distracted from one of these floating growlers (I think that's the term for them) by a black speck that danced up and down over the sea ahead and was certainly behaving in far too playful a way to be the lump of ice I had at first thought it. Putting my glasses onto it I saw to my excitement that it was a large open motor-boat. " Aha," I said, " company. The first for a month," and headed for it to be neighbourly, sticking up the ensign staff with its red ensign as I did so. The boat turned out to be a fisherman busily engaged in laying lines for cod. He had two big floats and a mass of line between them and in the sea that was running he was having difficulty in handling it. There were two men in the boat and they glanced up as I passed and I rather think that one of them was just going to wave, but over-balanced at the last minute and decided not to. I was upset by this, because I was feeling in a ' first day of holiday ' sort of mood and thought that everyone else should be as well. There were several other boats farther on and one of them did wave, but I still felt dissatisfied. ' Look at me,' I was longing to shout. ' Amn't I splendid. I've just come over from Scotland ' ; but instead all that I could manage and that only once was ' Lovely morning,' which seemed slightly inadequate.

I had decided to go to a little place on the Labrador side of the strait, partly because it was marked on my chart with the mystic symbol ' Tel. Off.' (which I apprehended to mean Telegraph Office), but chiefly because it had the charming name of Wise Man's Hole. It wasn't far from Cape Bauld, but it was the devil of a job to get there : first it blew a gale for twelve hours and forced me to heave to, and then a flat foggy calm descended and I drifted up and down the strait as the tide dictated. Wise Man's Hole maintained a lighthouse and I sighted this when the mist lifted, twenty-four hours after passing Cape Bauld. The lighthouse was built as far as I could see on a small island, and behind that there was a village of brightly painted houses with roofs coloured green and blue and red. I was so close I could even see people walking about.

With the dispersal of the mist it became a simply glorious afternoon, the colours supernaturally bright and the sea almost Mediterranean in its blueness. The coast was low and undulating and stretched into the distance to the northward in greyish-green waves : a desert of rocky tundra. Still there was no wind, and because the tide was ebbing I drifted farther and farther from my goal until I could no longer distinguish details, and the village became a mere white blob in the green line of foreshore. Darkness fell, and the lighthouse blinked through the gloaming, a tantalising reminder of harbour, fresh food and long uninterrupted sleep. Blink, blink, blink it went, and then again, blink, blink, blink.

At last a breeze came and I made headway once more. My blood was up and I was determined to make harbour that night. As *Salmo* hissed through the calm water, the sky over the crest of the hill to starboard grew lighter and lighter, as if the moon was rising, and then great green searchlights began to flicker and weave, eerily and silently, their reflections mirrored in the ink-black water.

It was the first display of Aurora Borealis I had seen on the trip, and I took it as an omen of welcome to this wild land.

The lighthouse grew closer and closer and I began to think of the mechanics of going into the anchorage. I had seen two motor-boats entering harbour during the afternoon, and each of them had gone round the far side of the lighthouse and disappeared, so I determined to do the same, wondering what the disappearing part of the manœuvre would be like. The lighthouse came abeam so I went about heading directly inshore, with the light just a fraction to starboard. " Here goes," I thought, " I wonder what on earth happens beyond the island ? "

The wind had freshened and we raced for the shore, a high black bluff, silhouetted against the sky. Beneath the lighthouse, blinding now in its intensity, I began to see the shape of the island forming ; it was steep to by the look of it, and fairly high, but the shoreline seemed to extend unbroken all the way from it to my bluff. Was it really an island, I wondered ? The chart didn't mark it but it had LOOKED like an island in daylight. And surely no one in his senses would put a lighthouse on that side of the land that he didn't want shipping to use. It MUST be an island and the entrance MUST lie on this side of it, I reasoned. But where was it ? No gap appeared in the wall of land and there had to be a gap. We were close now, very close and moving fast. I could hear the slap of waves on the rocks. The light was nearly abeam and 'way up in the air above me to starboard. I couldn't go on much farther. ' If I don't see a gap open up before I count ten,' I said to myself, ' then I'll turn round and go out again. That is if I CAN turn,' I added. ' Six, seven, eight . . .' and at last a gap appeared—a clear lane of water, but wow ! what a narrow one ! I pulled the tiller hard up and round we spun to starboard, bring-ing the wind astern, and I breathed a sigh of relief as the bow headed for clear water instead of the black wall of land.

'Going too fast,' I muttered to myself ; ' silly to come in at this speed. Haul the boom right aft. She'll be difficult to steer but easy to manœuvre if we have to do any quick turns ; and then . . . Time to get the stay-sail off.' I jumped from the cockpit and dropped the sail onto the foredeck, glancing aft to see that we were maintaining the course. Back to the cockpit to make an adjustment, then forward again to unhand the sail and stuff it down the fore-hatch. The anchor was cleared away and ready, the shore drifted past on either side, so close now that I could see the boulders on the beach and hear the gentle lap of water. We were sheltered from the wind and *Salmo* moved slowly. I took her as far as I dared, dropped the mainsail and let go the anchor. We had made our first foreign port, *Salmo* and I.

After a quick square-up on deck I went below to the cabin. It looked very homely and inviting as I sat on the bunk drinking a cup of cocoa ; I had lit the pressure heater so everything was warm and comforting and familiar. Slowly the realisation soaked over me that here I was at anchor at last, the crossing made and another dream accomplished. I scribbled a few lines in my diary and went to bed without a care in the world.

I slept late next morning and was still in the middle of breakfast when a boat bumped alongside and a man in a tartan shirt with a quiet voice introduced himself as the deputy lighthouse-keeper. He'd had breakfast he said and was going ashore to meet the weekly steamer. Did I want to go in with him ?

I said, " Thanks very much, I would like to, and would the steamer take mail direct, or would it have to go through the post office ? "

" No. No. They'll take it all right," he assured me. " You just come with me," and then added as an afterthought, " Do you like bake-apples ? "

I'd never heard of them and said so.

" Got a load of 'em in the boat. I'm shipping them to St John. They pay good prices down there. Everyone likes real Labrador bake-apples." He showed me some two-pound preserving jars filled with what looked like washed-out ginger-coloured raspberries. " You eat 'em with sugar and cream. Real good they are. Thousands of them here. We all pick them and preserve them. Everyone sends out one hundred, two hundred pounds in the season, maybe. They're over now though."

He'd told me so much, and had been so polite in disguising his curiosity that I felt I must reciprocate, so I said that I'd just come over single-handed from Scotland. He showed very little surprise at this.

" From Scotland, eh ? Most of our people come from there originally. Two, three generations back, mostly." That explained his accent, I thought. It wasn't Scottish, but to my ear at least it wasn't quite Canadian either.

We rowed ashore together. " Made this boat myself," he told me. " Spruce. But it's getting scarce now. Have to go way back for it, nine ten miles maybe. Used to have it right here by the village."

I looked at the rocky, barren and pathless countryside, rolling away moss-green to the skyline. " How on earth do you move the stuff ten miles," I asked, " across all that ? "

" Do it with the dawgs. We all have a team. Move anything with them in winter."

" Just what do you DO in winter ? " I asked.

" Well " (actually he said " Wall " but I can't attempt to reproduce the drawl), " it's quite a question that. Cut a bit of wood of course, and then some of us hunts a bit ; if the caribou are around, that is. Very few last winter, but the winter before that was great. Most everyone got himself one. And then there's a bit of trapping," he went on ; " but fur prices are down now. They boomed just after the war for a while, but nobody wants them now, seemingly. No. It's quite a question, what to do in winter."

The jetty was of timber, heavy logs bolted together to make a sort of cage that had been filled with rocks and decked over the top. By the time we landed the C.N.R. steamer *Northern Ranger* had arrived and the whole population was down to greet her. They called the village Red Bay, I discovered. Wise Man's Hole, the name I knew, hadn't been in use for fifty years.

The jetty seethed like an ant-heap, but I noticed that none of the women ventured onto it ; they stood in a group at the back laughing and chatting to each other, leaving the men to mill around the gangways and bustle up and down with boxes in their arms. The lighthouse-keeper and myself, staggering under the weight of two big crates of bake-apples, joined the mêlée and clambered on board. We found a gigantic man in shirtsleeves and a baseball cap who took delivery of the bake-apples, and then we fought our way aft to the mail room, only to find it locked. We cursed briefly and fought our way back to the gangway again where we asked baseball cap when it would open up.

" Goddam it ! " he bellowed. " That bastard's canned again. Happens all the goddam time. I'll fix it for you."

So we all went back and battered enthusiastically on the door, which groaned and rattled on its hinges until there were faint stirrings from within.

" Man here with some mail," yelled baseball cap, and went off muttering to himself. We gathered he didn't love his colleague.

After a minute the door opened and the mail officer peered out, blinking like an owl and looking unshaven and unhappy.

" Great morning," he said unconvincingly, " yes, sir. Simply great. Got some mail for me, eh ? "

It was a lucky guess, I thought, for it certainly WAS a

great morning ; there wasn't a cloud in the sky and it
was fine and warm, but how the mail officer knew it was
a mystery, for both his porthole and deadlight were firmly
battened down and the atmosphere of the office was like
the inside of a boxer's boot.

I got rid of my marathon masterpiece to Jill, and a
couple of other letters that I'd written during the calm
of the day before, and backed out as quickly as possible
to do some more looking round.

The lighthouse-keeper was away back to his lighthouse ;
I saw the green and red paint of his dinghy (like all the
boats and houses at Red Bay, it was beautifully painted)
bobbing away beyond *Salmo* towards the island. *Salmo*
herself, I noticed, looked rather like a Chinese laundry,
with blankets, mattresses, clothes and sails festooned all
over her, drying in the sun. It was the first good chance
I'd had to do this, and I'd quickly seized it before we
came ashore.

Most of the loading and discharging was finished by this
time and everyone had reverted to signing invoices, counting kegs of salt beef (from New York, I noticed) and
getting down to honest to goodness gossip. I wandered
vaguely into the background and stood watching everything
until an oldish man in a vivid green shirt came up :

" Hear you just come over from Scotland, eh ? "

I admitted it.

" Fellow came here, five six years back in a canoe," he
went on. " American, though, he was. Just arrived here
one morning, same as you've done ; spent a couple of
days and then moved on. Don't get many strangers round
these parts. Not since the war, that is. Used to be an
oil tanker stationed up here then and some destroyers
and such as well."

" Where's the telegraph office ? " I asked, for I'd been
expecting to see a wireless aerial and couldn't.

" Just up the road a step. In the yellow house," he

replied, " I'm the operator. Want to send something ? "

I said yes. I wanted to send a cable to England to
tell people that I'd arrived safely. Would this be possible ?
" Don't rightly know. But give us your message and
I'll try to get it moving." Messages, he said, went for
fifty miles down the coast by land-line and were then
transmitted by wireless to St John. But they'd been
having difficulty with static recently and communications
had been cut for a couple of days. They might be through
again now, though, he guessed.

I went with him up the road past an enclosure containing two goats and some hens and another with some husky
puppies rolling about inside it. A few people had tried to
keep cows from time to time, my guide told me, but it
wasn't really worth it. There just wasn't the fodder for
them.

I asked about the dogs : where they were kept, as I
had seen none except for the puppies. " Oh, they all
have to be kept enclosed," he said. " Wouldn't do to
have them roaming around. There wouldn't be a hen in
the place ; and they'd kill each other too. They're real
wild, most of them, you know."

We reached the house and his wife cleared a space at
the kitchen table and gave me a cup of tea and a plate
of bake-apples to keep up my strength while I wrote out
my cable on the back of a cigarette packet. They'd had
some telegraph forms once, she said, but they weren't
around now. The kids had got them, she guessed.

A bake-apple, I found, was one of those things that you
take a mouthful of, and then spend quite a while wondering whether you like it or not. Finally I decided that I
did. Quite genuinely and not just because it was the
guestly thing to do. They're hard work though, and it
takes several days to get all the pips out of your teeth
afterwards.

I left the operator wrestling with the telephone which was being recalcitrant, and went back to the jetty again. They'd tell me from St John's what the charges were, he said.

The steamer moved out and the crowd melted away back to their houses while a couple of motor-boats chugged out to go fishing, two men in each, like the ones I'd met on the way in. The cod trapping season which accounts for most of the catch was already over, I was told, and it was only jigging and fixed-line fishing that was going on now. I'd never heard of 'jigging' before and asked one of the men down on the jetty what it meant. It is, apparently, just what it sounds like. You don't use bait at all, you just bounce your hook. with a bright lead weight on it, up and down near the bottom where the cod feed, and they get so irritated with the performance that they snap at it and there you are.

There was another little island in the harbour besides the one with the lighthouse on it ; it was low and flat and stony, and had a house and couple of warehouses built on it. As I rowed back to *Salmo* two figures working in front of one of the warehouses saw me and one of them waved me over. He was dressed in long waders and was cleaning cod with a long handled broom in a tub of water. His assistant trundled the fish up to him in a wheelbarrow and then trundled the clean fish away again to be stacked inside one of the warehouses. They knocked off work as soon as I landed in order to show me round and then finally took me back to the house. Only two of the three brothers who ran the concern were here at the moment, I was told. The third man was coming back in their ship that evening with a cargo of salt and coal from Halifax.

" Ship ? " I asked. " Coal ? " What was this business that they ran ?

It was started they said by their grandfather, who

bought the island thirty years ago and it had built up since. Now they took the catch from several villages round about and ran general stores in them as well. The ship was used to bring up store goods as well as salt and coal. Coal was something of an innovation, but more and more people were using it now that lumber was so much scarcer. "Talking of lumber," the younger brother said, "we were running our own sawmill here a year or so back. There was a big lumber ship wrecked down the coast so we bought it, sawed and planed the wood up here and sold it. Good lumber's hard to come by nowadays."

Late that night, as I was going to bed, there was a drumming of diesels outside, so I came on deck to watch the ship nosing her way in as I had done the night before. It was another still, black night and the Aurora Borealis were again fingering the northern sky as she zig-zagged confidently in, showing me first her starboard and then her port sidelight. It was so still that I could hear them discussing my riding-light (I had put up an electric one for the occasion) as they came past, wondering what it was. Very gently she glided through the water and sidled up to the warehouses where they'd been cleaning the cod in the afternoon. Someone had a torch ashore there and was waving it backwards and forwards as a guide lamp. It was all done very quietly and easily and was a pretty piece of ship-handling. The captain, I was interested to learn, was seventy-four years old and had been on this coast all his life.

Sunday morning is visiting morning, and soon after breakfast the stream began. My first friend, the deputy lighthouse-keeper, was again first on board and brought two large loaves with him. "Heard you were out of bread," he said. "My wife baked yesterday and said to bring these along for you." How darned kind of them I thought. I HAD been trying to get some bread ashore, but hadn't then realised that everyone made their own. These two loaves were delicious and after two weeks without, I fairly revelled in them.

The three brothers were the next to come and they brought the skipper of the ship along with them. I asked about radar. Had they ever thought of fitting a set? " No. It's not worth it," the skipper replied. " I've got on without it up and down this coast for the last fifty years. And besides, the value of the set's as much as the rest of the boat's worth, so where's the point? Not that it wouldn't be handy sometimes," he went on. " A lot's fitting it nowadays. But I don't know that it profits much. We don't often have to stop for fog."

" It might have saved the *Ladybird* though," said the youngest brother who had been away in the ship the day before. " She was another boat that we were running last year, a new one. She was wrecked in fog after she'd only done a few trips. Young chap was skippering her at the time. I'd been running her myself before that." The others nodded sadly. " At the inquiry held by the Lloyds people they said he wasn't to blame. Put it down to abnormal compass behaviour. But it was a pity all the same ; there's work for the two boats and more. We're having to charter at the moment."

One of the features of entertaining on board that I noticed was the long silences. Nearly all day there were five or six people crammed into the cabin, as individuals drifted in and out at random, and for a good half of the time not a word was spoken. To begin with I felt I was failing badly in my duty as host, but soon realised that this was a community who don't go in for small talk. If they didn't have anything to say, then they didn't say it, and I must admit that what was said was worth listening to.

Another characteristic that impressed me was the completely local nature of their life. When I asked a question about a place ten miles away everyone knew all about it, though probably most of them had never been there, nor particularly wanted to go. Extend the radius to fifty miles and I'd know as much as anyone what the place was like. No one wandered or even felt the urge to, so it seemed. Indeed, the brothers, so far as I know, were the only people who ever did leave the village.

The war, I discovered, fascinated them. None had gone away to join it, but they never tired of asking questions about it : Had I seen ? Had I done ? and so on. And they were all remarkably well informed about world affairs; it was hard to realise that none had ever seen a car or a railway train, or even a street with a paved surface.

The weather had been fine all day, but just as it grew dark and all the visitors had left, fog rolled in from seaward and everything grew cold and damp and miserable. I had landed my battery at the post office to be charged and was frightened that I'd be unable to get it back if the fog grew really thick, so I rowed ashore while the going was still comparatively good.

The postmaster lived with his wife and baby daughter and also with his mother. The battery was ready whenever I wanted it, he said, but wouldn't I stay for a while ? I stayed ; the lamps were lit and we got talking. There were a couple of small generators in the village, I was told, and some of the houses had electric light, but most people still used oil-lamps. In a year or so they'd probably install a machine big enough to supply everyone. They'd probably put in a cold store at the same time so that the fish could be filleted and frozen instead of dried and salted. That'd bring a better price, with luck. But with fish you never knew. Prices fluctuated. So did values. You noticed that part of it particularly up here, they said, where so much had to be imported. They could grow a few vegetables, a very few, and they had fish to give in exchange for everything else that was needed were it clothes, flour or mousetraps.

A couple of neighbours drifted in without a word, took chairs and sat down. The postmaster took the baby from his wife and moved into the rocking-chair, where he swung backwards and forwards while she put a kettle onto the stove and rummaged about making tea and looking for plates. His mother came in at this stage, very tidily dressed (all the women dressed very well), having just been at the Church meeting. They were organising a garden party to raise funds for a new roof, she told me. The Church was a new one, less than two years old, but the roof was of poor quality and had been leaking so they were having to have it re-shingled. This was a three hundred dollar job and in such a small community three hundred dollars isn't an easy sum to come by. They'd got most of it now, she said, and they were full of hope that the garden party would finish the job off.

" What about a minister ? " I asked. " Is there one here all the time ? "

Apparently there wasn't at the moment. There was a travelling one who came every two or three weeks, and sometimes in summer they'd get someone on vacation from the Training College, but for the rest of the time they had lay readers.

" It'd be a fine thing to have a resident preacher," the postmaster said and everyone agreed with him. " It's sort of unsettling. Every time we get used to one, he goes and we get another. But we're a small place and there's more besides us that want someone."

I said that I'd been up to the Church—it's on the very top of the hill—and had been most taken with it. It's very plain, but the proportions are attractive and everything was immaculate down to a new coat of whitewash on the big-bellied wood stove which stood in the middle.

" Oh, you went in, did you ? " said the mother. " I'm

glad you liked the inside. WE've had all the women in the village repainting it for the last month. Did the whole lot ourselves right through. It was quite a job, what with being on the top of ladders and everything."

" The men just don't have time for anything like that in summer, you see," said the postmaster's wife, who'd come in to say tea was ready, and seemed afraid that I'd get a wrong impression, " It's such a short season that we get here that everyone's away at the fishing all week and it's only the women who can do any other work."

I left then, and the postmaster came with me to help carry the battery and lower it into the Prout. I was glad of his help, for the jetty was slippery and it's difficult to manhandle a heavy battery alone while standing in an unstable and dancing dinghy.

I rowed away into the fog. The bottom boards on which I sat were wet with it and I wished I'd had the sense to bring an oilskin with me. The lighthouse blared out its fog signal : a dull *eeeugh* sound which ended with a hiccough ; one four-second blast every minute, I made it, counting mechanically as I rowed. . . . My thoughts turned to all that I'd seen and heard during the last two days. They lived a hard life certainly, but by gosh, I thought, there are worse ways of living than fishing, gathering bake-apples and repainting one's Church. They called no man master and I heard not a single grouse throughout my visit. It wasn't really surprising that no one wanted to go and live in a city.

The fog was thick by this time and cut short my moralising. *Salmo*, lying anchored at the far side of the bay from the post office, was a difficult target to hit with the Prout. Yet find her I must if I wanted a bed to sleep in. My only guides to where she lay were the braying foghorn and the wind which I aimed to keep blowing on my right cheek. Thirty more strokes, I thought, and I should be there. . . . " Twenty-seven, twenty-eight,

twenty-nine, thirty." I looked round and saw nothing
but blackness ; heard nothing but the slap of water against
the canvas sides of the Prout and wondered which way
to go. Then, very faintly I heard another sound ; the
throb of the brothers' ship's lighting-generator. It sounded
farther away than it should have been, so I turned towards
the sound and rowed another thirty strokes. This time
when I stopped, though I could see nothing, there was a
new lapping noise to be heard, and one that I recognised
. . . *Salmo's* forefoot as she pitched to her anchor. Four
more strokes and I saw the outline of her mast and gratefully clambered back on board, hoisting the battery in
afterwards.

The cabin seemed even warmer and more comfortable
than usual by the time I'd changed my sodden clothes
and sat down on the bunk to plan my future programme.
The heating stove hissed on the table, the two lamps
shed a gentle glow on the polished mahogany, and I realised
just how much of a home *Salmo* had now become. With
this thought I glanced involuntarily at the calendar :
September the third. I had just two months left before
I married Jill. And there was so much still to do. Another
thousand miles to sail to Montreal, which had now become
my goal ; *Salmo* to be laid up for the winter ; passage
home to be arranged ; morning suit to be chartered. There
seemed to be no end to the list of things that I'd have to
do during those two months, so then and there I decided
to leave Red Bay in the morning, however foul the weather
might be.

CHAPTER FIVE

GOING UP THE RIVER

AND foul the weather duly was—a wet, cloying fog that later turned to rain with a biting northerly wind. Red Bay was swallowed up within minutes of *Salmo's* passing the harbour entrance, and only the dull *eeeugh* of its fog signal followed me out into the strait. Two hours later that too had faded, and once more I found myself alone, butting into the short steep seas.

A spell in port makes me careless, which is an unforgivable sin at sea. This time it very nearly wrecked us.

There was a headwind the first night out and I had to zig and zag across the strait against it. Each zig lasted about four hours and for some time all went well; I was close to the Newfoundland shore at supper time so I went about and left *Salmo* to look after herself while I slept. At one in the morning we were well in towards the Labrador side, so I went about again, expecting to repeat the performance at five. At five, however, I found that the wind had changed and that instead of being close inshore again as I had expected, we were still moderately well out and slanting in at a much less acute angle. 'Aha!' I said. 'Splendid. . . . That will be safe enough for another hour anyway,' and I crawled gratefully back into the warmth of the blankets. At six I looked out and decided 'Still safe enough. . . . She'll last another hour yet—I won't go to sleep, I'll just lie on the bunk for half an hour then get up and make breakfast and go about before I eat it.' And that's the last thought that I remember having.

Something woke me. I still don't know what; but every alarm bell in my body was jangling. For a moment I lay, half woozled with sleep, wondering where I was, what was wrong. And then the penny dropped. I glanced at my watch. Mercy on us . . . five past eight.

I flew into the cockpit. We were right on top of the land; I could see every crevice and patch of seaweed on the rocks ahead. I clawed at the tiller-lashing, almost weeping with mortification, and it jammed. It seemed minutes before I could free it (though it probably wasn't more than two or three seconds in actual fact), and then I slammed it hard down. I remember praying as the bows came round. ' O Lord, let us stay afloat. Please let us stay afloat.' It was a horrid cringing sort of prayer for my conscience was very guilty.

We didn't hit. But it was a matter of inches only. As I looked over the side I could see weed waving just below the keel, and jagged spikes of grey rock amongst it. My mouth was dry and my clutch on the tiller fevered as that of any drowning man.

Once round I had time to look about me, and the irony of the situation was such that I began to giggle shame-facedly. There was only one village for twenty miles in either direction on this stretch of coast. It was a glorious sunny morning. The sea was flat and there was a spank-ing breeze. And yet, if we had been wrecked, it would have been within twenty yards of the end of the one jetty belonging to the one village, in full view of the astonished villagers. I could see them gazing at me. They must have thought that I was the biggest show-off in the history of Newfoundland to come flying in as I had, at a good six knots, to within a few feet of the rocks.

It taught me a splendid lesson. Never again did I lie ' for just another half-hour ' in bed.

The seventh of September is my birthday and I cele-brated by spending the whole day hove to in a gale,

cursing. I had made myself a birthday cake the afternoon
before, intending to eat it politely, slice by slice at tea-
time during the forthcoming week, but I was so depressed
that I finished the whole thing off in one go. Not that
it did much good, I was just as gloomy at the end as I
had been before I started. My poor progress was getting
on my nerves, and I was beginning to realise that though
the Gulf of the St Lawrence looks nice and small on
English atlases it is in fact as large as the North Sea.
Even at Rimouski, for which I was aiming (where the
pilots come on board), the river is twenty-three miles across.

The fresh fish I had been given at Red Bay was soon
finished, so when I saw on my chart to the north of
Anticosti Island a shoal with the alluring title of the
' Natashkwan Cod Bank ' I decided to replenish the larder.
I had acquired a jigger from the postmaster at Red Bay,
so as soon as I thought I had reached a suitable position,
I hove to and began to jig as instructed. Within moments
I felt a bite and hauled a quite gigantic cod to the surface.
I dared not lift him from the water with the line, so I
leaned over and grabbed him by the gills as I'd seen the
Red Bayers do and then retired to the foredeck to clean
and fillet him : I had long ago given up attempting that
manœuvre in the cockpit, because all the bits and blood
and scales inevitably find their way into the cabin and
onto the blankets. I gutted that beast and I skinned it
and I cut its head off. Then I started on the business
of filleting, and the pile of meat beside me grew and grew.
For the rest of the trip I became almost entirely ichthyo-
phagous. I had fried cod in batter, boiled cod in white
sauce, cod roe on toast (my last piece of toast), curried
cod, kedgereed cod, baked cod and finally, to hide the
mounting smell, curried cod again. I never knew before
just how much eating there is on a very large fish. My
only comfort lay in considering all the dollars I wasn't
having to spend to replenish my tinned provisions.

A few nights later, after a kedgeree supper, I was sitting writing in the cabin while *Salmo* ploughed steadily on her way. Everything was quite quiet, peaceful and ordinary. We were twenty miles offshore, and I was just getting ready to spend a restful night when ' *Whoosh* ' went something just behind me. I jumped, almost literally, a foot in the air. All the ghost and ' Flying Dutchman ' stories I'd ever heard flashed through my mind as I scrambled on deck to see what was happening ; but when I got there nothing was to be seen. The sea spread empty all around, marked only by our wake, which bubbled out from beneath the counter and trailed away astern, ruler straight, in blotches and ribbons of foam.

Sanity returned with the familiarity of the scene. ' That was no porpoise,' I told myself ; ' could it possibly have been a whale ? ' With the thought, the sound came again. ' *Whoosh* ' it went, but from the starboard side this time instead of the port. A long, apparently endless black curve broke the calm surface of the sea, less than a hundred yards away. A small apostrophe of a dorsal fin adorned the after end of it, then a huge lazily lifted tail. A whale it was. I went below while the memory was still fresh in my mind, and identified it in my whale book. It was a fin whale, and must have been a good sixty feet long, three times the size of *Salmo*.

The darned thing stayed with me all night and two others joined him later on. I kept on wondering if they'd try to scratch themselves on the keel, and just when I'd decided that they wouldn't and that they'd gone away, ' *Whoosh* ' they'd go again. It was most unsettling.

Next morning they were still with me, so I decided to take some cine shots of them, but they weren't co-operative and persisted in sounding directly up-sun of me. I managed to get two short shots of one of them and then a large cargo ship came past and they must have agreed to follow her instead, because I never saw them again.

At long, long last I found myself sixty miles from Rimouski. For the first time I could see land on both sides at the same time, and it really began to seem as though I was getting into a proper river. This was in the evening, and just as I began to get excited about it, the wind dropped, and I decided for the thousandth time that the wind in Canada only has two speeds, gale or flat calm. Flat calm meant at least that I could sleep; so I slept.

The next morning was one of those unforgettable mornings when one suddenly realises that sailing, even single-handed sailing, is really rather fun after all. The sky was all pink round the edges with the rising sun. The mountains on either shore were a deep blue and the sea a fine burnished steel colour. It was very cold—nearly but not quite freezing—and a gentle breeze was just beginning to riffle the water.

'This,' I said, 'is a day to do things,' so I hoisted the spinnaker before making breakfast, instead of, as I had originally intended, the other way round. The time was half-past five.

Thus began a sail I shall never forget. For sixty miles the wind held, and I covered the distance in twelve hours. It was a joyous sail. Most of the time we were close inshore and the green farmland unfolded itself beside me. Farmhouses, villages, churches and motor-cars : I watched them all. A big German passenger ship overtook us, the rails lined with hundreds of passengers, waving handkerchiefs, shouting, brandishing cameras. Rimouski appeared, a nondescript, spread-eagled sort of a town ; and five miles short of it was Father Point, the pilot station, crowned with a lighthouse and with a jetty sticking out from the tip of it. I passed the end of the jetty just as darkness fell, and the lighthouse gave a few tentative blinks before settling down to its ordered rhythm. Three more miles to go : it was dark and the wind was falling ; two miles and we were barely moving and I began to grow anxious. Slowly, slowly we crawled over the water, and then the thin nylon spinnaker would collapse and wrap itself round the forestay threatening to leave me stuck and helpless . . . would we get there ? Wouldn't we ? As usual I was determined to get in. Also as usual I had no idea what the harbour was like, but this time our approach was so leisured that it didn't matter. The last dying puffs of wind carried me past the end of a large stone pier where a dredger was working, lit by arc-lamps. In the shadow beyond it I turned *Salmo* inshore towards what seemed to be a good berth, dropped the sails and then anchored. To my surprise I found the depth to be less than a fathom. It seemed unfair, for we were a long way offshore, but nevertheless I had to move. Painfully and slowly I reversed the anchoring process ; weighed the anchor, hoisted the sails and moved out to deeper water where I anchored again. I was very tired by this time and crawled straight into my bunk.

There was no one in the harbour-master's office when I went there next morning to ask if they approved of my anchor billet. I wandered round the deserted building wondering what to do next, and saw a car draw up. A lad of about eighteen got out. He was, he said, the harbour-master's son, and sure it would be all right to stay anchored there if I wanted to, why not ? This was a government harbour, wasn't it ? There seemed to be no answer to this, so I asked where the customs and immigration offices were and learned that " Those folk live in the post office building. I'm just going along there in the jalopy. Hop in."

I hopped, and was deposited outside the post office, which was in the middle of the town more than a mile away. It was a very chromium-plate establishment and someone had just broken the plate-glass door, leaving a pile of broken splinters on the doormat. It didn't seem to be anybody's job to clean the pile up and it stayed there for two days.

Upstairs behind a long counter lived the customs. They obviously weren't used to foreign visitors and it took time to find all the necessary forms. When it came to the crew list, which had to be filled in in duplicate and they saw that I was alone, they became very excited. " But you came over all the way from England ALONE ? " said the man who was dealing with me. " But how big is this boat of yours ? Oh, I see ; says here, five tons," and he summoned his chief to share the joke. They were both quite convinced I was crazy, and obviously longed to prod me to see if I was real or not.

I got away after a while with my passport duly stamped and went to see if there were any letters for me and there weren't. This was a big disappointment, because I had been counting on getting some. I needed reassuring that Jill hadn't changed her mind about marrying me. Money also was a worry. After much argument the Bank of England had allowed me to take one hundred dollars out of the country. Since this was to last the whole winter I wasn't at all keen to spend more than I had to, but my diet of fish had made me rebellious, so I went shopping and bought a huge steak, some onions, tomatoes, kidneys and fresh bread. As an afterthought I added a bag of oranges and another of apples. Thus loaded, and with my purchases brimming over the top of two big paper carrier-bags, I solemnly trudged the mile and a half back to the jetty, longing to be offered a lift, but too mean to take a taxi. No one obliged, so I loaded everything into the Prout and rowed back on board to make a mixed grill. I felt lonely, a sensation I never had at sea ; my first trip ashore hadn't been quite as I had expected it, but as I wasn't at all sure just what I HAD expected, I swallowed my disappointment and concentrated on the prospect of a good meal.

The onions, the steak, the kidney and the tomato sizzled in one pan while the chips were in another, and I was just beginning to drool over them when I heard a hooting and a shouting from ashore. I peered out and saw two cars and a little group of people waiting on the jetty waving and yelling, obviously trying to attract attention. Very, very regretfully I heaped my grill onto a plate, put the oven onto the stove and left the plate inside it. Then I rowed inshore in the Prout to see what the fuss was about.

"M'sieur," said the leader of the group, a dapper little French Canadian with gold-rimmed spectacles and a trilby, "I represent the Canadian Broadcasting Company. We hear from the Customs Authorities that you have just sailed here alone from England. Madame here is the accredited photographer of the local newspaper and this gentleman (here he indicated a very anæmic youth with a spotty face) is their reporter. We should like to have an interview."

"Well," I replied, "my dinner is still cooking on board. Would you care to come back with me?"

"With pleasure, M'sieur," said Madame, answering for everybody, though the other two looked doubtful. She was obviously the most spirited of the trio and equally obviously was enjoying herself immensely. She was very French, and had what I'm sure was a very chic hat perched above her fur coat. The ordinary-looking and battered Press camera satchel she carried looked quite out of place.

I ushered them into the Prout, which was bobbing in the water at the bottom of an oily iron ladder. I was invited to go first, the C.B.C. man followed, and Madame brought up the rear with a hitch to her skirt and a "Now, shut your eyes, all you, I command it." The spotted youth was unanimously chosen to be left behind. Prouting is quite an experience, particularly to the uninitiated, and with three on board can only be undertaken in the calmest water. Fortunately this was the calmest water, so we arrived without disaster in a haze of madame's " *Regardez moi ca-s.*" The Prout itself she considered " *Formidable.*"

I gave them cups of coffee and tried not to look embarrassed at the size of the helping of grill which I had given myself. One forgets the social niceties when living alone, and besides, I was hungry.

Madame took photographs and the C.B.C. man asked questions and wrote the answers down in a little note-book until overcome with seasickness. Sweating slightly and looking very wan, he asked to go ashore again.

Very reluctantly I laid down my knife and fork and rowed them back. The radio man recovered in the fresh air and asked if I would do a broadcast interview for him, adding in tones of the deepest reverence that it would be on the Coast to Coast network. I said yes, but added that I'd like to have a bath first because I hadn't had one for seven weeks. I half hoped that one or other would offer me the loan of their house for the occasion but it was not to be. " There is a hotel up the road," they said.

I went to the hotel up the road. They seemed surprised by my request but ushered me into a bathroom where I wallowed for an hour until I was whisked off to the Radio station. There the great broadcast was made and I returned on board for an early supper and bed. Making friends seemed to be more difficult than I had expected.

The familiar hooting and shouting began while I was half-way through breakfast. ' Well, the hell with it,' I thought, ' they can damned well wait.' The weather had become absolutely foul, rain lashed down and it was blowing hard. Prouting was miserable, particularly so because I wore a shoregoing suit beneath my oilskin, with the trousers rolled up, socks in my pocket, and my shoes slung round my neck by their laces.

Jumping from the madly prancing Prout onto the foot of the ladder, the painter grasped in my teeth, was much harder than it had been and seemed to amuse the group at the top of the ladder, so I arrived amongst them in a very bad temper and began to dance round on one foot while I put on my socks. The conversation was chaotic. By reason of my broadcast I had apparently become . . . *news* . . . and this group comprised—so they told me—the ' Big Boys,' the representatives of the Montreal and Toronto papers and the News Agencies. They all wanted my ' story ' and I wanted to know if any of them would give me anything for telling it, so, for a while we talked at cross purposes.

Slowly, however, I got the idea across to them that I was broke and they all became terribly helpful—up to a point. " What you want to do," said one of them, " is sell an exclusive." " But don't forget the serial rights," said another ; " You remember those mugs last year, Harry. They sold their exclusive to N.A.N.A. for five hundred dollars and N.A.N.A. serialised it straightaway and made ten thousand . . ." " Yeh," said Harry . . . " that was a laugh."

" But what is an exclusive ? " I asked, " and who would I sell it to ? And what are serial rights and who has them ? "

Then they all began to explain ' rights ' to me at once (we had moved into a bar by this time) until my head reeled.

At this point the telephone rang for me and I went to answer it, vaguely wondering whether this was someone wanting to buy an ' Exclusive ' and if so how much he wanted to buy it for. It wasn't. It was the harbour-master, who had apparently returned to his office after a two-day absence and disagreed with his son's views on anchoring. ' Would I please move *Salmo* immediately.'

One of the reporters took me back to the jetty in his

car, and I found that the Prout had filled with water, sunk, and that the oars had floated away. It took me an hour to recover them, to fish the Prout up, drain it, and get it back in working order, and all this time a crowd of nearly twenty people watched my every move with the greatest interest but without ever thinking of helping. I paddled back to *Salmo* in a fury, hoisted the mainsail, weighed the anchor and sailed round the end of the jetty and then up alongside a coal hulk which was where I had been told to go. . . . Single-handed ! . . . and single-handed it was a difficult manœuvre, and the latter stages carried out in a very confined space against the wind necessitated a good deal of scrabbling over the top of the barge's cargo of coal to lay out mooring lines. At the end of it all I was black.

No sooner was the last line secure when one of the photographers saw fit to come on board all agog with excitement. " You know when you were refloating that little canvas boat thing," he said, " on the foot of that ladder ? Say, you looked a scream. I got a real honey of a shot of you."

I would probably have killed him if the harbour-master hadn't intervened. He had some forms to be signed, so he took me off to his office, and when I got back, a man was sitting on my bunk reading my log of the trip. He rose when I came into the cabin. " Ah," he said, " I represent the ' Montreal Star.' I've just been reading your log and I think it's very good. Most interesting."

" Thank you very much indeed," I replied coldly. " Who asked you to come on board ? "

" Would you like a cigarette ? " he said.

" No. I don't smoke."

We seemed to have reached an impasse. I was absolutely livid. He was all charm. It says a great deal for him that he won the encounter in a canter and very soon I was eating out of his hand. He said he would have been

delighted to buy an Exclusive from me. Not only did
he represent the ' Montreal Star,' but he also represented
' Weekend Magazine '—The Magazine with the biggest
circulation in Canada—I knew ' Weekend ' perhaps ?   I
didn't. But it just so happens, he went on, that ' Weekend ' had run a big Transatlantic raft story lately and he
had been told by the Editor not to touch my story com-
mercially . . . but if I'd just give him a few details . . .
for the ' Montreal Star,' perhaps. . . .

We chatted for a while and then he said, " Why, I
know. Let's ring ' Life Magazine ' and see if they'll take
your story ? "

Like a lamb I followed him back to his hotel. We
went up to the bedroom and he picked up the receiver.
" Operator," he said, leaning back on the bed, his feet up
on the counterpane, " gimme long distance . . . long
distance ? Get me the Managing Editor of ' Life Magazine.'
Yes. In New York City."

In an incredibly short space of time, blow me down,
he GOT the Managing Editor of ' Life Magazine ' in New
York City. The Managing Editor thought that yes, it
sounded a simply great story. Yessir, simply great. But
(the inevitable but) no. ' Life ' had been doing a great
many sea stories just lately and couldn't use it.

" Well," my preceptor went on, into the telephone,
" now, sir, I'm sure you'll be able to accept this as a
collect call, won't you ? "

The Managing Editor said no he wasn't able to accept
it as a collect call, and that was the first and indeed only
time I ever say Roy Shields look in any way put out.

" But do you mean to say," I asked, " that the editor
MIGHT have accepted the charges for a call from here to
New York ? "

" Why sure he might," said Shields. " He should've
done. We were doing him a favour." I stored this
remarkable piece of logic away for future reference, and

later that afternoon, with the deliciously guilty excitement
of a small boy about to ring a doorbell and run away, I
picked up a telephone.

" Operator," I said in my best Erle Stanley Gardner
voice, " gimme long distance."

" Long distance," said the telephone.

" Long distance," I said, " get me the Managing Editor
of ' Saturday Evening Post Magazine ' in Philadelphia,
U.S.A., and make this a COLLECT call." As it turned out,
the Managing Editor of ' Saturday Evening Post ' wasn't
interested in my Exclusive either, but he did accept the
telephone charges and I left the call-box fairly hugging
myself with delight. This was real movie stuff, this was.

I started to walk back to *Salmo*, but as if by magic
a car swept up. It was my photographer friend, the one
who had been so delighted at my wrestling match with
the Prout.

" Have you a minute to spare ? " he asked me. " I
want you to get a load of this. It'll make you die."

He stopped the car and ushered me into the telephone
exchange, where he waved airily to the girl in charge and
then pointed to a big box like a gramophone which sat
on the floor with wires coming from its belly and into
the switchboard.

" Seen one of those before ? " he asked.

I admitted my ignorance.

" It's a line picture transmitter," he said. " Just hook
it into any telephone exchange, dial the number you want,
and set it rolling. It transmits the picture. See that
picture in there. I got it out of the office of this hick
local paper (it was one of madame's photographs and was
stamped on the back NOT to be reproduced without permission). They don't know I got it. Don't know I got
this machine here either. They flew their pictures off.
The aircraft won't arrive in Toronto for another two hours
yet and it'll be MY picture that hits all the morning editions.

Ain't it great ? If I'd taken the pictures myself I wouldn't even have them processed by now."

" Yes, great," I echoed weakly. All this big time stuff left me a bit out of my depth.

He dropped me beside the coal barge where a solitary figure was standing in the drizzle, peering down at *Salmo*. Most of the dockside spectators spoke only French, so I was quite surprised to be addressed by an obvious English-Canadian, who equally obviously wasn't a pressman.

" You seem to have been kept pretty busy up to now," said the stranger ; " you wouldn't care to come up to the house and have a bath and a quiet family supper, would you ? "

" Do you really mean that ? " I asked. My whole being was crying out for just those things, for a breath of sanity and a chance to unwind. I nearly fell on the stranger's neck, and my polite, " Oh, but you can'ts " rang remarkably hollow, even on my own ears.

Harold Price and his wife Pam, their dog and their daughter took me completely under their collective wing. He was, so he told me vaguely, in the family lumber business. He gave me a pint glass of whisky and soda to take into the bath with me, and after supper it became established that I should spend the night there. I told them something about my encounters with the Press and my total lack of success, so far, in turning the notoriety I had unwittingly gained, into hard cash. I also told them why I needed the money : to support Jill and myself during the forthcoming winter. We all laughed a good deal, and we also talked boats for they were keen sailors. It was a glorious evening.

The next morning I decided to sail for Quebec before I became involved in any more Press nonsense, so Harold ran me back to *Salmo* in his car and pressed a copy of ' The St Lawrence River Pilot ' into my hand. It was profusely annotated ' Filthy Tide rip this one. Keep right away from it,' and ' The best berth is the END one. All the others are badly exposed and you bump like hell.'

" Give it back to my brother Tony when you reach Quebec," said Harold. " I'll warn him you're coming. He'll be down to meet you."

I hoisted the sails, let go the mooring warps and pushed off. The peace, after the bustle and scurry of the last few days, was quite incredible.

The date was now the twenty-first of September, and judging by the rate of progress I had made so far, a month was none too long to see me up to Montreal and into an aircraft. I had already abandoned my original idea of returning by ship. But even with the best will in the world, it's a slow job going up the St Lawrence. The ebb is so strong in conjunction with the current that it's not worth attempting to buck into it (it runs at anything upwards of four knots), so I decided to go up on the flood in a series of bounces. There are no reasonable anchorages, but there are several jetties and I proposed on Harold's advice to use these as staging posts.

Coming up to an exposed jetty single-handed is a nerve-racking and athletic business when there's a strong wind blowing. There always WAS a strong wind blowing, I found when I came to do it, and to add to the difficulties the jetties were always deserted, so I had to take my own lines ashore. The occasion I remember best was my first attempt, at a little village called St Simeon. It was just getting dark when I arrived, and the wind was blowing strongly onshore, so that the only safe and Harold-recommended berth was the one on one of the inside angles of the T-shaped jetty. I spent almost half an hour cruising up and down off the end of it plucking up courage and hoping that someone would appear to help handle the lines. No one came, so I arranged all my warps very carefully, festooned the boat with fenders, and decided to try my luck. It was a very small jetty and had rocks

WAITING FOR A BREEZE TO TAKE ME AWAY FROM RIMOUSKI

all round about ; the problem how to make my approach was therefore simplified ; there was only one way I *could* approach it. The tricky part lay in deciding how fast to go. *Salmo* is a heavy boat and difficult to stop. Come in too fast and I would bash the bow against the stem of the T. Too slowly and I'd miss the ladder and be unable to get lines ashore . . . and thereafter bump, bump, bump on the rocks to leeward. In we flew with the wind on the quarter ; I dropped the mainsail and put a couple of gaskets round to keep it out of mischief, then went back to the tiller to square up for the final run in. Down staysail . . . edge farther up towards the jetty to be sure of reaching it . . . gather up the ends of the mooring warps . . . leave the tiller so that there's slight sheer out to throw the stern in, and to prevent any scraping when the weight comes on the lines . . . scramble up the ladder with headrope in the left hand, stern-rope in the right hand and spring in the teeth. Reach the top, find a bollard, drop the headrope, check the way with spring and stern ropes. Grab the headrope before the bow swings out, a haul on it and then secure.

I had hoped to make the passage in three days, but a day of calm and another of gale lengthened it to five. The last port of call before Quebec was called Ile aux Coudres. It's a real bottleneck and the island in the middle just adds to the jet effect on the ebbing water. There are several tide races in the vicinity, and in the main stream, out of the race, the flow is seven knots. No one, not even the bateaux, the big heavy lumber carriers with diesel engines, attempt to argue with the tide there. I spent a pleasant evening chatting and drinking wine with the crews of three of the bateaux and learned from them that the *moment critique* at which I should sail the next morning was half-past four. I sighed deeply. That was just what I had made it, but I hoped that they might disagree.

At a quarter to four I lit the Primus and made some porridge, for I was determined to get away before the mob. By the time the porridge was eaten and the sails set the bateaux were astir. Lights were switched on and showed as brilliant yellow squares and circles in the darkness. Sleepy figures called to one another as they singled up mooring-lines, and one by one the big diesels gurgled to themselves as starter buttons were pressed . . . the gurgles turned to rumbles and soon the whole air was filled with heavy throbbing. I slipped away, the sails filled, and I glided gently into the darkness towards the main stream, guided by the flash of a light-beacon. I had less than ten minutes' start. One by one, astern, I saw navigation lights switched on and I was passed in succession by six big belching monsters ; up ahead their white overtaking lights strung out like a brilliant necklace, curled to mark the line of the channel, and it was all so beautiful that I became reconciled to the early start.

It was a grand sail. The tide rushed and eddied past the buoys and it rushed *Salmo* with it. The sun rose, the morning passed, but still we maintained our progress ; until at last, as we went beneath a big suspension bridge linking Orleans Island with the mainland, I saw Quebec silhouetted ahead. An hour later we swept into a tidal basin and tied up alongside a gigantic crane.

I soon found that there were advantages to be gained from my newspaper publicity. The harbour-master knew about me and was absolutely charming. He suggested that I should move into an inner basin and tie up alongside an old lightship. There was a night watchman on board and he was sure that I could leave *Salmo* in perfect safety whenever I wanted.

That evening, when the time came to move, I impressed two ' news-hawks ' to act as crew, and they regaled me with details of a particularly gory murder which they had been covering earlier in the day.

"Now stand by to lower the foresail," I shouted to my new foredeck hand.

"Sure," he replied ; "I lower it with this rope here, don't I ? Yeh. As I was saying, you just SHOULDA seen that poor girl. Cut to pieces with a meat-axe. Right to pieces."

The photographer, who was with me in the cockpit, said, "And, do you know, there was still a lot of the bits they couldn't find. That's what they were at when I was there. Still looking. Like a jig-saw puzzle, they said it was."

"Would you drop the foresail ? " I asked.

"Yes. Down she comes. Did you get any pics., Harry?"

"No, not of the girl," said Harry sadly ; "they wouldn't let me. But I got a dilly of the meat-axe."

Quebec has only one skyscraper, and I was slightly startled to find that this was called ' The Price Building ' ; I'd never realised that Harold Price's ' Family Lumber business ' was that sort of lumber business. Tony had an office about three-quarters of the way up this impressive edifice, and he took up the job of chaperoning me where Harold had left off. One morning he announced that the Governor-General wished to see me. Tony's wife, Muffy, didn't approve of my shore-going suit after all its encounters with Rimouski's oily ladders, so she spent the time available before the visit in tidying it up, I being despatched meanwhile to find a barber. I hardly knew myself by the time we all reached the Citadel. Drinks on silver trays, immaculate A.D.C.s and the cushioned chairs on the balcony beneath umbrellas (where we talked) all seemed a very far cry from *Salmo* and her tiny cabin. H.E., Vincent Massey, was a most remarkable man. After five minutes I felt he knew more of *Salmo* and the sea than I did ; he was one of those people who always ask just the right question and leave one thinking ' I wish I'd said that.'

As we rose to go he invited me to the ball which was being held the following night.

" Now, what on earth can we find for you to wear ? " said Muffy as soon as we were back in the car.

" Well, I know Dad has a spare tail-coat," said Tony, " but his trousers wouldn't fit you."

" I've got a dinner jacket on board," I said, " with trousers attached."

" You've got WHAT ? " said Muffy. " Well, you Britishers are certainly the limit. You come ashore looking like a derelict scarecrow and now you tell me you've got a dinner jacket ! Well you just give it to me. I'll bet it's a wreck and all mildewed round the edges. You just give it to me."

It was a bit mildewed, but Muffy thought she could probably ' fix it.'

" Now you be up at our home tomorrow evening by five at the very latest," she said. " Harold'll be there by then, and Pam and us girls have got to dress too, you know, and we'll have to see if we've got you right before we start."

I was full of good intentions and undoubtedly would have been there by five had fate not been against me. The next day was a trying one.

I had at last managed to sell someone in Toronto my ' Exclusive.'

" Three hundred dollars," he had said on the telephone.

" Oh, come now," I had replied in my best Oxford cum B.B.C. accent, " make it a thousand."

" Well, five hundred, and you're breaking my heart."

I tried not to burst with excitement as I agreed : fifty dollars would have been welcome at that stage, let alone five hundred. The sum seemed astronomical ; but I didn't know what I was in for.

I was due to meet my benefactor, the ' Toronto Star Weekly's ' five-hundred-dollar-bearing representative at nine on the morning of the ball. He was a very large and

fat man and insisted on addressing me as ' Pete ' on all
occasions. He was also a great hand-shaker. We shook
hands once on the jetty, again just before we climbed
down into *Salmo*, and for a third time when we got on
board. I didn't realise it at that time, but I think he
was just as nervous as I was.

"Now, Pete," he said, "this fiancée of yours. Jill, you
call her. How old is she?"

"Well," I countered, "I've written a two thousand
word article about the crossing. If you'd just like to read
it through and. . . ."

"Yeh. Sure, Pete. Now about this fiancée of yours.
Now when you got engaged, where was that?"

I exploded. I said that I was very sorry but I had failed
to understand what I was agreeing to do on the telephone.
I had thought they wanted to buy what I wrote about
the crossing the Atlantic, not what somebody else wrote
about Jill. I said that I'd be grateful if he'd ring up his
editor and tell him to cancel the whole thing.

There was an awkward pause after this outburst, and
then the reporter said slowly, all the heartiness jerked out
of him, "Well, if that's how you feel we'd better just
telephone the office."

In silence we walked to a grubby dockside snack-bar.
The floor was littered with cigarette packets and the
window-sills were filled with empty Coca-cola bottles.
Half a dozen dockies wearing baseball caps and tartan
lumber-jackets lounged against the bar with cups of
coffee, and a juke box blared in the background. The
barman spat reflectively as we came in. This seemed to
me to be the last straw. I retired like a snail into a shell
of gloom and bad temper. I hated everyone, myself included ; my attempts to earn money were proving too
sordid altogether. The reporter got hold of someone on
the telephone, his editor presumably, and handed the
instrument to me, saying, "That's Mr Smith now, Pete."

Before the unfortunate man at the other end even had a chance to say good morning, I poured out all my woes upon him. "I'll send you the stuff that I've written," I finished off. "I don't care a tinker's curse if you publish it or not. And if you do, you can pay me any damned sum you want ... forget all about the five hundred dollars, but I'm not going to have my name appearing at the bottom of the sort of muck that your reporter is wanting to write."

I felt much better when I'd got everything off my chest, particularly since this unknown editor seemed to be taking it all very calmly, just interjecting an occasional "Why of course, Mr Hamilton," and "Why sure, Mr Hamilton," and at the end he asked to speak to the reporter again. I left them to it and waited for the reporter in the open air. As we walked back to *Salmo* he said :

"Well, Pete, I suppose you know that that was the Vice-President of the corporation that you were talking to ? He said it was twenty years since he'd heard anyone talk like that to him. He wants me to have a look at what you've written."

We were busy going through it when a head appeared in the cabin door and Harold Price remarked in a loud voice.

"What goes on here ? Oh, I see. Selling your life dearly. That's the stuff," and backed out again. I was still feeling a bit ashamed of myself and this remark flattened me completely. The reporter, who on closer acquaintance had turned out to be a very amusing man, was delighted by each new happening of the day, and kept chuckling to himself at intervals and murmuring :

"Just wait till I tell them about this back at the office. Just wait. It's been a riot." Riot or not, he kept my nose hard to the grindstone of photography all afternoon. He took shots of me eating, steering, hoisting sails and making 'Land Ho' gestures on the foredeck. He took shots of *Salmo* from every conceivable angle, and it was half-past five before I could persuade him that he had done enough and that Muffy would probably kill me if I didn't appear. I grabbed a spongebag and leapt into his car and we careered up the hill to Tony's flat, where I arrived breathless, the reporter's ' goodbyes ' and ' good lucks ' ringing in my ears as I raced up the path.

Just as I entered the lift I heard his final benediction : " Now don't you worry about that article, Pete. They'll take it all right. Just leave it to me."

To their eternal credit they did, and the five hundred dollars which resulted just tided us over the winter.

As soon as I entered the flat I was grabbed and more or less pushed into a bath. The organisation was immense. When I was clean, clothes appeared as if by magic. The shirt, trousers and shoes were mine, but a tail coat, white waistcoat and a collar without rustmarks on it had all been borrowed for the occasion, and what was more, they fitted. In twenty minutes the transformation was complete, and we sipped elegantly at iced drinks as if ball-going was an everyday occurrence. . . .

I told Jill about this in a letter. ' You were very full of all *your* finery,' she said, " what did the girls wear ? ' For the life of me I couldn't remember. Indeed the whole evening, after this first frantic rush, passed in some sort of haze, pleasurable but indistinct.

The next morning saw me back in the docks beside the coal dump, wrestling with an outboard engine which the local dealer, with incredible generosity, had lent me to push *Salmo* against the current to Montreal. The trouble was that its stalk wasn't long enough and the screw didn't reach the water when I mounted it dinghy-wise on the transom. I finally had to bolt a heavy wooden bracket through the hull and secure it to that ; it looked horrible and stuck out dangerously, but it was the best I could manage at short notice.

The passage to Montreal was a nightmare. Time had mysteriously slipped away the way time does, and as I pushed off from my nice sheltered basin, the engine purring on its bracket, it was already October the fifth. All the maples were ablaze on the bank, and less than a month remained to W-Day.

' I'll do this passage, split or bust,' I decided, and had airy visions of completing it in two and a half days. . . . ' Now that I've turned into a motor-boat,' I told myself, ' nothing can delay me. I'll just keep chugging along.' I was soon disillusioned : all sorts of things delayed me. The first was petrol, and it nearly wrecked *Salmo*. I had borrowed a chart that marked a jetty just at the point where I wanted fuel. It was dark when I reached it and I was surprised to find no lights. However, I nosed in towards the shore and in due course the jetty loomed up black and mysterious. I eased alongside, jumped ashore with my lines, and was just about to walk away with a can in each hand to find a gas station when I saw a ship going up the channel. What made me wait I don't know ; the ship was going slowly and was some way off so I didn't expect much wash from her, but for some reason wait I did.

Without any warning the wash arrived. Some strange formation of the bottom must have magnified it, for it came in as a great tidal wave. The head rope snapped, the bow flew out, and by the time that the second wave arrived, *Salmo* was stern on to me. There was nothing I could do. That was the worst feature. I just stood transfixed in the darkness, watching. Up she went, up and up until she seemed to tower above me, and then charged in towards the concrete wall. ' Well, the engine's a gonner ; that's certain,' I remember thinking. Sticking out on its bracket it looked as if it was bound to take the impact ; but somehow it didn't. The bumpkin did and snapped like a carrot, and the end hung down like a broken

arm. I leaped on board taking the stern-line with me
and shoved like a madman before another wave should
arrive. It wasn't much of a shove, but it stopped us from
hitting a second time and the engine, being an American
one, started like a bird. Back to the channel I went,
petrol-less but safe. " So that," I said, " is why they
built a jetty and don't use it. It's a wave trap."

Two hours later, still without petrol, I anchored. It
was when I came to weigh the following morning that I
found just how strong a pull a four-knot current exerted
on the chain. Link by link I hauled it in. Link by link,
thirty fathoms of it. By the end of it I was dead beat
and my hands half raw.

Part of the time I sailed, for I found that when the
wind blew, *Salmo* pitched and this made the screw lift
from the water and race. Mostly, however, the wind was
from ahead and the current was so strong that if I tacked,
I made no progress or even went astern. When that
happened I simply had to anchor and wait for an improvement, and always as I did so, I thought of the
agonising effort entailed in weighing.

The weather for some reason seemed to be better by
night than by day, so most of my progress was at night.
In the early stages, after being on watch for only an hour
or two, it was rather pleasant to sit in the cockpit and
steer, keeping the rangemarks in line, swinging round the
curves and watching the big ships pass up and down. The
Aurora Borealis played in the northern sky on most nights,
and the stars were reflected in the calm water. But as
the long hours went by, all the early pleasure used to be
superseded by tiredness and I would set little targets for
myself. . . . ' Go on until you reach Trois Rivières ' I
would say, naming a town just two hours ahead, and then
when I got there would change it to ' Well you can keep
on just a bit longer—try another hour.'

One full day I had to waste, just beyond Trois Rivières,

when it blew a gale against me. I could make no head-way either with sail or with the engine. The day after that, or rather the night after, for the weather moderated at dusk, I ran into duckweed. Great drifts of weed came floating down with the current and wound themselves round the engine where they blocked the water-cooling inlet. The first time this happened the engine seized and we drifted back nearly a mile before I found out what the trouble was and threw the anchor over. An hour later, things had cooled sufficiently for the engine to start (what a sigh of relief I breathed when it did so, for borrowed engines are a big responsibility !) and then link by link up came the accursed chain once more. How I hated it ! For the rest of that night I hung shivering over the side, clawing free the weed before it caused another blockage.

At Sorel we ran into fog, thick and choking. I had wasted so much time already that I was determined not to anchor if I could help it. Two big ships thought the same and each in turn passed me, unseen, within a hundred yards. The braying of their sirens, down my very neck as it seemed, made me want to scream, but screaming would have been of little help.

On and on I went. The trip seemed endless, but I couldn't afford to delay ; every day wasted on passage meant a day less for laying up, for my air passage was booked.

Montreal appeared round a bend in the river at four in the afternoon, five days after my departure. I was sailing at the time ; the wind was too strong to allow the engine to be used, but because it was against me, progress was unmercifully slow. Inch by inch we wormed our way towards the city—a long tack which won me distance, and a short one straight across the current where I lost nearly all that I had won on the tack before.

I reached a great collection of oil-tanks as darkness fell ; they were massed along the bank, hundreds and hundreds of them, Shell, Gulf Oil, Texaco, White Rose and many others. The wind fell and I began to lose some of the ground I had been so long in gaining. I dropped the sails and started the engine.

Slowly, slowly, I began to win again. Tank after tank slid past, but it soon became obvious that I could never reach the great mass of the Jacques Cartier Bridge without more petrol than I had on board. Besides, I was dead tired. I decided to go in and have some sleep, for I had been on the move since ten o'clock the night before—twenty-three hours.

I slid into a basin and began to put out lines but was hailed by a voice. " Hey, you can't tie up there. Get out of it."

I left the basin, cursing, and went out into the stream again. The engine failed. The current snatched us and whirled us downstream while I tried to discover the trouble. It turned out to be an airlock in the fuel system—I had waited too long before putting in my last drops of fuel. An hour later I won my way back to another possible billet and thankfully eased in out of the current and was promptly hailed again :

" Hey, you, we're expecting a tanker there at six in the morning ! You'll have to get out before then."

" All right," I replied, " I'll move at five." In my exhausted state a sleep even until five was to be valued beyond diamonds. The watchman wouldn't help me take my mooring lines ashore so I had to climb up a slippery wooden pile, which soaked my clothes so badly in oil that I had to undress on deck, but cold as this caper made me, I was asleep within seconds.

At five, rubbing the sleep from my eyes, I moved again. I had found an all-night garage which sold petrol, carried a tin of it back to *Salmo* and was feeling sorry for myself. Fortunately it was such a glorious morning that the feeling didn't last, and I soon began to get the joy of making a final landfall. One last hurdle remained—St Mary's current, which sweeps beneath the Jacques Cartier Bridge at seven knots.

At my first attempt it beat me. The engine just couldn't manage it, even though I kept so close inshore that I could touch the dock wall. I crossed the current and crawled up the other side towards the massive stone pier which carried one leg of the bridge. Several times we stopped, momentarily, but each time it proved to be merely the result of a stronger eddy than usual. I counted every one of the great stones from which the pier had been built as we inched past them . . . I prayed that the engine would not suddenly fail . . . on we went, and on and on. Once past the bridge the speed increased. I could have shouted with delight. A few more minutes and I swept into the basin and put out my lines. A car drew up and a charming woman got out of it.

"Are you Peter Hamilton ? Pam Price told me to watch out for you."

And so it went on. I was handed from one kind friend to another until I hardly knew if I was on my head or my heels. *Salmo* made a final trip through the Lachine Canal onto Lake St Louis, where the Royal St Lawrence Yacht Club lies in glorious woody grounds on the fore-shore. I worked like a black to unship the mast, empty the water-tanks (in case they should freeze and burst) and to prepare *Salmo* to spend the winter ashore and alone. Masses of bedding and books and charts were lugged out and stored in basements belonging to people who until moments before had been strangers. Everyone was kind and helpful.

When all was ready, I went to the office of the boatyard attached to the club and said to them :

" Please will you be sure that when you bring her from the water you leave her ready to go back first of anyone ? "

and I asked for the bill there and then ; for I feared that
by the spring we might be penniless and I didn't want
to run the risk of being unable to sail for reasons of debt.
The yard must have guessed I was hard up, for their
bill was an absurdly low one ; but they presented it with
a straight face. With an equally straight face I paid it.
I hope they realised how grateful I was.

The day for departure came and I flew round in a mad
flurry of last-minute remembrances until the family who
had been acting as my hosts-in-chief drove me up to
the airport. Their name was Coristine and I found it
hard to believe that I had only known them for four days ;
they were so kind that they seemed more like close relatives.
As I left the baggage hall for the aircraft, Bobby Coristine
said to me :

" Now when you and Jill get back to Canada, just
come here right away and stay for a while until you have
a chance to look around." He little knew what he was
in for.

Ten minutes later the aircraft roared off the runway
and headed eastward. The next morning I was in Prest-
wick. This time the Atlantic crossing had taken one night
instead of one month. Jill was at London airport to meet
me, and suddenly Canada and *Salmo* seemed very far
away indeed.

CHAPTER SIX

A WINTER INTERLUDE

THE days between landing at the airport and November the Third flickered past in a whirl. It seemed to be no time at all between the moment of touching down and the moment that I found myself standing listening to the organ as it rumbled in the background and wondering why my new and immaculate (though borrowed) trousers should feel so strange and unfamiliar round my hips. The hairs at the back of my neck prickled with the impact of hundreds of pairs of eyes, and I kept wishing that Jill would hurry up and put in an appearance. At intervals, too, I tried to remember where I'd left my top-hat. Was it in the vestry, or underneath a pew, or even out in the porch ? I couldn't for the life of me recollect WHERE it was, for the third of November seemed to have become the sort of day when it was hard to concentrate on anything for more than a second or two . . . but that was hardly surprising because, so I kept reminding myself, it was the day on which I would stop being a bachelor and would become instead that strange new sort of a being, a married man.

There was a rustle of " Oh-isn't-she-sweetering " from the packed congregation, and it didn't need the choir to break into a hymn for me to deduce that Jill, in all her glory, was coming up the aisle.

It was a short service, and as soon as it was over, the ring in place and the register signed, we bundled ourselves and our bouquets, our lace and our top-hats (which had mysteriously reappeared) into the back of the waiting car. The driver tootled melodiously on his horn and off we glided towards the reception, thrilled and excited and delighted with ourselves. " Did you hear the driver," Jill bubbled at me, " when he helped me into the car just now ? He called me ' Ma'am.' He said, ' Let me help you with your veil, ma'am ' ; but when I got out at the church before the service he said, ' Good luck, MISS.' Oh wasn't it nice of him ? Wasn't he sweet ! "

That driver, I decided, was clearly a professional. No doubt about it . . . he'd learned a thing or two about technique at all the weddings he must have assisted at. But it WAS nice of him none the less, and it put us into high good humour as we stood shaking hands and respectively assuring people that " No. We hadn't really been in the least bit worried while Peter was away by himself," and that " No. It had really been a very pleasant, quiet sort of a trip, thank-you-very-much."

Our official honeymoon was spent in Sussex, but somehow, all the time, we felt guilty about it. We had decided that for the next two or three years anyway we'd make our home in *Salmo*, and even though we knew that the ice would now have locked her into Lake St Louis for the winter, and even though our passages were booked in the *Empress of France*, sailing within two weeks, we still felt that we should already be out there to give her moral support and company and to prepare her for all the voyagings that we could picture so rosily in our mind's eyes.

The voyage to Canada was uneventful, and Liz and Bobbie Coristine welcomed us back to Montreal most characteristically. " First you must have a bath," they declared, " and then breakfast. We've had an idea while you've been away."

It was during breakfast that they told us what the idea was, and all at once it shattered our plans of spending a rather sordid and very-much-on-the-cheap sort of a winter.

" Why OF COURSE you must use our cottage," Liz said. " It's only a SMALL one you know, but it's warm and we hardly ever use it. It's up in the Laurentian mountains at a little place called St Sauveur. . . ."

So we used it, and three weeks later, when we woke up, the pipes were frozen and Jill had to make coffee from melted snow which she shovelled from the garden. It was a long and tedious operation and ruined both our tempers. Mine was in no way improved later on by the plumber who told me, on the telephone, that he had fifteen other freeze-ups to attend to before he could get round to ours. It was a Friday and St Sauveur always filled up on Fridays with weekend skiers from Montreal.

" You must realise," said the plumber, " that the visitors expect to find their houses in good order when they arrive."

We did realise. The Coristines were amongst those due, and we didn't want to hand their house, a little timber-built chalet, over to them in a waterless state. During their occupancy we were to move down to Montreal and use their town house. It was a Box and Cox sort of a set-up.

I spent the day pottering round the basement with boiling kettles pouring them over the pipes, and finally at dinner time I succeeded in freeing the system. It was too late to think of settling down to any work, so as soon as we had finished our meal we walked the half-mile to the post office, clumping through the snow in brilliant sunshine, to see if there was any mail waiting. We most earnestly hoped that there would be, for we had both been writing streams of articles and were eagerly waiting to see if anyone had bought them. As usual there were no takers, and we tried not to feel depressed about it as we turned our steps towards the main road where the Montreal buses stopped.

HONEYMOON COUPLE

Our dollars were getting fewer and fewer. Even though we had no rent to pay (thanks to the Coristines) living was still expensive. We both liked to do ourselves well and invariably did so, vaguely imagining the whole time that tomorrow someone would buy something that we had written. Now, however, the situation was becoming half-way desperate, because in addition to our ordinary living expenses we had set our hearts on buying a pair of skis apiece, and ski boots, and most of the other glamorous clothes and gimmicks which the local ski-shops displayed. Neither of us liked borrowing, and it was misery to live in a ski resort without being equipped for it.

The bus station was in the next village, two miles down the road, and as we walked we began to consider further ways of raising money.

" Well, I think we should try television," said Jill ; " quite obviously no one wants any of our articles. Not that I blame them really ; they're all pretty dreary. But we might get someone to give us something for a tele-vision appearance. You could show them some of those films you took on the way over, the whales spouting and that Paraguayan ship in the rough sea, and the iceberg. They all came out quite well. I think we should try it."

I wasn't keen on the idea. It sounded as though it involved going to see people . . . and who did one go and see anyway ? I hate organising things ; I like them to come to me on a plate . . . so I said crushingly :

" Well, all right. If appearing on television is as easy as all that, off you go and arrange it."

" All right," said Jill, nettled, " I will."

That weekend, while I sat in the Coristine's house and thought great thoughts, Jill disappeared into the blue to see people and to find out about things. The temperature outside was thirty below, and I felt that I was far better employed than she was. I had made a great decision. I would stop writing articles . . . no one bought them anyway . . . I would write a book instead, and we would immediately become rich and be able to buy enough stores to leave Canada with. (It wasn't for several months that I realised that no one would buy the book either . . . the un-co-operative brutes !)

We returned to our ski house the next Monday, Jill still maintaining a dignified silence about her television negotiations, and I settled down to write my book. I didn't have any idea how long books ought to be, so I started off by counting the words in five of the Penguin books we had about the place. They averaged, I found, seven words to the line, thirty-two lines to the page and anything from two hundred to three hundred pages to the book.

" Good gracious," I said, appalled, when I had worked it all out on the back of an envelope, " that means I'll have to write something like eighty thousand words."

" Well, go on," said Jill unfeelingly, " write them."

I started off with a big rush, the idea being to describe first the trip I made in *Speedwell* from Singapore back to England and then finish off with *Salmo's* adventures so far. It was an uninspired theme, but I couldn't think of any other and I soon slowed down. The trouble was that nothing worked out as I wanted it to. As I read through each chapter I kept thinking ' well surely no voyage could have been all THAT dull,' but then I'd comfort myself by thinking that if one came to the book fresh, instead of after hours and hours at a typewriter, it might be a bit better. Unfortunately the possibility remained with me throughout the winter, so on I went with that darned book, and on, and on and on.

Jill, meanwhile, had returned to sanity, deciding that since we were obviously going to remain broke throughout the foreseeable future, we might as well be broke but happy. She therefore stopped writing and concentrated on Christmas, which was nearly upon us. About her tele-

vision enquiries she remained silent and quite soon I forgot
them.

One day she burst into the house after an expedition
to the village, staggering beneath the weight of an enormous
cardboard carton.

" Look what I've got," she said ; " fairy lights and
twenty-seven paper chains and some big bells and masses
of sparkly stuff. We'll make that our Christmas present
to the Coristines, to decorate the house for them. They're
all coming up on Christmas Eve. We can go and dig up
a Christmas tree from up on the hills. It'll be splendid."

" Where on earth did you get all the money to pay for
it with ? " I asked her.

" Oh didn't I tell you ? I got a letter to say we're to
go to Toronto the day after tomorrow to appear on the
programme called ' Tabloid.' And we're to get a hundred
dollars each for doing it, so I've just cashed a cheque on
the strength of it."

This was terrific news. We sat down at once to have a
conference about the disposal of the money. Half of it,
we prudently decided, we would bank. With the other
half we'd have a splurge, so off we went that afternoon
and had one. We lost all our inhibitions and bought and
bought and bought. Skis and boots came first, then
gloves ; a windcheater for Jill, Christmas presents for
each other, and finally food. This last item was memorable. For weeks we had gone into the local supermarket,
crept round it rather furtively and come out again with
porridge oats, butter and liver (which we had found to
be the cheapest form of meat). Now we swept in with
a trolley apiece and had a real go at things, and by the
time we'd finished our trolleys were as full as anybody's.

We met at the cash desk and each looked at the other
reproachfully :

" Well, haven't you been just a LITTLE extravagant,"
we said, both in the same breath. The girl at the desk

whisked our items expertly into cardboard cartons, punch-
ing at her adding-machine as she did so ; a bell rang at
the final punch, the machine whirred unemotionally and
produced a ticket which we both grabbed at at once . . .
' Forty-three dollars, twenty-five cents.'

" Well," I said to Jill, as we walked back home, " we
won't be able to bank quite half of the money we make
from Tabloid, but at least we should have a bit left over
and we won't have to buy any more food for some time."

Because we were going to have our fares paid by the
television people we thought we might as well travel in
comfort, so we had a neat little compartment on the train
all to ourselves and arrived in Toronto in gala spirits.
The broadcast was at six in the evening, and we spent
the day having a conducted tour of the countryside
(arranged by my old friend, the reporter from the ' Star
Weekly ') and at five turned up at the studio.

The place was in an uproar. Where had we been all
this time ? They'd been phoning Montreal and no one
there knew anything about us . . . had we got the film
with us . . . we had ? Good. I produced a cardboard box
containing all the eight reels I had so far taken, and
invited the young man who was chaperoning us to take
his pick. He reacted as if a bee had stung him :

" Oh, my golly ! Do you mean you've not had the
stuff edited ? " and he began to tear his hair in a frenzied
sort of way.

We tried to comfort him by suggesting that he could
have written us a letter stating his requirements, and
learned that this is what should have happened but that
there had been a Nonsense in the organisation.

" Well, we'll just have to use one of those reels, that's
all," he finished off. " Choose one of them and I'll send
it off to the screening room for a check-up."

I gave him what I thought was the most interesting reel,
the one with my iceberg, my whale and the Paraguayan

in a storm, and we were then rushed off to the make-up room. Jill, so said the experts, was to be glamorised, and I had to have the shine taken from the top of my head where it might distract the audience.

Gulping slightly but trying to look unconcerned, we soon found ourselves in the studio proper. It was a vast barn of a place like an aircraft hangar, and our corner contained a desk and a few chairs. We were surprised to see that it also contained a rather scruffy-looking artificial palm-tree stuck into a forty-gallon oil-drum ; opposite to it was a blackboard where a little man was hard at work drawing a weather map in coloured chalk. Camera men and electricians milled everywhere and the floor was covered in trailing wires.

We sat as directed, in chairs, while grinning monsters of cameras carried out dummy runs at us and made chalk-marks on the floor to get the distances right. We spoke into microphones and were told we weren't speaking loudly enough, and at intervals our question master pulled feverishly at a cigarette and told us to remain perfectly natural, quite relaxed, and to take it easy. He also prac-tised smiling when he thought no one was looking. At length the show started. We had been married, we said, on the 3rd November and come over to Canada very soon afterwards. Yes, we had changed our plans and now intended to sail to the Pacific via the Panama Canal ; and yes, we did hope to circumnavigate the globe.

The lights blazed down at us, making me sweat ; the cameras ground away, and out of the corner of my eye I could see the screen of the monitor set displaying us as seen by the cameras. This I found unnerving and studi-ously averted my gaze.

Suddenly the question master said, " Now, Mr Hamilton, perhaps you'll be kind enough to give a little commentary on this film of yours . . . this film, ladies and gentlemen, shows Mr Hamilton crossing the Atlantic in his tiny craft."

As it happened it showed nothing of the sort ; I had apparently chosen the wrong reel. The film that flickered on the monitor showed *Salmo* lying at Rhu being loaded by Jock and myself ; it jumped disconcertingly to a bleary view of Rhu anchorage disappearing astern, and then finished off with Ailsa Craig in a rainstorm. All my carefully thought-out jokes and descriptions were now made useless, and I sadly ' oohed ' and ' er-ed ' my way through the display trying to make it look as if I knew what was happening. Fortunately it didn't last long, and as soon as the film was over we were signed off and were able to relax, while a man made twanging gestures at a guitar in front of the palm-tree (the noises mysteriously being supplied for him). It looked quite realistic on the screen and was fun to watch. We even enjoyed the little man with the blackboard and the weather, which concluded the proceedings.

As soon as the lights went on everyone made a dirty rush for the door and we found ourselves wondering what we ought to do next.

" Don't they even take our make-up off ? " said Jill, indignantly.

They didn't. We had to scrub it away with paper towels and cold water, and as a consequence reached the street looking more than a little smeared and remarkable. We were also upset by our final interview with the office, where we had learned that our hundred dollars apiece was intended to cover our travelling expenses instead of being additional, as we supposed.

As a result we travelled back to Montreal steerage class instead of in luxury, and made do with a fifty-cent sandwich for supper in the restaurant car where everyone else was guzzling at three-dollar meals. Two young men next to us nearly drove us mad by leaving most of their food on their plates and then sprinkling cigarette ash over it, thus defeating our intention of waiting until they had gone and finishing it off for them.

Back once more at St Sauveur we carried on living much as before, making daily pilgrimages to the post office in the hopes of receiving even the most modest of publishers' fees, and after a few days of Hi-life, resuming our diet of porridge and liver. The big difference now, however, was that when we grew bored with the house we used to go out and ski. At least we called it ski-ing, though one man whom I inadvertently knocked down called it a lot else as well.

By February the sun began to regain its power, and because it had been an unusually snow-less year the snow melted and patches of green appeared. We had brought all the tattier of our sails up to the house for repair (the Coristines had nicknamed it ' Honeymoon Villa ') and as soon as the front lawn cleared, took them out and spread them on the grass. The Genoa we very nearly rebuilt altogether and were very proud of our efforts. It looked rather like a patchwork quilt with big blotches of white on a tan sail, but it was a strong job and lasted well. The mainsail, too, we spent much time on, renewing yard after yard of the steam stitches which had given way. As we worked, we kept noticing a strange new smell about the place and it worried us. Had the drains burst in the big freeze at Christmas, perhaps ?

The smell grew worse and worse until it really became difficult to work outside in any comfort, so we went to consult the plumber with whom we had grown friendly. He was a great big man and spoke little English. On a particularly virulent afternoon we brought him back to the house and said proudly :

" There, do you smell it ? " He sniffed for some time and then pronounced gravely, " That ? It is just the spring."

The remark became a great favourite with us, and later on, whenever *Salmo* began to develop any more than ordinarily unpleasant odour we would assure each other gravely that it was just the spring making itself felt.

The day we left St Sauveur there was a snowstorm in Montreal, and *Salmo* looked very sad when we went to visit her to make a list of the jobs to be done before she went into the water. It was the first time Jill had seen her since the day after we became engaged, and her heart brimmed over with sympathy.

" Poor old thing," she said, shovelling six inches of snow off the cabin-top so that we could get at the hatch. " You must be cold lying out in the open like that."

The frost had played havoc with the paint, raising it in great big blisters both above and below the waterline. I had hoped just to do a touching-up job, but saw at once that this was a case of taking everything off and starting again. As usual Bobby Coristine proved to be our guardian angel. He produced for us the most gigantic belt-sander I have ever seen. It was all that I could do to lift it, and the sandpaper belts that it used would fit over my shoulders. First with a blow-lamp and then with the sander we took every morsel of paint off and left *Salmo* naked as the day she was built. It was the first view of the bare hull that I had had and it was beautiful. Pitch-pine below and mahogany above and not a bad strake anywhere. It was a comforting sight when we thought where she would have to take us.

The paint-scraping was mostly a one man job (Jill couldn't even lift the sander, let alone hold it over her head) so she concentrated on the inside. The first objects of her attack were my biscuit-tins for holding the bulk provisions.

" But these are QUITE DISGUSTING," she said. " It's bad enough sailing in a boat without a lavatory without having to eat out of rusty tins as well. And where's your washing-up basin ? "

" Well, I usually use the pressure-cooker," I replied. I had known this was going to come sooner or later. The one thing that interests women in a boat, so I have discovered, is the washing-up gear. In their minds everything else is of minor importance.

"The pressure-cooker, indeed," she snorted. "That's absolute nonsense! One thing's flat. I'm going to buy a washing-up bowl. That is, if we ever get the money to buy anything at all," she added, after a moment's reflection.

For the sad truth was that we were stony-broke. Our bank account now only held six dollars, and those I wanted to keep so that the account remained open. In cash we had seventeen cents, and that included a nickel which I found in the turn-up of my best pair of trousers, a relic from church at St Sauveur when I had dropped my collection money. We were so desperate that we even contemplated taking jobs, but one last hope of an idle life remained. I had made an appointment to see the editor of 'Weekend Magazine,' who, so the bush telegraph of our journalistic acquaintances suggested, might possibly buy a story from us.

We dressed with extreme care for this interview, though the effect was slightly spoiled by the time we arrived; for the 'Weekend' office was two miles from the Coristines' house, we hadn't the money to pay for the bus fare, and the Montreal pavements were covered with slush.

"Now you do the talking," said Jill, as we stepped from the lift and headed for a window marked 'Enquiries.'

We were shown into the office of a Mr Shaw and it soon became obvious that he knew a great deal more about us than we had suspected, so little time was wasted on preliminaries. "Now I'll tell you what I want, Commander Hamilton," he said. "If you'll excuse me saying it, and of course, I intend no offence. The interesting part about this set-up of yours—what makes it something a bit different from the usual run of cruise—is that you've got your bride along with you."

Jill winced. She hated being called a bride and longed to graduate to being a wife.

" Oh yes. Quite," I replied, slightly baffled and wondering what was coming next.

" Now I'll tell you what," said Shaw (he was obviously very frightened of treading on any corns) ; " well what I mean is . . . that's to say, what we'd like is a diary by Jill, not by you ; what she thinks of it all, day to day sort of things. You see, most of our readers won't be sailors at all." He hurried on, " And colour photographs of course. We specialise in colour photographs. We'd run it as a sort of ' Sailboat Honeymoon ' story."

By this time neither of us really cared a damn what he ran us as, so long as he paid for it, but we felt it would be impolite to say so. Besides, Honeymoon Scenes in Sailboat *Salmo* seemed to be a theme that offered scope for considerable embellishment if we didn't come to some sort of understanding on the subject.

" Now, if we do this," I asked, " can we take it that you'll publish what Jill writes and not what you'd like her to have written ? "

" Oh surely," said Shaw ; " would five hundred dollars an article suit you ? And we'd have a series of four or maybe five ? "

Would it suit us ! We nearly turned cartwheels in the office. In fact it was only with the very greatest difficulty that we restrained ourselves from cheering when we heard him continue. " Now what I suggest is this. Most of your expenses will come before you start, as I understand it. Would it help any if I give you an advance for the amount of your first article ? "

He rang for his secretary and in a matter of moments the cheque was in my pocket. There was a bank just opposite the entrance to the ' Weekend ' offices and we darted over to it and stood hugging ourselves as the cashier counted out fifty ten-dollar notes. Without hesitation we went off and bought a gigantic lunch with the appropriate wine, and then we drove back to the house in a taxi.

I had filled *Salmo* with paint before leaving England, so it wasn't long before we had brushes in our hands instead of scrapers. We decided to give her four coats above the waterline and three below. As each went on, the job began to look more and more professional, and passers-by would pause as they saw us at work to say :

" Why, you've got her looking real nice. I remember last year about this time there were two boats at just the same stage as you are and then the frost came. They had to burn the whole lot off again. Right down to the wood. Wasted three weeks' work they did."

Fortunately the frost didn't come, or not too much of it anyway, and the lake began to clear of ice. The weather at this time was glorious ; day after day of brilliant sunshine which attracted big crowds to work on their boats at weekends. Everything was bustle and scurry and anticipation. Jill spent a whole morning making paper stencils and then did a masterly job of signwriting on the counter in gold paint : ' *Salmo :* O.C.C.'

" Thank goodness we belong to the Ocean Cruising Club," she said at the end of it, " and not to the Royal St Lawrence Yacht Club. It saves two letters and a lot of difficult spacing."

The last drifts of ice left the lake in the second week of April and we slithered *Salmo* into the water. It was a Saturday, and quite a crowd gathered round to watch the show. I had the mast, all glittering in new varnish and with the standing rigging oiled, lying ready beneath the sheerlegs, and in half an hour it was stepped. *Salmo* began to look alive once more and we felt it was time to have a small celebration. Two or three friends drifted on board to help the party and work was forgotten for the afternoon.

"Don't just sit there drinking beer," said Jill to me, "get the guard-rails reshipped or someone'll go overboard."

I was provoked by such a remark from one who was also drinking beer.

"Well, if anyone goes, you'll be the first," I said, grabbing her and holding her over the side.

She wriggled. I lost my balance, stumbled against the non-existent guard-rail, and disappeared with the most almighty splash. To my absolute fury Jill managed to grab the gunwale and remain inboard. The water, only two days unfrozen, was shattering. With a yell, I swam to a ladder and clambered out, much to the delight of all the club members on the balcony above.

"Well, you Britishers are certainly the hardy ones," they greeted me; "why, out here we don't open the bathing season for another three months."

Three days later we were ready to sail, though everyone said we were crazy. "What you don't realise," they told us, "is that when you leave here to go down river you have to go nearly four hundred miles north before you can clear the Gaspe peninsula and start getting south again. It may be spring here but it'll be mighty cold up there."

"Well, the thing is," we replied, "that we HAVE to go now. If we're going to spend any time at all in the States on our way south we can't afford the delay. We'd rather be cold here than mixed up in hurricanes by the time we reach the West Indies. And besides, we don't mind the cold, we're used to it." This boasting wasn't long in rebounding upon us. Less than three weeks in fact.

On the twenty-fifth of April we sailed. The weather, having been beautiful for nearly three weeks, broke and the day was cold, wet and stormy. When we reached her on the early morning bus *Salmo* was rolling madly at her moorings and we had great difficulty in getting on board with our suitcases. It would obviously have been hopeless to try to beat out of the narrow yacht harbour with the gale in our faces, so we asked the club motor-boat, the only other craft afloat, to tow us clear.

"O.K., we're fine now, thanks," I shouted. "Let go the tow!" The rope splashed into the water and Jill hauled it in. 'How splendid to have a fo'c'sle hand!' I reflected, thinking of the scampering which I would be engaged in had I been single-handed.

"Now can you remember what they said about the channel?" Jill asked me, when she came aft again. "I couldn't understand all of it, except that we had to make a big zig-zag before we reached the main channel."

"Oh yes," I said, "it's quite easy. I remember how I went when I came in. The buoys were laid then of course, so it was easier, but we have to go down this way for a mile or so and then we can go straight out. In fact, I think we're about far enough down now. Ready about."

We went about and started threshing offshore towards the middle of the lake. We could see the lake steamers busily passing up and down and had very nearly reached them when CRASH! There came a shattering impact and we stuck. "Go down and see if we're leaking," I said to Jill as I jumped for the halyards to drop the sails. It had been such a terrific wallop that I wondered if we had cracked the stempiece.

"No. There's no sign of any water," said Jill, coming out of the cabin.

She was looking a bit shaken, and I didn't blame her. I was pretty shaken myself. I'd never run aground as hard as that before, and at the moment of impact it had crossed my mind that it would have been a singularly undignified way of ending a world cruise, to go and sink in the middle of a well-charted fresh-water lake just because I hadn't bothered to listen to instructions carefully enough.

We got towed off eventually by the club motor-boat, whose faith in the uncanny skill of world voyagers had also taken a knock.

" Say," he said, " I thought you KNEW those rocks were there."

" No," we answered, " we didn't, but we know now."

We'd had a bad fright but our morale was not long in returning. The Lachine canal passes through some busy industrial areas and the lock operators had been warned of our advent. They weren't used to boats without engines and obviously mistrusted our powers of braking. No sooner did we appear on their horizons than bridges swung open and streams of traffic built up on either bank. ' Weekend' had been doing a bit of publicity promotion on our behalf, so the passage developed into a triumphal progress. Motors tooted to us, pedestrians waved and there were great shouts of " Good luck ! "

" Oh isn't this FUN," said Jill ; " I've never been famous before."

We secured for the night in a basin above the Jacques Cartier bridge in order to hold a farewell party. All the friends we had made during the winter came down on board, including of course the Clan Coristine, who had brought with them the most enormous basket of what they called ' Emergency Rations ' that I have ever seen. We started glancing through the labels ' Smoked Oysters,' we read ; ' Peaches,' ' Tongue.' It looked as though we'd have to have plenty of ' emergencies.'

It was late before we went to bed, and suddenly we both felt very sad. It was just like leaving home all over again. We hated making all the goodbyes. Jill became quite sniffly.

" The worst of it is," she said, " that we won't be

coming back here again. So that most of the goodbyes we've been saying are real goodbyes not just ' *au revoir* ' goodbyes. Oh, it's horrid."

It was on this rather sombre note that we spent our last night in kind-hearted Montreal.

Our start was at five. It was light by that time, and ' Weekend ' had particularly asked us not to go earlier as they wanted some photographs. We took the opportunity of giving both our cameras to their photographer so that he could take some for us as well. It is so rare that one has a chance to have an outsider take photographs of one's own boat.

Apart from the photographer the quay was deserted when our lines were slipped. A light breeze filled the sails and we rippled gently out of the basin into the main stream, which snatched and whirled us through the bridge. The photographer's launch circled twice, once for his photographs, once for ours, we opined ; then back he came to return our cameras and, with a cheerful wave and a " Well, I'll be hearing all about you," he left us. The oil-tanks flashed by, and I remembered the battle I had had to get past them when the current was against me and I was single-handed.

It seemed to be a good omen, this easy, leisured progress. I turned to Jill :

" Well, now we're really off," I said, " any regrets ? "

" Of course not," she answered ; " it's going to be wonderful."

CHAPTER SEVEN

SPRING AND THE ST LAWRENCE

THE channel is narrow as far as Quebec, and we found that we had to pay close attention to the marks and beacons. During the day this was easy enough, but at night, being strangers, we found it more confusing. Jill in particular could hardly have chosen a worse place to stand her first night watch alone. It was at Trois Rivières, rather more than half-way to Quebec, that I handed the boat over to her.

"Do you see those two white lights up ahead?" I asked, "in transit? Well, keep them that way until you get the next red flashing buoy abeam. You turn a bit to port then and should see a couple of green flashing lights which are the next transit marks. And watch out for these unlit buoys. There are usually three between each pair of lit ones and they're not very easy to see. And you see those two ships out there ahead? They're coming up channel. Give them lots of room."

"Yes," she said, rather breathlessly. "Look, you don't mind if I have to call you up sometimes, do you? There seem to be such a LOT of lights."

Half an hour later I heard a voice saying, "Could you come up a minute, please?"

When I arrived Jill was apologetic. "We got round that first bend all right and there are the green transit lights, but I don't know what all those other lights are. They look terribly close."

I didn't know either. It looked as though we were blundering into the middle of Piccadilly Circus. There was a great mass of lights and in amongst them black shapes ; we were flashing down upon them at ten knots, five knots of our own and five of current and it all looked mighty alarming. As we gazed at the mass, trying to disentangle it, a huge unlit buoy loomed up right ahead. Jill swung the tiller hard over and we missed it by a hair's-breadth. " Ooh ! the darned thing," she said, " I never saw it. I was too interested in the lights."

Suddenly we found ourselves in amongst them all. They were dredgers and spoil-barges all moored together in a tangle of cables on either side of the channel, widening it in readiness for the Seaway. The gap between the clusters was narrow and there was a bend in the channel at the same place. In daylight it would have been easy to see what was what, but in the darkness it all seemed sinister and alarming. We swept through and into clearer water and I went down below again busy wondering. . . . " Is it fair to leave Jill up alone there or isn't it ? " I knew that if I did leave her and we survived the watch unharmed she'd never be frightened of a night watch again ; she was most unlikely to meet another when conditions were so beastly. But if something did go wrong, what then ? Would it give her such a fright that she'd never want to keep a night watch ? There was no real answer to these conundrums, so I cold-bloodedly left her to it, trusting to her good sense to keep us out of trouble.

We spent two days at Quebec renewing old friendships and buying fresh provisions, for we planned to press on as hard as we could thereafter. The thought of West Indian hurricanes haunted us, and we were determined to keep as much time in hand as possible for seeing something of the U.S.A.

The weather had broken with a vengeance, and the day we left Quebec we ran into a gale which brought driving rain and sleet with it. Blowing straight in our faces it made watchkeeping a misery, and for all the progress we made it seemed silly to martyr ourselves. Instead we decided to anchor at a place called St Anne de Beaupré, which is a town much venerated by the local Catholic Church. We went ashore to try and get warm and have a bath, and while we were away some little boys stole the rowlocks from the Prout, which infuriated us, because we were reduced thereafter to paddling instead of rowing. This loss, the only one we sustained throughout the trip, left a bad taste in the mouth, and we were very pleased to be able to sail with the tide early next morning bound for my old staging-post, the Ile aux Coudres.

The channel hugs the left bank for ten miles before bending to starboard across the mouth of Baie St Paul and leading thence to the Ile. The shore is hilly, almost mountainous, and we found that the wind came whistling off it in vicious squalls which made us heel till the gunwale was deeply buried. The tide was running strongly with us and we hoped to make our passage with a couple of hours in hand before the flood began. Jill was on watch, and I was brewing up some Bovril to keep us warm for lunch when a particularly vicious squall arrived bringing hail with it. *Salmo* heeled far away over and flew through the water. Suddenly there was a BANG and it was followed by a mighty flogging from the mainsail. It had split right across and tatters of sail flew from the mast like streamers; the boom hung limp on the guard-rail and all in a moment we had changed from a vigorous sailing-boat to a hulk. Sadly remembering all our hours of toil restitching the seams, I gathered up the mangled remains and set the tri-sail, which was a heavy flax canvas sail, cut with a big belly to it and nearly useless for going to windward.

The next three hours were miserable; for we had ten miles to cover before the tide turned and the wind did everything in its power to see that we didn't cover them. It increased to a full gale and brought drifts of stinging sleet along with it. It shifted from fine on one bow until it was from right ahead and it whipped up the sea to an angry chop. Depressed, cold and angry we sat in the cockpit together looking at our watches and coaxing *Salmo* every way we knew. There is no slack water at this bit of river. The stream changes from ebb to flood in a matter of minutes, and once the flood started we knew we'd have to go back all the way to St Anne de Beaupré, and the thought of doing so was gall and wormwood to us. We had developed a hate for the place out of all proportion to the wrong it had done us. And besides, it's always infuriating to lose hard-won distance.

Nearer we got to the Ile aux Coudres jetty, and nearer still. Our watches pointed to five to five. The tide was due to turn at a quarter past.

At ten past exactly we edged in to the jetty and wormed our way to the most distant and inshore corner, so as to be clear of the general post which would take place at midnight when the ebb began again.

"The hell with going on tonight," we said, "there's not all that much hurry. It's been a perfectly foul day, so let's have a rest."

We brewed up an enormous curry supper, lit the heater in the cabin, and after supper settled down in our bunks to talk and read and enjoy ourselves.

"This heater does make things snug," said Jill; "I'd no idea the cabin could be as comfortable as this. Just listen to the rain outside, it's fairly lashing down. I love hearing it when I know I don't have to go out into it." She snuggled down beneath the blankets and quite soon I saw she was asleep. Reaching from my bunk I blew out the two lights and left only the heater hissing on the bulkhead to shed a dim glow in the darkness. The rain drummed down on the deck and I too felt strangely at peace. Certainly this was a better way to sail than single-handing had been.

I'd hardly closed my eyes, so it seemed, when I was awakened by shouts, the flashing of a powerful torch and the frenzied drumming of a big diesel. Rubbing the sleep from my eyes I stumbled into the cockpit and nearly put my hand onto the towering stem of a bateau. Surmounting the stem, miles and miles above me, was a frantically yelling figure brandishing an aldis light.

It didn't take long to grasp the situation. The bateau, for some inscrutable reason, wanted to use our bit of wall ; and, with the wind that was blowing, if he didn't get a line ashore his stern was going to be hard on the *sacrés* rocks in a matter of moments. That was what the dervish-like figure on the fo'c'sle was trying to explain to me.

Pausing only to stick my head into the cabin to yell at Jill :

" Come - and - get - a - ruddy - fender - out - don't - just-lie - there - like - a - dormouse - dammit," I leaped for the ladder, clambered up it onto the windswept jetty and began to do some impassioned line-handling while thanking my stars that I always went to bed in an ankle-length red sweater.

Some moments later, by which time the bateau had manœuvred himself in astern of us, the situation calmed down sufficiently for me to spare a thought for my wife. I peered down over the edge to see how she was getting on, and there she was skipping nimbly about on deck with a large motor-tyre on a lanyard and dressed only in a very elderly vest of mine. The hand not needed for fending was clutching the hem of the vest, and every time the wandering aldis beam strayed towards her she'd leap for a patch of shadow.

" I don't think they COULD have seen me, do you ? " she asked anxiously when I got back down below again.

While we were having breakfast the next morning the captain of the bateau, a courtly man, came on board to thank us most sincerely for all our help. He hoped, he added, that we had not been inconvenienced in any way.

The fields had all been green at Montreal, but by the time we passed Rimouski they were white, and the Shick Shack mountains, farther downstream, looked icy and aloof. We kept the heater going day and night, and while on watch wore layer upon layer of clothing. We had been given specially quilted jackets while in England, ' Yot-Jaks ' they were called, and now they really came into their own. Life without them would have been a misery, but huddled into their grateful warmth we felt like bugs in rugs, and only our noses and our ears suffered too badly from the icy winds. The turning point was Cape Gaspe ; once past there and we hoped to run into warmer weather.

We reached it early one morning, about a fortnight after leaving Montreal. For once the wind was favourable and we were sporting a spinnaker, I was on watch and it was a grand thrill to watch the lubber line walk round the compass all the way from north-east to south. Our route lay through the Northumberland Straits and down to the narrow Gut of Canso which separates Cape Breton Island from Nova Scotia. Beyond the Gut lay the open Atlantic and we longed to reach it. The constant watch-keeping and the ever-present fear of meeting ice was beginning to weigh on our nerves.

The last landmark before reaching the Gut is Cape St George, a big bold headland with a lighthouse on it. We swept past this in grand style at suppertime one night without a care in the world. The wind was increasing from ahead, and in the middle of supper I had to leave my plate on the stove and go on deck to reef and change head-sails. Half an hour later the wind began to head us so that we could no longer hold our course for the Gut, the flash of whose light we could see quite plainly fifteen miles ahead. It seemed as though it was one of those evenings when nothing goes right. Just as we had come to this conclusion its accuracy was confirmed when one of the foresheet leads pulled out of the deck and left the staysail flogging like a mad thing. It was the only piece of permanent gear that ever did carry away in two years' cruising, but as I crawled forward to rig a jury lead I didn't know that, and merely decided for the thousandth time that I hated sailing.

Things went better for a while after that ; the moon came out and Jill turned in, for she was doing the middle watch. With any luck I thought we should by that time be almost up to the causeway which the energetic Canadians have built across the strait, and for the rest of the night we would have a nice flat run through sheltered water.

It was a fine night, though blowing moderately hard, and *Salmo* cut her way through the short, steep seas like a racer, with a moonbow of spindrift arching from her bow. Every now and then little black clouds scudded across the sky and made the night seem very dark when they passed across the moon, hiding it completely and wiping the silver glitter from the water. This happened once soon after ten o'clock, just when I was thinking of going about, and when the moon shone clear again it lit up an iceflow less than a cable ahead.

Instinctively I pushed the tiller down and hove to with the staysail aback while I considered the situation. It wasn't a particularly big floe, about the size of a tennis-court maybe, but it would have been an ugly thing to ram at six knots, for it was eight feet thick at least.

" What's the matter ? " Jill asked as she felt the motion change.

" Ice," I replied. " You'd better come up and have a look at it."

So up she came, and we sat there for a while watching the beast, all white and silent in the darkness, as we slowly drifted away from it. To go racing on, even in

moonlight, seemed to be foolish. And though it was the
only floe we'd yet seen, it seemed most unlikely that it
would be on its own. Far more likely that there were
lots more in the area somewhere. So we decided to stay
where we were until daylight.

We did this, and when dawn came (we'd had to dodge
four other floes in the meanwhile) things looked better
than we had feared they might. True there WERE some
big floes in sight, but for the most part the water seemed
to be open. With only ten miles to go to the causeway
we would be crazy to turn back without making some sort
of effort to discover whether there was a passage. The
chief snag which we foresaw was fog. It wasn't exactly
foggy at dawn but the visibility was poor : something
like a mile we reckoned it to be.

Breakfast was a silent meal. We passed some more
floes and took photographs of them, because after all it
isn't every day that one goes sailing in amongst such
monsters, but all the time we kept wondering what lay
ahead. The fog had turned to a thin drizzle and it was
bitterly cold.

Ahead of us a whitish glow appeared through the murk
and the word ' Iceblink ' leapt to mind. Neither of us
was quite sure what iceblink was, but we had an idea it
was something like this glow of ours and that it indicated
the presence of solid ice.

I climbed the mast to see if I could get a better view
and found I could. The whole horizon ahead (not that
it was a very extensive one) was a solid mass of enormous
floes, each the size of a rugger-field and all tumbled and
jaggedy in contour. The gaps between them were nasty
narrow-looking canals of black water, and we didn't like
the look of them at all, at all.

We cruised right up to the edge of this barrier, keeping
a good lookout for projecting ledges, to see if things looked
any better, and they didn't. Even the sight of a mass

of seals on one of the bigger floes totally failed to cheer us up and the rain was now coming down hard.

We tried first of all to see if we could work our way round the edge of this barrier by going close along the Cape Breton side of the bay. Inshore, however, we found ourselves in amongst a veritable river of floes, grinding together in the tideway which ran far more strongly than we had expected. Next we tried to sneak up the mainland side, and for a while that looked more promising. So promising did it look, in fact, that by late afternoon we reckoned we only had another five miles to go, and we were in comparatively open water with the wind from right astern.

" It's getting late," said Jill, " and I don't want to spend another night in amongst all these floes. " They're far too eerie for my liking. And besides you never know where the damned things are. Do they move with the tide, the current, the wind, or WHAT ? "

I didn't want to spend another night in the ice either, but we were so very nearly through that I felt we really OUGHT to go on. So on we went, and found, with only two miles to go, that there wasn't a passage after all— at least not the sort of passage that I'd dare to push an engineless wooden boat into in darkness. The floes kept writhing and turning, and when they did so the little canals of open water would open and close, and sometimes they shut altogether with an ugly grinding noise as a few tons of jagged ice fell away from each bank. To take *Salmo* in amongst them would be lunacy. We'd be bound to end up in a cul-de-sac.

But as soon as we decided to turn back and head for open water the wind dropped completely.

As it grew dark we lay completely motionless on an inky lake of open water with floes all round us. We weren't unduly worried, for no floe was within a mile, and it was only to the south and east that the barrier was really formidable ; to the north and west the floes were more scattered.

Jill had the first watch, which we hoped would be a peaceful one. Without any wind we expected to behave very much like an icefloe ourselves. If the ice was a mile away when it grew dark, then it should darned well stay a mile away. So she began to read a book down in the cabin where it was warm and dry, while I went to bed. Every ten minutes or so she stuck her head out and had a good look round.

After an hour the wind blew up and it seemed best to set no sail unless we had to. We still hoped to behave like an icefloe and drift as they did. As a precaution, however, I bent on the tri-sail and Number Two staysail, so that if we did have to start moving we could do so without delay.

Very conscientiously, every ten minutes, Jill laid aside her book and went on deck with the binoculars to look round, and every time she saw nothing but an empty circle of blackness. The wind whined gently in the rigging and it was all rather eerie. The book she was reading was rather eerie, too, so she laid it down and wished there was someone to talk to ; she didn't want to wake me, for I was going to take over the watch in another hour and she knew I wanted all the sleep I could get.

Quite suddenly she heard a noise. Water slapping against something—and it didn't sound as though it was against the hull. Not quite sure what it was, but with a dreadful premonition that made her tummy feel all empty inside, she bundled up into the cockpit and there, less than six feet away, was the edge of a floe, white, jagged, and very frightening, with the waves slap, slap, slapping against it. How she missed it I'm not quite sure, but miss it she did—and then saw another floe, dimly out on the beam. Quite obviously we'd drifted in amongst the group, so I set the sails and got under weigh to try and nose into open water.

I took over the watch and we stayed like that for the rest of one of the unpleasantest nights that either of us had ever spent. The wind rose nearly to gale force and sleet came with it. It was bitterly cold and the visibility dreadful.

Jill tried to sleep but it was hard to stop imagining things. Every lurch made her feel we were going to be flung against the side of a floe, and every strange noise or alteration of course suggested that we were hemmed into a ring of drifts.

Up top I nursed *Salmo* along just as slowly as ever I could, peering and peering into the darkness, craning my neck to see first on one bow and then on the other. The sleet whirled down, stinging my eyes and soaking through the leather gloves until my hands were numb. The worst of it was that I had no idea where the main mass of floes might lie. We could only guess at their movement from our knowledge of the tides and the wind.

Once I blundered in amongst them. After two hours of seeing nothing but blackness, I caught a faint greyish loom to starboard. More appeared ahead, and then to my horror I saw another floe to port. All this was miles from where we had last seen the close-packed ice, and it was desperately hard to gauge the line of it. I dodged between two big floes, dimly seen, and found myself in a perfect litter of small stuff which ranged in size from a dinghy to a football. All the time I was terrified that I'd bump into one of the small bits and bring Jill out on deck. It was sufficiently alarming to me, after two hours spent in getting used to the idea ; to come up from below and be confronted with ice all round would have been shattering. We skiddered through the bits some-how or other, gybed, and found our way back into open water, and I sighed a breath of relief. It was a mercy, at any rate, that the ice did at least keep the sea moderately flat.

Not a light was in sight, the visibility was so poor, and after all our twistings and turnings I was not in the least certain of our position. I THOUGHT we were still more or less in the middle of the bay but it was hard to be sure. If only we could get a glimpse of either Cape George or the Gut of Canso light it would have been a comfort, but no light showed. Nothing but rain and inky water.

Slowly the blackness lessened and became grey. Our circle of visibility grew and I could see half a mile of yeasty water and the rainswept cheerless deck. Above that the sails swelled in dark curves and little streams of mingled spray and rain ran from them. The mast swung in spirals against the sky and after watching it for a while, half hypnotised, I realised just how cold and tired I was. There was no ice in sight, and with daylight to help us, the danger of running into a flow was slight. Jill, who had managed to have a few hours of uneasy sleep, now took over the watch and I stumbled gratefully into the warmth of the cabin, stripped off my oilskin and clambered into the little warm nest of blankets which she had left on her bunk.

By nine o'clock the rain stopped and we saw that the wind had broken up the floes far more than they had been the day before. Once more we tried to find a way through them to the causeway. This time, however, it was rather a half-hearted attempt. Whatever happened, we were quite determined not to spend another night like the last one. We were both very cold and very tired, and by now we hated the very sight of ice. As soon as we found that the way was once more blocked by thick stuff we decided that we'd had enough, turned tail and headed for a little port called Pictou, fifty miles back in the direc-

tion from which we'd come. It was a wrench to lose all
that distance, but we felt that we needed a break.

Needless to say, having had to beat against the wind
all the way from Pictou to reach the ice, we had to beat
against it all the way back again to Pictou, and it took
twenty-four hours to do it. We spent two days there,
warming up and reprovisioning, and then we heard that
the approaches to the Gut were reported to be ice free.
We didn't believe it but sailed all the same. Strangely
enough the reports proved to be correct and we had a
glorious sail back past Cape George and down to the
causeway. As the lock-gates opened to let us out into
the Atlantic (we looked rather like a beetle swimming out
of a bath) we heaved a great sigh of relief :

" Now," we said, " we should REALLY start to get
warm ! "

CHAPTER EIGHT

FROM THE ICE TO THE TROPICS

THE most notable incident of our passage through the Gut of Canso came when we set the spinnaker.

" Have you got the sheets secure ? " I shouted to Jill, who was down aft.

" Yes, they're O.K.," she replied.

" Well, just give them a check-over before I hoist. It's infuriating if they slip when the sail fills."

" I've told you already," she said, " they're all fast."

I hoisted and the starboard sheet promptly zipped off its cleat and ran through the block at the boom-end. The spinnaker flew ahead like a flag. Jill was furious. " But I DID check it. I did," she kept on saying ; " Oh, it IS unfair. Why did you have to go and ask me THAT time of all times if it was properly secured." I felt incredibly smug, and silently remembered all the other times in the past when I had allowed the same thing to happen and had had no one to blame for it. *Salmo* having done her best to teach me to behave myself properly, was evidently in the process of taking Jill in hand as well.

It was somewhere off Halifax that we met our first spell of really foul weather. The wind was from astern and we held onto the spinnaker as long as we dared, but our nerve cracked soon after supper. As ever with a strong wind from aft, the motion was horrific. We rolled gunwales under each way, and steering was difficult. It was Jill's first experience of carrying too much sail on a run and she hated it. I went forward and dropped the sail, smothering it quickly as it came in and bundling it

down the forehatch. It was quite dark, but the foredeck
had become very familiar by this time and I thought
nothing much of it. I set a small staysail in its place
and the tri-sail, and then came aft again making some
trite remark such as, " Well she's a good deal more comfortable now."

" Oh yes, it's quite all right NOW," Jill said, all of a
rush ; " but why can't you SAY something some of the
time when you're working up forward there. I can't see.
you when you're up there. I asked you twice if you were
all right and you never answered, all I could hear was an
awful flapping noise and some bangs. And the boat dances
about as if she's a sort of bucking Bronco, and you never
wear a lanyard round yourself : and now you come back
and say ' She's quite comfortable.' What about me ? "

I had rather forgotten that it is much easier than it looks
to work on a bouncy fo'c'sle. Always after this, on dark
nights, I used to carry on a sort of running commentary
when I went up there.

We had a cup of cocoa as we talked things over, for
I wanted to be quite sure that Jill was happier about
steering now that sail was reduced before I turned in.
There wasn't much danger in actual fact. Without a
mainsail set a gybe wouldn't be a very serious matter,
and the sea wasn't rough enough to poop us.

" Is this a gale ? " Jill asked, looking out at the spindrift and the rushing wave-crests. " It feels like one. I
always wondered if I'd hate it in a gale. But I don't
think I will. This IS a gale, isn't it ? "

" Well I don't quite know," I said. " It's a pretty
strong wind, anyway."

The next day we were off the southern tip of Nova
Scotia, heading for Cape Cod, when a U.S. coastguard
cutter saw us and came steaming over. He had a great
ungainly helicopter-deck built on his superstructure, and
was rolling forty degrees each way. Life on board must

have been a misery, but he had no thought for himself :
only for us.

"Hey!" he shouted on his loud-hailer, "you're heading all the wrong course. You should go up that way.
North-west ; into the wind. If you haven't got a compass,
just keep headed into the wind and you'll find land up
ahead of you." He was just like a mother hen reproving
an errant duckling, and it took a long time to convince
him that we were capable of looking after ourselves. It
was our first encounter with the U.S. Coastguards and we
were highly impressed both then and later with the trouble
to which they went to be wet-nurses to yachtsmen.

Cape Cod and the Nantucket Sounds were shrouded in
fog when we reached them. We had only one chart of
the whole American coast from Virginia to Maine, and it
was of such a small scale that it didn't mark buoys, so
we never really exactly knew where we were. This was
a fairly common occurrence, and we rarely worried about
it, but this particular stretch of coast is dangerous and
littered with off-lying shoals and dangers. I had chosen
a route that took us clear of most of them, but there was
one that I was worried about, a shoal called The Stone
Horse shoal. The fog was particularly thick as we felt
our way towards it, a warm clammy blanket that hid
everything. Little streams of moisture ran down the sails
and dripped from the boom ; our faces shone with water
droplets, and even the inside of the cabin was misty and
sweated from condensation. Neither of us felt like sleep,
so we shared the watch poring over the chart, checking
the course, and, above all, listening. The sea seemed to
be alive all round us. Three separate foghorns boomed
and burped ; a bell rang and astern we could hear the
throb of a diesel.

"That bell is probably a bell-buoy," I remember saying to Jill. "Nothing else ever contrives to sound quite
as mournful. I think we'd better try and find it. It

may have a name painted on it and that'll tell us where
we are." Ding, went the bell, dinga-donga-ding, ding.
It sounded quite close and we wondered if it might mark
the end of our Stone Horse Shoal.

We sat in the cockpit very silently. The few remarks
that we did make were spoken in undertones, as though
we were afraid of awakening somebody ; the bow-wave
lisped from the stem and the boom creaked gently, while
we strained our ears, striving to draw every mite of
information that we could from the noises round
about.

" One of these foghorns is a navigational one," I murmured. " Do you hear it . . . THAT one, the vulgar sounding
one ? The other two are ships."

" Those engines sound as though they're coming mighty
close," said Jill.

They did. Our attention removed from the buoy and
the foghorn and concentrated instead on the engine. We
peered and peered into the fog astern trying to make out
the shape that we knew must be there, for the sound
seemed to be almost on top of us. We kept imagining
shapes in the swirling greyness . . . looming bows . . . but
nothing appeared. Only the beat of the engine grew louder
and louder. Quite suddenly we heard voices. They can't
have been fifty yards away yet still we saw nothing. A
tidy line of waves swept towards us from the starboard
side, the wash of the unknown vessel, the voices faded
and the throb of the engine died away ahead.

" Well, at least we seem to be in the fairway," said
Jill, breaking the tension.

Dinga-dong went the bell again, startlingly loud ; and
then, there was the buoy looming indistinctly ahead. We
both jumped to see what was written on it as it slid past
five feet away. Barnacles grew round its waterline and
its top was white with seagull droppings. The legend,
however, was disappointing. ' No. 7 ' was all it said.

Departure from Montreal—" We're off "

Looking down on an Ice-Floe from the Mast

That, we reflected sadly, would be a lesson to us that short-cut methods of navigation rarely work.

We found our Stone Horse at last, worked our way round it and down through Nantucket sound to Newport, Rhode Island, where we spent a pleasant four days. From Newport we went to Milford in Connecticut and from there, still in fog, we hopped to City Island, where the New Yorkers keep their yachts. We had several matters to attend to in New York, but chief amongst them was our mainsail, which was steadily driving us crazy.

It was a specially made one of my own design, but like so many patent ideas it just didn't work. It was made from flax canvas and the cloths were vertical instead of horizontal as on more normal sails. The whole thing had stretched, and do as we would the boom sagged down until it rested on the guard-rails. Ever since we had split our original mainsail in the St Lawrence we had been forced to make do as best we could with this . . . thing . . . this sack . . . this scarecrow wrapping. I knew I'd never make a really good job of recutting it, but I was determined to do what I could, and what was needed was space in which to work.

Ratsey and Lapthorn have their American sail-loft just down the road from where we lay at the Morris Yacht Club, at moorings which hospitable friends had lent to us. Certainly we could use their loft floor for our butchery, Colin Ratsey told us when we sought permission ; so every morning off to Ratsey's we trudged and squatted cross-legged on the floor with palm and needle. All round us, speckless and spotless, stretched great billowing acres of shiny white Dacron being turned into impeccable sails for the aristocrats of the American racing fleet. There we crouched in our corner guddling away at our heavy grey canvas. Every now and then the loft foreman would come along and peer down at us. " Don't you think that

if . . ." he would say, as he saw our struggles, and then
he'd usually take a hand himself and in a few moments
achieve what had been baffling us for an hour or more.
The women with the sewing-machines, too, helped at
intervals, and great lengths of seam would magically fly
beneath their needles.

" We can't have you take anything out of here looking
TOO bad," they would all say. They lived for sails, all
of them, and we learned much from their comments.

At last the whole thing was finished, so we borrowed
a push-cart and loaded the finished sail on top of it to
wheel it back on board. On the way we passed the Ratsey
signboard, so we had to stop for a photograph. After
all, it's not every yacht that can boast of having Ratsey-
handled sails to its name.

New York itself was like an oven, for it was mid-June
before we were ready to leave. On our visits to Manhattan
we sweltered and sweated and began to think longingly
of getting out to sea again where breezes blew, so one
day we slipped our moorings at the Morris Yacht Club
and headed for Hell's Gate, the back-door entrance to
New York harbour. The sun blazed down and there was
hardly a breath of wind to set us on our way. We drifted
down East River, and somewhere off the vast United
Nations building a breeze found us.

It freshened as we passed the Battery, and by the time
we took our farewell photographs of the Statue of Liberty
we were skimming and chuckling through the water. A
Coastguard launch came alongside when he saw our Blue
Ensign and asked where we were going.

" Jamaica," we shouted.

He went off, but must have been turning things over
in his mind, for he came straight back again and said,
" Did you say Jamaica ? In the West Indies ? "

" Yes," we shouted back, delighted as children at having
surprised him ; " Jamaica in the West Indies."

The days slipped by as we made our way southward.
A hurricane passed up the United States coast, the first
of the season, but having no wireless we knew nothing of
it save that we had more headwinds to contend with than
we had expected. It was a slow sail but a pleasant one.
One morning Jill was on watch, and while I was cooking
breakfast and chatting to her through the hatch she
suddenly said :

" Come up here a moment. There's something funny
floating on the water."

Up I went and she pointed it out to me, a strange
whitish brown lump about the size of my fist. We had
passed the thing by this time and another appeared and
then another and another one again. " I wonder if it
could be ambergris," I said, " I know that you meet that
floating about the ocean in lumps, but I always imagined
they were bigger lumps and more of a greyish colour."

We decided to stop and investigate, for ambergris sounded
both romantic and lucrative. We'd fill a biscuit tin with
it, we decided, or two if we could find enough pieces, and
take them to Jamaica and sell them. We'd buy a fishing-
rod with the proceeds and enormous quantities of rum.

I gybed round and we worked our way back to the
thickest cluster of lumps. To our delight we saw there
were far more than we'd thought at first.

" Golly," said Jill, almost bursting with excitement,
" there must be fifty of them at least," and she dived
down to the cabin to get a saucepan to scoop them up
with. " Even if they're only worth a couple of quid a
lump it'll always be something," she went on ; " but
probably it'll be far more than that, and we could get
dollars for them too." Quite obviously, in her mind's eye
the money was as good as spent already.

As we reached the first of the pieces she lay flat on her
tummy on the foredeck and lunged over the side with the
saucepan. " Got two of them," she announced delightedly,

and scooped again, " and another one," she added, and began to sniff her prizes cautiously. A long silence ensued.

" Well, what are they like ? " I asked. " What do they smell of ? "

With a snort of disgust she threw the three pieces back overboard. " It isn't ambergris at all," she said sadly, " they're bread rolls. Isn't that the limit. Here we are a hundred miles from the nearest land and we have to go and find someone else's bread rolls."

We were so disappointed at the way this lovely fortune had melted from our fingers that we decided to call in at a Bahama to console ourselves, and for some reason that I can't remember we chose Inagua.

I took a sight in honour of the occasion and found that we were ninety miles from Crooked Island, which obstructed our direct approach to Inagua. If all went well, I thought, we should sight land at dawn, coast round through the Crooked Island channel (a ten-mile channel that separated that island from its nearest neighbour) and then make Inagua on the day following. We were feeling light-hearted now that we had decided to work in an extra port of call, and our chief worry was that our whisky wouldn't hold out until we made port. At six o'clock promptly, but never a minute before, we used to open the bar and treat ourselves to a drink apiece, and it had become one of the favourite moments of our day. If the whisky bottle died (and there were only four very small tots left in it) we would have to make do with a ghastly substance which Jill had bought by accident at City Island. It was called Lo-cal and was, of all things, a calory-free orange squash for not fattening you. We had tasted it once and been appalled by it.

At dawn next morning I began to peer through the gloaming, and as the sun rose we lifted high on a swell and I saw a palm-tree sprout from the horizon ahead. Another one joined it as next we lifted, and another after that. " Land ! " I shouted down to Jill, who was still asleep, " I can see Crooked Island."

" Eeugh ? " said Jill, then feeling perhaps that she hadn't rated my achievement quite highly enough, added, " Well done : what time is it ? "

" Half-past six," I said.

" Well, give me a shout when breakfast's ready," and down she went to periscope depth again : a mound amongst the bedclothes.

It began to worry me as I fried the eggs that I couldn't see a lighthouse. I knew that there was one at the northern tip of Crooked Island, but the northern tip never seemed to appear. Every time I decided that the latest palm-tree of the series to poke over the horizon was the last one, another would come up beside it still farther off. It was most depressing.

" I suppose it's the right island," said Jill, as we began our meal.

" Of course it's the right island," I said rather snappily. " What other island could it be ? It arrived just dead on time. Of course it's the right island."

" Oh all right, all right, I only asked."

Palm after palm appeared and sand-dunes and more palms. Whatever island it was it certainly didn't boast very many distinguishing features. I eased the bows round a further five degrees northward to keep clear of the latest of an apparently never-ending series of right-hand edges of land, and Jill began her complaint anew.

" Well, I think it's Long Island," she announced.

" Oh, ha ha ! " I said. " Very funny. I suppose Manhattan's just round behind those sand-dunes."

" No, not THAT Long Island," she answered patiently. " Haven't you even looked at the chart? The island on the other side of the strait we're meant to be going through is called Long Island."

" Oh," I replied, " why didn't you tell me ? "

She was, of course, perfectly right. The first palm we had seen turned out to have been the southern one of Long Island instead of the northern one of Crooked Island, so we had to retrace our steps for twenty miles. Worse than that, we had to drink Lo-cal before we reached Inagua and it nearly choked us.

Inagua is just as flat as Long Island had been, and the only thing on it more than one palm-tree high is the lighthouse, which looks gigantic for lack of all competition. We arrived at six in the evening and secured to a convenient buoy. No one had come out to see us by the time we'd stowed the sails and put on shoregoing clothes, so we Prouted in and found the local policeman standing on the beach scuffling the sand with his bare black feet ; but his uniform was otherwise so immaculate that we expected to hear the starch crackle as he walked. He conducted us a hundred yards along a dust road leading between palms and white, red-roofed, bungalows to the police-station, where he took our passports from us, saying that Mr Parker would like to see them and would give them back to us in the morning. Mr Parker, he added, was the Resident Commissioner.

We signed a few forms, answered a few questions, and then the policeman said, " Well, I expect you'll be wanting to have baths and a meal ashore. I'll take you along to the club."

The club turned out to be a chummery where the bachelors and the grass-widowers of the American Salt Company, which was the island's chief industry, lived, played poker, and drank beer.

We were ushered into the verandah by the policeman and introduced. He then retired discreetly ; to go and get his tea, he said.

" That's one of the nicest dicks I've ever seen," said a red-haired young man with a fruity voice. " If we had some of the dicks I've known back home come here, Oh, lordy, lordy, lordy. . . ."

This young man became our host, and, Oh, lordy, lordy, lordy, he showed us the works of that 'goddam island,' as he called it. Actually, I think, he loved the place, and certainly was a mad enthusiast on salt-panning. . . . "Why, the new salt-harvesters we have pick the stuff up out of the pans at a twenty tons an hour" (or it may have been twenty tons a minute, he avalanched us in statistics). "And to do it by hand, why lordy, lordy, lordy, you wouldn't get more'n a teaspoonful in that time." We wandered amongst the pans in the broiling sun and heard how the gypsum is removed, and how the poor long-suffering brine is pumped from pan to pan to do this to it, and that to it ; and we watched the little white clouds floating overhead like cotton-wool balls. Some of the pans were blue, but the porridgiest of them, just before they turned to salt, were brilliant red and looked most uncanny.

On the way back to the boat, Lordy Lordy stopped the truck and dived into the scrub, which was as prickly and spiky as a porcupine's back, to gather a little bunch of flowers for Jill. His wife always picked them there, he said, handing over the most unexpectedly bright and delicate looking posy.

" I bet she doesn't wear shorts when she goes to get them," Jill remarked afterwards, surveying her legs ruefully. " Look at what those thorns did to me, and I hardly left the road, even."

That evening we had a party on board for the chummery wallahs. Glasses glugged cheerfully, jackets and ties were abandoned, and photographs of absent wives and families were produced, compared and handed round. " What happens with you folks," asked our friend, " if you find you have a family arriving when you're in the middle of the Pacific ? Oh, lordy, lordy, lordy, what a fix you'd be in then."

" Oh I expect we'd manage somehow," we replied stiffly. " But we don't think there's too much fear of it." Everyone threw that joke in our teeth and we were getting tired of it.

There was a full moon that night, and as we rowed back on board after ferrying the last of our guests ashore, we saw the black shapes of the palm-trees silhouetted against the dark indigo of the sky. Their fronds whispered gently in the breeze and we could hear the wavelets lapping against the beach. The setting was almost improbably tropical-islandish, and it seemed hard to believe that it was only two months since we had been wrestling with ice-floes and fog.

The trade wind whirled us joyfully down from Inagua to the Windward Passage. We had been warned to keep away from the Cuban shore, because a revolution was in full swing and the inhabitants were inclined to be trigger happy, so we stuck to the middle of the strait and in due course became becalmed there. It was so hot that we made an awning from some of the tatters of our old blown-out mainsail and lounged in the shade beneath it, drinking lime-squash made from our stock of Inaguan limes. It was a lazy interlude and lasted two full days. Everything was thoroughly peaceful and pleasant, and I was able to finish reading the book on chicken-farming which I'd begun at New York. The whole business of making a fortune from hens now seemed delightfully simple, and I determined to set about it as soon as we got home again. Me an unemployable, indeed! I harked back scornfully to the caustic comments thrown at me when I left the Navy.

Jill at this time was much occupied with fish. She thought it was quite absurd that we didn't have a fishing-rod on board, and the swarms of yellowtail and tunny that hovered round us drove her nearly mad with frustration. They seemed to annoy the sharks a good deal, too, for there were dozens about, drifting like sinister shadows, deep below us. Normally the fish would follow the boat at a respectful distance, fanned out on either side like motor-cycle escorts to a V.I.P. car, but often a sort of electric ripple would go through them and they'd huddle in close beneath us. Nearly always, on these occasions, we would see a shark rising out of the depths in a slow glide, but not quite summoning up the courage to come close enough to seize a meal.

We never bathed when we could see a shark, but at other times we used to go over happily enough. When there was a breeze we'd hang on to a line trailed from the stern and spin and turn at the end of it, shouting and bubbling. In very light airs we could dive from the fore-deck and grab the line as it trailed past, but it was only in calms that we could manage to do without the line altogether. It was in calms, however, that we usually seemed to have the sharks about, so we never ventured far afield, and always felt slightly uneasy until the last toe was dragged back inboard.

Port Antonio on the north coast of Jamaica is the best harbour on the island and a picturesque place to approach. There is a red - and - white - striped lighthouse standing amongst palm-trees to mark the entrance, and the mountains tower behind it, ridge after ridge, changing from green to blue as they grow more distant, and over all there is usually a ragged canopy of clouds. We swept past the lighthouse into a green and sheltered bay behind an island. Slowly and peacefully we moved through the mirror-flat water, looking at the palm-groves that lined the shore and the huts scattered in amongst them. From the town a loudspeaker boomed out dance-music and we could see two girls dancing together at the edge of the palms. They paused a moment to watch us pass, and then resumed their graceful rhythm, swinging and sway-ing to the music with easy grace. Half a cable off-shore I flung the anchor over the side, we dropped the sails, and decided that we were going to like Jamaica.

We stayed two weeks and would have stayed longer,

but we had made a resolution to leave the island before
the end of July and we stuck to it. We both thought it
was silly to go out of our way to look for trouble, and
though we were prepared to do the best we could with
Salmo if we ran into a hurricane, we hoped we wouldn't
have to. Besides all that, the Pacific was really the magnet
which had drawn us out of England, and we found its
pull growing stronger and stronger as we drew closer
to it.

The trade wind blew strongly, and we made a fast,
though a wet and uncomfortable passage from Jamaica
to the mainland. Night and day we hurried along without a falter, leaping, plunging and reeling in the wild
seas, keeping watch all the time so as to make the best
possible speed.

It was about this time that I began to notice that Jill,
though an excellent crew in all other respects, had one
most irritating failing. No sooner did she settle down
at the tiller than she would ask me to pass her something
from the cabin : her hat, a box of matches or a book
from the shelf. I bore it as long as I could, and then one
day as I was cooking supper I came to a decision to
broach the subject. I didn't want to hurt her feelings,
but I felt that it was one of the irritating little quirks
that can ruin a close companionship unless it gets nipped
in the bud. The pressure-cooker, full of potatoes, was on
the cockpit seat beside her, so while I cast about in my
mind for a suitable opening to my little homily, I thought
I'd start to boil them. They were out of reach so I asked
her to pass them down.

" Now, for GOODNESS' SAKE," she exploded, " stop asking me to pass you things the whole time. You're always
doing it. I've not been up here five minutes yet and you
want me to pass something down to you."

I was flabbergasted and began to splutter, " But what
do you mean *I* keep asking you to pass things ? It's you

who keep on asking ME! I was just going to tell you about it."

Jill was just as indignant as I was, and we relapsed into silence for a few moments thinking things over. Then slowly it dawned on each of us that, though the other was unquestionably the worse, there were a couple of instances . . . well rather more than a couple perhaps . . . well a few instances anyway . . . when we might have erred ourselves. We began to giggle about it, and thereafter any opening gambit of " Will you just pass me . . ." would be met with a delighted howl of " There you are, you see YOU'RE doing it." It cleared the air wonderfully, and we never had any more morbid moping sessions on the other person's shortcomings.

We made our Panamanian landfall on the mainland at a lighthouse called Isla Grande, twenty miles east of Cristobal. We sighted it soon after daylight in a weird looking world. Great towering banks of black cloud loomed up all round the horizon, spitting lightning. The sun rose in a blood-coloured sky and the sea looked black as ink. It was as hot and sticky on deck as in a Turkish bath, and the wind fell away to nothing. We lay and wallowed, watching the fireworks all morning, and found to our fury that a strong current which set along the coast was drifting us farther and farther from our destination. In the afternoon five thunderstorms raced down in quick succession, and as each passed over, the wind whined in the rigging, thunder crashed, and flashes of lightning split the whole world open. As the storms passed we would win back a mile or two of lost distance, only to drift back as the lulls came. It was during one of these lulls, while we both lay panting on sweat-soaked bunks, waiting for the next storm or a breath of wind to reach us, that the fishing-line, our new Jamaica-bought fishing-line and the pride of Jill's heart, went zzzzzZZZZZTTTTT . . . and we both leapt for the cockpit with thoughts of a fresh-fish supper.

It turned out to be a porpoise which had taken the line, and just as we were losing all hope of recovering any of it, he shook himself free and I began to reel back all that he'd run away with. As I did so, I glanced idly round at the gently heaving, oily water. All at once I felt the bottom falling out of my tummy; for directly ahead of us, less than a mile away, a waterspout was forming. A long drooping feeler hung down from the cloud overhead, swaying and groping. As it groped, the oily surface beneath was whipped into fine spray higher and higher and higher.

Jill had gone back to the cabin again, so I shouted to her and darted forward to the halliards, determined that if we became entangled with the spout it should be with the sails furled tightly. Jill, frightened by the urgency of my tone, came bundling up on deck to see what had upset me. Silently I pointed to the spout.

At that moment a breeze came. I was torn with uncertainty. Should we furl the sails so that if we did run into the spout it should harm us as little as possible, or did we try to sail away from it?

The breeze strengthened and made up our minds for us, we began to heel over and drive through the water. At the same time the spout began to move off to starboard. I turned *Salmo* so that she was headed in the opposite direction and just kept going until all danger of collision was past. Then we resumed our course, considerably shaken. A horrid, anxious hour followed, for the cloud above us seemed to spawn spouts. There were literally dozens of them about, but all of them tiny. Most never formed properly at all, but just looked like small squalls on the water. One of these we ran into and it knocked us every way as the wind shifted right round the compass. The boom crashed from one side to the other and back again, all in a matter of moments, and then we were out on the far side, for the whole disturbance can't have been more than two hundred yards across.

Afterwards, when we had time to think things over rationally, we realised that probably the reason why none of the spouts ever quite managed to form up properly was because there were so many of them, all trying to do the same thing. While we were in amongst the brutes, however, we were less sure about it, and all the time expected to be caught up by a big one.

The spouts were the last adventure that the Atlantic had in store for us. During the night we sighted the lights of Cristobal, and very early in the morning we sailed in past the long breakwater. A coastguard came out to find out who we were, and then handed us over to a Canal Company boat who led us to the anchorage. An hour later we went ashore to find out the details of a Canal transit.

CHAPTER NINE

PANAMA

THE man in the Canal office was quite emphatic. He was sorry, he said, but unless we carried an engine of some sort we wouldn't be allowed into the Canal. In vain I described to him how we had gone through the Canadian canals under sail without blocking the fairway. He couldn't help that, he said, the regulations were quite clear . . . no engine, no passage. " Of course you could always take a tow," he suggested; " the banana boats often tow people through. They'd probably do it for fifty dollars."

Unfortunately we hadn't got fifty dollars : we were reduced to twenty and needed them all to buy stores. " Well, just leave the date of our transit blank," we said. " We'll let you know when we've worked something out."

During the afternoon a company measurer and his mate came on board to work out the Canal charges. They had huge steel tapes with them and measuring-rods and notebooks. They measured *Salmo* from end to end and muttered to themselves as they made allowances. The first figure they arrived at seemed to displease them, so they started again. Our hearts sank. We'd always heard that Canal charges for a boat as small as *Salmo* were very reasonable, but the measurement seemed to be such a serious business that we began to have doubts. Would our twenty dollars get us through ?

" Er, excuse me," I said to the senior measurer, " but can you tell me yet about how much we'll be charged ? "

He sucked his pencil. " Well, no . . . we're still checking it. But I guess it'll be either two dollars ten or two dollars twenty cents."

We sighed with relief. Actually it turned out to be two dollars twelve, and that included a pilot, so the Canal Company can't have grown very fat at our expense.

We had directed our mail to the consulate, so as soon as we'd been measured and received permission to move to the Cristobal Yacht Club, we decided to go and collect it. Mail is such a big event that we honoured the occasion by taking a taxi, and we swept through the streets in most unaccustomed glory. The consulate when we reached it was a slightly seedy looking building with peeling plaster and a general air of decay. The entrance hall was deserted, except for a few sad-looking posters that adjured us to Take Our Holidays in Historic England, so we charged upstairs, where we found the vice-consul sitting behind a large desk.

" Our name's Hamilton. We're in a yacht called *Salmo*. Have you any mail for us ? " we panted out at him, for it had been a long flight of stairs.

" Oh, you've come at last ? " he smiled. " I was beginning to wonder if you were just another of the yachts with big ideas who don't get this far." He handed us a thick wedge of letters and we scrabbled quickly through them.

" Three from home," said Jill, " and a couple for you, and oh look ! here's one from ' Weekend.' I wonder if there's any money in it. Oh, I wonder if there is. Open it."

I opened it. Inside the letter there was a cheque for five hundred dollars. " Blow me down." I said, " what splendid chaps they are. It's another advance. They've taken what you sent from New York, all about the ice-floes, and they like it. Oh, well done ; isn't that terrific."

The consul, whom we'd rather forgotten, had been an interested spectator of this discovery of treasure trove.

" Well, that's just about a record," he said. " Nearly
all the yachts who arrive here are broke. By the way,
I suppose the two of you are still on speaking terms, are
you ? That's another of our specialities here. As soon
as yachts arrive, as often as not every member of the
crew packs a suitcase and catches a ship back home. The
owner then sells the boat for a quarter of its value and
follows in the next ship but one."

" Oh no," we assured him, " we're not in the least fed
up with things yet. In fact we're rather enjoying ourselves."

Indeed, we were so delighted with life that we took a
taxi back to the Yacht Club again and had lunch ashore
for a change.

There's no tide at Cristobal, so the Yacht Club have
built finger-jetties in front of the clubhouse where the
boats lie moored in tidy rows. The masts made black
romantic patterns against the sky as darkness fell, and
we often used to sit and speculate on the stories of each.
For nearly every boat had a story of some sort attached
to her. Some, like ourselves, were merely pausing. Others
as the consul had told us were dreams that had come to
a sad end : boats which had started off on a long voyage
and ended up here unexpectedly, sold to provide the passage
money to take their crews home. Others again were lying
uncertainly, wondering which category they would fall into.

Our next door neighbour was one of these. A big ketch
called *Wapi*, she had been sailed from England en route
for Australia by a charming couple and a penniless Spanish
author. The boat's owner was an eccentric individual who
had failed to give them any money, and they were now
stranded, waiting to see if any would turn up. Jill used
to go on board to do her ironing and to talk to Marjory,
the captain's wife, for they had a large table in their
saloon. In return for the use of it, Jill lent Marjory her
iron, a paraffin one of which we were very proud.

DINNER TIME: THE CABIN WITH ALL STORES EMBARKED

There was quite a village atmosphere about the whole of the yacht harbour, and a great deal of visiting went on between the crews. Besides *Wapi* there were two other boats in our neighbourhood with whom we became particularly friendly. The first of these belonged to an American called ' Skip,' who was engaged in pottering round the world, pausing here and there for a year or two in the process as the spirit moved him. He always kept his boat speckless and immaculate, and he was busy wondering, when we first met him, whether to sell her and build another bigger, better, faster one. Jill, of course, wanted to marry him off. " He's such a NICE person," she said, " he SHOULD be married." The final member of our circle was the tiniest boat in the Club, called *Taki O Autohi*, which, so her owner told us, means ' Southern Cross ' in Maori. He had built her himself in England, and was now going home to New Zealand with an American as crew. We took a particular liking to them, because after an hour or two spent in their cabin *Salmo* seemed as big as a liner when we got back to her again. They left to go through the Canal four days after we arrived, and I went with them to help handle ropes and to see what the Canal looked like, before we embarked on the journey ourselves. There wasn't room on board for Jill to come too, so she stayed behind with a very bad grace, and, so I later discovered, threw a gigantic party to make up for what she thought she had missed.

Thanks to our five hundred dollars we were able to spend two arduous days reprovisioning. Most of our wants came from a Greek ship-chandler with a name like Popoulopoulos, but it was in the market that Jill really enjoyed herself, haggling with the old ladies who sold fruit and vegetables and indefatigably going from one stall to another comparing the great gaudy heaps of oranges, lemons, bananas and peppers while the crowds pushed and shouted and spat all round her. Some of the peppers she bought nearly proved our undoing, for she made them into a salad under the mistaken impression that they were cold ones. We had both filled our mouths before we realised that they weren't. Cold water wasn't the slightest use in dousing the fires they made, and we learnt caution the hard way.

One day a large American yacht called *Seafarer* came into harbour bestrung with washing lines from which hung festoons of nappies and children's clothes. The crew, so we learned, consisted of two families with five children between them, ranging in age from eight down to practically nothing. They had come from Miami and were bound for Los Angeles.

The whole ship's company came on board to visit us the next morning, and after showing them round we told them of our engine difficulties, wondering if they would give us a tow. They were delighted with the idea, and said it would make a good incident to include in the film they were making of their journey. They hoped, they said, to sell it to a television show called ' Bold Journey ' when they got back to Los Angeles.

We didn't think much of this remark at the time, but later on we were to hear more of the scheme.

The Hathaways (as they were called) didn't stay long on board, for the children grew restless in *Salmo's* cramped quarters and soon began to demand to go back. "Besides," said Charles, the skipper, " we've a lot of work to get through. The pilot's due on board at half-past five to-morrow morning. You'd better come alongside tonight and then we'll be all ready to get away quickly."

We did this, and arrived to find *Seafarer's* deck fairly bustling with activity. Although there were only five altogether, there seemed to be children everywhere ; clambering in the rigging, falling over ropes, and dragging fenders everywhere more or less as directed by their elders. They seized our lines enthusiastically and we moored *Salmo*

very securely, so that we could forget about her on passage
and transform ourselves into extra crew for *Seafarer* who,
being inboard at all the locks, would take any bumps that
were going.

It was very early indeed when we got up, and still quite
dark. Jill made breakfast and then we hung about impatiently waiting for the pilot to arrive, while mosquitoes
buzzed viciously round our heads and dived at our bare
legs. Alongside we could see that *Seafarer* too was astir.
Their saloon porthole was open and we smiled as we
heard a voice come floating out of it, " But, Mummy, I
don't WANT any more." They too, apparently were having
breakfast, and the younger members were crotchety about
such an early one.

Slowly the sky began to lighten. It turned from dark-
blue to green, the stars faded and we began to see
things more plainly. A car drew up in front of the club,
its headlights blazing, a figure left it and came striding
towards us with an attaché case in his hands. It was
the pilot.

Seafarer had her engine ticking over by the time he
arrived, and a few minutes later, still in the half-light,
we slipped quietly out from the jetty and headed for the
first lock. The approach took us close past thick over-
hanging jungle, and two parrots squawked and flew low
over our heads, while brown pelicans dived into the water ;
everything seemed wild and tropical and exciting.

The lock looked huge as we came into it. Two tiny
figures high overhead threw heaving-lines which snaked
down and hit the deck with heavy thuds. Then they
hauled our mooring-lines up and up and up to the top
of the wall. The gates shut astern, and almost before
we could get our battery of tyres into position against
the rough-hewn rock walls, the sluices were opened. It
was just as if our two boats had been matches in a pot
of boiling water. First we swung out until the mooring-

lines twanged like harp-strings, and then an unexpected
sheer made the pair of us rush crazily at the wall while
Charles Hathaway stood biting his lip with worry. Two
big lorry-tyres took the impact and it flattened them like
pancakes, while the pull of the boats rising with the water
dragged them against the masonry. Nothing but a tyre
would have stood such treatment, but they survived it
and saved the hull from damage. There was a big cargo
ship in the lock ahead of us, held central by four ' mules,'
which are just little funicular engines with winches on
their roofs. As the lock-gates opened they shunted the
ship forward, climbing up steep ramps between the lower
and upper levels, while we followed quietly astern, using
the engine.

After the turmoil of the locks it was a relief to get out
into Gatun Lake. I had brought a large lump of ice
from the club in a bucket and put six cans of beer round
it, so we shared these out to give us an appetite for lunch.
Charles Hathaway had heard that you can catch some
sort of fearsome fish in the lake, so he trailed a hook the
size of a small anchor over the stern and the children
retired to the fo'c'sle where they blew bubbles. So each
of us was occupied after his own fashion. The pilot,
who wore purple socks and a baseball hat, steered. He
said it was a pleasant change from taking tankers through.

During the afternoon we went through the Culebra cut,
which is the bit of Canal that you usually see in photographs, where great slices of hillside have been dug away.
The pilot had great fun waving to his friends in the ships
bound the other way and having ribaldries shouted at
him in return ; he was one of the senior pilots, we discovered, and was assured by three people in succession
that if he got us through safely he could expect to graduate
to a banana boat within a year or two. Banana boats
apparently are used to give young pilots experience.

The downward locks were child's play so long as we

remembered to check out our mooring-lines. We just
sank gracefully, instead of diving about like restive colts
as we had done on the way up. We went in to the last
lock just as it was getting dark, and as the gates opened,
the pilot turned to me (we'd been talking ' Navy ' together,
for he too had been a regular) and said, " Well, there you
are. You're in the Pacific now." He said it jokingly,
but it gave both Jill and me a very real thrill ; for it
meant that another milestone had been passed and we
were on the threshold of a new and exciting stage of our
journey.

We had a farewell supper with the Hathaways at the
Balboa Yacht Club, and waved as they left the next
morning, motoring out into Panama Bay to make a good
offing before turning north. The last that we saw of them
was a glimpse of one of the children earnestly fishing over
the stern.

We wanted to paint ship. There's a good rise and fall
of tide at Balboa and we knew it would be our last chance
to have a cheap look at the bottom for many months to
come. Not having a copper sheathing we were always
worried about the state of our bottom-paint, for even a
small bare patch is enough to let Teredo worms get into
the wood ; and once in, they're dangerous shipmates, for
they eat their way backwards and forwards through the
planking, leaving just a thin crumbly skin instead of a
plank.

The beach beside the Yacht Club looked too rocky and
exposed for our purpose, so we scouted round and soon
found a good spot on the other side of the Canal up a sort
of sandy backwater. I chose a good billet where the sand
was clean and hard, and marked it very carefully by sticking up two pairs of driftwood marks above the high-water
line. By bringing the first pair of marks into transit we
knew where to leave the main channel, and then we simply
went along the line until the second pair came in line.

Once arrived at our chosen spot I laid out two anchors, and then we waited until the tide dropped us onto the bottom.

Jill had never done this before and was slightly worried by the procedure. " But how do you stop the boat falling over on her side when the water's all away ? " she asked. It was quite simple, I explained, we just lashed the two spinnaker-booms into position on either side so that they acted as legs.

As an afterthought I added that there wouldn't be much weight on them because the boat naturally wanted to sit upright on the flat of her keel.

" There you are, you see," I said proudly, two hours later, as we climbed over the side. *Salmo* had settled comfortably onto the sand and the water had dropped below the turn of the bilge. She looked as though she was standing on stilts.

" It doesn't look very secure," said Jill.

We were out of the boat now, wading up to our waists with scrubbers, rubbing at the thin green slime of weed at the waterline, and the few barnacles and other growths that the anti-fouling paint hadn't been able to cope with. I stepped back to have a look, and certainly *Salmo* DIDN'T look too secure. She seemed, in fact, to have developed a definite lean to port ; climbing overboard must have unsettled her.

Thirty seconds later there was a splintering crack and she subsided with a most almighty ' flump ' flat on her side, while the port leg, our beautiful spare spinnaker-boom, lay beneath her, snapped in two. Evidently spinnaker-booms weren't quite such good legs as I'd thought they were.

By midday the temperature had soared, and we were roasting after all our scrubbing. There wasn't a spot of shade on the whole beach, so we set up a camp ashore by standing Prout on his end and leaning him against two

oars. We then brought out our ice-bucket, a large jar of
water and a picnic lunch, and sat in the tiny patch of
shadow that he provided, surveying our poor prostrate
boat. The bump hadn't damaged her, but it was a
nuisance, because it prevented us from getting at the
underneath side, and besides that there was always the
thought of sleeping on board, tipped at a fifty-degree angle.

" Well, I'll be all right, anyway," said Jill brightly,
" my bunk's on the downhill side, it'll be you that gets
rolled out. What'll you do ? sleep on the deck or trust
to your leeboard ? "

" Use the deck, I think," I answered gloomily. I'd
done it before and remembered that the side of Jill's bunk
which would take half my weight became remarkably hard
after an hour or two.

After our picnic we roused ourselves reluctantly and
finished our scrubbing ; then we dragged out a tin of
undercoating and spent two long hours painting while the
sun glared down from overhead and the white sand
shimmered with heat.

Rather unexpectedly, it turned out to be green paint
instead of the red we had ordered, and after we'd finished
we spent a long time standing back and comparing the
port side with the starboard, wondering which we liked
best.

By teatime there was nothing more that we could do,
and as we didn't expect to refloat until ten we had a lot
of time on our hands. The thought of spending more
time than we had to in a standing-on-its-side cabin didn't
appeal very much, so we decided to go beach-combing
instead, and soon found it was an excellent beach for the
purpose. Not only was there a mass of shells, but the
sand itself was alive with hermit crabs. Each one of these
strange little creatures had found a shell for himself, which
he carried round on his back, but often managed to do so
only with the greatest difficulty. Quite obviously there

was a good deal of keeping up with the Jones's in their way of life. Some of the most unsuitable crabs had moved into enormous country mansions of shells when what they needed was clearly a much more bijou little residence which they could move about in comfort. We spent hours, off and on, in the next few days, watching them and comparing our finds. We also began to collect margin shells to take home as poker counters. It was our aim to get five hundred and quite soon we'd got them.

It was while we were sorting these through on our return on board that Jill turned all sentimental. She found that some of the shells contained very tiny hermit crabs, and the thought of them dying on board from lack of food horrified her.

" You must put them all back," she said.

" But we've just spent an hour and a half collecting them," I remonstrated, " and, besides, it's only a few of the shells that have crabs in them."

Finally we came to a compromise. Jill solemnly took each of the five hundred shells in turn and checked it carefully for inhabitants. Those that had them she ceremoniously tipped back into the water. Those that remained, we put into a tin and stowed in the bilges.

The moon rose after supper, so we went for a last walk beside the water to discuss our future plans. Everyone in the Balboa Yacht Club had been very depressing about our prospects of making the Galapagos under sail alone. It was quite the wrong time of year for one thing, they told us, Christmas was the right time to go, and besides, how would we manage when we found ourselves in the Humboldt current ? Didn't we know it ran at four knots right through the Galapagos ? And how would we ever get clear of Panama Bay with no engine ? People had often been becalmed there for weeks on end.

" Well, what do you think ? " said Jill. " Are we mad to try and go, or aren't we ? "

" No, I don't think so," I replied, " I think, almost,
that we'd be madder if we DIDN'T. After all, it's one of
the places that we've come all this way especially to see.
It'd be rather feeble to give up without even trying. And
besides, most of these people who talk the loudest don't
really KNOW anything. It's not as if any of them had
ever tried to sail there at this time of year in any sort of
boat, let alone one like *Salmo*. How can they know what
it'll be like ? "

We sat down on a log of driftwood, our minds made
up. To hell with what people said. After all, it was we
who would suffer if we did something silly, so surely it
must remain our privilege to decide what was sensible
and what wasn't. " We'll always listen to advice," we
decided, " but won't necessarily take it."

" Do you know," said Jill suddenly, after we'd sat silent
for a while, " I think it's an awfully good way to start
married life, this. It gives you a terrific sort of ' It's us
against the world ' spirit. At least not ' against ' exactly ;
that's the nice part about it, most people are terribly out
to help us. But it's we who are doing things, everyone
else just says how much they'd like to. But I bet they
wouldn't really, most of them."

" No," I agreed, " mostly they just think we're crazy.
Harmless on the whole, but definitely odd."

We fell silent. It was utterly lonely on the sandspit.
Two miles away, across the Canal, the lights of Balboa
shone like yellow pinpricks in the blue-black sky, but on
our side all was dark. Inshore there was a high bluff, and
in the moonlight the outline of the palms clinging to its
crest made a jagged frieze of the skyline ; the water lapped
nearly to our feet, and all the thousand night noises of the
tropics made a background to our thoughts.

" Yes," I said at length, " it's lovely now—just what
we'd hoped it would be. That's the glory of sailing. The
nasty bits and the frightening bits seem to fade very

quickly and just leave the pleasant times to linger in the memory. And another thing. I really do believe that this living right on top of each other that we do crams years of ordinary married life into just a few months. It's a kill or cure sort of experiment, I suppose, but it's certainly terrific fun if it turns out cure and not kill."

We rose to go. " Yes," said Jill, " we really ARE lucky. Just think of all the people there are in the world who HAVEN'T ever sat down on a log at night in the tropics, and looked at the stars and listened to the frogs booming. And all our worries are such NICE worries. They're real and concrete. Will the wind blow, or won't it ? Will the sea be rough ? Will we be hungry ? They're worrying enough in their way, I suppose, but at least they're straightforward."

A crab scuttled over her bare foot. She gave a yelp and we came back to earth again. " Race you back to the boat," she said.

By the time we'd climbed back on board and got to bed our mood of introspection had passed. The mechanics of life-on-a-severe-slant were too complicated to allow thought for anything else. Even the problem of disposing of tooth-paste water was magnified by the almost impossible tilt of the cockpit ladder.

At last our preparations were made, I blew out the lamp and we clambered into our respective places : Jill to her bunk, me to the deck.

Almost immediately there was a sharp " Ooh " from Jill.

" Well, now what is it ? " I asked.

" Bilge water," she replied crossly. " You can't have pumped her out this morning and it's all in the foot of my bunk. There's a great big pool of the stuff."

There was silence for a while, until I was very nearly asleep, and then she said, " You know, I think that the deck's probably a better place than the bunk to sleep. You wouldn't like to swap, would you ? "

" No," I said, remembering her earlier cockiness about owning the downhill bunk, " I wouldn't. Not in the least."

In due course we refloated, but this time I was quite determined that when we touched down again we should remain upright. Jill, if anything, was even more determined on this point than I was. She said she thought that she'd almost certainly develop rheumatism from lying in a damp bunk, and that if she did she wasn't going to do any more painting. No, not even if I begged her, she wasn't.

We had found a huge bamboo pole on the beach and were going to use it to replace the broken spinnaker-boom as a leg. In addition we intended to run out lines from the masthead to anchors dug into the sand to act as additional stays. As soon as we felt the keel bump gently on the bottom once more after two short hours of vertical existence, we clambered reluctantly from our bunks and out on deck into the darkness. The moon had set and a chilly pre-dawn breeze made us shiver through our pyjamas.

It was agreed that I should lay out the two anchors while Jill lashed the legs, so I tumbled over the side and splashed my way through the neck-deep water carrying an anchor in my arms. First one and then the other, I laboriously dug into place, and then returned to find Jill peering over the stern in a crestfallen way, a bit of rope dangling in her hand.

I was shivering with cold by this time and impatient to get back to bed. " Well, have you finished lashing the legs yet ? " I asked.

" No. At least I've done one all right, but it's a very funny thing, I can't find the bamboo. I lashed it to this rope before we went to bed and now it's gone."

" What sort of knot did you use ? "

" Well, I thought it was a rolling hitch, but I suppose it couldn't have been. They're funny things, rolling hitches with me, sometimes they do hitch and sometimes they don't. Oh I AM sorry."

I was sorry too. Absolutely livid in fact, and I stumped off down the water's edge in high dudgeon to see if I could find the pole again, muttering ruderies about Jill and her something, something, rolling hitches. Fortunately it hadn't strayed far, and I returned on board slightly mollified to find that she had some cocoa waiting as a peace offering. We finished off lashing the pole in place, tested the pull of the lines to the anchors, and then retired to bed again with cups in our hands, quite well pleased with ourselves, saying that it would need something really quite remarkable to happen to let us topple over again this time.

It was soon after lunch that the remarkable duly began happening. A thunderstorm, black as ink, came coursing down the line of the Canal from the direction of Gatun. Still in blazing sunshine, we worked feverishly to get the painting finished before we should be engulfed. Terrific peals of thunder and streaks of lightning heralded the storm's approach, and then quite suddenly it hit us. We had finished painting by this time and had taken all our bits and pieces back on board *Salmo*, so we clambered on board ourselves, pulled the spray hood over the hatch, and settled down to sit the storm out.

A quite terrific lightning flash blinded us for a moment, and right on its heels came a deafening peal of thunder : a roar like a fifteen-inch gun.

" What do you think ? " I asked. " I know that trees attract lightning. Sitting all alone on the sand like we are, do you think we'll attract it too ? "

Neither of us knew the answer to that one, but we didn't like the idea in the least. After some discussion we decided to bail out and go and sit on the beach until it blew over. Better to be cold than electrocuted, we felt, and scrambled hurriedly down onto the sand as further blinding flashes and shattering roars assailed us.

The rain was pelting down like a waterfall, carving runnels in the sand, roaring on *Salmo*'s decks, hissing in the sea, and it battered at us through our thin clothes. In thirty seconds we were as wet as if we'd been swimming and it was bitterly cold in the wind. Down below we hadn't realised how strong the wind was. The beach seemed quite untenable. " Let's go into the water," we shouted to each other, above the uproar. Cowering in the sea with only our noses exposed it was certainly warmer, but we wondered very much what happened if lightning struck the water. It was a case of being perfectly certain that each place we chose to stay in was the wrong one. *Salmo* was wrong, the beach was wrong and now the water was wrong. So we stayed in the water.

The very centre of the storm soon came. The roar of thunder was almost continuous, and the wind fairly shrieked in *Salmo's* rigging. The palms on the bluff, seen through the rain dimly, though they were only two hundred yards away, were turned inside out like broken umbrellas, their long fronds flung before the blast. One of the mast-lines we had rigged was now taking all the strain, it was as taut as a bowstring, while the other hung limp and slack.

There was a final squeal of wind. The anchor pulled itself out of the sand, and *Salmo* was hurled flat onto her side once more.

We forgot our fright in worrying about her, wondering whether the jar would spring her planks apart, but there was nothing we could do till the storm passed.

At last it did. The intervals between the flashes and the thunder grew longer and longer ; the wind and rain eased ; and then, quite quickly, it grew light again. In half an hour things were back to normal, the sun shone, and we fearfully went to inspect the hull for signs of damage. Almost miraculously there was none. Even the paintwork hadn't been marked, so far as we could see, and this time our new-found bamboo pole hadn't been broken, it had just fallen flat beneath the hull and was dug into the sand undamaged.

When we got back to the Yacht Club next day we found that we had been luckier than they had. Their jetty was lined with big steel lockers for boat-owners to keep their sails, their spare gear and their outboard engines in, and the whole massive contrivance had been lifted bodily up in the air and flung into the water, tearing away a long length of tubular railing as it went. For days afterwards disconsolate owners were trying to recover their property with borrowed aqualungs.

CHAPTER TEN

INTO THE WILDS

JILL had a mass of ironing to do and swore that she couldn't POSSIBLY be ready to sail by nine o'clock, so I left her to it and rowed ashore to the Yacht Club, where the secretary had collected a bunch of letters for delivery among the Galapagos Islands. I thumbed quickly through the pile he gave me, and even the addresses sounded romantic and last frontierish : Wittmer, Floreana Island ; Angermeyer, Academy Bay : and one quite simply was directed to ' Kastdalen.'

I rowed back to *Salmo* mouthing the names over to myself, wondering what sort of people they would turn out to be. It was like reading through a theatre programme before the curtain rises.

Somehow or other Jill WAS ready in time, so we slipped our mooring and headed seaward, the ebb bustling beneath our tail to make up for the lack of wind. One by one we passed the channel buoys marking the Canal approach, and by dinner-time we were well out into the bay. The weather was roasting, but it was a moist clammy sort of heat that bred thunderstorms.

For four days and four nights storms passed over us one after the other, spitting lightning out of inky clouds, roaring thunder, and spewing rain that hissed and pelted into the sea, turning the surface from black to silver with its impact. Sometimes we'd climb into the cockpit during these downpours with bars of soap, lather ourselves all over and sluice ourselves clean with buckets of rainwater collected from the sails, but at other times we'd be kept too busy reefing. Slowly, however, thunderstorm by thunderstorm, we slid farther and farther from Panama and deeper into the Pacific.

Between the thunderstorms we just lay idle ; the idleness of a ping-pong ball on a jet of water. Poor *Salmo* used to lean and toss and roll in the tired, left-over waves, the boom, in spite of all the lashings we could contrive for it, creaking and banging, and the foresail slatting against the rigging with petulant flicks. It was a wearing time both for the sails and for our tempers, for we longed to get moving.

One morning, while a larger than usual thunderstorm was approaching, it sent out as its harbinger a strong north-easterly wind. To us, scrabbling desperately for south-westerly miles, it was too good a gift to neglect, so we quickly set the spinnaker and wondered, as we did so, how long we would dare to carry it. Just as I'd finished hoisting, zzzZZZTT went our fishing-line and Jill grabbed up the rod from its lashing. At once it bent nearly double and . . zzZZTT went the reel once more. " Oh, I can't hold it. I can't hold it ! " she yelled ; " you come ! " I dived aft and grabbed the rod from her. This time, certainly, we were on to something big. I applied the brake to the reel as hard as I dared, and worked furiously at the rod, dipping and hoisting it, winning a few inches of line at each dip. *Salmo* in the meanwhile had come to life with a vengeance. The spinnaker was dragging her through the water like a team of mustangs ; the bow-wave foamed and roared.

" Hurry up and get the fish in," said Jill, " I'd like to get the spinnaker off her again."

I looked up at the approaching cloud, black as ink, the rain joining it to the sea like a dusky pillar, and I looked at the fishing-line stretched taut as a bar, and I felt the thrilling tug of a big fish fighting.

We were both torn with indecision. Should we hold onto the fish or the spinnaker?

At that moment the fish leaped—a blue and silver flash from the dark water—and in doing so signed his death warrant. We couldn't let him go after that.

A flash of lightning lit the world and a roar of thunder came hard on its heels. The fish was tiring and at each dip I was able to wind in more and more line. *Salmo* tore through the water. " Oh, hurry up. Oh, DO hurry up,". murmured Jill; " but isn't he a WHOPPER! We'll be able to live on fish for days. Oh, DO get a hold of him."

One last furious heave and I got the fish alongside. Jill, her eyes riveted on the straining sails and one hand holding the madly vibrating tiller, reached the gaff over to me and I hooked it into his gills. A moment more and the brute was inboard. I dumped him flapping in the cockpit just as the rain reached us, and with it the wind —hard, angry wind. I leaped for the halliard, dousing the sail before it should be torn away. Free of its pull *Salmo* calmed down, and we had leisure to admire our catch. It was a big blue dolphin (the fish, not the mammal) and must have weighed all of twenty pounds. They are beautifully coloured creatures when newly caught, having all sorts of brilliant blues down the back and shimmering silver underneath ; but out of the water they quickly lose all their beauty and after an hour become quite drab.

As soon as we managed to fight our way clear of the Panamanian calms and into an area of steadier breezes (albeit from ahead) our thoughts began to turn towards the problem of Crossing the Line, for Jill had never yet done this.

I spent hours trying to remember the more important points of procedure from bygone courts I had attended in various H.M. ships, but it was hard work. It was complicated, too, by the fact that I realised I'd have to do most of the talking. Jill, a neophyte, could hardly be called on, for example, to be her own bear and barber.

Gradually the scheme took shape, so I drafted out a rough certificate for Jill (the ship's artist) to turn into something pretty, ready for later presentation, but with blanks left in it for the date and other such last-minute details.

The Equator runs slap through the Galapagos group, and we were uncertain which would come first, landfall or Line, so on the appointed day, twenty miles from Baltra Island, I took a sight and found we had only three miles of northern hemisphere left to go. It was a glorious morning, sunny and calm with a steady breeze ruffling the water, we therefore left *Salmo* to look after herself and she trotted on shorewards at a steady four knots while we played.

I had already written out the dialogue for the occasion so, while Jill made a trident from three forks stuck through a crossbar lashed to our broom-handle, I retired to the cabin to put on a baggywinkle beard, a paper crown, and our regal-looking yellow oilskin embellished with a sexy black nylon sailbag by way of a cloak.

At eleven o'clock, as nearly as I could calculate, we had reached the right spot, so I flung open the fore-hatch and in my rôle of Neptune addressed *Salmo's* ship's company :—

" I am King Neptune, the Lord of the Deep.
All who sail through my realm must my ordinance keep.
My Kingdom extends from the ice of the Poles
To the tropical depths where the Coelocanth rolls ;
But by precedent, custom, and ageless belief
Of all of my Palaces, THIS is the chief.
Here on EQUATOR in grave majesty
I receive at my court those who sail on the sea.

I administer justice and homage accept
From such of my subjects whose wand'rings have
    kept
Them exclusively (so far) on one side of my line
And neglected attending a levée of mine.

Whose is this ship ? And what is her name ?
Why do you come here ? And which of you claim
To be Seafarers true who have paid to my court
Obeisance proper and thus furnished sport
For my bears and my barber, my wife and myself
And received in exchange neither lucre nor pelf
But CERTIFICATE proper of CROSSING THE LINE.
Declare yourselves straight : Are ye subjects of
    Mine ? "

To which, as *Salmo's* captain (my crown and trident had
to be hastily stuffed back down the fore-hatch for this),
I replied :—

" O Master of the stormy main
I bid you my respects again
This vessel *Salmo* is yclept
And, Sire, I trust that you'll accept
Her crew of two. In order due
I'll give account of them to you.

The first is me. I've sailed the sea
Since the age of one (nineteen twenty-three).*
I crossed the Line in 'thirty-nine,
But I come here now with this wife of mine ;
She's a comely lass, and brave and true
But she has some faults, I must own to you.

* I was brought back from India in a P. & O. liner at this age. The
rhyme was too good a one to miss.

NEPTUNE replies :

> " What are these faults ?   Be they great or small ?
> Come speak up, man, I must hear them all
> That I may judge if she be fit
> To receive of me a CERTIFICATE."

ME: "Well, Sire, the first is a wondrous thirst
At the strangest times it afflicts her worst
In bed or on watch she's like to burst
Unless I flap to a pump or tap
And draw a draught, her drought to stap
Or she's far too cold (if she's not too hot)
She's never happy with what she's got.
But sire I pray (for my brain is weak)
May I stop this verse and plainly speak ?

NEPTUNE : " Certainly, my good man. It's beginning to
pall with me too. But it's customary, you know, on
these occasions. To start with at any rate. But come,
come. What other offences has the girl committed.
These sound mere feminine trifles ; why my Good
Queen is just the same. Only last week she. . . . "

SCRIBO (the Clerk of the Court, and rather a nasty bit of
work, interrupts) : " HRRRRRRRRMPH."

NEPTUNE : " Of course. Of course. Let me consult the
records. SCRIBO ! "

SCRIBO : " Sire ? "

NEPTUNE : " Have we any charges against this wench ? "

SCRIBO : " Yes, Sire. It has been represented to us (by a
brown Pelican named Percival, who observed the incident with abhorrence) that on the 21st day of August
this GILLIAN HAMILTON did willingly, wantonly, and
wholly without grounds, refuse passage to certain of
your Majesty's subjects desirous of seeing the world,

to wit certain hermit crabs residing at the Port of
BALBAO.   This woman, Sire, despite and notwith-
standing the directly expressed wishes of her MOS1
EXCELLENT HUSBAND, did cast back these crabs from
the accommodation provided for them in the forepeak
of the aforementioned YACHT *Salmo* and now, Sire,
they languish still, most miserably, at BALBOA."

NEPTUNE : " Is this true, Woman ? "
JILL (who at last has a chance to speak) : " It is, Sire,
but . . ."

NEPTUNE : " It is a grievous and wanton crime.   And
grievously must you be punished therefore.   I shall
consider the sentence."

He pauses.

" The Sentence is decided.   Thou art to be DUNKED
by our Royal Hand, three times, over the stern of
thy vessel.   After that, when, with proper humility,
you have confessed yourself repentant of your un-
kindness to my subjects, the hermit crabs, you may
consider yourself a fully-fledged seadog [my wife dis-
likes the term seabitch] and you may SPIT TO WIND-
WARD whenever you have the inclination and ability
to do so."

After pronouncing sentence, I duly picked Jill up and
retired aft to dunk her as scheduled.   It turned out,
however, to be a remarkably difficult operation.   Having
manoeuvred her, at last, into a head-down position, I
shifted my grasp to her ankles and placed one foot on
the bumpkin.   Dunk one.

It was during dunk two that disaster nearly overcame
us, for *Salmo* gave a most unexpected lurch and flung me
off balance.   My only hope of staying on board seemed to
be to let go with one hand and grab the backstay.   I
did this, praying that my left hand would be strong enough

to retain its grip on Jill's ankle. It was, but only just. Considerably shaken, we completed dunk three and returned to the cockpit, Jill still slightly spluttery and wondering what the something, something I'd been playing at to go and dip her in as deeply as all that during the second dunk. " I thought for a moment you'd dropped me," she said.

I explained to her that I'd slipped and very nearly gone overboard as well. " Wow," she replied, " what a way to finish off the cruise. Give me that certificate quick before anything else happens to us ! "

We had a drink to stiffen our morale. As I went to get it so we sighted Baltra Island, a greyish-green lump fine on the starboard bow. Baltra was one of the islands we didn't intend to visit, because we'd rationed ourself to a month for the whole group, deciding to concentrate on two or three places we were particularly interested in and leave the rest until, perhaps, a later occasion. We therefore started a brisk discussion as to where we SHOULD go to. A place called Wreck Bay was the official entry port, and the consul at Cristobal from whom we'd got clearance papers had been most insistant that we should go there first to report ourselves. " It will avoid unpleasantness," he had said.

Wreck Bay is nearly forty miles from Baltra, and against the current at that, so we weren't at all enthusiastic about going. " What do you suppose will happen if we don't bother ? " Jill asked. We discussed the point for a while and decided that, since there was a gunboat stationed in the area, they'd probably find us sooner or later and then arrest us. Goodness knows what would happen then. Probably, we said, we would be given a million peso fine : five hundred thousand for the government and five hundred thousand for the man who levied it.

We were still feeling a bit doubtful about Ecuadorian government ethics after our fortunate discovery at Panama that entry papers taken out at Cristobal (where the Consul was new and presumably inexperienced) cost fifteen American dollars, whereas exactly the same thing at the Embassy at Panama cost eighty. We, needless to say, had got the cheap variety.

" Oh, well," we finally decided, " since we've been legal so far, we might as well go on being," so we rather reluctantly shaped a course for Wreck Bay, consoling ourselves with the reflection that it was a course which *Salmo* could hold without attention and that we should get a good night's rest.

At breakfast time it was misty, then, suddenly, halfway through the meal, out of the mist loomed Barrington Island. Now Barrington was one of the places we *did* want to go to, so we sat looking at each other for a few moments with our mouths full. " Well, shall we ? " we said. " Yes, let's," we answered. " To hell with legality, we'll forget about Wreck Bay and just see what happens." For obviously it had been an omen that *Salmo* should have strayed here, five miles off her course, while we slept.

We had been told that there was a wonderful anchorage at Barrington but didn't know where it was, so we aimed for a likely looking spot and steered inshore to investigate. The sun came out and sucked the mist away as we washed the dishes, and soon we began to see the land more clearly. It was a rugged place, pocked with old volcano craters and overgrown with thorny scrub. The water seemed deep, so we closed to within a hundred yards of the shore and began coasting along, our binoculars eagerly scouring the hillside for signs of life.

The first things we saw were a couple of sea-lions asleep on the rocks, and soon afterwards a goat picking its way through the bushes. Of the anchorage, however, there was no trace at all. The island is only about three miles from end to end, and we had nearly reached its southeastern corner when we suddenly stumbled on what we were looking for : a little lagoon blocked on its seaward side by an island with a row of prickly cactus-trees sticking up from it. I climbed to the masthead to see if I could see how to get in.

From that height, and with the sun behind us, the shallows showed up plainly, a dull brown colour, in contrast to the deep blue of the open sea and the brilliant luminous green of the sand-bottomed lagoon. The entrance stood out very clearly and consisted of a narrow channel on the far side of the island which, on its nearer side, was entirely foul (indeed, at low water, so we later discovered, one could wade across). I directed Jill from my lofty perch, conning her in and giving a running commentary at the same time :

" Port a little, no a little more. That's fine. Oh, look ! There are two turtles swimming just up ahead. And do you see, out to port there, there's a sea-lion asleep on the rocks. My gosh, it looks a lovely sandy beach up at the end there. Perfect for bathing, I should think. Lot of rocks all over it, but white, white sand in between. Oh, look at the gannets. Fairly whizzing down. Just like dive bombers. . . . No, back to starboard again a shade."

" Oh for goodness' sake come down from there," said Jill. " You haven't got the anchor ready or anything, and how on earth CAN I look at all the things you're talking about when I'm trying to do all the work down here alone. Oh gosh. Is that the turtle you were talking about? Just LOOK at him, he's right alongside. Could we eat one do you think ? "

I climbed back on deck again, but only very reluctantly. Never in my life had I seen so many birds and beasts and fishes all at one time before. And none of them seemed to care a damn about us. Even the turtles hardly bothered to swim out of the way.

We anchored in a sort of trance. The water was so clear that as I let go the chain I could see it flying down into the luminous depths and the anchor dragging up a cloud of sand as it dug itself into the bottom thirty feet below.

As we lowered and stowed away the sails two small birds came on board and one flew straight into the cabin, where it sat, quite unperturbed, on the edge of the table. " Oh, the little devil," said Jill. " It's made a mess on my clean shirt " ; but there was more affection than anger in her tone.

We could hardly wait to get the Prout into the water and then bundle into it ourselves, loaded down with cameras, spare films and exposure meters. " Where shall we go to first?" I asked. " Let's go in to the beach there," said Jill, " and see if we can stalk back out along the rocks and get close to one of the sea-lions and take a photograph of it. That's where they mostly seem to lie, on the rocks."

I was rowing and Jill sat in the stern wriggling about with excitement as we went in, determined not to miss anything. " Oh, look," she said, " Pelicans. White ones this time. They're much more fun than the brown kind. Aren't they clumsy compared with the gannets. Just look at them landing. They come flying in close to the water and then just sort of stop and seem to fall over themselves and trip on their noses. Just as if the engine had failed unexpectedly."

Suddenly she seemed to freeze where she sat, and her mouth fell open. " What on earth's the matter ? " I asked.

" Oh, my goodness ! " she said ; " you know all those rocks we saw littered about on the sand ? Well they aren't rocks at all. They're sea-lions ! There must be HUNDREDS of them. Literally hundreds. Oh heavens, what do we do ? Can we go and land all in amongst them ? "

I stopped rowing and looked over my shoulder. Sure enough, now that we were closer, I could see plainly enough. The whole beach (it was only about a couple of hundred yards long) was absolutely packed, five and six deep, with a mass of sea-lions.

" I know what we'll do," said Jill suddenly. " You land me here in among the rocks at the side, and I'll creep up very gently to the edge of the beach. And then you row the Prout right into the middle of them and we'll see what they do. It should make a perfectly SPLENDID movie."

" Like hell," I said. " They're probably fierce. They've got young ones with them and they may not like people Prouting all round them."

" Oh, go on. Surely you're not FRIGHTENED, are you ? "

" Yes, I am," I said, " very frightened. You do it and I'll take the film."

" Nonsense. It was MY idea. On you go."

Very reluctantly indeed, on I went. Jill crept over the rocks like a senile and rather overloaded Red Indian, and then set up shop with the camera, tripod and exposure meter just offstage of the beach in the prompt corner and gave a sort of ' On men, follow me ' wave to indicate that she was ready. With a sinking heart I started Prouting.

Very, very clearly in my mind's eye I was able to visualise what would happen in the next minute and a half. First the sea-lions would gaze at Prout with surprise, and then with anger. As I began to disembark they would charge, surrounding me, and Jill in her corner would film and film as they sank their teeth in my legs. I could even hear, in my tortured imagination, young voices shouting on a wet winter afternoon, " Oh, Mummy, DO let's see that LOVELY film of daddy being bitten by the sea-lions."

I gritted my teeth and rowed on, but much to my surprise all went very well indeed. The sea-lions behaved just exactly as I would imagine the members of the Athenæum might behave if someone stalked into their smoking-room without any clothes on. One-half, those nearest to me, hooted furiously and lumbered from their armchairs and into the sea ; presumably to complain to the secretary. The other half, after a couple of scandalised glares and a hoot or two apiece, just relapsed once more into slumbrous positions, and I could almost see them lifting up their copies of ' The Times ' to block out this appalling intrusion upon their privacy.

We went nearly crazy for the next few days and filmed and filmed and filmed. The sea-lions, as subjects, were unbeatable. They loved to lie in the sun at the water's edge and go to sleep. As the tide rose, small wavelets would reach them and they'd stir uneasily and glare around disapprovingly as if to see who it was that was taking liberties. Finally, by the time that their tummies were awash, they'd rise with great dignity, lumber six feet up the beach and then slump back on the warm sand, ready to repeat the performance ten minutes later.

We tried, two or three times, to go in amongst them, but unless we actually found one asleep, as we quite often did, it was only the young who were willing to make friends ; the adults would wait until one was about six feet away, and then waddle into the sea. The babies had no such qualms. Jill used to love turning herself into a brightly coloured sea-lion in her red shirt and blue trousers and worm her way up to the young ones and pet them on the nose and talk to them and let them sniff at her hair.

On my birthday we decided to be really energetic, to tear ourselves away from the beach and climb to the top of the highest crater. We had heard that Barrington was one of the places where there are still a few Galapagos (the giant tortoises) left, and we hoped that we might meet one.

It was a weird climb. Underfoot the ground was all of broken lava, and every few hundred yards we found little baby craters rearing up from the scrub. Acacia and huge bloated cactuses grew everywhere, and so did some sort of lichen, so the effect was of walking through a greyish-green dream-world. Dead trees lay in gnarled and impossible shapes like modern sculpture, and it was almost with relief that we reached the lip of the big main crater which was our goal. Ahead and beneath us stretched a vast bowl, fully two miles across, misty green in colour and mottled with smaller craters. " The mountains of the moon must be just like this," we said to each other as we gazed out over the desolation. It was very silent up there ; almost uncanny in fact, and it was reassuring to turn round and catch a glimpse of *Salmo*, no bigger-looking than a toy, floating in her glittering green lagoon a thousand feet below.

After taking some photographs we began to trundle down again, rejoicing in the easy movement after the gruelling ascent, loaded as we were with our movie-making bits and pieces. Jill had baked me a birthday cake, and the prospect of tea was alluring, so we began to trot.

Quite near the beach we stumbled on a huge iguana with a dragon-spiked collar which scuttled from beneath our feet into a crevice beneath a boulder ; but there were no signs of any Galapagos. There had been so much else to see, however, that we hardly missed them and burst onto the beach in high good humour panting and with the sweat pouring off us. The sea looked cool and inviting, so heedless of the sea-lions we tore off our clothes and dived in. It was gloriously cool and invigorating, for the Humboldt current that sweeps through the islands, bringing fish and penguins with it, makes the water Mediterranean rather than tropical in temperature.

I grew tired of the water sooner than Jill and idly thought as I began to dress in the sunshine at the back of the beach what a wonderful existence it was that we were now living : eating when we felt hungry, bathing when we felt hot, and with nothing and no one to dictate to us. Jill was now engaged in sticking out her tongue at a particularly large and choleric-looking sea-lion who was swimming just beside her.

'Just look at her,' I thought to myself, 'there goes the ci-devant stage manager of the Theatre Royal at Windsor. It's less than a year since she was working in the theatre. Wouldn't all her audiences be surprised to see her now.'

Possibly they might have been, but if they'd stayed on for just another few moments they'd have been positively electrified. The sea-lion suddenly grew bored with his purely passive role in the game and decided to enliven it. He leaped from the water with an almighty splash and flung himself straight at Jill, hurtling along the surface of the water for all the world like a water-polo ball, powerfully flung.

Jill never hesitated. She gave a blood-curdling shriek and dashed out of the water. With a great flapping of arms and legs she galloped over the silver sand to where I stood gaping with astonishment.

" Did you see that ? " she said indignantly. " He CHASED me ! "

The sea-lion grinning enormously through his whiskers, swerved seaward and departed looking pleased with himself. " That'll teach her to make faces at me," he seemed to be saying.

We left the next day, and having determined to forget all about going to Wreck Bay and being official, headed for Post Office Bay in Floreana, about twenty miles away. Post Office Bay is one of the touristic musts of the Galapagos Islands. It is a bay that was much favoured by the sperm whalers in the days of Moby Dick, when voyages might last three years or more, and those who put in there for water and fresh meat used to leave mail in a barrel at the back of the beach in the hopes that the next arrival might be homeward bound. The barrel, so we had heard, or A barrel anyway, still existed. We half

hoped too that there might be some mail in it left by some
other yacht that we could deliver.

Apart from that, all that we knew of Floreana was that
it was a much bigger island than Barrington, being about
twelve miles long and more than two thousand feet high
in places ; and that there were two farms on it, one of
which belonged to the Wittmers whose mail we carried.

We had no idea whereabouts on the island the Wittmers
lived, except that it was ' up back in the hills,' so as we
coasted along looking for the post-office barrel we kept
our eyes skinned for signs of life ashore. There wasn't a
trace of it. There were no sea-lions, no goats, no smoke,
nothing. Nothing but thorn-bushes.

At length, late in the evening, we sighted a strange
white erection like a totem pole in the scrub at the back
of the beach, and conning carefully from the masthead
(for we had found some nasty outlying ledges), stood in
and anchored a short way from the shore. As soon as
the sails were stowed we flung the Prout in the water and
paddled in to investigate. On close approach the object
looked more like a totem pole than ever, and we saw that
it stood in a little sand clearing bordered with white-
painted stones. Finally we found that it WAS a barrel
after all, mounted on a two-foot length of telegraph pole,
but it was so much covered over with baroque doodlements
and diddlements that it was hard to discern the basic
core from the later additions. In the front of the barrel
was a little hinged door, and over the top was a jaunty
canvas roof painted red and marked, ' Brigantine *Yankee*
Seventh World Voyage.' Much to our disappointment
there were no letters inside, so we settled down to a detailed
study and saw that the whole structure was covered with
the names of yachts ; carved on little signposts ; written
in pencil ; painted ; nailed ; everything. It didn't take
long to realise that visitors could be divided into three
categories : the painstaking, who made tallyplates of their

own ; the unimaginative, who used paint-brushes ; and the downright lazy with pencils. Determined that future visitors should class us amongst the industrious, we rowed back on board and spent the rest of the evening carving a wooden *Salmo* fish, which we proposed to fix like a weathercock to the top of the roof on a length of copper tube which I dug out of the repair-locker.

At the price of a badly cut thumb we completed our carving, painted it white, and rowed ashore after breakfast to add it to the already massive collection. While I fixed it in place Jill wandered round looking at some of the other contributions. Suddenly she said, " Hullo, what date is it ? "

" Tenth of September," I replied, " why ? "

" Well, look at this," she said. " There's been a yacht here only last week, on the 4th. She's called *Pandora*, from Green Bay, Wisconsin."

She pointed first to one inscription then to another, and another after that . . . the *Pandora* sure had been a-visiting. Looking round I found it hard to believe that I hadn't noticed her ' spoor ' before. She was one of the paint-pot brigade, and there was hardly a boulder for a hundred yards round that hadn't been Pandorinated, Green Bayed, or Wisconsignatured.

" Brash," we murmured, comparing these scrawls, this crude, vulgar daubing with the careful engineering and impeccable taste of our weathercock, " Definitely brash. I wonder if we'll meet them." We practised making ' not quite-our-class-dear ' faces at each other for a while, and then began to giggle and decided to go and find the Wittmers. We hadn't the faintest idea where they lived, but felt that there was bound to be a path somewhere that would lead to their house. After all, the prickles were so thick everywhere that if the Wittmers ever moved around the island at all, then they'd HAVE to make paths for themselves.

There was a ruined building behind the barrel (the remains of a Norwegian whaling-station we later learned) and after poking about and round it for a while, we found a perfectly splendid path and sauntered up it.

Two hours later we found we had stopped sauntering and it had become a walk. By lunch-time Jill was beginning to say, " How much farther do you think it is ? " and soon after that it began to rain, what they call at home A Scots mist. The Galapagans call it a *Garua* and say it makes the crops grow, but we said all sorts of other quite different things about it and wished we'd brought waterproofs with us. We'd climbed well over a thousand feet by this time and walked about six miles ; six miles by the path that is, but a great deal farther if we added on all the donkey tracks that we'd blundered into by mistake and had to blunder out of again afterwards. The island was infested with donkeys, and they all seemed to make tracks for themselves into the prickliest and rockiest bits of country and evaporate when they got there. At least they either evaporated or else backed out ; we weren't quite sure which, for they certainly left no room to turn. My shirt was in ribbons and so were Jill's legs. We hated donkeys.

" The damned animals," said Jill, as we struggled back onto the path again after one of our periodic strayings, " I believe they do it on purpose. Just LOOK at this path of theirs. Here, where it leaves the proper path it's twice as good as the real one, but that clump of cactuses that it finished up in would have torn the hide off a rhinoceros. That's your last pair of trousers," she added as an afterthought. " If you split them as well as your shirt, you'll just have to do without. I'm fed up with sewing your clothes together. You shouldn't go dashing on the way you do. You should go carefully. Never choose one leg of a fork till you're CERTAIN it's the right one."

The path was pretty indistinct everywhere, but when

we reached a more open stretch of country where there
were occasional patches of coarse grass amongst the scrub
it gave up the struggle entirely. Someone had taken the
trouble to mark the last recognisable part with a small
cairn. Beyond the cairn was a mass of open glades and
impenetrable thickets criss-crossed with donkey tracks,
which we christened ' Donkey Circus,' and by the time
we'd unaccountably repassed the cairn four times we began
to think it was enchanted.

It was five in the evening and we were feeling very
weary indeed before we finally blundered out of the Circus
and onto a path that was a path. The sun had returned
during the afternoon, dried up the *Garua* and proceeded
to roast us as we laboured to find our way. The sweat
poured down our backs and soon we had raging thirsts.
The new path ran straight up the side of a hill, and just
as we reached it we saw a tin-roofed shed down by the
sea and a boat moored offshore beyond it. With the
choice of going either up our new path or down it, we
unanimously chose down, and at the thought of finding
somewhere to rest and drink our steps instinctively
quickened.

The first sign that we were approaching a human habitation was a crumpled newspaper lying underneath a bush,
but our next find was infinitely more exciting . . . a well-
sucked orange-skin. We nearly danced a jig round it.
They must have oranges on this island, we chortled—
oranges, oranges, oranges. It was the most cheering
thought we had had all day.

Beyond the orange-skin, half a mile beyond, was a pig-
sty with five pigs in it, and beyond that again a small
village of wood and corrugated-iron shanties round which
lounged some Ecuadorians in ragged-looking clothes.

" Wittmer ? " we said to them, " Wittmer ? "

They pointed disinterestedly to a house that stood away
from the others, much more robustly built and painted

green, and as we approached it a plump, jolly-looking woman came running out of the door to meet us.

"Hello, hello . . . I am Frau Wittmer," she introduced herself, speaking excellent English ; "welcome to Floreana. Where have you come from ? "

We told her that we had walked over from Post Office Bay and had brought some letters for her. She looked at the scratches on Jill's legs and at our general dustiness and decrepitude, and obviously thought we were crackers, but all she said was :

"Ah, but you must be hungry. I have been baking ; come in and eat."

Jill, especially, she took under her protection, and almost carried her up the steps that led to the front door, "Come on in . . . come on in," she kept repeating. "That path aiee . . . it has not been used in years. You must be exhausted."

Still talking she sat us down on the L-shaped bench that ran behind the table and brought out two teacups and an enormous brown china jug full of water. "Now," she said with the air of a genie offering an oasis to a caravan of camels, "you must drink."

We took her at her word, and would probably have finished the jug off then and there had she not intervened with a large bowl of oranges ; lovely, juicy, sucky oranges brought down that day, so she told us, from the farm up the hill where the *Garua* could get at it. We quartered the oranges and unashamedly sucked at them, little dribbles of juice running down from the edges of our mouths and splashing onto the scrubbed wood of the table. It was the most glorious sensation.

While we were still eating the door opened and a girl came in, square and strong, wearing grey shorts, a khaki shirt and a baseball cap. This was Floreana, the Wittmer's daughter. Rolf, their son, was up at the farm with his wife and Herr Wittmer.

It soon seemed to be taken for granted that we were to spend the night ashore (the first time since New York) and certainly the thought of not having to find our way back to *Salmo* through the prickles in the moonlight was a welcome one. We settled down to enjoy ourselves.

They wouldn't let us help to get supper ready, so we were left to our own devices for a while and had a chance to rummage round the living-room. The walls were covered so thickly with photographs that there hardly seemed to be room to squeeze in another. Photographs of ships and yachts predominated, but running them a close second were sea-lions, Galapagoses, flightless cormorants and all the strange fauna of the group. We noticed too that nearly every picture was autographed : ' To the Wittmers from the . . . Scientific Expedition, 1934,' or ' Yacht *White Heather*, thanks for such wonderful hospitality.' Frau Wittmer also kept a visitors' book, now entering its second volume, in which all the yachts made entries. We were left with this and invited to make a contribution.

" Come on," I said to Jill ; " you think of something to say in it. My mind always goes blank on these occasions."

So did Jill's. We sat with the book open on the table in front of us for nearly half an hour seeking inspiration from previous entries. All the Americans seemed terribly good at it. ' Well, it's been swell knowing you folks. Be sure to look us up if you ever visit back in the States, just remember that the address is Pat and Willie Blair, 437 Lexington Avenue, Waukegan, Illinois.'

We gave up in the end and simply wrote ' Sailing Yacht *Salmo* ' and then signed our names ; later on, when we brought *Salmo* round to their bay, we gave them a photograph to go with it.

Supper was stewed goat with potatoes, cauliflower, and carrots from the farm, and after supper a bottle of ' Whisky ' was brought out. As it was inside a ' White Horse ' bottle we were slightly startled by the taste which, while good, certainly wasn't what the Lagavulin Distillery in the Island of Islay would have produced. At the first mouthful we must unconsciously have made considering faces and what-have-we-got-here faces, for Frau Wittmer burst out laughing and said, " Do you not like our whisky, then ? "

" Oh, yes," we both rushed to explain. " Oh yes, very much indeed. Yes. Quite excellent, er . . . er . . . what is it ? "

It was apparently all their own work, distilled from sugar-cane and flavoured with oranges. This particular vintage had been brewed for Rolf's wedding two months before, when there had been a gigantic gathering of the clans at Floreana. The Kastdlaens, the Angermeyers, the Hornemanns had all been there, all the people whose names were on our mail delivery list. It had been the biggest gathering ever, so Frau Wittmer proudly told us, but at the last moment the wedding had nearly been cancelled because the priest (who lived at Wreck Bay) had found his motor launch had broken down and he couldn't get across. I forget how the difficulty had finally been solved, but it had been somehow.

We were nearly dropping with sleep before we finally stopped talking and lit our candles. Our room was up a very steep stair and, as Frau Wittmer ushered us in, the draught from the open window made the candles flicker and throw strange shadows on the bare plank walls. There were two goatskins on the floor, dark pools on the scrubbed white wood, and against one wall stood two beds. Outside we could hear the waves washing on the beach and the whole room smelt sweet and clean. " Thank you," we said to Frau Wittmer, " yes, we shall certainly sleep very well in here."

There were sheets on the beds, and blankets, for the Humboldt current makes the islands cold at night. We tumbled underneath them and just before I went to sleep I heard Jill saying slowly, " You remember when Frau

Wittmer told us that she had to sleep on the floor when she visited Guayaquil because the beds were all too soft. I can see what she meant. I feel as if I'm sleeping on a board now. I wonder if I am. . . ."

It was daylight when we woke up ; the sun was shining brilliantly outside, and someone was feeding hens underneath the window. The problem of the beds was still worrying Jill, so as soon as she got up, she turned back the bedclothes to see what happened underneath. " Oh, THAT's what it is," she said. " Strips of rawhide woven across the frame and no mattress. No wonder there isn't any give in them. Oh! my poor back."

After breakfast we decided to walk up to the farm to work the stiffness out of our limbs. Floreana had already gone. She was going to marry an Ecuadorian wireless operator in a month or two and was clearing more ground for them to farm on, so Frau Wittmer told us, then added :

" She is extraordinary, that girl. When she was twelve a woman in a yacht gave her a pretty dress and Floreana was terribly upset. She said she would much rather have had a machete."

Jill, remembering that she had already given Floreana a pair of ear-rings (her favourite ones too) the night before, as a sort of advance wedding present, blushed and looked uncomfortable. I knew she wanted to ask Frau Wittmer if there was any chance of getting the ear-rings back, so that she could replace them with a saw or a chisel. Later she said to me sadly, " But I thought she'd LIKE something pretty, to wear to be married in. I know I would."

The walk to the farm was easy enough, straight up the hill on a Rolls-Royce path (the one we'd come down on the day before). The country to start with was dry and thorny, but above a thousand feet it grew green and lush and we were able to fill a bucket with lemons from the trees that grew wild beside the path. After about an hour's walk the path split and a small white-painted signpost,

startling in its unexpectedness, said ' To the Wittmers.
25 minutes.' We followed its direction and soon dived
into a real tunnel of undergrowth where the light was as
green as in an aquarium and the track grew muddy underfoot. At length we reached an open field, hedged with
bananas, and a hundred yards or so beyond we found
Floreana sitting on the ground with another girl, feeding
sugar-cane between the wooden rollers of a home-made
mill, while a donkey plodded slowly round and round
them, turning the beam which drove it. More whisky
was in the making.

Herr Wittmer was a splendid-looking figure with a long
white beard, and he showed us all round the farm, cutting
and pruning with a pair of secateurs everywhere he went.
" This was the first field we cleared," he said. " The straw-
berries sometimes do very well here, but this year we have
potatoes." He reached a row of coffee-trees and passed
down them snipping here and there. " Before I came
here I knew nothing about farming. First I was an officer
in the machine-gun corps in the war against your country
in 1914, but afterwards I became secretary to Dr Adenauer,
who was the Burgomaster of Cologne. Ach, you see what
the ants have done? Always they eat my plants, the
onions also they attack."

Rolf took us in hand and showed us the new ground
that he and Floreana were clearing in readiness for her to
set up a separate establishment, but he didn't seem very
enthusiastic about her choice of husband.

" Do you know," he said, " I do not think that he could
even build a house. I expect he will come to ask me to
do that."

" Dreadful," we murmured politely, " quite dreadful,"
and began to wonder just how, if invited to start, WE
would set about building a house for ourselves.

We passed a deep cave set amongst massive boulders
which made me think somehow of Minotaurs, but which

now housed nothing more fearsome than two pigs that Rolf fed with a bunch of bananas. " That was where I was born," he said, " four months after my parents reached this island. That was their first home."

Later on, when we got back on board, Jill said to me, " I always knew that they lived a hard life out here, but I never realised before just how completely self-sufficient they would be. They seem to make everything for them- selves. Every single thing. I've never felt very pampered before on this trip, but, my goodness, I do now."

CHAPTER ELEVEN

ISLAND LIFE

THE sea was blue and dappled with white horses on the day that we went to say goodbye to the Wittmers. We had shifted *Salmo* round to their bay soon after our arrival at Floreana, so we rowed inshore, just before we sailed, to make our farewells and collect some letters for delivery to Academy Bay.

Jill, for some inscrutable reason, had decided to wear a skirt for the occasion, a bright cotton one, newly washed and pressed. Prouting and skirts never really agreed with each other, so I watched with some amusement as she manœuvred its billowing folds over *Salmo*'s guard-rail and daintily stepped into the stern, spread a handkerchief on the floor-boards and then wrapped herself up into a sort of parcel before sitting down.

She must have seen a smile hovering on my face; for as we pushed off and began to bob shorewards over the wavelets she said, " Well, I LIKE to try to look nice, sometimes. Why shouldn't I ? "

There was quite a surf running at the beach, and from experience we knew that the secret of a dry landing was to wait until a big wave came, rush in on the top of it, and then leap over the side and drag Prout above the waterline before the next wave came. It was all easy enough, but required timing.

This time everything went very well indeed, until the dragging started, and then, just before we were clear of the water, Jill stood on a sharp stone with her bare feet

" Ooн ! " she said, and forgetting that she was holding
Prout in one hand and her well-parcelled skirt in the other,
tried to pick up the damaged foot to look at it and give
it sympathy. The result of course was that she dropped
the boat and this gave her such a surprise that she very
slowly lost her balance and sat down in the water beside
it, just as the next wave arrived.

Frau Wittmer and Rolf had come walking down the
beach to meet us and saw the whole thing. Like me, they
collapsed with laughter, and poor Jill was left to scramble
to her feet unaided, wringing water from her skirt in
streams.

" And I was being so careful," she said. " Oh STOP
laughing. Oh, it IS unfair."

We sped away from Floreana on a glorious reach. *Salmo*
spread her wings ; she flew and danced over the water ;
tossed the spray from her stem and heeled joyously to the
breeze while the sails, silhouetted against the deep blue,
were arched into perfect curves. We were looking forward
eagerly to Academy Bay, and the boat seemed as though
she, too, longed to get there.

During the night the weather changed completely, and
the dawn came red and angry with big white crests racing
over the water and bursting in a deep fringe of foam all
along the grey cloud-covered coast of Santa Cruz Island,
which stretched across our bows. Academy Bay, we knew,
lay somewhere in this fringe, but for a long time we were
unable to pick it out.

At last it opened up. From the masthead I could see
that the surf had a break in it, and as we reached this gap,
so we sighted the masts of a large sailing-boat anchored
inshore. We drove in towards this other boat, lifting
high on each successive swell, wondering whether we'd be
able to find a calm corner to anchor in, for everything
looked very exposed. It was a deceptive place. Suddenly,

as we came up to the other boat (we saw, to our amusement, that she was the paint-daubing *Pandora* of Green
Bay, Wisconsin) the swell was cut off, at the same moment
the wind dropped, and we had a better chance to look
round.

" Oh, look ! " said Jill, " what a lovely little house ! "

I looked as directed and there, down by the very edge
of the water, perched on rocks, stood a small stone-built
bungalow with a windmill beside it. There were flowers
in the garden and the general effect was more of a ' desirable
suburban residence ' than of the backwoods.

Beyond the house stretched a low cliff with deep water
right up to its base, and beyond the cliff again, spreading
from it at an angle to form the back and other side of
the bay, was lower ground, sandy and dotted with fifteen
or twenty wooden and corrugated-iron houses. One, we
noticed, had a flagstaff in front of it from which flew an
enormous Ecuadorian flag, and our hearts sank, for this
surely heralded the advent of officialdom and explanations
about illegal entry.

Sure enough, very soon after we'd anchored, a rowing
boat put out from shore and came towards us. It contained three extremely grubby Ecuadorian sailors who
asked, by signs, for our papers. We handed them over
and the boat departed shorewards followed by our anxious
glances.

We were still sitting in the cockpit nursing our guilty
consciences when a dinghy bumped alongside, unobserved,
and an American voice said, " Hi. My name's Divine.
Bud Divine. Don't you folks have an Ecuadorian ensign ? "

We had intended to buy one at Panama, but the only
size available had been more suited to a battleship than
to a twenty-footer, so we'd decided to do without. " Well,
for Gosh sakes don't tell them that at the Navy Offices,"
said Bud when we'd told him this. " They're touchy as
hell about that sort of thing. The last person they found

without one they fined a hundred dollars. Didn't they say anything about it when you went to Wreck Bay ? "

" Well, as a matter of fact, we haven't been to Wreck Bay."

" Oh, my Lordy," said Bud. " Aren't you the ones. You'd best nip ashore and try to explain things to the commandant. He lives in that office there by the flagstaff. But you'd have to get there quick. He knocks off work at eleven and if you go to see him after that you get charged overtime rates—four dollars an hour."

With these few cheering remarks he pushed off and said he'd be seeing us, adding for good measure, " Probably in gaol."

The row from the anchorage to the Navy Office felt like the long, long walk to the headmaster's study after an official summons at school.

We had dressed for the interview with extreme care. Jill wore a very garden-party dress with a purple sash that she'd bought in New York, and she had nearly put on stockings as well, but had decided at the last moment that would be carrying the glamourising process too far (besides they were packed in a ' Not wanted on Voyage ' suitcase underneath the sails). I had on a clean shirt and khaki trousers with knife-edge creases, while I could have shaved from the shine on my shoes. This, we had decided, was an occasion that called for the utmost formality, so I promoted myself one rung on the retired list and became Commander Hamilton, Royal Navy. I even began to think it was all wrong that I should be rowing. I mentioned this to Jill, but by that time I think that she had become no less a person than Lady Hamilton and declined to take the hint. We didn't even smile at each other the whole way in, and landed with great dignity and quite undamped.

The same cheerful but ragamuffinly sailor who had taken our papers came forward when we reached the gate of the compound (there was no fence, just a gate with an arch over it) and led us to the office.

There was a man sitting at the desk, a lieutenant-commander, I noticed with satisfaction, making a great play of being busy with an ' IN ' tray, though the mail-ship hadn't called for three months. " Good morning," I said, " I am Commander Hamilton, and this is my wife. We are very pleased to visit your island."

The man seemed much impressed by our entry; thereafter the interview went very well indeed : deep calling to deep, brotherhood of the sea, was the theme of our talks. Without an engine in the boat, the commandant suggested, we must indeed find it difficult always to go just where we wanted to.

Sometimes, we said, we had to battle for days on end to make headway against these terrible currents. The commandant was quick to comprehend, and endorsed our papers ' Entered Academy Bay from stress of weather,' and presented us with a letter for the Governor explaining the situation. The currents in these parts, he said, were really VERY bad. We thanked him for his courtesy. He thanked us for our visit. He bowed to Jill and the interview was over.

" Whew," we said, as we walked back to the Prout again, " what a relief ! " It was the last we ever heard about papers or going to Wreck Bay.

The crew of *Pandora* were feeling sorry for themselves. They rowed over to tell us this as soon as we got back. The trouble was, they said, that they'd paid deposits of two thousand dollars to the owner back in the States for the privilege of joining him on his world cruise, and they weren't getting their money's worth. They were suckers to have paid it, maybe, but they had paid it, and what would happen to it, goodness only knew. It was to have been a share and share alike cruise, and now here was the owner trying to sign on some bum to act as professional mate. They were giving up, they said—quitting. Besides, half the time on board they had to spend in washing dishes or cooking.

We asked how they were going to quit ; and that was a difficulty too apparently. There wasn't a ship due back to Guayaquil for another two months. But they weren't going to stand for being pushed around ; no, sir, that they weren't.

The story seemed to be a long and involved one, so we made ' there, thereing ' noises and suggested that probably it might be better to give things a longer trial ; surely they couldn't be as bad as all that, could they ? And they rowed sadly back to *Pandora* again, the droop of their shoulders proclaiming that . . . yes, indeed, things could be as bad as all that. Worse in fact, if anything !

Their skipper was our next visitor : a small man, very cocksure of himself, but clearly worried. He didn't know what was wrong with people nowadays, he said. Why, this crew he'd taken on in Panama were talking of leaving already. Just the very same thing as the crew before had done. There was no spirit of adventure left in people nowadays, no give and take. " Why," said the skipper, " I've got eighty thousand dollars tied up in that boat there," he nodded to *Pandora* anchored half a mile to seaward. " Echo-sounder, two-way radio, radar, the lot. Finest boat we've ever built. Composite construction, galvanised hull-plating, latest control devices, dacron sails. . . ."

Jill interrupted him, " You built it yourself, did you ?" she said.

" Yes, ma'am. We own the biggest shipyard in Wisconsin. Right there on the lake. We've built P.T. boats, minesweepers, yachts, lake craft, anything. You want it, we build it."

" Er, yes," said Jill, slightly overcome by all this. " How do you like this boat of ours ? "

He looked round for a moment, " Why fine, fine. But back in the States we don't go for this sort of thing much. No engine in this you say ? No, you'd not get two thousand dollars for a boat without an engine. Why in *Pandora* now we've got four engines. Need the power, you see. Two main driving-engines, two generators. There's a generator running day and night. We carry ten tons of gasoline. Yes, ma'am, ten tons. And food, why we don't have to buy a thing, not a thing, till we get back to the States again, maybe in two years."

He rowed away again and we could see him clambering up *Pandora's* ladder and pottering round on deck for a while as if summoning up the courage to go below and come to terms with his recalcitrant crew. " What a rotten shame ! " we thought. " Three people over there in that boat. All of them nice enough, and yet all absolutely miserable and with no way of letting off steam except at each other."

" Yes," Jill added, " and to make it even worse, each one of them probably has been dreaming and looking forward for years to doing just this . . . sailing across the Pacific in a yacht, and now they're doing it they don't even have the spirit to go ashore and see the things they've looked forward to ; they just sit on board moping and hating it all."

Two days later they left. We watched them motor out beyond the breakers at the point and then turn away northwards. They'd come to some sort of agreement amongst themselves we'd heard : Joe, the ' bum from ashore to act as professional mate,' had bullied them into it, and they were off to paint their names on the rocks of Tagus Cove, another of the places where the habit was fashionable, before leaving for Tahiti. We wondered if they'd be any happier by the time they reached it.

Joe had come on board the evening after we arrived. He was an effervescent Austrian with a craggy face, a ragged

straw-hat and a wonderful smile. Jill thought he was a
' duck,' and wherever he went we found he left a thick
trail of shattered female hearts. We gave him supper and
then, because no one felt like refilling the lamps, we sat
in the half-darkened cabin talking and talking of people
and places and boats and dreams, until the one lamp we
had lit grew red and smoky for want of fuel. We blew
it out and Jill lit a candle which she stuck in an empty
rum bottle ; and still we sat round the table to hear of
Joe's shipwreck on the other side of the island, a year
and a half previously. Jill, I remember, was sitting with
her face cupped in her hands, leaning on the table, the
candle-light thowing shadows on her hair, while Joe sat
back in the darkness, his glass held on one ragged knee.
Every now and then as he talked he would lean forward,
and the flickering light would catch a flash from his happy
smile.

" But what on earth did you do ? " said Jill, " when
you found yourself stranded on the beach at three in the
morning ? "

" Vell, I joost wait until daylight, you see, and then I
realise that I cannot get the boat afloat again myself, so
I walk along the shore until I reach Academy Bay. It
took four days, you know. And I haf no vater with me.
And it vas hot. I vas plenty tired when I arrive."

That was all he said about what must have been a
shattering experience. By the time he had rested and
could get helpers to come back with him, the boat was a
total loss, so he sold her timbers, rigging and engine to
the highest bidders, bought a shack for himself with the
proceeds, and settled down to write a book and see what
would turn up.

We kept a special corner of our visitors' book for interesting people, so when we asked him to sign it he wrote :
' My proud ship, the *Sunshine*, I have left on the rocks
of the Galapagos. Now has come the staysail schooner

Pandora to Academy Bay, and her I take, if God is willing, to Tahiti, the Earth's last Paradise.'

The pioneering example set to us by the Galapagos was such that we became infected with a fit of ' Do-it-yourself-ism ' and decided to economise on stores by laying in a gigantic stock of langoustes which we intended to salt and use as delectable midday meals for the rest of the voyage. The normal method of catching these, we knew, was to dive for them in goggles, but since we didn't have any goggles I decided to trap the creatures by securing a very high bit of fish onto a shallow basket and leaving it on the bottom overnight. It was a method I used with great success as a small boy for catching crayfish in the River Wey at Guildford ; one simply hoisted the basket very carefully in the morning and the crayfish didn't know any-thing about it until he was out of the water, when it was too late.

The bit of fish that I laid aside for the purpose on the cabin-top grew very high very quickly, and it soon became oppressive even in the cabin itself. Jill stood it for a while but was eventually driven to remonstrate and asked me to remove it. " The trouble is," I said, " that I can't think of what to make the basket part of the trap with. It's got to be fairly porous and net-like to let the water run through without the langouste noticing when I hoist it."

" Well," said Jill, " if that's all that the trouble is then surely we can think of something." We considered, in turn, all the available materials and rejected them for one reason or another, until Jill remembered the petticoat that she'd bought with her New York dress. It was fine in the shop, she said, but definitely wasn't designed for yachts. It made the dress behave like a parachute when-ever the wind blew. I could have it if I wanted.

So I had it : it was made of a window-net sort of material and was absolutely ideal. We fastened it onto a wire frame, secured the fish, and lowered the whole contrivance over the side at a place which we'd heard was a good one for langoustes. Unfortunately, however, in spite of repeated attempts we never caught any, and finally we gave up in disgust and decided to try diving after all. We knew that Bud Divine had a spare mask and a pair of swim-fins, so we walked over to his house one afternoon to try and borrow them. Bud's house, one of the largest in the village, was made from a mess hall transported from the wartime airfield on Baltra Island, and it stood on a little sandy peninsula about half a mile from the anchorage. The door was open so we walked in, and found a quite gigantic man sitting down inside and looking rather nervous. He got up at our entrance and introduced himself as Alf Kastdalen : " I am waiting," he said, " to have three teeth pulled out by Bud. Freda Hornemann is in there with him now. She too has two teeth to be removed."

He pointed to an ominously closed door and we realised why he looked so nervous.

The door opened at that moment and Freda Hornemann came out. She was a pretty girl, small and slight and about fifteen years old. She said Hullo to us rather wanly, and then drooped into one of Bud's chairs, holding her head between her hands, while the next victim went through the door.

Bud, so we learned, though he had no anæsthetics, owned the only dental forceps on the island so he had a lot of customers.

It was such a frightening thought that we grabbed the goggles and ran before any of our teeth could join his collection.

I found that I couldn't catch the wretched langoustes even with goggles. There just didn't seem to be any, though I cruised amongst the dim, dragon-green rocks and seaweed until my lungs were bursting. There were fish there by the dozen, of every hue of the rainbow, and once

I met a very small shark which made my tummy turn over; but not a sniff of a langouste did I get until Gus Angermeyer and his son Johnny came out from shore to join us. Gus was the local langouste expert, and within seconds of entering the water he waved to me to come over and join him and Johnny. He had a sack tied to his waist and he handed it to me as I came up, saying it would be better that he should have both hands free. He'd soon fix us up for as many as we needed, he said; there were, for example, twelve under the rocks he was standing on. He and Johnny, a strongly built boy of about thirteen and as brown as a seal, dived competently down at the rock and rather less competently I joined them. The scene reminded me of the illustrations in Cousteau's books; Gus and Johnny hovering like aquatic angels over a huge rock, while fishes darted, cruised and hurried among the weeds. Working as neatly together as the girls of a chorus, they each dived down at his own side of the rock, and as they did so, strange black shapes came exploding out from underneath it. Determined to take some sort of share in the party I grabbed wildly at one and much to my surprise got it and came spluttering and triumphant to the surface. Gus and Johnny were up before me and each had two, one in each hand. We stuffed them into the sack and then off flashed the Anger-meyers to another rock and yet another. At each one they found langoustes, and at each one after the first, I didn't; any grabs that I made at the flitting forms that fled the Angermeyer onslaught closed onto nothing more substantial than water. In half an hour they had collected a sackful. So large a sackful in fact that it nearly anchored me and I stumbled ashore puffing, blowing and slithering onto the rocks where Jill sat watching the performance.

"It's incredible," I panted, "they never miss, those two. And I would swear there was nothing under those rocks when I looked there first."

Gus and Johnny came out and joined us, laughing at me gently for my clumsiness, and told us how to preserve the langoustes by pickling them in salt. Talking of pickling, Gus said, would we like some smoked goat to take away with us ? He brought some on board the next day, looking like hunks of brown leather with bones sticking out of it and smelling strongly of wood smoke. Six months earlier Jill would have ditched it thirty seconds after he'd gone ashore again, but now she put it happily into a biscuit-tin with the air of a miser adding another pot of gold to his store.

One of the things that we wanted before we sailed was a replacement for the spinnaker-boom we'd broken at Balboa. The Kastdalens were alleged to have some good bamboos growing on their farm, so one day we trudged off to see them. The path wound up the hill from the dust, sun and cactuses of the coast, through thick woods higher up, and finally it ran through rank jungle where the ground was all oozy underfoot. It was from this sort of country that all the farms had been hacked. The Kastdalens's was the biggest and most prosperous of any of them, being nearly eighty acres in extent, and they had recently added dairying to their other activities by importing a Friesian bull from America and crossing it with some of the wild cattle brought in originally (I believe) by the Spaniards. Being the only milk producers in the group they were terribly proud of their wares, and we were both given glasses of milk to refresh us after our climb. As we sat down opposite each other at their big scrubbed table, the glasses in our hands and our minds buzzing with all the questions we wanted to ask, Jill shot me a fascinated glance and then quickly averted her gaze. She knew that, above all things, I hated milk. She also knew that I wouldn't be callous enough to refuse it and wanted to see how I'd try to wriggle out of drinking it.

She took a sip. " Delicious," she murmured. " How

lovely to get a glass of REAL milk again," and again I saw her shoot me a look, " So creamy, too. Oh Bliss ! "

For a few moments I had been praying that the Kastdalens might leave the room. Then I had wondered if I could spill the glass (but there was a whole jug of the stuff on the table as well) and then finally, as a last resort, I had steeled myself to the sacrifice.

' I WON'T be sick. I WON'T be sick. I WON'T,' I told myself, and seized the glass.

To my tortured imagination all eyes seemed to be fixed on me as I raised it to my lips. Gulp, gulp, gulp, gulp and there it was down. I shakily replaced the empty tumbler, a ghastly smile rivetted onto my lips, while the room seemed to heave up and down and a greenish mist blurred the edges of everything.

A voice penetrated into my private Hell. It was Mrs Kastdalen : " Please, will you not have some more of our milk ? It must be a long time since you have last had some. Really we have lots, you know."

" No, thank you very much, Mrs Kastdalen. It's very kind of you indeed, but really I won't. No, really. Really."

Almost in a fever I put my hand across the top of the glass, and soon afterwards we took our leave. We were ushered down to their bamboo grove where we cut ourselves a simply splendid pole, dead straight, strong, and twenty feet in length.

The Kastdalens had asked us to spend the night with them (it was a three-hour walk from the beach), but I was so frightened of being offered more milk that we declined and went instead to visit Sandy, the New Zealander, who was the only Commonwealth representative amongst the settlers. Like Joe, Sandy had been shipwrecked, but at the neighbouring Cocos group, where he had been engaged in the traditional pastime of hunting for pirate treasure. He had somehow begged a passage to the Galapagos, and having arrived (three years previously) had decided to settle. He bought a boat and fished for two years with such success that he had been able to give up fishing and buy a rather derelict farm next door to the Kastdalens.

The path leading to this farm we soon found to be a nightmare. Not only was it steep (all paths on the Galapagos are steep), but it was knee-deep in gluey mud and subjected to a terrific bombardment of avocado pears which hurtled down onto it from the tops of very high trees. We ran, or rather waddled, the gauntlet for a hundred yards, then decided that the risks of concussion were too great and struck off into the undergrowth clear of the avocado trees. " Ah ! " we said happily, " that's better," and then ran into a bushful of fire ants. They are tiny little beasts, bright red, and they sting like mad. With no hesitation at all we shot back to the path again and scuttled and slithered up it, scooping and slapping to stop the devilish stinging. It was as if we had been rolled in a bed of nettles without any clothes on. The newly acquired spinnaker pole which I was carrying on my shoulder interfered with my antics and swung wildly backwards and forwards, until a louder shout than usual from behind announced that Jill had got mixed up with the end of it. " Stop waving that thing about," she yelled, " you nearly knocked my head off . . . oh, mind yourself ! "

An avocado landed in the mud between us with a whistle like a blockbuster and cut short the conversation ; in a grim silence broken only by puffs and wheezes, we burst out of the trees and onto Sandy's farm.

Sandy was moodily attacking some giant grass with a machete as if he expected it to get the better of him anyhow, but felt he ought to make some effort to beat it back. He stopped as soon as he saw us and ushered us into the house. " Aw come on in and have some coffee. I don't have tea."

We went into the kitchen where Jill was given the chair and Sandy and I sat on boxes. The floor was mud and wasn't very flat, so the boxes wobbled up and down as we shifted our weight and tried to get comfortable. A line of yellow ants walked steadily up and down one leg of the table and into a hole in the wall, carrying grains of sugar from a little heap that had been spilled at break-fast time, and Jill could hardly take her eyes off the grey line of dishcloths which hung on a string over the stove. I knew she was longing to try Persil on them. Sandy was a keen reader and had collected heaps and heaps of books and newspapers which lay stacked knee-deep every-where. " Have you read this ? " he kept on asking, " or this ? or this ? " and each time we had to admit that we hadn't. Sea books he seemed to be keenest on, and books about the war. He had been in the Long Range Desert Group and had a mass of literature about it.

After our coffee we went out to pick oranges to take back on board. The island had been hit by blight, but Sandy's trees had survived it. " The damned things were so deep in creepers that the blight couldn't reach them," he said ; " I'm still trying to cut them clear of the stuff, but it's hard work alone."

" Poor Sandy," said Jill, later on, " he needs a wife. But I suppose that with twice as many men as women on the islands some people are bound to suffer. We should ship a few girls out here when we get back." She paused for a moment, then added, " But they'd have to be pretty tough ones. I don't know that I'd like it much, living in a hut in the jungle and hacking back creepers all the time. I'd get claustrophobia."

Sandy very gallantly lent us his bed and dossed down himself on the camp one. There was only a paper-thin plywood partition between the bedroom and the kitchen where Sandy was, so we couldn't talk to each other above a whisper. I felt Jill shaking beside me and heard muffled gasps and bubblings. " Have you ever seen such a bed ? " she finally hissed out. " Where on EARTH did he get it ?

All the brass knobs on it and the twirly-wirlies and everything. And getting it up that path on a donkey. That
was how he said he did it, you remember? Oh, I'd LOVE
to have seen it. Through all that mud." She relapsed
into silence for a moment, then renewed giggles hit her.

I grew rather cross. I wanted to get to sleep. " Now,
what is it ? " I asked.

Jill was nearly choking by this time. " You know when
you told me about the sanitary arrangements ? "

" Yes," I said, for Sandy had tactfully drawn me aside
and asked me to explain to Jill that there was a spade
leaning against the door to the garden and a roll of paper
on a shelf above it.

" Well," she breathed into my ear, fairly wriggling with
delight, " it was PINK paper and it said on the wrapper
that it was designed to blend with ALL schemes of bathroom
decor."

I must admit that I exploded that time, and we lay
stuffing the sheet into our mouths for fear that Sandy might
hear and misunderstand.

We had a wonderful breakfast of fried eggs, for the
local hens were at the top of their form, and then we
shouldered our oranges and our spinnaker pole and headed
through the avocadoes for the long road back to the sea
once again. The Hornemanns stopped us on the way down
and insisted that we should have some fresh vegetables
and pots of home-made jam, so we were heavy laden,
and for almost the first time we wished that *Salmo* was
a little bigger. In a bigger boat, we felt, we would have
been able to carry a few extras that we could have left
behind in return for all that had been done for us, but
Salmo of necessity carried only the barest of essentials, so
we could do no more than promise ourselves to send things
later to show our thanks.

We sailed that same evening, slipping quietly out of
Academy Bay as the sun set in a blaze of reds and purple

and gold, and headed for our last port of call in the Galapagos, Elizabeth Bay of Isabella Island, where we knew
there were penguins. Our first impression of the islands
had been of their fauna ; our next interest had been the
settlers, so we felt it right that we should finish off by
seeing more animals.

Isabella is the largest of all the islands and consists of
a string of huge volcanoes (one still active) that tower up,
Fujiyama-like, to eight or nine thousand feet. The 'string'
between two of these giants is cut by a stretch of low
sandy ground that runs right across the island, and it is
at one end of this valley that Elizabeth Bay is situated.

It was only about seventy miles that we had to go
from Academy Bay, but the winds were fluky and the
currents bothersome, so it took two days to cover the
distance. We had been so filled with stories of wreck and
disaster by Joe and Sandy that, though we both went to
sleep for the whole of both nights, leaving *Salmo* to look
after herself, we only did so with rather guilty consciences,
and I found myself bobbing up, time and time again, to
gaze at the black loom of the mountains silhouetted against
the sky, just to make quite sure that no mysterious agency
was pushing us in towards the rocky and inhospitable
islands. Each time I felt slightly ashamed of my fearful-
ness, for in my heart of hearts I knew we were always safe
enough ; but these are enchanted islands ; and surely, I
used to plead to myself, with enchanted islands one must
be allowed to indulge in a few foolish fears.

It was once again late evening when we arrived. The
bay was large, and though well enough sheltered it was
disappointingly featureless, just a long stretch of mangrove and sand with no perfect little corner crying out
loud to be used as an anchorage. We finally chose a place
at random ; threw the anchor over the side and dropped
the sails.

" Well," said Jill, " supper. What shall we have ? How

about catching a few fish from the Prout ? there's no sense
in starting off using tinned stuff yet awhile."

So off I went with the rod while she started peeling
potatoes and making soup. In less than half an hour I'd
caught five of what the Galapagans call cod : splendid
fish to eat, with nice flaky white meat. I rowed back
very pleased with myself and began to gut them while
we had a drink apiece to celebrate. No sooner had I
tossed the first handful of bones and guts over the side
than there was a strange swssh, swssh, swssh noise overhead, and out of the gloaming swept a brown-and-white
pelican, which flumped down on the water and scooped
up a beakful of the cleanings.

After holding the whole consignment in the pouch of
his beak for a while he tried to swallow it, but the backbone seemed to catch in his gullet and he gazed reproachfully at us while he coughed it back into his beak again.
I threw him another backbone to see how he'd get on
with it, and with one great gollop he snatched it up and
held it with the rest.

" Oh, don't be such a swine," said Jill, " he'll choke.
Give him a proper bit of fish. There's far more there
than we can possibly eat."

The pelican had by now made another attempt to get
the bones down his throat, and after a considerable struggle
he managed it, though I still felt that the look he gave
me wasn't altogether one of gratitude, so I relented and
gave him the smallest fish of the five I'd caught to see
what he'd do with it. This time the rat-trap beak just
opened and closed with a click like a refrigerator door,
and we saw the lump slide straight down his throat for
all the world as though he were a Guinness advertisement.
He seemed so delighted by this offering that he clumsily
splashed off the water, flew once round the boat and then
landed with a crash and all of a heap on the end of our
spinnaker-boom which, for harbour use, we kept stuck

over the bow like a bowsprit to give more room on deck. There he stayed, belching gently while we had supper, and then at the end of it he flapped off into the darkness, swish, swish, swishing as he went.

The next morning was so perfect that we decided to have a day in the Prout hunting penguins. Jill made a few cod sandwiches from the remains of supper, while I loaded up with cameras, spare films, tripod and all the other paraphernalia that we seemed to need when we went animal-filming.

The likeliest place for penguins seemed to be a little miniature Ailsa Craig that lay a mile offshore and whose top was white with bird droppings, so off we went, chattering like magpies, wondering what we'd find there.

A mile is a long row in a Prout, and we'd sobered down by the time we arrived. We clambered ashore unscathed onto a tangle of black boulders, the water surging round our knees as we disembarked. Calm as the day was, there was still quite a swell running over the rocks, so as soon as we'd carried the cameras clear of the splashes we came back for the Prout and lifted him bodily out of the water and laid him out of harm's way, a brilliant red blotch amongst the basalt.

The place was alive with marine iguanas, charming little black dragons eighteen inches long, which scrambled over the rocks or simply sat sunning themselves in statuesque attitudes waiting for someone to take their photographs. We obliged several times and were just wondering if we'd find any penguins when we met a cormorant looking at us rather indignantly. Jill snatched the ciné-camera in a frenzy of excitement, and tried to set the tripod up and keep the camera trained on the cormorant at the same time in case he decided to go away before she was ready.

" Oh, do you think it's a flightless one ? Do you think it's a flightless one ? " she kept on asking as she got more and more tied up in the legs of the tripod, which for want of anywhere reasonably flat to stand on were flapping about happily.

Flightless cormorants were things we'd heard of but never so far met.

" Looks pretty ordinary to me," I said, and at that moment, bored I presume with Jill's ineptitude, he started bouncing over the rocks towards the water exactly as though he was on springs. As he bounced so he flapped a pair of silly little wings, all stunted and wasted away, to help him keep his balance, and then with a splash he landed in the water, dived and shot off like an arrow through the clear blueness.

Jill, having abandoned her attempts with the legs, managed to get a picture of this little episode and was terribly delighted with herself. " Oh, did you see him bouncing ? " she chortled. " What a splendid little creature ! And he was flightless. Oh, isn't this fun ? "

We had a wonderful morning after that, mountaineering round our rock. We found a rookery of blue-footed boobies, which are gannets with Cambridge-blue feet. Most of them had chicks on their nests, all covered with terrific itches that required incessant scratching. The parents got terribly worried when we went close, and shrieked and squawked but never seemed to think of moving away. I'd heard that you could actually touch the creatures, so I tried it out rather gingerly. The one I chose for the experiment can't have been a very good one, for though he let me pick him up, just as I was asking Jill if she'd seen how clever I'd been, he rounded on me and gave me a terrific peck on the chin which made me drop him. He then danced off over the rocks in a towering rage, yelling curses over his shoulder as he went.

The penguins, when we finally happened on them, were the most difficult to photograph of any of the creatures that we met. They lived in holes at the foot of inaccessible cliffs and liked to scuttle back inside them as we tried to get close. We tried doing it by Prout, and we tried doing it by holding onto the cliffs with our eyebrows, and we nearly succeeded in dropping the camera before we finally found a colony that didn't seem to care a damn what we did or how close we came to them. They were funny little beasts, only about a foot high, and very full of their own importance, like after-dinner speechmakers. They were standing, about a dozen of them, by the water's edge with their shoulders hunched up looking straight ahead. Having come to a suitable place we set the camera up and waited for them to do something. " Go on. Move ! Do Something, Shoo . . ." we shouted, and they didn't even turn their heads.

" Chuck a rock at them," Jill suggested. So I chucked a rock, and though it bounced beside them they very properly ignored such a silly trick. I hadn't the heart to throw another in case it should hit one by mistake, so I finally had to climb right down to within a couple of feet of them and practically push them into the water. The result in the film was the advent of a strange disembodied pair of feet, cut off at the knee into an otherwise purely penguinic picture. It looked most odd.

All the time we had been playing, the wind had been getting up, and as we finally sat down in a sheltered corner to share our lunch with some iguanas, we began to have doubts about the return trip. The Prout, after nearly two years' misuse, had developed a leak and we only had our shoes to use as bailers.

" Well, I think we should wait until the wind drops," said Jill. " If we go now we'll only fill the boat up and soak the cameras. And besides, I don't want to go in swimming here ; there are far too many sharks about."

" Oh, come on," I said, " you can bail and keep the cameras on your knees. We may have to wait all day before the wind drops. Besides, I'm hungry."

" You CAN'T be hungry. You've just had four sand-wiches."

That remark I took to be a sign of capitulation, so off we went, dragging the Prout into the water and then very carefully loading the cameras and ourselves in afterwards, and trying to stop it from being washed up on the rock-ledges as we did so. With a final heave and a leap I shoved off, grabbed the oars and began to row. The wind was dead against us and had thrown up quite a chop which, if we went too energetically, broke in over the bluff canvas bows. If, on the other hand, we didn't go energetically, we never moved at all, so it presented a nice problem.

Jill had to start bailing almost immediately, but I soon grew very angry with the way she did it. She rocked the boat too much, I said, and shipped splashes over the sides.

She retorted that if she didn't bail then we would just sink anyway, and that doing it her way she got rid of more water than she caused to be shipped, and besides it was she who was sitting in the water. Up amidships I was all right. Just LOOK at her trousers, she said.

Very soon I was in water, too, though not quite so much as Jill, and we began to discuss the best method of abandoning ship should we ever have to. What we wanted was a method that would keep the cameras dry, but since none occurred to us, we just went on as we were. Fortunately, as we drew closer to the shore, although the freeboard grew less, so did the waves, so in the end we made it. But only just. We paddled through slimy mud up to a huge mangrove, hauled the Prout out onto its roots and tipped the water out of him, then paddled along as close inshore as we could manage until we regained *Salmo*. We were both soaked, though it was such a hot day that that hardly mattered, but at least, we told ourselves, we had managed to save the cameras and that was the main thing.

We had intended to spend three more days at Elizabeth Bay, but quite suddenly, that evening, an urge for the open sea overcame us. Pitcairn was our next port and it lay three thousand miles away. Those three thousand miles of open water, instead of being a barrier, seemed suddenly to become desirable in themselves : a vast stretch of kindly water, of peace and quietness and ordered routine where we would have no subconscious voices breathing threats of shipwreck into our hours of sleep . . . nor worries about the safety of our chosen anchorages.

On the impulse we weighed the anchor and set the sails. The waves chuckled beneath the forefoot and two hours later we were lifting and swinging to the rhythm of the open ocean.

CHAPTER TWELVE

BLUE DAYS AT SEA

THE moon sank lower and lower in the sky, smothering the neighbouring stars and turning the sea into a golden fan. At last it slid beneath the rim of trade-wind clouds, and left the night seeming very black by contrast and the ocean very large and very empty—our little world on board the only speck on its surface for hundreds upon hundreds of miles.

Salmo rushed and dived and swooped through the darkness, twisting and shouldering the waves from her forefoot, revelling in her wild race south. I leaned into the doghouse and peered at the luminous dial of the clock : five to two —time for Jill to come up and take over the watch.

Down in the cabin the Primus was hissing gently as it heated up the cocoa water, and its dull glow silhouetted the cups as they swung from their hooks on the plate-rack. I lashed the tiller, gave a last look round on deck, then clambered down the ladder and took off my oilskin. All the sounds were familiar ones : Jill's steady breathing from the lee bunk ; the *sssh, ssh sssh* of the stem cutting through the waves ; the steady sigh of the wind in the rigging and an occasional creak from the tiller as it strained against its lashing. My hand strayed to the sultana jar where the fruit felt squashy and luscious beneath my fingers, so I scooped up a handful and chewed happily as I made two cups of cocoa.

" Two o'clock, Jillie. Lovely night but a bit cold still. You'd better wear an oilskin."

The shapeless bundle in the bunk wriggled unhappily and Jill's head appeared. " Any cocoa ? "

I handed the cup to her and she clambered out and began to dress. " What course is it ? Still two-two-five ? "

" Yes," I said, " we've another couple of weeks of that to go yet. She's sailing fine, though. Shake me if you want to take the Genoa off " ; and then I pulled off my jacket and trousers and crawled gratefully into the little warm nest that Jill had made in the bunk. In a matter of moments I was asleep, lulled by the rush of water past my ear, the thickness of a plank away.

We had run into the south-east trades two days after leaving the Galapagos, and thereafter made wonderful time, each day's milage being well into the hundred-and-thirties instead of the sixties, seventies and nineties we had grown used to on the way from Panama.

Jill had decided that it was time she learned to navigate, and the process brought pain and grief to both of us. She couldn't add up straight. " Well, of COURSE you get a funny answer if you add seven and nine and make thirteen out of them," I used to snap at her.

" Well, don't be so horrid about it," she'd reply, " I didn't MEAN it to make thirteen. It just happened . . ." and then after a pause, " Oh, I hate all this messing about with figures and tables and everything. It doesn't seem REAL at all. I can't picture a Greenwich Hour Angle, so how on earth can I remember whether it's one of the things one adds things onto or takes things away from ? "

I had always sworn that a child of six could learn enough about navigation in half an hour to get a boat to A from B across an ocean, so Jill's reluctance to support my theory used to make me crosser and crosser, and the crosser I got the more she couldn't understand what I was trying to explain, and I could only unwind myself again by thinking how lucky it was that I had never become a schoolmaster. Finally, just as I had decided that there was no

earthly use in going on with such a painful process, she
got it. I could hardly believe it the first time, but then
the next day she took another sight and got it again.
It was just like ' My Fair Lady,' which we'd heard records
of in Canada, and we began to chant to each other :
     " She's got it. She's got it, I really think she's got it."
     Day after day we scudded south-westwards, each day
superficially very like every other, and yet each one just
sufficiently different to prevent monotony. A great grief
to us was our lack of success at fishing. Nothing seemed
to be in the least bit interested in our line, though we
trailed it day and night with odds and ends from Jill's
sewing-bag tied onto the hook as bait : red wool, white
cloth and yellow silk from an old blouse. Then one night,
soon after I'd gone to sleep, there came a great commotion
on deck and shouts of " Peter, Peter, quick, come up, it's
a HUGE one."
     " What's a huge one ? " I grunted. The bunk was very
comfortable.
     " It's a fish—a huge fish. He jumped on board and is
in the scuppers. Oh DO come up and get it."
     " No, YOU get it. It's your watch."
     " Oh, but it's flapping. I don't want to get it. It's
right up forward and I can't see it, but it's flapping like
anything. Oh, please come up."
     With a very ill grace I started to clamber out of bed,
and just as I did so a big wave scooped itself onto the
deck and I could hear it rivering aft overhead. Then
came Jill's voice, sadly, " Oh ! It's gone again."
     I climbed back to bed thinking longingly of our escaped
breakfast. Jill was heartbroken, so heartbroken that the
Lord must have taken pity on her, for she caught a tunny
on our rod the very next morning. We fried it in batter
and had fish and rice for supper.
     Supper-time was always conversation time. Most of the
rest of the day we seemed either to be busy or else asleep,

but supper was the big meal of the day and we made a social occasion of it. One evening Jill had been doodling with a pair of dividers while she waited for some of Gus Angermeyer's smoked goat to finish stewing and said, " Do you realise that by the time we reach Pitcairn we'll be almost exactly halfway across the Pacific ? "

I hadn't realised it, but she was quite right, and a little private glow spread through both of us. We really WERE getting somewhere now.

Halfway across the Pacific. There was magic in the thought, but a certain amount of anxiety as well. How infuriating it would be to reach Pitcairn and then find we couldn't go ashore there. The Pilot, describing the anchorage, was terribly gloomy about it and suggested that at this time of year landing was impossible on very nearly half the days, but then the Pilot was always a bit depressing about everything. It obviously had to be.

" What'll we do," Jill once asked, " if we can't land ? Shall we hang around and see if it gets better, or shall we go on ? "

We discussed this for a long time and finally came to the conclusion that we'd wait for a few days at least, for Pitcairn was high on the list of places that interested us. We'd bought the three books, ' Mutiny on the *Bounty*,' ' Pitcairn Island ' and ' Men Against the Sea,' which described the whole of the *Bounty* episode, and we had become very thrilled with the whole terrible story. We MUST see the place in real life if we possibly could.

" Perhaps if we can't anchor," I suggested, " we might be able to get some of the islanders to sail *Salmo* off and on for a while just to let us go ashore. They're supposed to be terrific seamen, so it should be safe enough."

There was no end to the speculation we indulged in. The navigational problem, too, was a more enthralling one than usual, for Pitcairn is such a tiny blob of land in such a huge expanse of ocean that we couldn't afford

to miss it. " You must be crazy," the *Pandora's* skipper
had said to us in the Galapagos, " to go sailing round the
world without a radio and just relying on that chronometer
of yours to tell the time with." He'd been a great one
for ' figuring,' as he called it, and had at once whipped
out a sheet of paper and after a few moments intensive
calculation said triumphantly, " Why if that clock goes
just two seconds a day faster or slower than you think
it does during your passage, do you realise you'll be sixty
miles out in your calculations. But with a radio you'd
be right on. Bound to be. They give more than eighty
different time-signals every day that you could pick up."

I hate wireless sets. Not only do I find that they don't
usually work for me, but they seem to take all the interest
out of sailing. One of the great joys of life in a small
boat is the feeling of independence that it gives, the knowledge that one sinks or swims (quite literally, very nearly)
by one's own unaided effort. Wireless sets take that feeling
away, if one KNOWS the time, then landfalls become a
mathematical certainty instead of a glorious and exciting
occasion.

Nevertheless, as time went by we became more and more
anxious about our position. I had checked the chronometer by observation at the Galapagos and the results
had been slightly disconcerting. Instead of losing three
seconds a day, as it had been doing up in Canada and
America, my sights suggested it had been losing seven
seconds, and I had attributed the change to temperature.
Now that we were coming south, out of the tropics, I
thought that the rate should grow progressively less again
and allowed for it accordingly, but there was no way of
telling, until Pitcairn either did or didn't appear, whether
this theory was the correct one. That nasty remark kept
straying back to my mind: ' If your chronometer loses
just two seconds more than you think it does, you'll be
sixty miles out in your calculations. . . .'

On we went, and on and on. It looked as though it would be a three-week passage, though we had allowed for four when we sailed. The trade wind blew steadily day after day, and every day we ran a hundred and thirty, a hundred and thirty-five, or a hundred and forty miles. The daily crosses of our noon positions and the weekly dots inside a circle (when we took a sight) trailed their way down the chart, and on our fifteenth day at sea there were only another thousand miles left to go. We started to eat our salted langouste, and after being enraptured with it for the first two or three meals grew tired of it. We had it cold first, with salad dressing, on a day when we did our weekly bread-bake. Then we had it hot with white sauce over it. We made fish pie from it, and finally decided that, although we had nearly a biscuit-tin left we'd have to give it a rest or we'd never be able to look it in the face again. " And I ALWAYS used to order lobster when anyone stood me an expensive dinner," Jill lamented, " I'll never be able to again. I'm sick of the beastly stuff."

Meat had been the most difficult of our supply problems. We had intended to take on board a big consignment of dehydrated goods from an experimental factory in England, but there had been some terrible mix-up over import regulations in Canada, and though we had been allowed to take huge quantities of dehydrated cod, dehydrated fruit and dehydrated vegetable, the meat had been forbidden to us. All the other items had been such a huge success that we were miserable at the loss and often used to brood about it and plan terrible hunger tortures for all customs officials to undergo. Had it not been for the langouste and the smoked goat (which took a bit of getting used to but was then quite good) we would have been in a fix for stores, meaty stores anyway, because neither of us liked tinned meat very much and rarely bought any.

Baking bread in an over-lively boat is a wonderful panto-mime, particularly when, as in our case, we weren't at all sure how to do it and had to keep on comparing recipes the whole time. We used to mix the dough in the pressure-cooker and then put it out into the sun in the cockpit (when there was any) to rise. The kneading, too, was a problem, because we always seemed to have to break off at a crucial point and put out a hand to stop ourselves from falling over, so the whole boat rapidly became covered in a thin layer of doughy flour. We used to make four loaves in a batch, but since only one at a time could go into the oven it was a lengthy operation. As the first loaf neared completion we'd both find our mouths watering as the smell spread throughout the cabin, and we'd be waiting, poised with knives and butter, for it to come out of the oven. We both lost all our inhibitions and fairly tucked into that first loaf, so we really found ourselves with only three loaves to last the rest of the week. But oh! the joy of fresh bread in a boat : it just makes all the difference to life.

Another trait which we used to note in ourselves was an obsession about fair shares. Each of us, ever since our marriage, had tended to cast suspicious glances at the other's drink when it was poured out, but now we found we had descended to counting the number of peach segments and raspberries that we doled out at supper-time. A tin of peaches, for example, allowed twenty-six apiece, while eighty raspberries constituted a ration.

" Where have all the sultanas gone to ? " Jill asked accusingly one day. " Do you come down and eat them during the night watches ? "

" Well, I sometimes have a few, I suppose," I answered, privately trying to add up the number of handfuls I'd taken out recently. I'd meant to fill the tin up again, but had forgotten.

" A few indeed ! " Jill snorted, " it looks like about a pound and a half in the last three days."

" Well, what about fruit juice ? " I retaliated. " There

was nearly half a saucepanful of plum-juice left the other
night and I was saving it for breakfast. Where did it go
to ? "

"Oh, but that was different," said Jill, "I was thirsty."

Five hundred miles left to go, three and a half days,
and we realised that in spite of all our good intentions
we hadn't taken a single shot of life at sea to put into our
film.

"We must get some," said Jill, suddenly businesslike,
"or else we never will. Go and get the camera."

"No," I said, up in arms at once, "I got it the last time,
when we took those shots of the storm petrels following
the wake. Don't you remember ? It's your turn."

"Oh, I'm always getting it," said Jill (which was a
lie), but down she went, nevertheless, and unstrapped the
big unwieldy camera from its stowage, wrapped it in polythene in case it should get splashed, and came back on
deck with it and with the book in which we wrote down
the sequences as we took them. She flipped through some
of the back pages refreshing her memory of the shots
we'd already taken, then said, "Well, we're still short of
some good linking shots . . . things like the bow-wave,
and the lee-rail fizzing along in the water, and the sails
and that sort of thing : and we also need a bit of a reefing
sequence. Any ideas ? "

We thought about it for a long time and finally decided
to start off with a shot taken from the cabin of me steering. "Taken from the cabin it'll make a change," said
Jill. "Most of our shots of sitting in the cockpit have
been taken from the upper deck."

She wrote down in her book 'Open with seven second
Medium shot . . . Peter steering.' Then she went on,
"Peter looks up at mainsail with worried expression—and
for goodness' sake try to LOOK worried," she threw in, in
an aside to me, "not just all stiff and embarrassed—Close
up, three seconds, Peter worried."

" What'll we have then ? " she asked. " A shot of the
sail or one of the lee-rail getting wet ? "

" Better have the lee-rail," I suggested ; " if you just
show the sail no one will know that it looks any different
from usual. We can't introduce noises-off of wind shrieking in the rigging. And if you do that—take the lee-rail,
I mean, then I'd better not look UP and look worried, I'd
better look ALONG."

She scrubbed out her last entry and changed it to ' Peter
looks at lee-rail, worried.' And we went through our little
scene trying to imagine what it would look like on a
screen, and to give the whole sequence continuity. After
we'd done that, we wandered round the boat with the
exposure-meter to the places where we planned to take
the shots from, working out the camera-settings, so that
when the shooting began we'd have as little to do as
possible and consequently lessen the chance of wetting
the camera. It all took quite a long time, and in the
process we changed two or three of our original ideas.
" Now, when you do the close-up shot of a hand on the
reefing handle, winding it, you'll have to use the telephoto
lens and take it from the cockpit. If you came up close
to take it with the standard lens your shadow would be
all over everything."

We'd been reading lots of filming books and took all
our shooting very seriously, often spending days arguing
about the best way of getting some particular sequence.
It was all rather fun, and added immensely to the interest
of the whole of the film idea.

At length we took our shots of the reefing of the mainsail and began to think how to take one of the bow-wave.
It was a very difficult task, because from the deck you
couldn't see the bow-wave at all, while if you hung over
the side the camera just got soaked. The angles were
wrong too. What was needed was a very long bowsprit
on the end of which to perch to get back a bit from the

subject. Even with three lenses our camera needed some
room to take a picture.

We tried this way of doing it and we tried that way,
and none of them was any good, but just as we decided
that that was one of the shots we would have to do without,
I was struck with an idea and dived into the cabin.

" What on earth's wrong ? " said Jill, as I scrabbled at
her bunk and stripped the bedclothes off it.

" My darling," I replied, " do you not yet realise that
you're married to a genius ? "

From her rather blank expression, it was obvious that
she didn't, so I had to go on and explain that by lashing
the foot of her bunk-spring (which was on a steel frame)
to the gunwale and securing the top of it to the spinnaker
halliard I could make a sort of movable drawbridge on
which I could lie, well out from the side and yet above
the danger line for splashes, holding the camera trained
on the stem. It felt slightly wobbly when I got there
and the spring was uncomfortable, but it certainly did
give a lively view of the white plume of water splitting
away from the forefoot . . . the bone in our teeth.

I took the camera out and got several shots, varying
the exposure very slightly each time, so as to be sure of
getting some at least which would be perfect, and then
when I finished I just lay there for the joy of watching.
Above the main plume of white, a little rainbow hovered,
and tiny droplets of water shimmered and flashed as the
sun caught them. The sea itself was a deep blue, and
Salmo's hull, cream above the waterline and red below,
made a lovely contrast. The curve of the stem-piece,
rising and falling gently, and steadily slicing each wave
that passed beneath it, seemed perfectly shaped for its
function of splitting a furrow through the water. A long,
long furrow it had split already, I reflected, one which
stretched nearly ten thousand miles back to the Clyde.
I rolled over on my perch and gazed aft to look at the

wake. It wasn't like a furrow at all, it was a flashing white ribbon that sprang from the stern, made up of patches and blotches of silver foam, and dark flattened water, unmarked by the wind. Fifty feet astern, the wind riffles reappeared, but the foam patches stayed : *Salmo's* signature written in the sea.

" People always say we must find life terribly dull at sea," I said to Jill from my strange perch, " but it isn't, is it ? "

" Dull ! " she said. " Good gracious, no. That's the last thing it is. Don't you think you'd better come back inboard now, it's nearly lunch-time."

CHAPTER THIRTEEN

PITCAIRN

LUNCH-TIME—and I put a triumphant little cross on the chart, the twenty-third since leaving the Galapagos, and said to Jill, " Just another hundred miles to go. Wonder if we'll sight it tomorrow ? "—' it ' of course being Pitcairn.

" You know that patent allowance you applied to the chronometer rate ? " said Jill; " you know ? when you said you thought it had taken to going faster in hot weather, or slower or something ? Well what happens if it doesn't ? "

" Doesn't what ? " I replied helpfully, then suddenly remembered it was Jill's supper that night so changed it to, " Well, I suppose it means we'll get there earlier or later. Depending on whether it's faster or slower than we think it is."

" I think it's slower. Which is it if it's slower ? Are we easter or wester than we think we are ? "

I was afraid she'd ask that. I never can remember which is which. Even if I have an old envelope handy to do calculations on. But then Jill never remembers either, so I gravely pronounced, " Slower, easter. Faster, wester," and changed the subject.

Jill had the ' dogs ' next evening and was steering. Well, sort of steering, but reading a book mostly, for the wind was light. So I offered to come up and give her a spell if she'd cook the supper. Privately I thought it was about time that Pitcairn turned up, and it would be much easier to keep an unostentatious look-out for it when on deck than while cooking supper.

" Oh no, you don't," Jill replied. " It's my watch. You get on and cook the supper and I'll tell you if anything appears. I'm looking round every quarter of an hour. How far away did you say it ought to be now ? "

" Twenty-five miles."

Fish curry. Fry the onions, fillet the fish, and flake it on to them. Add curry powder, flour, and some of the water the fish was cooked in. Sultanas, chillis—and a dash of lime-juice. Lime-juice. That was it. The limes lived, all brown and shrivelled-looking, in an old beer-crate on the upper deck by the mast. I went forward to get one. Not to look round about naturally, just to get a lime. And then, BINGO ! there it was. Very fine on the starboard bow, a dark-blue hummock rumpling the line of the horizon.

I sauntered aft again, bursting with smugness and the great and holy joy of making a landfall : the joy that drags people into boats and sends them sailing ; the joy that is just that little different, that little bit more joyous than anything else in the world.

" I've seen it," I said

" Oh you RAT ! " said Jill. " Oh WHERE ? Oh yes. Oh how wonderful. Oh isn't it splendid ? Oh why didn't I see it. Oh it IS unfair."

We had an extra sherry on the strength of it, and chattered like children until long after it grew dark and the smudge on the horizon had melted into the blackness. What would the islanders be like, we wondered. Would we be able to anchor ? Would they row out to meet us in a longboat ? Would it be safe to leave *Salmo* untended ? And if it wouldn't, then would one of the islanders be willing to act as a boatkeeper ? There were lots and lots of things that we wondered, but always whenever there was a gap in the conversation, we'd come back to, " Oh, isn't this wonderful ! Here we are at Pitcairn. It's US and we're nearly there. We've found it. We've got there.'

At two in the morning a blacker bit of blackness loomed
up ahead, so we hove-to and both slept like logs while
Salmo bobbed and danced her gentle dance with the ocean
as she waited for daylight. But when it came the sky was
grey and lowering, and rain-squalls chased one another
across an ugly and tumbled sea. Alone in the middle of
it stood Pitcairn, blue and fierce-looking, with wisps of
cloud streaming away from its shoulders.

" By gosh ! It really is tiny," we told each other ;
" smaller than Ailsa Craig even. How can people live on
an island as small as that ? "

The squalls gradually departed as we closed Bounty
Bay, which the Pilot described as ' a practicable landing-
place in fair weather.' The sea grew calmer and at last
a watery sun shone through the overcast and lit up the
greenery ashore : rich and lush and bursting with life.
First we were able to make out wireless masts, some
corrugated-iron roofs, then cultivated squares of garden
that looked like pocket-handkerchiefs laid out to dry on
the hillside, and finally some goats scrabbling uphill from
the beach. Our eyes followed them upwards and we both
shouted together, " Gimme the binoculars ! "

Jill grabbed them from their hook. " They look like
women. Yes, I'm sure they are. All in bright-coloured
clothes, standing in a big bunch. And there's a flagstaff
there. That must be the landing-place just down below
them in among all the rocks and things. Yes, I can see
some thatched roofs down there. Boat-houses probably.
But there's no sign of a boat coming out."

" Lots of time for that yet," I said. " They'll not want
to row farther than they have to. At least, I sincerely
hope they do come out to meet us, because then they can
show us where people usually do go to. From here it
doesn't look as though there's a scrap of shelter anywhere."

Nearer we approached, and nearer still, and at last
there came a flash of white from among the rocks and

surf of Bounty Bay. Oar-blades caught the sun, glittered
and then dipped back into the sea again. Our smugness
returned ; for clearly we were being accorded the full
welcome routine.

We MUST take some photographs as they come out,"
said Jill, " otherwise we'll never do it and we'll kick ourselves for ever after." So we argued for a while as we
always did about whose turn it was to get the camera
and whose turn to take the photographs, for neither of
us wanted to waste a moment of this rather special arrival.
We wanted to have the photographs but didn't want to
do anything so humdrum as to take them.

The men in the boat were nearly as colourful as the
women up at the look-out station. Each of them wore
something a little different from his neighbour : a bright
scarf, an old uniform cap or a tartan shirt ; they really
looked the part of mutineers' descendants. Fred Christian,
who was steering, was particularly eye-catching as he stood
grasping the steering-oar and inching his ponderous craft
in towards the diminutive *Salmo*. " Oh, I think he's a
DUCK," said Jill, " with those lovely features and dis-
tinguished-looking grey hair." The postal authorities must
also have thought he looked a bit duck-like ; for we later
found that he featured (in an agricultural pose) as star of
' Island Scene ' on the eightpenny stamps.

" Where do we anchor ? " we both shouted as soon as
they came within range.

" We'll show you," they replied, and two figures jumped
neatly on board from one plunging craft to the other, just
as easily and quietly as one might step from a stationary
train onto the platform.

" I'm Vernon Young," said the first man, " and this is
my brother Andrew."

Two hours later, ready to go ashore, we sat in the
cockpit waiting for Vernon to return and fetch us. Months
before, in Canada, we had been shown a film of Pitcairners

flinging their boats through the surf, and it had given Jill the heebie-jeebies on a major scale. Now that we knew we were about to find out what it felt like, we were both rather silent. Besides that we had worries about *Salmo's* safety. Should we leave her to look after herself or shouldn't we ? Would she drag her anchor or wouldn't she ?

The longboat had left us some time ago ; they wanted to get themselves ready for church, they said ; but Vernon had promised to return and fetch us when we'd had time to change and make sure that the anchor had taken a proper hold.

At last we saw movement on shore. Two figures moved here and there among the boat-houses and we saw them dragging a long canoe-like boat down towards the water. Here goes ! we thought.

Our own motion was terrible. It was quite the most uncomfortable berth I've ever anchored in. The rocks roared and spouted at what seemed to be little more than an arm's length away, and what made things worse, the backwash turned and fought with the main ocean swell beneath our keel, wrenching at the anchor-cable and throwing up vile pyramidal waves all round about. *Salmo's* antics combined with everything else to make us edgy.

" Look ! " said Jill, " we can't possibly take the camera with us. It's bound to be ruined."

I wasn't too happy about taking it either, but I did long to have a record of what it felt like to go surfing in for the first time. If we didn't take the sequence today, would we ever have a better chance ? Would we ? wouldn't we ?

Vernon and his companion had the boat in the water now and were standing up in it, facing seaward, just inshore of the surf-line. A huge wave broke, all white and frothy, and roared in towards them. They paddled a few strokes towards it ; the canoe rose in a light splatter of foam and the wave passed beneath them, racing for the beach. Still they waited, holding the canoe in the same position. Another wave came at them and another and another.

We thought of our camera and we thought of the film that we wanted to take, and *Salmo* wheeled and danced beneath us like a thing demented.

Suddenly the two figures began to paddle furiously. The paddles dipped into the water at a terrific rate and the canoe shot forward. Two little waves went underneath them and then a great big black grandfather of a sea began to rear up to seaward. Higher it rose and higher still. Curling forward, toppling, toppling, toppling . . . the canoe rushed to meet it before it should break. It seemed so unfair that they should have to meet this wave, this monster, just when we thought they were through the last line of surf and clear of everything. And then they met : the sea and the canoe. And as quietly as a seagull, the canoe lifted up over the wave-top without shipping a drop. The wave broke with a roar a boat's length astern of them, and the tempo of their paddling eased down. In a minute more they were alongside no whit worried . . . no, no, it had been a very quiet trip out this one, and we were at once ashamed that the palms of our hands should be sticky with sweat.

We bundled into the canoe, Jill aft and myself for'ard, with our loads of clothes and washing-gear and cameras clutched to our bosoms, and before we were really aware of it we were speeding back for the beach again. But this time Vernon and Reynold Warren (as Vernon's crew had been introduced) were sitting down and rowing the boat instead of standing and paddling.

After so much anticipation the trip turned out to be a bit of an anticlimax. A wave crawled underneath us and broke ; the bows went down and we shot inshore in a flurry of broken water. Close on our port side a line of

rocks spouted as the wave hit each in turn. Very fierce
they looked, and it was hard to realise that it was our
wave that was causing all the bother. As the last of the
rocks rushed past us, Vernon gave a mighty heave on
his oar ; the wave passed beneath us and we slewed to
port into the sheltered water left by the rocks, and then
all of a sudden we found that we were there. Ahead lay
the beach, covered in a fan-shaped skidway of roughly
squared logs and beyond the skidway lay the boat-houses.
We leaped ashore, steadied the boat while a spent wave
lifted her onto the first baulk of timber, and then we ran
her easily up the beach. We were ashore. We had arrived.

Vernon squelched up the muddy path ahead of us, the
red clay squeezing itself like toothpaste between his
knobbled and calloused toes. We slipped and slithered
in his wake, determined that we'd never wear shoes again,
and wondering how much higher we'd have to go before
the path began to flatten out a little. The only thing
that kept us going was a delightful steaming white vision
that floated before our eyes—the bath that we'd been
promised. It was more than two months since we had
been able to indulge in one.

At last we reached the top, a sort of flat platform with
a large shed on it, close to the flagstaff where we'd first
seen the crowd of women gathered.

" Well, there she is," said Vernon. " Better take a last
look at her before we go on. You can't see the bay from
my house."

Far, far, below us lay *Salmo* rolling at her anchor. Even
at this distance we hardly dared to watch her frantic
curvetting and plunging. The mast wove giddy spirals
through the air, round and round, and down and up and
down again. We thought of the anchor chain and we
thought of the anchor and we thought of all that *Salmo*
meant to us and very nearly decided to go back down
the path again and back out through the surf to her.

But common sense came to our aid. We weren't anchored quite as close inshore as we had seemed to be. Seen from this height she was really quite well out. And the anchor wasn't dragging. *Salmo* plunged and she swooped but she never moved at all. We agreed that she looked rather like a celluloid duck in a very large bath, and decided that she'd be able to look after herself unless the weather grew worse, so we followed Vernon up the path, where it led through the trees to Adamstown.

At once we found ourselves in a totally different world from the one of cliffs and sky and seabirds and water that we had known for so long and just left. Everything was lush and green and flamboyant. There were flowers everywhere, hibiscus and lilies and convolvulus. The houses of Adamstown stood in little clearings all dappled where the sun shone through the trees, and hens pecked and scrabbled around them. For the last fifty yards the path grew even steeper and more slippery, so that it was almost on hands and knees that we finished off our journey. Vernon's wife Lillian stood waiting for us at the doorway and gave us a terrific welcome which ended up with the wish that we should make ourselves ' at ho-am.' It's a funny trick of speech they seem to have, the splitting of all long vowel sounds into two : things on Pitcairn are never all right, they're always ' ri-aht.'

The bath was a large two-handled zinc affair (not at all like our vision of chrome and enamel) and we filled it with buckets from a cauldron of boiling water conveniently built over a brick fireplace just outside the bathroom door. We wallowed for a long time, lathering ourselves all over, then tipped the water out with a wondrous hoosh onto the concrete floor, from where it rushed down a sort of chute affair and out among the hens.

Feeling very spick and span we went in to join Vernon and Lillian, but my complacency was rudely shaken when Vernon immediately offered to lend me some clothes to

go to church in. When I saw the knife-edge creases in
the borrowed trousers and felt the starch crackling in the
shirt, I realised that we'd have to raise our standards of
spick and spannery very considerably while we stayed on
the island. Jill passed muster in her skirt and blouse,
but only just ; for all the time we slithered downhill to
the church, Lillian kept on assuring her very kindly that
she was ' Quite all ri-aht ' and that she wasn't to worry
about not wearing a dress. Vernon, I noticed, had immaculate white tennis-shoes, but as a concession to the
breadth of his feet, they didn't have any laces in them.

During the service our minds wandered slightly and we
looked round at the congregation. It was at once obvious
that everyone else was suffering from shoe trouble as well,
as Vernon and all round about we watched toes being
stretched luxuriously while the shoes themselves remained
beneath the pews.

Besides ourselves, the pastor—from Sydney—was the
only one whose feet seemed quiescent. Above the shoes
he wore a particularly virulent blue business suit. We
met him next day stripped to the waist and sweating like
a bull as he dug the foundations for the low wall that was
to go round the church. It was a very hot day and he
invited us to his house to have some orange-juice from
the refrigerator.

" Yes," he said, " me and the schoolmaster are the only
two foreigners on the island. Both of us come for three-
year tours. He's from New Zealand."

We asked how he liked it. " Oh it's grand," he replied.
" They're wonderful people, the islanders, as you've probably discovered. Very nice, terribly generous ; they even
lend me this house, you know. When I go the owner
will move back into it and then someone else will lend
HIS house to the next pastor."

We wanted to know about money, for we'd never seen
any being used. " No, none is used. Not on the island,

that is. Only for buying stamps or for anything that's
needed from outside. That's what all the souvenir-making
is for. They work like blacks at that, you know. Stay
up half the night sometimes if a ship's expected in and
stocks are low. I often think they work too hard at it.
It's a dead-end sort of life carving a never-ending series
of flying-fish or making baskets or whatever it may be.
No one ever seems to think of branching out into anything new. There used to be cows on the island at one
time ; did quite well too by all accounts. But it was
too much trouble . . . didn't leave enough time for making
souvenirs . . . so they have to buy canned milk and canned
meat all the time. And that means they have to sell still
more souvenirs to pay for it. A very vicious circle."

Underneath his house the pastor kept a sort of Pitcairn
museum. No one knows who the first inhabitants of the
island were, though everyone has theories on the subject.
Whoever they may have been they seem to have been an
industrious lot, for the pastor hauled out box upon box of
stone weapons and instruments, and finally a darned great
length of barnacled timber. " That's the stock of the
Bounty's anchor," he announced, " do you see ? There's
still even a bit of the rope cable left, secured to the ring.
Some Americans with aqualungs from the yacht *Yankee*
fished it all up a year ago. The anchor itself is down at
the landing still. You probably saw it on your way up."

As a matter of fact we had seen it. Vernon had told
us, slightly aggrievedly, that the pastor and the schoolmaster were always on at people to drag it up to the
square outside the church and set it up on a concrete
base. But, Vernon had gone on, it was a very heavy
thing to move, and most people thought it would be far
better to cut it up into small bits where it lay. " But
what would you use the bits for ? " Jill had asked. " Oh,
we'd mount them on wooden bases, you see, and sell them
as paper-weights to the tourists."

Clearly the *Bounty* anchor was a big bone of contention in local political life.

The *Bounty* herself was not nearly as 'lost' as we'd imagined her to be when we read a long article about her 'finding' in a number of British papers. She lies, what's left of her, just where Fletcher Christian beached her and burnt her, right next door to the landing-place. The chief remaining pieces are the pigs of ballast that litter the shore. Periodically the Admiralty get very upset about it when they think that people are improperly making away with them. Not that they do very much about it except write aggrieved letters to the British consul at Tahiti, telling him to put a stop to the practice forthwith. "And the remarkable thing is," said the consul when we met him months later, "that I once DID find a pig of the stuff in one of the yachts that came in here. How they got it on board was a mystery, it weighed nearly three-quarters of a ton, as I discovered as soon as I had seized it on the Admiralty's behalf. It took twelve Tahitians to lift it into a lorry and another twelve to lift it out again. Then I asked the Admiralty what they wanted me to do with it, because it was lying in the middle of the lawn at the consulate and everyone was hurting themselves by falling over it. I never did get any answer, so I finally shipped it back to them in a cardboard box."

One day Jill and I were sitting writing letters in Vernon's house. Vernon had gone up the hill to his garden to pick oranges, because a ship was expected to call in a couple of days and he wanted to have some handy to sell to them. Lillian was outside in the kitchen baking, and we had the room to ourselves. The most conspicuous object in it was the baby who lay asleep in the bath. We had thought for a while that it was Vernon's baby, because it seemed to be so very much a member of the household : it was some days before we found that it was a rather distant cousin or nephew or something like that. The parents,

Lillian had announced calmly, were away at Oeno. The pastor, when we visited him, had apologised that his wife wasn't there to give us a meal. She, too, was ' away at Oeno,' and it wasn't long before we found out that very nearly half the population of the island was missing. These migratory urges seem to hit the islanders once or twice a year and off they all go, either to Henderson Island (to collect wood to make into flying-fishes) or, as now, to Oeno where shells (for necklaces) are the attraction. Now, Oeno is closer than Henderson, a mere seventy-five miles, but its highest point is the top of a palm-tree eighty feet above the water. It is a perfect example of an atoll, complete with a very fine surrounding reef, and there's never a man of all those men in Pitcairn who knows the first thing about navigation in its more widely accepted sense. Apparently they don't need to. They just go on the principle of ' Oh yes. Oeno's over there. We always go this way.' And, what's more, in all the years that they've been doing it, no one has ever got lost. To add to the excitements, neither island has a proper landing-place : in each you not only have to land, but also have to get back to sea again by waiting for a wave sufficiently large to come crashing over the reef and provide an adequate depth of water for floating purposes. And it's not just the men who do this. The women go along, too, and children down to four years old. They're tough, mighty tough in the South.

As we sat and wrote our letters and Jill made clucking noises at the baby in its bathtub-bed, I couldn't help noticing that the weather was getting filthier and filthier. The tops of the palms were bending farther and farther over, and more and more white horses appeared on the small patch of sea that was all that Vernon's window commanded.

A blatter of rain drummed against the glass of the window and I felt I could stand it no longer. We made our way out to the kitchen. Like all the island kitchens it is an outside affair, a simple thatched hut over the top of two open stone fireplaces, where huge wood fires burn almost continuously. Lillian had just reached the stage of raking the embers out of her oven before she put the bread in. Anxious though we were, we had to pause to watch this operation. It's really very simple. The oven is made of huge stone slabs and the fire is lit inside it. When the time is judged to be ripe the embers are raked out and the heat left in the slabs of stone does the baking. Lillian thrust in her pans of dough and put the heavy iron door back in place across the oven's front. Then she turned to find out what was bothering us.

We told her it was the weather, and she considered for a few minutes. Vernon could not be got at for another hour. Reynold would probably be at home. Andrew might be, but he might have gone out fishing. If he wasn't at home then Charlie might be, or Willie or Dick. She'd ring up and find out.

The telephone is an astonishing contrivance, presented to the island by (I believe) the city of Auckland, though it looked as though someone had raided a museum to get hold of the bits. Calling is done by a complicated series of longs and shorts on the crank-type bell, but it doesn't really matter if you forget the code, for everyone seems to listen-in anyway. Very soon a crew was organised— Reynold and Andrew. Jill and I had meanwhile had a rapid parley in which it had been decided that she should stay behind and I would go out alone.

As we started off down the path I found that I was going faster and faster until I was nearly running. At each new vista of sea that opened up through gaps in the trees my heart sank further and further. Surely, surely, *Salmo* should be in sight in that gap. By the time I finally reached the place where you get the first glimpse of Bounty Bay I had firmly convinced myself

that I'd left my return too late, and that *Salmo* had long
ago dragged her anchor and joined the *Bounty* among the
rocks and surf. But, of course, she hadn't. There she
was, bouncing and wheeling as wildly as ever, but still
firmly anchored, and I felt ashamed of my foolish fears.

It took a few moments to reach the landing-place and
launch Andrew's canoe. Very soon we were waiting inside
the surf for a calm spell that would let us dash out without
a drenching—or worse. At last it came (though to me it
didn't look much calmer than it had done five or six
waves before) ; Reynold and Andrew paddled like maniacs.
Bang ! and we went through a small one : Bang ! through
another ; Whoosh ! and over a third, and there we were
at sea and heading towards the frantic *Salmo* who was
worrying at her cable as a dog worries a bone. It was
an enormous relief when I got some sail onto her and
broke out the anchor and headed away offshore to where
I could no longer hear the pounding of the surf.

It was a glorious, still, blue day when I returned, and
Jill was bursting to tell me about the birthday party she'd
been to on the night before.

" The amount we all ate ! " she said. " I've never seen
such quantities of food. There was breadfruit and fish
and corned-beef and taro and jelly and peas and new
bread and eggs." She sounded just like the Water-rat
preparing for a picnic. " And during the meal," she went
on, " I couldn't understand a word that anyone said
because they were all talking Pitcairn ; except occasionally
when they remembered and then some of them would
speak English to me for a bit. I'm beginning to understand Pitcairn a bit too. It's a sort of shorthand really.
' Wathingyugwendutama ' means ' what are you going to
do tomorrow ? ' But it's terribly difficult to understand
when they go at it hard. I believe the children get beaten
when they do it during school hours." Evidently she had
enjoyed her time as a castaway.

It was our last day. A ship was due to come in (there's
one every ten days or so, we were astonished to learn)
and we wanted to see what went on during these
visits.

The wireless operator had said the ship was due at ten
o'clock in the morning, so at nine we posted ourselves on
the landing-place. Fred Christian was the first to arrive ;
he strode down the path with a pole on his shoulders and
two baskets slung on either end of it, oranges and bananas
at one end, flying-fish, grass skirts and wooden tortoises
at the other. After him came Andrew Young, and then
in ones and twos they all arrived, all with baskets and all
chatting. A few of the women also gathered, but by island
custom (law almost) they don't go out to cargo-ships and
they sat a little apart in a patch of shade and laughed and
joked among themselves.

" The bell's been rung," said Vernon to me.

" What bell ? " I asked.

" Oh, the sighting bell," he replied. " It's always rung
by the first person to sight any ship and everyone who
wants to go out and meet it has to get down to the landing-
place within a quarter of an hour."

" Was it rung for us ? " Jill asked him.

" Oh yes," said Vernon. " It was young Donald over
there who was the first to see you when you appeared
that morning. He was just on his way down to go fishing."

We felt flattered. It was the first we had heard of this.

By a quarter to ten we could even see the ship—one
of the New Zealand Line—from the landing-place. Everyone gathered round one of the huge longboats and with
much shouting and laughing she was launched.

Vernon was very worried about Jill. He knew she was
longing to go out in the longboat, but he couldn't bring
himself to go against the island tradition of ' no women,'
and he was greatly relieved when Jill told him that she
quite realised she couldn't go. He had wanted her to

say that but hadn't been able to summon up the courage
to tell her so.

The confusion of loading up the boat was enormous.
Twenty-five people, a hundred baskets of this and that,
mail, the pastor, me, a boy who was going to New Zealand
to study medicine—all were finally crammed on board
somehow and we were ready to start. Everyone fumbled
for oars and shouted at everyone else and told them what
to do, not paying any attention to what anyone else was
shouting. Somehow, miraculously, the boat stayed afloat
and pointing the right way. More shouting, more laughing, more abuse of the coxswain, " Ach ! you couldn't
even steer a wheelbarra " (wheelbarrow seems to be a
Pitcairn jokeword—something like ' Wigan ' in English
music halls) and then, mysteriously, everyone began to
row. It was a calm day and we barely noticed the surf
as we went through it. We passed *Salmo* as she lay to
her anchor, and then everyone began to curse the captain
of the ship. " Ach ! silly old fool, never will bring his
ship in nearer than two mile," and " Ach ! he used to
be the mate in the old So-and-So. Crews always hate
him. Drinks like a fish." There's not much that they
miss, down in Pitcairn, of what swims within their ken.

Still arguing, shouting and laughing, we came alongside
the ship. A jumping-ladder was lowered and there was
a mad dive and devil take the hindmost to get on board
first. In a twinkling the boat was empty except for the
coxswain, the pastor and myself. Coxswains miss all the
trade on these occasions, so a strict rota is kept. More
sedately the pastor and I climbed on board to find that
everyone was already squatting on the deck and had set
up shop. Passengers thronged round them to ask
questions and to buy grass skirts and baskets, and money
clinked cheerfully. More corned beef, I thought to myself,
and then busily denied to an elderly Auckland lady having
any connection with bygone mutineers.

The ship stopped for only an hour and a half and we soon found ourselves back in the longboat and arguing furiously whether the wind would or wouldn't allow us to sail back. Obviously it wouldn't. It was dead in our faces and the longboat only boasts a very elderly lugsail and no keel or leeboard. I felt myself completely at home now and argued with the best of them : " Ach ! we couldn't even sail a wheelbarra back with the wind like this, let alone an old tub of a boat." We couldn't either. We had to row it back. All three miles of it.

Then Jill was collected and heaps of presents, fruit and bread and wooden flying-fishes, and letters for delivery to here and there and everywhere, and back to *Salmo* they took us.

We hoisted the sails, weighed the anchor and wondered at the ease with which it came up. No wonder it was easy ! The fluke had caught beneath a coral-head, and the tug, tug, tugging of the cable, as *Salmo* swooped and plunged when we were shortening-in, had sheared the shank clean across.

We breathed a prayer of thanks that it had happened no sooner, and turned our stern to the landing-place. Smaller it became and smaller still. The waving crowd at the lookout hill went back to their houses, and when it grew dark the island was once again a tiny smudge on the horizon.

CHAPTER FOURTEEN

THE Oeno party of Pitcairners was due to come back the day we sailed, so we thought we'd run along their route in the opposite direction to see if we could spot them. If we didn't, or if our navigation wasn't as good as theirs and we missed the island altogether, we'd pretend we hadn't been trying and just go on to Mangareva, which is the most southerly of the Tuomotus.

As it happened we did find it. Palm-trees poked their distinctive tops over the horizon while we were having breakfast, so we aimed for the middle one and went in to see what was what.

It was a perfect day, brilliantly blue, with a fresh breeze dusting the water with white cockades and spinning *Salmo* before it. I climbed to the upper crosstrees to get a better view, rejoicing, for the thousandth time, in the blocks which I'd screwed ladderwise to the fore-side of the mast for this very purpose. Climbing the mast of a lurching boat by scrambling up a bunch of halliards (as one usually has to) is a miserable and painful process.

From the deck all that could be seen of Oeno was a row of palms with the thinnest possible fringe of sand stretched beneath them, but from the crosstrees everything changed completely. The whole island and lagoon were spread out like a map. " I can see the reef," I shouted down, " and what a surf ! It's colossal."

A white ring of foam, unbroken, so far as I could see it, encircled a shimmering green lake, with the island,

crescent-shaped and golden as a new moon, forming its
far shore. Huge combers raced onto the reef, roaring as
they broke. They were an awe-inspiring sight as they
reared up like snakes about to strike, the curved leading
edges bending themselves further and still further forward,
white manes of spindrift streaming behind them until they
smashed themselves onto the coral.

For a long time I gazed entranced, for never before had
I seen such breakers. It seemed quite impossible that
any boat could get through them and into the lagoon.
Yet somewhere, somehow, the Pitcairners had done so.

" Any sign of a camp ? " Jill called up to me, " or boats
anchored anywhere ? "

I scanned the shore with the binoculars inch by inch,
my feet twisted round the mast and the harsh angles of
the crosstrees biting into my buttocks. " Can't see anything," I replied at length. " We must have passed them
during the night. Better head for Mangareva."

Jill pushed the tiller down and we swung away westerly,
leaving the palms, the golden sand and the spouting, angry
reef to their solitude. There weren't even any birds in
sight.

" Our first Pacific Island," said Jill when I reached the
deck again. " It's just exactly what I'd imagined it would
be. Most satisfactory. Hadn't you better check the chronometer since we know where we are for a change ? We
never got a check at Pitcairn, remember ; it was always
going to be ' tomorrow.' "

I dug out the sextant and took a sight ; we had lunch,
and then while I lay back at my ease in the cockpit with
a book, Jill went down to her bunk. We had settled
back to sea life again and the familiar problems associated
with it filled our heads once more.

It wasn't a long trip, three days only, and at breakfast
time one morning we threaded our way into the Mangareva
lagoon and on towards the village, following a tortuous

path through ledges and outcrops of coral. It was a glorious morning, all that a Pacific morning should be, and the hills looked green and inviting. The lagoon viewed from the masthead (from where the coral showed brown) was every imaginable shade of green and blue. White houses with red roofs gleamed among palm-trees, and at a nearby jetty lay a big white schooner with tall, tapered masts looking infinitely romantic. It was all too good to be true, too like a storybook of pearl smugglers and high Adventure. We scarcely spoke to each other for fear of breaking the spell.

A boat with an outboard engine came skimming towards us as we neared the anchorage, a French flag fluttering bravely from its ensign staff, and the romance died abruptly as an immaculate gendarme stepped on board.

" You will anchor here, please," he said.

" But can't we go in closer ? " we asked, fumbling through our rusty vocabularies for the unfamiliar words and phrases. *" Plus prêt du quai. Notre bateau a rames "* (here we indicated poor battered Prout, sunbleached and cocooned in lashings as it stood against the guard-rails) *" n'est pas convenable pour des voyages allongés."*

It wasn't either. The poor thing was leaking like a sieve after being used as a surf-boat at Pitcairn and a rock landing-craft at the Galapagos.

" You will anchor here, please," said the gendarme.

Sucking our teeth, we anchored. " Now," said the gendarme, " your papers, if you will be so good ! "

We handed them over, our passports, the Certificate of Registry and our clearance from Pitcairn, carefully obtained and beginning, ' To whom it may concern. Greetings. These presents are to certify. . . .'

He placed them all in his brief-case, saluted us ceremoniously, and stepped into his boat. The coxswain gave a flick of the outboard starter and off they skimmed. We watched the boat draw alongside a little jetty in front of the Gendarmerie and out stepped the gendarme, very upright, and strode into his office, leaving the coxswain to moor up the boat.

" I wonder if he's going to be difficult," said Jill ; " he seems to be a terribly super-efficient sort of a man."

I wondered too, but there was nothing we could do about it, except have lunch and hope for the best. We had, after all, visas for entering French Polynesia, even if they were two days out of date, owing to the unexpected length of our stays at Panama and the Galapagos.

Our summons to the Gendarmerie came during the afternoon. The coxswain came out to fetch us, very animated and friendly now, in the absence of his master, asking where we'd come from, how long we were going to stay, how big the boat was. Like all Polynesians, he was fascinated by boats.

The Gendarmerie stood, very clean and square, in a little compound. A white-painted flagstaff stood in front of it, embedded in a forty-gallon drum filled with concrete, the paths were all bordered with white-painted coral blocks, and even the flowerbeds were formal and regimented.

The gendarme greeted us from behind his desk, which was placed with mathematical exactitude in the centre of the room. Our papers lay tidily in front of him, neatly tagged together.

" Mangareva, you realise, is not the Port of Entry for the French Oceanic Possessions," he began. " You will have to go to Papeete " (it was the first time we had heard the word pronounced by a Frenchman, Papé-été, he called it).

" Of course," we replied, " we are going there. But we have come from Pitcairn, and we wished to visit your island first, since it is on our route. To go to Papeete first would add more than a thousand miles to our voyage."

" That," he said, " is regrettable. Entry here is not permitted, however. You must go first to Papeete ; after that you may come here if you wish to. You will sail this afternoon, perhaps ? "

" This afternoon," we both exploded, " but we've only just arrived and we've a parcel to deliver from Pitcairn. We want water and fresh vegetables ; we. . . ."

" Very well," he said, " you may sail tomorrow morning, but except for the necessary replenishments you will not stay ashore, please. It is the elections, you comprehend," he added, as if that explained everything. " If it were not for the elections it might have been possible to arrange that you stayed, but as it is. . . ." he made a deprecatory gesture, handed back our passports and certificate and once more saluted smartly.

We suggested radio-ing to Tahiti ; we suggested lots of things, but he countered everything with " *C'est les élections vous savez ?* " and that was the end of the matter. We found ourselves out on the verandah muttering " What the hell have the elections got to do with it ? " It was a mystery we never solved, and we walked sadly back to the jetty once more, oblivious of the whispering of the palm fronds, the bougainvilleas that had so delighted us half an hour earlier, and the flaming hibiscus trumpets that nodded their heads as we passed. The savour had gone out of life. We felt flat and angry and deflated.

" Probably very good for us," we reflected wryly as the coxswain motored us back over the sparkling lagoon to *Salmo*. " We've grown terribly spoiled after all this time, being greeted as something a bit special, everywhere we go, and being charming and modest about it. Do us both a power of good to be kicked out as undesirables." That's what we said, but in reality we were very upset. Mangareva is an interesting island and we'd been looking forward to exploring it. For many years it was governed by a mad Catholic priest who built a huge cathedral and tried to convert all the Polynesian girls to chastity by enclosing them in a nunnery up in the interior. He had even constructed special lavatories for them, we had been told, hewn from rock, and now that the whole building is abandoned they stand there still. . . . That's what we had heard, but we wanted to see for ourselves, and now we couldn't. It was very galling.

There was a tap sprouting from the ground in the middle of a palm-grove near the jetty where the schooner lay, and from it we replenished our tanks, laboriously trundling a ten-gallon can from the tap to the beach, from the beach to the Prout and then from the Prout into *Salmo*. Quite a crowd gathered to watch these proceedings, all of them very friendly, cheerful and inquisitive, and all, so far as we could see, supremely disinterested in the elections which were presumably in progress. We delivered our parcel (to the wife of an erstwhile Pitcairner) and were given a rather elderly hen and four drinking-coconuts in exchange, and then we reckoned that our ration of shore-leave as allocated by the gendarme had expired, and we rowed back on board.

It was late by that time, and the light was rapidly going, or we would have up-anchored there and then ; but as it was, the thought of attempting the rather tricky passage through the coral purely on memory and in the darkness daunted me, so we went early to bed and nursed our grievance until nearly midnight.

"What do we do next? " was the burden of our thoughts; for we wanted to go and visit Rapa, eight hundred miles farther south-west, the most lonely of any of the French islands, but it, too, was no port of entry. It, too, would probably be holding elections, and the thought of being kicked out of yet another place without even being able to have a look round was not an attractive one.

" Well, if we never go there, we'll never know if they're a friendlier bunch than this lot, so let's," was our final decision.

Very early the next morning we weighed, I climbed the

mast, and with sun shining as brightly as ever, the lagoon just as glorious and the schooner just as romantic looking, I conned Jill through the coral, and back through the reef into the deep blue of the open sea.

Jill had decided that she would do the navigation on this leg. It would give her confidence to know that she could find a lonely island seven hundred miles from anywhere, she said. I privately wondered what it would give her if she didn't find it, but had the sense to hold my peace.

" And what's more," she said, " I'm going to do it properly. None of this sloppy stuff that you go in for, taking sights only once a week. I'm going to take sights every day."

Her enthusiasm goaded her on and on. She didn't approve of the chart we carried. Wasn't large enough scale, she said, so she set about building herself a real super-dooper model on the back of one of our old ones. She put a cross right in the middle of the paper and then looked up Rapa in the ' Pacific Pilot.' Then she proudly labelled her cross 28 degrees 05 minutes South ; 144 degrees 42 minutes East. Then a thought struck her. What part of Rapa do you suppose that is ? The middle of it ? Or Ahurei Bay or what ?

I told her I didn't think it mattered very much what bit it was. We could leave details to sort themselves out when we got there. Just so long as it was Rapa was all that mattered.

Jill seemed doubtful, but decided to go on with the chart anyway. Making charts was a newly learned achievement she was very proud of. She drew a line at twenty-eight degrees angle from the bottom edge of the paper and began dropping perpendiculars from it and measuring like mad until she'd drawn a nice grid on the paper and could include another cross at the top right edge to represent Mangareva. It still looked pretty bare, so she decided to mark in the Marotiri rocks though, as she explained, it wasn't much use putting them in because we wouldn't see them anyway. "They'd be," she wielded her dividers for a moment, " eighteen miles south of our line."

I had not heard of these rocks before, so I started to read them up in the Pilot. They sounded desolate in the extreme—three big rocks that stuck up a hundred feet above an empty ocean, and a mass of shallows and foul ground all round and between them. It was one of the richest fishing-grounds in the world, said the Pilot, and seabirds abounded. We could well imagine it. Here if anywhere birds and fish should be uninterfered with. One ship a year goes to Rapa, and probably not one in twenty years would go near Marotiri.

The weather defeated Jill's good intentions of taking daily sights. In fact, we never saw the sun after the first day out. Instead, we ran into a dank and miserable gale, with streaming rain that never seemed to end. It drummed on the deck and on the canvas of our hatch-cover. The cockpit lay bare and streaming with water for days on end, littered with an untidy tangle of mainsheet and our red plastic bucket, which rolled forlornly to and fro in the well. We barely poked our noses out, and steered entirely from the cabin with the tiller-lines, while *Salmo* raced and plunged and leaped on her headlong way, her mast weaving crazy spirals against the low-flying clouds. Gradually the sea built up, rolling in from the quarter, each wave crowned with white, and seemingly enormous as it loomed up over the spray screen that encircled the cockpit. Every now and then I had to make a cautious trip forward to reef or to change sail, but it never blew so hard that we had to heave to. Mostly we just flew along with the trysail and Number Two staysail, chasing the miles away, one hundred and forty a day for five consecutive days.

It cleared slightly one afternoon so we both took sights ;

Jill to work out, and I just so as to have one in case it might come in handy. And then we started in on cine-photography, trying to get some shots to remind us, in after years, what it felt like on board in weather like this. It was a chancy game, for the camera, even though swathed in polythene, was far from watertight. The best view-point and the driest we found to be right forward, so forward Jill crawled, cradling the camera to her bosom. Then she sat on deck, her back braced against the pulpit supports, to take her shots, while I steered and did my best to avoid shipping a green one.

We got our movie without disaster (it turned out to be a darned good one too) and then rather reluctantly worked out our sights. The sun, by this time, had once more retired, so the sights were not as useful as they would have been if we'd had another position line to make a cross with, but we were left with the impression that we were south of Jill's intended track. Perhaps we would see the Marotiri rocks after all, we decided.

We did. Just as dawn broke the next morning, they appeared out of the murk and mist, right ahead, instead of eighteen miles to the south as she had intended them to be. They made a weird picture. Three huge rocks like a giant's teeth, vicious looking and very lonely, stood in a grey welter of mist and wave-crests. Huge breakers crashed against their bases, flinging the foam half-way to the summits, and everywhere round were clouds of sea-birds, mewing and calling, diving into the sea and circling over *Salmo*.

It was such a dramatic-looking picture that I called Jill up to have a look as I altered course. She stuck her head out and considered for a few moments. " Looks like something out of a nightmare, doesn't it ? " she said at length. " At any rate I'm glad we got here in daylight. I wouldn't care to go much closer to them. Thank you very much."

The rain eased in the late afternoon and Rapa material-
ised out of the heart of the flying scud. We had spent
the day in drawing charts of Ahurei Bay from the description given in the Pilot : ' A rocky spit extends two miles
south-eastwards from the harbour entrance and inshore of
it, a rock carrying a depth of five feet fouls the channel. . . .'
We had each made out our own interpretation of all that
was written and not very surprisingly the two pictures
seemed to have little in common. As a result, as we
closed the land, each of us brandished his own piece of
paper and dabbed at it triumphantly. " There you are.
Just as I told you. There's that rock that looks like a
castle when viewed from seaward. You've got it all wrong
on YOUR chart."

" No, I haven't. That's not the rock at all. It's THAT
one. Look, can't you see ? It's just like a castle. Well
fairly like, anyway."

Rapa is a wild place. It is fantastically mountainous
and each and every mountain towers up into a needle-like
peak. Seen as we saw it for the first time, with a ragged
curtain of clouds streaming from the higher mountains,
it looked like some enchanted pantomime island. We
coasted along for some time looking for a bay that would
fit our description of Ahurei, but the Pilot had been
delightfully vague on where to find it. Normally they
give you some clue, like ' is situated midway down the
eastern shore '—but here they said nothing and we just
had to guess. Suddenly a red-roofed building appeared,
and soon afterwards more buildings. There was only one
village on the island, so we assumed we'd come to the
right place.

" O.K.," said Jill, " I still think your chart's all wrong.
But on you go. You take her in."

I rounded up towards the entrance and found that the
Pilot's description—now that we could really see all the
features—was not as bad as I'd thought it was. We had

to zig first and then zag, in order to get in. The zig would take us in behind a rocky (but submerged) spit, and the zag avoided some coral clusters close to the channel. The gale had blown itself out at last, but a good fresh breeze remained and we fairly flew inshore. Jill had the Pilot open on her knees and suddenly began to quote : ' Owing to the utter unreliability and frequent absence of all marks, the dangerous nature of the approach and the fact that the disturbed nature of the water makes it impossible to detect by eye the presence of dangers in time to avoid them, no vessel should attempt to enter Ahurei Bay without local knowledge.'

" I say," she added, " I've only just seen that bit. Don't you think we ought to try and get someone to come out and pilot us ? "

" Too late now," I replied. We had already embarked on our zig and I was tensely awaiting the moment to zag when two distant hills came in transit.

Two rather tired and rusty bits of iron scaffold-pipe passed down the port side and dozens more stuck up ahead. These, we presumed, marked lumps of coral. More pipes flitted past.

" You're too far over to port," said Jill.

" No, I'm not."

" Oh PLEASE go over to starboard a bit. It says here there's a rock with four feet over it on the port side of the channel."

" Yes, I know it does. If you read on a bit further it says that the starboard side is ' Continuously foul.' "

" Oh yes, so it does. Sorry."

Finally we skimmed through the lot and were able to relax. Ahead the bay stretched calm and peaceful for more than two miles, ringed all round with jagged peaks ; and from the village at the end a convoy of canoes came speeding out to meet us. There must have been a dozen of them, two men in each and all paddling fit to burst.

One by one they came alongside, the occupants leapt on board and dropped their craft astern on painters. By the time we had six in attendance, conditions on board had become cramped, and what was worse, we couldn't talk to them. We tried them first in English and then reluctantly in French, and grins were the only response. One obviously fancied himself as a pilot, and since I knew we had already passed the dangerous bit of the entrance I handed the boat over to him. The rest retired to the foredeck, where they squatted down and began to chatter among themselves, and each in turn hung head downwards through the forehatch to see what the cabin looked like. To judge from the roars of laughter when they emerged they found it a first-class joke.

They were a ragged-looking bunch of villains, dressed for the most part in shorts and vivid shirts, though one or two had *pareus*, and most wore either flowers or strings of shells as decoration round their straw-hats.

At length we anchored, and our supercargo joined enthusiastically in helping to stow away the sails and secure up on deck. So far as boats were concerned we didn't have to tell them anything ; they knew just what to do and did it with a will. When all was finished an awkward pause ensued. We doled out two cigarettes apiece and hoped that they'd go ashore again, but not a bit of it. They just settled down comfortably and waited for something to happen.

We went down to the cabin and two or three of them politely followed and made themselves comfortable on the bunks, while the rest remained perfectly happily on deck. Once more we tried to talk, but once more it was a lamentable failure. We offered cups of coffee all round, but though they were accepted very little was actually drunk and soon we were back at grinning at each other.

After three-quarters of an hour this grew very wearing. " I wish to goodness they'd go away," said Jill ; " it gives me the creeps sitting like this, as if we were in a zoo with those strange disembodied and upside-down heads bobbing down through the forehatch all the time. Tell them to go away."

" How the hell can I tell them to go away ? " I said. " They wouldn't understand, and if they did they'd only be mortally offended. We'll just have to wait till they want to go themselves."

We started to cook supper, and this was such a major attraction that half the fo'c'sle brigade abandoned the upper deck and crowded down into the forepeak to get a better view, still grinning delightedly. " Oh, I can't bear it," said Jill, " I'm going to explode in a minute."

Very fortunately at this juncture a boat bumped along-side and two much older men came on board. One of them, a great tall man with grey hair and distinguished features, introduced himself as the chief, and to our great delight spoke French. His companion was the local shop-keeper who, besides speaking French also miraculously had a little English. We asked him where he'd learned it and he said that he'd been cook in an English schooner for many years.

The chief, who was a great charmer, signed his name in our visitors' book with a flourish and said that we were very welcome to the island, and that he hoped we would enjoy our visit. When we came ashore, he said, we must certainly visit him and he would take us then to visit the Frenchman.

We asked who the Frenchman was. Was he a gendarme ? After our Mangareva experiences we weren't too keen on gendarmes. " No, this one lives here. In fact, there are two, but one is very strange. He lives always by himself and lets no one come near him, not even the *vahines*. But the other you will like ; he is a very friendly man, though today he is ill and lies in bed."

With this the chief rose to go, and to our great relief ushered all the rest away with him.

We woke early next morning, and as we were cooking

breakfast a canoe came alongside with a single girl in it
wearing a rather beautiful wreath of white and purple
flowers in her hair. When she came on board she gave
this to Jill, who was very touched by the gesture. Like
the rest, the girl spoke no French, but we learned that
her name was Fa-Au and she explained by gestures that
she had just been gathering the flowers from which she'd
made the wreath. We also learned that it was a very
rare event for a white woman to come to Rapa. Jill
at once began to preen herself, and with the wreath
perched above her ears tried to look suitably dashing and
adventurous. The effect was odd.

It was a long row to the little jetty, for the coral stretches
far from the shore, and the Prout was half full of water
by the time we arrived. It was beginning to feel its age
and the leaks were growing worse and worse. We never
seemed to have the time to repair them. Half the village
seemed to have come down to meet us, and our progress
towards the chief's house was processional. Most of the
houses in the village were of the traditional pandanus
thatch type of construction but the chief had a rather
ugly corrugated-iron house of which he was obviously
very proud. We barely paused here, however, but were
hurried on to meet ' Le Français.'

' Le Français ' lived in a sort of corrugated-iron shed
that from the outside looked like a garden toolshed. The
chief knocked at the door and then ushered us inside.
It was dark after the brilliant sunshine of the village
street, and for a few moments we could see nothing, but
a thin voice immediately greeted us. " Ah, you are
English, yes. Me, I spik ze Eenglish ver well, understand
ver well. You know ze Lord Mountbatten and 'is wife,
yes ? Zey 'ave visit me. Ver' nice people. You will
'ave a peep wiz me ? And you too Madame of course.
Hey, Elbake Tuoria " (this to the chief)," *veuillez chercher
une pipe ? Là bas, sous la table.*"

The chief fished under the table and came out with a bottle and some glasses and we all had a ' pipe,' and after that several more ' pipes ' while the figure in the bed apologised for not being able to greet us properly. " It was ze Japonais you know. I am ze prisoner in Indo-Chine and I get ze fever. Ze beri-beri. From time to time 'e come back and zen, *zut*, I am feenish. I must lie in ze bed. But tomorrow perhaps, I will be again orrright."

While we were being engulfed in this torrent of words we had a chance to peer round. The place looked more like a garden shed than ever. There was a vast bed, a table and a mass of junk everywhere. A gramophone and records fought for *lebensraum* beneath the table with a forest of bottles and glasses. Clearly Le Français liked to have all his possessions readily available. Clothes were piled in heaps and so were books and newspapers. Before we left he handed us his card with a flourish. Our eyes, accustomed now to the gloom, were able to read ' Comte Des Champs de Verneix ' and underneath that ' Cusset (Allier).' " We are ver old familee Les Verneix," he said ; " but 'Amilton too is ver old familee, no ? I 'ave 'eard of the 'Amiltons often, often. Ver good familee."

" Yes," we said as we finally left. " Yes. I think that the Hamiltons are a very old family."

The silence of the outside world seemed to be infinite when we reached it. The Count, though a very entertaining host, left one with the feeling of having been run over by a steam-roller.

We saw a lot of him in the next few days. His beri-beri seemed to get better and he quickly organised a party of enormous dimensions at the Pharmacie. This was the biggest house on the island, and it was presided over by a young Tahitian who had been General De Gaulle's cook throughout the war. The Chief was there and the shop-keeper, the Count and the wireless operator and countless hangers-on. We were plied with great platefuls of fish of several kinds, exquisite omelettes, sweet potatoes, raw-fish salads (which are quite excellent), ' *poi* ' which taste like glue and all sorts of other things. ' Pipes ' arrived with unnerving frequency, and after we'd finished eating, guitars were produced on every hand and a concert-cum-dance developed. It was all terrific fun, and at the end we were ushered into some spare beds in the Pharmacie's verandah where we lay for a few moments before sleep arrived, with the thrumming of guitars ringing through our heads while we tried to sort out our impressions of the day. It was too difficult. We had seen and done too much and all that remained was a pleasurable blur.

There were distinct signs of the party reviving immediately after breakfast next morning, so we hastily excused ourselves, saying we must see something of the island. A path led steeply uphill past the hut of the island's other Frenchman, ' *Le Vieux Celibataire* ' as he was generally known, a retired Paris taxi-driver by profession, and he gave us a brief wave as we passed. He was engaged in washing a pile of clothes in a barrel beside a stream. Not for him the noisy chatter of the *vahines* who looked after the Comte.

We left the village behind and found ourselves on a steep hillside covered with grass. Panting, we dragged ourselves to the top, a razor-edged ridge one thousand feet up. We perched there awhile, gazing round at the fantastic countryside, the crags, the pinnacles and the precipices, and then looked back at the village and the bay which was spread in a riot of colour beneath our feet. *Salmo* lying at her anchor looked like a tiny dot in the blue water and the village and its gardens were a sort of patch-work edging to the picture.

There were streams everywhere, tumbling down from the hills in rapids, pools and waterfalls. We were so hot after the climb that we longed for a bathe and made our way through sugar cane and banana plantations to a steep ravine. The sun shone greenly through the foliage as we scrambled down its bank to a stream that tinkled and burbled over rocks. We found a pool where the water was deep enough for diving, threw off our clothes and plunged into the icy water. It was a glorious sensation. Three strokes took us from one end of our pool to the other, and as we swam we could see small fish flit over the sandy patches on the bottom. It was too cold to stay in for long, so we climbed out on to rocks and dried as best we could with handkerchiefs before making our way back to the village to make our farewells.

Most people were gathered near the head of the jetty, and for a change the scene was one of frenzied activity instead of the more usual sleepy lethargy to which we were accustomed. Old men with hammers straightened rusty nails. Children dashed hither and thither with pandanus fronds ; women sat plaiting them into thatch and the younger men dug holes and stuck posts into the ground. The Chief, who had been directing operations, drew us into the group and explained that they were building a new church hall and meeting-house. They had started work that morning and hoped to finish it all in a day. " That is the way with our people," he laughed. " We love to do big things in which everyone can take a share. That house will be finished today. If only a few people tried to make it they would grow bored before they finished, so work would never be done."

The Count arrived : " Ah, I 'ear you go today. When you reach England and you see ze Mountbattens tell zem I remember zem ver' well. And ze American Captain Byrd. 'Im too I remember. 'e is Admiral now, I believe. But I 'ope you 'ave enjoy your stay 'ere. It is best island in 'ole Paceefic. Ze climate 'e is good. Ze girls is good also. I 'ave many sweet'arts here. I come 'ere before ze war. I was in ze, what you 'ave ? yes—ze air-race to

Australia. Your Amy Mollison she was also in ze race. But me, I love it 'ere so I stay. Always I shall stay."

We rowed back to *Salmo*. During the week that we lay at anchor, dozens of visitors had come out to us and all had brought gifts of some sort. A leg of mutton, baskets of fruit and of sweet potatoes, two hens, and fish beyond numbering. We had been worried at first by all this, but the Count had told us to take everything. " You 'ave give them cigarettes on ze way in I believe. Zey 'ave all like zat. Zey weesh to 'elp you."

The cabin was now filled with our piles of loot until we could hardly fit into it. It took only a few minutes to pull the Prout inboard, weigh the anchor and hoist the sails. The crowd ashore round the new church hall had stopped work by the time we were ready to leave and had moved down to the beach and into canoes. We swept through them waving goodbye, as close to the coral as we dared to go, and then we turned our bows towards the harbour entrance. " Goodbye," we shouted. " *Au revoir*," said the Count from the stern of a huge rowing-boat. " Be sure and remember me to ze Mountbattens and to ze Admiral Byrd."

CHAPTER FIFTEEN

TOWARDS TAHITI

THE day was grey and windy. Drifts of rain strayed over the valleys and the hill-sides and lay in smudges on the sea. The whole atmosphere reminded me of Scotland, a wet summer day in the Kyle of Lochalsh, perhaps.

We flew down the loch (we always called it a loch, though the Pilot talked of it as a bay) and as we approached the tricky part of the entrance saw that the whole sea was covered with white horses and looked bleak and cheerless. After a week in port we knew we'd soon be seasick and began to feel depressed and edgy.

" Oh you ARE being silly," Jill kept saying, " you're FAR too far over to starboard. Can't you SEE ? "

" I'm not," I snapped. " Don't fidget me."

The marks we'd used to come in by were hidden by cloud, and we had to rely on memory to guide us through the perplexing forest of iron pipes that stuck forlornly from the water on every side. Right in the middle of the forest we had to zig ; we both knew that, but just exactly where, had been in dispute. I knew my line was right. Jill knew her's was, and we both remembered the awful crash we'd given ourselves in Lake St Louis at Montreal. Our mouths were slightly dry ; for here, if we hit anything, there would be no one to come and tow us off and the swell would soon pound the boat to pieces.

One after another the pipes flitted past, *Salmo* surging along at her maximum speed while I held her as far to windward as I dared, for the wind was onshore.

" Perhaps you were right, after all," said Jill at length. The last piece of pipe passed astern, and we found ourselves breathing normally again, back in the comparative safety of open sea. A wave crashed onto the foredeck and we both ducked for shelter beneath the spray hood before the splashes should reach us. " How about lunch ? " Jill asked. " Do you feel like having any ? I don't. Not after all those ' pipes ' we had to have with the Comte. I'm going to bed, then perhaps I'll feel a bit more interested in life by the time my watch starts."

She dived down below, pulled off her oilskins and lay in the lee bunk determined to go to sleep before sickness intervened. Alone in the cockpit I huddled myself into a ball and coasted along, a mile offshore, gazing dully at the waves pounding on the cliffs and at the black forbidding mountains as they showed themselves and then melted away again in the driving mist. Valley after valley opened up between them, each one with a floor to it no wider than a tennis-court, and flanked by crazy pinnacles and slopes too steep to seem possible.

The last hill of all was the most dramatic. It had been sliced away on its seaward side three-quarters of the way up and fell sheer to the water as a cliff two thousand feet high. Mobs of seagulls screamed and circled off its face, soaring on the wind eddies like a cloud of wood-ash rising from a bonfire, while the waves dashed themselves to spindrift at its foot. Some freak blast of the wind opened a gap in the clouds as we flew past, and a wandering searchlight of sunshine strayed wanly over the rock, etching shadows on its surface from the cracks, gullies and the ledges. The gap closed, the cloud lowered, and very soon a rain-squall hit us and blotted out the land altogether. All that I could see then was *Salmo's* heaving deck, gleaming with wetness, and a small circle of dark water striped with foam, ever changing in its pattern as the waves chased across it.

Between Rapa and Tubuai, where we were bound, lies a group of rocks, lonelier even than the Marotiri rocks, their tops no more than a foot or two above the water. It was the sort of place to give one nightmares in poor visibility ; so, since the rain continued unabated for three days and we had no chance to take a sight, we had to give it a wide berth. At the end of the three days, when we reckoned at last that we must be safely clear of the area, the sun came out. We took a sight, just to make sure, and found, as is usually the way on these occasions, that I had been unduly pessimistic and that we had gone farther from our course than perhaps we had needed to. People sometimes accused us of being slapdash in our navigation, but things that we were really frightened of we always treated with the greatest respect, and though unexpected things happened sometimes, we never really had many serious worries.

' Tubuai,' said the Pilot, ' makes like two islands when raised from the South'ard.' After constant reading of these fascinating publications we grew extremely fond of their literary style, and sometimes even found ourselves talking the same sort of language. " That mountain," we'd say, " makes like a gunner's quoin from here." To my mind the Pilot reeks of jib-booms and bobstays, and I shall be very upset if they ever decide to modernise their phrases.

Sure enough, a week after leaving Rapa, two islands duly appeared to the northward late one evening, so we closed in on them until we could hear the roar of the reef and then hove to to wait for daylight. The dawn came fine with a booming wind, and while Jill tidied up the cabin to impress visitors, I steered inshore towards the pass, which was a wide one and easily seen. The two islands had joined themselves together by this time and in the early morning light looked most attractive ; two big whale-backed hummocks, green and grassy on their

tops as Sussex Downs, but fringed round the shore with
the darker green of palm-groves. Two white beacons
marked the entrance to the pass so we flew into the lagoon
without a care in the world, turned sharply to port and
then coasted along in smooth water until we reached the
village. On shore the sand was golden, brilliantly so, the
houses looked clean and well cared for and everything
seemed to have a friendly, welcoming air. " I'm going
to like it here," Jill announced firmly. " Bet you anything
you like there won't be any nonsense over papers."

For once in a way her feminine intuition was quite
correct. No one came out to see us, so we rowed ashore
in the Prout to be greeted by the usual crowd of delighted
small boys, all obviously longing to have a go in it. These
lads all had little model aeroplanes in their hands and
were having a wonderful time with them, for the trade
wind made the propellers spin in the most satisfactory
way. They jostled and shouted and pushed and giggled
as we clambered onto the jetty, and then formed themselves
into a sort of procession to escort us ashore.

Just as we reached the first houses there was a toc,
toc, toccing noise and a huge gendarme appeared, mounted
on a very small bicycle with an outboard engine on it.
He hung over its sides in ample folds and it seemed astonish
ing that it should not only support his weight without
crumpling, but should bowl it along at a goodly clip as
well. He wobbled to a stop beside us, took off a pair of
dark glasses and then propped the bicycle up on its stand
so that he could salute properly.

" Good day," he said, " I do not care for small boats,
for their motion is disagreeable to me " ; he patted his
midship section fondly. " So I have waited for you here.
How long will you remain with us ? "

We had developed a terrific thirst for mail by this time,
our last consignment having been at Panama three months
ago, so we decided to stay only twenty-four hours at

Tubuai, even if more time was offered to us. The gendarme was disappointed. He obviously liked visitors.

The Gendarmerie, he said, was a short distance off, so he conducted us up one sandy road and then down another at right angles to it, past gardens ablaze with flowers, and neat, pandanus-thatched houses. Two women saw us passing and came out to give Jill a large bunch of bananas and some coconuts tied together with creeper. What with this and our delighted escort of yelling children, we felt as though we were being given a ticker-tape reception in Broadway.

As soon as he'd shoo'd the children out of the garden and returned our passports, the gendarme fished in a rather untidy drawer and pulled out a printed form which he signed and stamped before giving to us. " This," he said, " will enable you to buy wine should you wish to do so. You like our wines ? " he added anxiously, remembering suddenly that we were British.

We reassured him hastily on this point and he seemed much relieved. " Well, in that case I will suggest that you go to Ah Kee," he said. " There are two traders on the island permitted to sell wine, but this month Ah Kee has the better vintage. His is the shop down there." He drew us to the doorway and pointed out a green-painted corrugated-iron building, half hidden by breadfruit-trees.

" If, however, you should wish to have a meal ashore, then I would recommend Wing Su, whose shop we passed near the quay. His omelette is passable and always his fish is the best. They are caught by his nephew. But he should be warned of your arrival in advance."

We thanked the gendarme for his kindness and were just turning down the road to have a look at Ah Kee and his wine when we were called back again, " One thing more," he said, " do you like the green vegetables, the salads ? "

We had been expecting some further query about passports and were slightly taken aback. " Yes," said Jill, recovering herself quickly, " we do."

" Ah," said the gendarme, " then, in that case, I shall send you down some small onions, spring onions, you understand, this afternoon. I am thinning mine and shall have some in excess. That is my garden over there." He pointed over a low hedge to a business-like plot laid out with the greatest care with little criss-cross paths. Between the paths were rows and rows of beautifully tended vegetables : lettuce, tomato, cabbage, onions . . . everything. We realised why Jill's raptures over all the flowers we passed had not seemed to strike a chord . . . had they been vegetables now, that would have been a different matter altogether.

Ah Kee's shop was a wonderful jumble of tins and umbrellas and bales of brightly printed cotton. Hurricane lanterns hung in festoons from the ceiling, jostling against clusters of garlic sausage, two or three anchors, and some flypapers that had twisted into spirals. The counter was piled with toothpaste and radios and sweets, and a glorious smell of baking wafted in from the back premises. We hadn't done a bake since leaving Rapa and our mouths began to water.

We bought six bottles of wine and five loaves and a tin of butter and another one of cheese and then began to wonder how we would get everything back to the boat, for the bananas and the coconuts were already beginning to weigh heavily. Ah Kee, however, afraid perhaps of losing custom to his rival Wing Su with his shop near the quay, at once volunteered to have everything delivered out to *Salmo* for us. His son would take it, he said.

A very small boy of about six was summoned. He took our load from us, item by item, and made a cache by the roadside. He was half Polynesian and had big round eyes and, inevitably, a wooden aeroplane. We never did discover if it was he who took everything back out to *Salmo*, or whether he had an elder brother.

It was now nearly midday, so, extracting two loaves, the butter, the cheese and a bottle of wine from the pile, we made our way down to the beach. The bread was still almost too hot to hold and we were longing to have at it. The gendarme was not the only one on the island with a deep interest in food.

Carefully choosing a palm - tree whose ammunition appeared to be expended (for coconuts reach the ground with a tremendous wallop) we parked ourselves comfortably and settled down to a picnic. It was pleasantly cool in the shade with the strong trade wind to fan our faces, and we felt that life really had very little more to offer. " This is just EXACTLY what I've been looking forward to," said Jill. " Rapa was fun, but it wasn't a South Sea Island. Just look at the perfect blue of the sea and the brilliant white of the reef. Oh ! and the sand's gold, too. It's almost too much." She scuffled her bare toes luxuriously.

It may have been the wine, or perhaps we were more tired than we thought we were, but whatever the cause we became more and more drowsy. Two fishermen walked past with hand-nets and began flinging them just a short way down the beach. The nets swung away from them spinning gracefully, and then landed in the water with a plop, to be carefully gathered up again and the catch placed in a sack. It was small fry for bait that they were after. Ahead of us, half a mile away, the reef was dotted with figures armed with spears, wading thigh deep in the spent breakers, pausing by the pools and occasionally lunging. We watched them lazily, the surf roared, the palm fronds sighed, and quite soon we were both asleep.

It was late afternoon by the time we woke ; the sun had swung round to seaward and we were no longer shaded. Our mouths felt parched and our faces burning, so we had a long and lazy swim, cruising face downwards over the coral watching the fish, and Jill found a Tiger Cowrie, as big as my fist, brightly polished as enamel and beautifully marked in chestnut and black.

A clopping noise came faintly to us as we dried, so we walked through the palms where the sunshine and shade threw dappled patterns on the grass, to see what was the cause of it. It was a man with an adze making a canoe. The main body was already hollowed out and he had pegged two wash-strakes to the top of it to give more freeboard and was now engaged in smoothing these off. A great heap of newly cut chippings lay round about him, and the whole of the small clearing where he worked was littered with trimmings from the trees he had used. We went to admire his handiwork and he was delighted to show it off; he spoke a little French and explained how he lashed the outrigger into position. His last canoe had been too small, he explained, so he was making a bigger one. His family heard our voices and came out to join us, sitting on nearby logs, grinning and friendly. The women all wore brilliant *pareus* and beside them Jill, in a plain red shirt and blue trousers, looked like a sparrow among a group of kingfishers.

They must have thought we looked thirsty, for one of the younger girls was sent off for drinking nuts and came back with four of them which she split open with a few neat bangs on a steel stake stuck in the ground. We'd tried to do the same thing in Rapa and found there was a knack to it. Our nuts had looked as though they'd been run over by a tank, and most of the juice was wasted; those we now had were perfect.

We would have stayed longer, but duty called in the shape of a bucket of dirty washing that Jill had brought ashore and wanted to get on with while there was still sun to dry it. Up the hill, slightly above the village, we found a spring bubbling out of the ground into a rocky pool beneath a group of breadfruit-trees. Washing, I reckoned, was not my ' part of ship,' so while Jill rubbed and scrubbed and darkened the pool with a scum of ' Tide,' I lay back like a gentleman on a bed of moss and told her just how she SHOULD be doing the job, until she got annoyed and threw a dishcloth at me.

She finished at last and while the clothes flapped and fluttered from the crest of a thorn-bush Jill came and joined me on my perch. " Do you realise," she said, " that supper tonight will be the first meal that we'll have had in a restaurant since Panama ? I love having meals that are surprises. On the boat, even when you do the cooking, I always KNOW what I'm going to get. I wonder what we WILL have tonight ? "

The restaurant was at the back of Wing Su's shop, which was, in fact, almost indistinguishable from Ah Kee's. We hadn't expected to meet a restaurant on an island as isolated as Tubuai, so were deeply interested to know what we'd find.

It turned out to be a big barn of a room with about fifteen very home-made tables set out in it and with orange-boxes to sit on. The floor was earth, more or less levelled off, and the roof was of pandanus thatch supported by wiggly rafters. A Tilly lamp hissed from one of these and beneath it was what was obviously intended to be our table, covered with shiny oilcloth and with a tumbler of flowers on it. There were no other patrons, so before we sat down we went for a tour of inspection to admire the advertisements that lined the walls : they were all of the rather lurid variety and showed a charmingly cosmopolitan taste. Coca-Cola, for example, was represented in Chinese, French and English. Our table was underneath the Chinese one, of an improbably enthusiastic young lady in a *cheong san* drinking a bottle of the stuff.

The meal was brought in by the various members of the Wing Su family in turn, though father tended to cheat slightly ; for, having introduced himself with the soup, he returned again in a purely social capacity with the fish, and stayed chatting for the rest of the meal. He was a native of Hong Kong and was highly delighted to find that I knew it.

The meal, as the gendarme had forecast, was excellent, and we blessed him for his suggestion. It was a pleasant change to sit in a spacious room again instead of in a tiny cabin, and the hiss of the Tilly lamp and the flickering cloud of insects that fluttered round it made it not just another meal but a pleasantly unusual and intriguing occasion.

The moon was shining as we rowed back on board, and *Salmo* danced and plunged in the chop of the lagoon, her mast swaying blackly against a background of stars. Wavelets broke against the bows of the Prout and splashed inboard wetly, gathering into a large puddle down aft, where Jill sat on top of the upturned bailer to keep herself dry. Some of the magic seemed to have gone out of our evening. Things grew worse when we got back on board, for our pile of groceries had been left as a pile by Ah Kee's son, the motion had toppled them over and the cabin was a shambles—loaves and bottles rolling backwards and forwards on the deck. A jar of pickles had burst and some bananas had mysteriously squashed themselves and spread over everything in a thin and slippery paste. We tidied up, glissading like drunken skiers from one end of the cabin to the other as the rolling and the bananas dictated ; then we tried to repack our shoregoing clothes in their suitcase, which was taking up far more than its share of room in the forepeak. The battery had nearly run down, so we were reduced to oil-lamps which, when used in the forepeak had no permanent holders and had to be jammed. Our tempers suffered considerably. " Sometimes," said Jill, clinging desperately to a handrail and trying to fold her skirt at the same time, " I hate boats."

" So do I," I replied, " nearly always. But some of the places they take you to are rather fun."

It was raining the next morning. Driving rain whirled over the lagoon and the palm-trees were turning themselves nearly inside out as they leant away from the wind. The lagoon was no longer green, but a yeasty grey and the reef looked fierce and frightening.

The motion on board was frantic, and it took a long time to get everything secured for sea. Just as we were nearly ready to sail, a canoe with two men in it pushed off from the beach and came slowly towards us, bursting through the chop in clouds of spray, the two paddlers heaving furiously at their paddles to maintain headway. At last they came alongside and began showering us with vegetables : cabbages, mangoes, tomatoes, lettuce and carrots. They were a present from the Seventh Day Adventist community, explained one of the paddlers, a young man with a charming face who spoke excellent English. " I am their pastor," he added. We thanked him as best we could, but with the two boats leaping and diving as they were, it was rather an incoherent business and much interrupted by the need for fending off.

They cast off at length and headed back for shore. " May God be with you," said the young man with simple sincerity. It was the most touching parting we had ever had.

We hoisted the sail, reefed almost to the limit, and with infinite labour broke out the anchor. *Salmo* heeled far over and then, with Jill steering, raced like a stag down the lagoon. On the foredeck I worked feverishly to get the anchor and chain stowed away below and the canvas cover on the forehatch before we should reach the pass. Bitter experience had taught us that if we failed to get this done before reaching open water we always regretted it. A dry boat stays dry, but a wet one is almost impossible to improve, it just firmly stays wet.

Just as I hauled the last lashing taut it was time to go about and head seaward : the two white beacons had lined themselves up astern of us. We plugged our way into the incoming rollers as they heaped themselves up and fought in the pass with the lagoon water that was trying to force its way seaward. Battering our way through the turmoil we finally reached open water. " My goodness," we said to each other, " let's hope this doesn't go on for long. It's quite disgusting."

It remained quite disgusting for the next five days, and instead of the south-east trade promised to us by our chart, the wind remained persistently northerly and therefore straight in our teeth. The fifth of the days was Jill's birthday. As the distance from Tubuai to Tahiti is only about four hundred miles I had confidently promised her to be in port for this, and since we weren't I felt guilty about it and had spent nearly the whole of the previous day building her a birthday-card. Jill has always been a great one for birthday-cards, and had made me a splendid one in the Galapagos (but then she can draw), but when I sat down to consider the project my mind went totally and absolutely blank.

" What are you doing down there, just sitting on the bunk with a pained expression ? " she asked me. " Are you feeling all right ? Would you like to come up and get a breath of air for a bit ? "

" I'm thinking," I replied with dignity.

" Oh, what are you thinking about ? Can I help ? O what is it ? "

I declined her offers and continued to think, and I kept seeing her peering down anxiously, but covertly, to see what was going on. " I'd lie down for a bit," she advised me. " Have a dry biscuit with Marmite on it. That's what I always do when I'm feeling a bit seasick. But lie down anyway. That's bound to help."

" I'm NOT FEELING SEASICK," I shouted at her at last ;

" leave me alone ! "   Still nothing came to me, so I tried doodling. I wrote ' A Happy Birthday ' on a plain sheet of paper to see if it would give me any inspiration and it didn't, so I dug out Jill's paint-box and did it over again in blue to see if that was any better.

Jill glanced down again.   " Oh, I know what you're doing," she said.   " Well, if that's what you're doing, I WILL leave you alone.   By the way, it's your watch in half an hour , you know, and it's still pouring with rain . . . just to remind you, that is."

With only half an hour left, I was driven to desperation and fairly splashed colours onto my card, trying to draw little scenes of Pitcairn and Rapa and Tubuai.   I knew what I wanted the little scenes to look like, but they resolutely refused to look like it ; even my final one (a topical one), which was meant to represent *Salmo* in a rainstorm, was barely recognisable, and I went up to take over my watch feeling more depressed than usual.

I had my revenge on Jill, though, for her gibes about the rain.   I had the first watch that night, so when I shook her at two (we ran a patent system of watches) I was able to do so by shouting down to her, " A Very Happy Birthday to you.   It's still pouring."

" Eee . . . uugh," was all the reply vouchsafed to me.

I remember that birthday vividly.   All the other four days of rain had been bad enough, but this one was worse than any of them.   As if the rain itself wasn't enough to depress us, there was the additional worry of not knowing where we were, for in five days of tacking to windward in rough water it's difficult to keep a track of exactly how far one has travelled.   All we knew was that we must be getting somewhere near Tahiti.   Then, half-way through the afternoon the island loomed up out of an ink black cloud, and a short time later Moorea appeared to port of it, just as I had expected it would.   Later they both disappeared again, and it was only next morning, when the sky suddenly cleared after an anxious night spent listening for surf, that I was able to convince myself that my Moorea and my Tahiti were both wraiths.

The real Tahiti appeared almost immediately we had disposed of the imaginary one, and that evening, to make up for all the filth we had suffered, there was the most glorious sunset we'd yet seen. Little fleecy clouds changed from white to pink to gold and to fiery red. Purples, mauves and greens spread themselves away from the central finery, and beneath it all, the sea grew gradually darker. Through all this brilliant colouring *Salmo* sailed, slipping gently through the water with the Genoa set, the bow-wave whispering secrets to the stem, and the rudder plucking at the whorls and eddies of wake as they slipped astern. Fine on the starboard bow loomed the huge bulk of Tahiti, spiked and turreted like a castle, dark blue against a greenish sky. We sat in the cockpit wordlessly, sipping our drinks and glorying in the stillness and the beauty.

The whole night was magical. It was one of the nights when the water seems to come alive with phosphorescence. A white glow surrounded the hull, while under the stern great curving flakes of blue-white fire played and danced and faded again. The wake shone for a hundred yards astern, and everywhere we looked the black water flashed and winked as fishes passed through it or wavelets broke. At one stage I dipped my hand over the side and it came back alight, and even the drips as they fell to the cockpit scuppers were winking like jewels.

Towards midnight we drew level with the end of the land and heard a low-pitched murmur from the reef. Ashore, on the black hillsides, a few lights flashed, and out on the reef were more of them where men stood on the coral with blazing torches and fish-spears. Even the swell seemed to have died and we slipped through the water as if it were asleep and unaware of our presence.

At last the sky began to lighten in the east where the land lay, and the most wonderful scent came wafting out to us, the sweetest I have ever known, millions and millions of flowers joining together to throw their fragrance onto the breeze. Jill came on deck to marvel at it, for it had even reached below into the cabin, and we sat together to watch the mountain-tops grow pink and the stars fade. Slowly the rosy tints spread farther and farther overhead and the darkness on board faded into greyness. We had set the spinnaker overnight, a white one, and its ghostly outline became clearer and clearer, swaying gently as it tugged at the restraining sheets. Fingers of sunlight lit up the mountain crests ; colour returned to the hillsides and quite soon it was full daylight. The magic left the world, but it left behind it a longing and an expectation, for were we not approaching the island that Joe the Austrian had described in the Galapagos as ' The Earth's last Paradise ' ?

CHAPTER SIXTEEN

EARTH'S LAST PARADISE

THE wind fell away almost completely at breakfast time, and we just slid through the water with the sails hardly filled. Out to starboard the reef lay with its teeth bared, growling at the ocean, while beyond it rose the huge bulk of the island, green, lofty and mysterious.

We scrubbed the boat from stem to stern and then turned our attention to ourselves, sloshing about in great bowls of fresh water to soak the salt from our skins. Clean shirts completed the treatment and we felt like different beings as we sat in the cockpit, our eyes glued to the binoculars trying to pick out every detail of what went on ashore.

Quite soon Papeete appeared, a cluster of white houses with red roofs, tree-lined streets, and a mass of schooners and yachts moored along the quayside. An island, like a little toy Japanese-garden sort of island, but with palms on it instead of pine, lay out in the brilliant blue bay, and an ugly scar of newly excavated earth and a litter of steelwork showed where an oil depot was being set up. "It doesn't look very BIG," said Jill doubtfully. "After all we've heard about the place I thought it would be far larger and not quite so sleepy-looking somehow."

I agreed with her. Everyone we'd met for the last year, so it seemed, had always breathed, "But wait till you see Papeete . . ." as soon as they learned that we planned to come this way, and to each one the place had obviously been magical in one way or another. A Canadian

had shown us coloured slides and hinted at Bachanalian
joys past counting. The gendarme at Mangareva had
thought of it as head office where permits in triplicate
for this, that, or the other grew on every bush, while at
Rapa our friend Monsieur le Comte des Champs De Verneix
had ranked it as a sort of mid-Pacific Birmingham. "Now
be sure to let zem know zat I need four tons of ze wot
you 'ave, yes, ze concrete. And also ze crane which I
'ave on order from zem. But especiallee ze concrete."

A large white motor-boat shoved off from its moorings
in front of the harbour office and came ploughing towards
us, a red-and-white pilot flag fluttering from a staff in
the bows. We'd never taken a pilot on board before (at
Panama he'd been in our companion craft), but it looked
as though we were going to get one now, willy-nilly.

The launch swept alongside and the pilot, a trim figure
in khaki with a brief-case in his hand (full of charts in
case he forgot the way in, we supposed), stepped on board.
"I am ze pilot," he announced, rather superfluously, "you
will start ze engine, please."

He was deeply shocked when we told him that we hadn't
got one, and stood for a moment or two, arrested in mid-
stride, clucking at us for such carelessness. He appeared
to think we must have mislaid it somewhere and left it
lying on a far-off dockside. But then he recovered himself,
and with an imperious wave invited the launch to come
back to take us in tow. As it swept round to pass a line,
the pilot completed his downward step into the cockpit,
whipped a large white handkerchief from his pocket, and
having spread it carefully on the seat to protect his shorts,
sat down and took the tiller with the air of a television
cook about to make an omelette. Jill, who had watched
me scrubbing the seat for nearly an hour after breakfast,
began to make choking noises as she caught my eye, and
then hurriedly retired to the foredeck to receive the towline before she disgraced herself. *Salmo* jerked as the

strain came onto the line, and then off we went in a flurry of wake sweeping in through the pass.

The pilot thawed once he had things arranged to his satisfaction, brought us competently into our berth, stern on to the quay, and introduced us to the customs and immigration officers. A whirl of paperwork ensued. Had we noticed any remarkable casualties amongst the rats on board ? What was the date of our last de-ratisation certificate ? Where had we obtained our visas ? Where had we come from and where would we go to ? What stores did we carry ? We signed this, we signed that and we signed the next thing. Jill got so excited that she signed one paper in her maiden name and blushed deeply when the immigration officer asked, with great Gallic charm and understanding, whether we were married or not. Our heated protests of our utter respectability seemed merely to deepen his conviction that we were having a rather clumsy ' affaire,' and that, I am sure, remained his opinion throughout his stay.

Fortunately we seemed to comply with all the regulations, and were just getting ready to go ashore to see if we could find our mail when there was a yell from across the street and a figure which had been flying along on a motor-scooter with a *vahine* on the pillion, skidded to a stop and greeted us : " Aahiee ! So there you are at last." It was Joe, the shipwrecked man from the Galapagos.

With a slap on the bottom he despatched the *vahine* to take the scooter back to *Pandora*, which was moored three or four boats farther down the line, and he sprang nimbly on board.

" What sort of trip did you have ? " we both asked in one breath, for we had been longing to hear how such an ill-assorted seeming crew had got on together.

" Ach ! Terrible, terrible," said Joe happily, his grin flashing brilliantly as ever from the mahogany of his face ; " One of the silly boggerts decided he would steer no more

one day. He joost leave the tiller and we nearly jibe, so
I had to knock him down, you know."

" What happened then ? " we asked, much intrigued.

" Oh, he still would not work so ve joost do vithout
him. He lie in his bunk and read all day. The skipper
he vould let him come to meals, but I say ' No.' No
vork no food, I say. So he joost cook for himself all the
rest of the time. Anyvay, that is done vith now. He
has found a *vahine* and he is gone. The other he vill go
too, I think, I don't know. The skipper says he must
now go home to the States to get lawyers on to these
boys. It is all damn silly. I say to the skipper, ' you
forget this lawyer nonsense. Go on vith your cruise I say,
or else take your boat back now to the States.' But he
say ' No,' so he gets the lawyers onto the boys and the
boys they get lawyers onto him and I don't know what
all . . . Haieeee. . . ."

He broke off to wave to a girl walking past with a
flower behind her ear, but his mind wasn't on her, it was
a purely automatic reaction ; he was still thinking of
Pandora and he went on as if there had been no break :
" but me, I like it here. My book is nearly finished now.
I tell the skipper I vill vait here for him and look after
the boat, but you . . . how did you get on ? "

We told him something of our own doings, and we
could see him drinking it all in, shooting questions at us,
how had the chronometer behaved ? what was the anchorage like at Pitcairn ? what weather had we met near
Rapa ? Joe was an enthusiast and a perfectionist. He
was fascinated by the sea in all its aspects, and determined
to cram himself with every scrap of knowledge of it that
he could find.

Quite suddenly, as suddenly as he had arrived, he left.
He sprang ashore and strode off down the quay, and a
few minutes later we saw him flying back up the road
again on his motor-scooter, his *vahine* up behind him once

again, her hair streaming in the wind, both their faces animated and happy as he talked to her over his shoulder.

We too leapt ashore and turned our steps towards the Consulate, thirsty for mail that we knew must be waiting for us. The vice-consul, a timid-looking little man, gave us a great pile of letters, but before we settled down to them we felt we should call on the consul himself. The vice-consul, looking as though he expected to have a knife stuck into him, went to see if we could be received, and in a few moments we were ushered down the rather decrepit verandah which led to the main office. At a desk in the window sat a large and distinguished figure with greying hair. We introduced ourselves.

" Good morning. Our name's Hamilton. We've just arrived here in a yacht."

" Good God ! " said the figure ; " MORE bloody yachtsmen. Well, what have you been up to ? "

We retired at once beneath our umbrage-tree. " What do you mean, ' What have we been up to ?' " I asked. " We just came to pay you a courtesy visit, to thank you for looking after our mail for us."

" What I mean," said the consul, pushing his spectacles down his nose, so that he could glare over the top of them, " is this : have you been marrying anybody ? Or casting anybody ashore on uninhabited islands ? Or arriving here without any money and expecting me to ship you home again as Distressed British Mariners, or any of the other peculiar antics that yachtsmen get up to in these parts ? "

We searched our consciences carefully and found no such blots on our escutcheon. " No," we said, " we heard about the man being left on an uninhabited island with his chimpanzee. In fact, we met him while we were at Pitcairn. But we didn't drop him in the first place. And certainly we've never married anyone. Why ? Is it a common practice ? "

" Not common exactly," said the consul, " but it has happened. An American did it a few years ago and there's a terrific lawsuit still raging over it. No one knows if the marriage is legal or not. But if you HAVEN'T been doing anything strange and rare, then I'm quite delighted to meet you. My name's Devenish. Come to dinner tomorrow night."

The interview was over. Freddie (as we soon learned to call him) was very busy that morning. He was always busy, so we discovered, always in a rush. The days were never long enough for him and he was a familiar figure, flying through Papeete at any time of the day or night, in his car or on his motor-scooter, his distinguished bearing and his brief-case never deserting him even when he went bathing.

Back on board once more we divided our mail into two piles, a big one for Jill and a much smaller one, mostly in brown business-envelopes, for me. I opened the first one, which was from the Ministry of National Insurance. ' Dear Sir,' it read, ' There is no trace in this office that you ever returned the form C.F.I.C. (National Insurance Card) issued to you on release from the Services. This form is now twenty-one months overdue. An early reply, with remittance, is requested.'

I looked at the postmark and saw that the form was no longer twenty-one months' overdue, it was twenty-three months. I had no idea what it was or why, so stuck the reminder into the ship's attaché-case beside all the rest of our ' nonsense papers.' Perhaps, I reflected, they'll have forgotten about it by the time we get home again.

Jill, in the meantime, seemed to be getting on a good deal better. " Isn't that SPLENDID," she burbled, " Anne's getting married. Oh I AM glad."

" Who," I asked, " is Anne ? "

" Anne ? " she answered vaguely; "oh, just a girl I

knew at school. Very dull really. Quite ordinary. She wasn't at the wedding. You won't know her."

"Well, who's she marrying, then ? "

"Oh, I don't KNOW who she's marrying. Just someone. Oh what does it MATTER ? " And then she struck a new vein : "Hullo . . . Jane's having a baby and she wants me to be Godmother. Oh what fun. What shall I give her . . . now I wonder . . . a table-napkin ring perhaps . . . no that's dull . . . or a brooch, or some pearls . . . my Godmother gave ME some pearls. . . ."

"Well, don't you think," I said cautiously, "that you could just write a letter now, and send a present later on when we get home again. We haven't got very much money just now, and things'll probably be pretty expensive here, and we have to get the boat provisioned and buy more ciné film and the Genoa's getting worn out and we should really order another and . . ."

"Oh, I don't mean NOW," she said impatiently ; she was on to another letter by this time : "I MEAN when we get back. Of course I wouldn't buy her anything now."

My next letter was from the bank and it said that as per my instructions of the fifteenth ult. (what on earth does ult. mean ?) they had remitted five hundred pounds (£500) to their agent in Papeete, La Banque Nationale de L'Indo-Chine. Well, that was a mercy anyway. Money, as ever, was a worrying subject. We were spending huge sums on taking films, and even buying provisions was costlier than I had imagined it would be, and at the same time nothing was coming in to the kitty to make up for all that went out. Some day, perhaps, if we were getting our exposures right and the film wasn't melting in the heat, someone might give us something for it ; and some day we might get another couple of payments from ' Weekend,' but it was the gap that was so disturbing. Money yesterday, money tomorrow, but never any money today seemed to be a chronic affliction of ours.

As soon as we'd wrung the last drops of news out of all our letters and re-read some of the more entertaining ones, we wandered ashore again to look at our neighbours. The quay runs beside the main road, separated from it by a broad strip of grass planted with flame-trees and dotted here and there with old cannons dug in as bollards. A Chinese ice-cream vendor had a barrow set up in the shade of one of the trees and the whole length of the quay was crammed with yachts and schooners and fishing-boats. Our next-door neighbour was an Australian ketch built on the general lines of a washtub and painted a rather ugly blue. There seemed to be a crew of three on board and she swarmed with Tahitian girls, while a gramophone churned out ' Singing the Blues ' from down in the cabin. We walked past, and there, hidden behind her, was the tiny little *Taki O Autohi* which I had helped to take through the Panama Canal. It was our turn to shout " Hullo there " and jump down on board, and soon we were all firing questions at Bill Mangan. " Where have you been ? . . . how long did you take ? . . . when are you leaving ? " There's a great freemasonry among small-boaters and soon we were being filled with information in return. " You can get baths over at the Continental Hotel, but if you do, then they like you to have drinks in their bar . . . there's a public wash-house just down the road where you can take your clothes for dhobey-ing. You can hire bicycles at Wu Chong's, and the cheapest place to eat is the Trois Hirondelles restaurant."

We soon settled down to harbour routine and the days just drifted past as we played at renewing worn rigging, restitching a few sails, and painting the hull.

The Australians beside us were beginning to grow restive. " Could I come down and write a letter in your cabin ? " one of them asked as we were going ashore one day. " It's kind of difficult to do that sort of thing aboard us." We could well believe it. The girls had now taken possession of the boat completely. The three original ones had invited all their sisters and friends and cousins to keep them company. ' Singing the Blues ' never seemed to stop for a moment, and the cabin was always bought up for them to wash their clothes and their hair, or just to sit gossiping in, while the Australians were banished to the upper deck. " And the amount they EAT," said the skipper to us one day, " why, they get through a whole forty-pound bunch of bananas every day, and we have to buy fish and meat at the market very nearly by the hundredweight. It's TERRIBLY expensive."

" Well, why don't you just tell them to get out ? " Jill wanted to know.

The Australian seemed embarrassed by this. " Well, it's kind of DIFFICULT to tell them that," he said. Quite obviously Tahiti had been the magnet that had drawn these three from Australia, and now that they'd got here they weren't sure that they liked it. They left, finally, after a week instead of the month they had planned, to see if any of the more outlying islands would measure up more nearly to their expectations. We doubted if they would.

One morning, after we'd had a shower, we stood leaning over the balcony of the Continental Hotel. Below us stretched the long line of yachts and schooners, awnings spread, flags flapping gently, while on board each one, figures like ants moved backwards and forwards, scrubbing or painting. Beyond the boats lay the brilliant blue lagoon, fringed with the white lace of breaking water on the reef, the island like a green splinter at the edge of it. Moorea, blue with distance, broke the horizon, and as we watched, a ferry, overcrowded as usual, punched its way seaward through the built-up swell that swept in at the pass. On the road, dim in shadow beneath its row of trees, bicycles passed up and down in a never-ending stream; girls with flowers in their hair ; young men with loads of fish flapping from the carriers ; matrons with children perched on the handlebars, policemen, yachtsmen—everyone seemed to have a bicycle. Today, too, there was an unusual bustle everywhere, for a cruise ship was due and all those who had nothing better to do were being drawn to the cobbled stretch of quay that lay in front of the harbour office.

We, too, had nothing better to do, so we joined the crowd and soon found ourselves jostling and pushing with the best of them. Everywhere there were flower-sellers : old ladies in from the country with huge baskets of hibiscus, lilies, and gardenias which they deftly wove into wreaths and garlands. At the outskirts of the mob stood the taxi-drivers with rags in their hands, languidly wiping their battered vehicles, tooting the horns to attract the attention of their friends, and laughing, shouting and joking among themselves. At the very front of the quay there was an open space roped off and guarded by gendarmes, and inside this space we saw a band and beauty chorus assembling to give a welcome. The girls all wore yellow and red grass skirts and skimpy brassieres, and prominent amongst them we were amused to see several who had been our neighbours in the Australians' boat. Everywhere there was an air of excitement and expectancy.

A stir went through the crowd when the pilot (still with his brief-case full of charts) boarded his craft and shoved off seaward ; it was as if the conductor had just joined the orchestra, and even though we ourselves had no flowers, beer, or taxis to sell, we found we were getting just as worked up as everyone else.

Suddenly, round the corner of the point, the *Mariposa* appeared, huge and immaculate, gliding along close to the reef. The pilot scrambled on board up a ladder and round she came, through the pass and up to the quay. Her rails were lined with tourists, and every figure seemed to be wielding either camera or binoculars. As established residents of nearly a month's seniority we felt delightfully superior, and smiled indulgently as the band struck up and the girls swung into their routine, twisting, swaying and writhing as though they hadn't a bone in their bodies, in perfect rhythm with the guitars. It was only a short performance, *hors-d'œuvre* to whet the passengers' appetite and lure them into the waiting bars, shops, and taxis ; and as soon as the gangway was lowered, band and chorus together leapt onto it and rushed aloft, helter-skelter to offer their services as guides and hostesses.

We, too, felt that it was time to go, and just as the first passengers, flower bestrung already, began to come ashore, we fought our way out into the open and back to *Salmo* where we started to paint the upper deck. It was all part of a deep-laid plan ; for not only did the deck need painting, but we had decided that we wanted to be invited on board the *Mariposa* for dinner. Painting, we felt, was a suitably glamorous occupation for shell-backed mariners, and also, of course, it allowed us to keep an eye on what went on ashore ; surely amongst all the *Mariposa's* passengers there would be some whom we could entertain and who would reciprocate !

It wasn't long before we had our first bite. A solitary figure came striding down the line of boats with a self-assured swagger ; binoculars were strung round his neck and he wore a pale-blue yachting-cap.

" Say," he accosted us, " you didn't come here in that thing, did you ? "

" Yes," we replied, " we did. Would you care to come on board ? " We'd set our hearts on that dinner, and it would have needed more than this rather odd greeting to deter us.

He came on board and accepted a glass of beer. " Why, I wouldn't go to sea in a craft with a stern like yours," he said. " No. Not if you paid me, I wouldn't. The sort of stern you need for real seagoing is a canoe-stern.

It parts the seas instead of blocking them, you understand ?
It's the natural sort of stern to have. Now I've read very
nearly every book that's been written about small-boat
voyages and not one person who's had a canoe-stern has
ever had any trouble in a following sea. No, sir. Not one
of them."

I stifled an impulse to say that we'd never had any
trouble from following seas either, and he went on accusingly : " Now, I hope you both realise how lucky you are
to be able to undertake a voyage like this. When I was
your age I'd have given my right arm, yes sir, my right
arm to go away like you're doing. But I couldn't do it.
I had to work. I had a wife to support and I had to
work." He finished his drink thoughtfully as he considered
all the work he'd had to do in his life and rose to go.

" Well, I must be getting along now," he told us ;
" but remember, next chance you get, you change this
boat for one with a canoe-stern and you'll be all right."

He jumped ashore, the binoculars flapping against his
chest and his cap askew from bumping it on the backstay ;
then he strode off down the road, bound we presumed for
the *Pandora* to advise Joe about canoe-sterns.

" The stinker," said Jill, eying his retreating figure, " I
wouldn't even have accepted if he HAD asked us to dinner.
Or at least," she added, after a moment's reflection, " I
shouldn't have ENJOYED accepting. Give his right arm
indeed to go sailing round the world, why he wouldn't
even give up his JOB to do it. Why," she went on fiercely,
" does everyone have to call us lucky because we've come
here ? Why can't they realise that we had ruts to climb
out of too ? "

We had several more visitors after that and enjoyed
ourselves hugely, showing off the boat and talking of some
of the places that we'd visited and hearing about life in
the *Mariposa*. " The food on board's terrific," said one
elderly couple from Detroit who'd been saving up for years

to come on the cruise. " Real American cooking. Now why don't you two come on board tonight and join us for supper ? "

Here it was. The invitation that we'd been working so hard to be given. So hard had we been working for it, in fact, that as soon as it came we began to feel ashamed of ourselves and very nearly refused. Nearly, but not quite, however.

Painting was forgotten for the rest of the day, and at six o'clock, dressed in our newest and bestest, we walked along the front amidst a salvo of jeers from all the other boats : " All toffee-nosed tonight, eh ? " they shouted to us ; and Jill, in her one remaining unladdered pair of stockings and high heels, earned a " Whee-wheeu " from Joe.

After *Salmo's* tiny cabin the sun-deck lounge in the *Mariposa* seemed enormous. Enormous, and cold as well, for the air conditioning was running full blast, but our host and hostess, sitting at a table near the bar, seemed to be quite comfortable, so we supposed that we would be too in due course. Drinks appeared as if by magic (no grubbing under the floorboards to look for bottles hereabouts) and we sat back and enjoyed ourselves while a stream of new arrivals filled the room and sat down at the tables to open parcels and compare purchases. Grass skirts seemed to have been the favourite buy, but mother-of-pearl shell ornaments had also done well and so had pictures. All the cafés ashore were filled with the works of aspiring Gaugins, and thanks to our extensive researches among the lowlife of Papeete during our month's residence, we recognised several of the canvases that were being handed around.

" Wouldn't be seen dead with any of them," our host said cheerfully as we moved towards the dining saloon past a very remarkable portrayal of purple palm-trees and orange mountains, " some of the people on board here just seem to go crazy whenever we reach port."

Dinner, as promised, was a sumptuous affair, served by waitresses, and we waded delightedly through course after course, turning our noses up in horror at the 'Special Low Calory Suggestions' that appeared as an addendum to the menu. Boat life had almost made us forget that such things as diets still existed in the world.

The waitresses, we were told, wanted to go ashore, and our hosts had to change before going on to a dance at one of the hotels, where the shaky state of our finances wouldn't permit us to accompany them, so it was still early in the evening when we found ourselves back on the quay once again. The bars were doing a roaring trade, and we paused at one or two of the doorways to peer inside and watch the dancers swinging and swaying their way round the floor while the drums and guitars of the various bands poured their rhythm out onto the warm evening air. Over Moorea the sky was still a light and luminous green, outlined in fading splashes of pink : a perfect background for the exciting tangle of straight lines made by the silhouetted masts and rigging of the moored boats. Two or three riding-lights had been lit, and these shone like jewels in the gloaming. The whole romantic pattern sent a stir of restlessness through us ; the first itch to the soles of our feet that we had felt since our arrival. " Let's not go back on board just yet," Jill said. " Let's decide on our future programme."

There was a café just across the road, so we turned into it and took our bottles of beer out to a table on the pavement where we could sit in darkness and talk and watch the world go by. After Christmas, we decided, we'd get down to work seriously. We'd paint the boat, we'd buy provisions, and we'd finish patching the sails. That, we estimated, would take two weeks and at the end of that time, on we'd go. On to the west, to the Cook Islands, to Palmerston, Tonga and Fiji. The very names of the islands were exciting. We'd finished our beer by this time, and were just getting ready to go when our attention was caught by one of the tables at the far side of the café. It was a large table and there was a party of six or eight girls sitting at it, American girls by the look of them, and all looking slightly lost and at a loose end. We wondered who they could be, and then suddenly recognised them as the waitresses from the *Mariposa*, the girls who had been giving us dinner an hour or two previously.

On an impulse we crossed over and invited them to come back on board with us, and soon we had them crammed into the cockpit and the cabin, with glasses in their hands, while they told us of life in the *Mariposa* as they saw it, a different life from the one we had heard about earlier in the afternoon from the passengers. But they were enjoying themselves, by the sound of it, and were proud of the fact that the company had decided to have girls instead of men in the dining-saloon. " You see, we're much politer than the men are," they told us, " and the passengers prefer it." They also told us that they had a male steward to make their beds for them, and left us speculating happily on who it was that made the bed of the steward who made the beds of the stewardesses who made them for the passengers.

Before we had time to resolve this interesting problem my eye was caught by one of the rats that lived in a hole in the wall close by the stern. He was happily walking up one of our mooring-lines to see if there was any food lying in the cockpit, and I wondered if I ought to do anything about it. I decided not to, and thought that probably when he found we had company he would just go ashore again without being noticed. He probably would have, too, if one of the girls had not chosen the particular moment that he was poking an interested nose over the cockpit coaming to put her glass down right on top of him. There was an earsplitting scream of " Oh, my gosh, QUICK. QUICK, it's a RAT," and a great crash as the glass broke and the peaceful scene of a moment before was

transformed. Three of the girls who had been sitting in
the cockpit leapt onto the seats and began dancing round
like dervishes, shouting advice and encouragement to each
other. " Oh where is it ? Oh QUICK. Oh push it overboard.
Oh THERE it is. . . ."

Jill, also in the cockpit, was trying to calm them, " It's
quite all right. It's just looking for greasy plates. It
ALWAYS come on board. Leave it alone and it'll go back
ashore again. Oh now you've frightened it." There was.
a scampering noise, and the poor rat, thoroughly un-
nerved, made a dash for the fo'c'sle and went to ground
beneath a pile of sailbags we'd put there to leave more
room in the fore-peak.

The girls down in the cabin weren't at all sure what
the fuss was about (one of them, indeed, had happily been
asleep, propped in a corner) and weren't in the least reassured by such explanations as were forthcoming from
above, and the party broke up with extreme abruptness.
We were full of apologies for the incident, but found that
it had made our stock soar to undreamed of heights. In
their eyes we were now real backwoods adventurers ; Jill
particularly they regarded as some sort of a super-being :
" Why, I just don't know how you COULD live in a boat
with those things around. I just couldn't, I COULDN'T."

The rat having been finally ushered ashore again, once
order had been restored, we were taken back to the
Mariposa. " Well we've seen your boat, now you just
come and see ours." The quartermaster at the head of
the gangway was heard to murmur something about being,
" not really supposed to allow visitors back on board after
one in the morning," but was quickly silenced with a
suggestion that the girls would get him " two, three
cinnammon rolls " if he just didn't make a silly fuss, and
we swept through the now dark and deserted dining-
saloon into the galleys. Here everything was a hive of
industry as the night shift worked at baking. Everything

was super-clean and super-modern, and delicious smells wafted to our nostrils. A general conference of the chefs on duty was called, paper bags were produced, and soon we found ourselves loaded down with cakes and rolls and fruit, and out-of-season vegetables from the icebox. A thick wedge of menus was thrown in for good measure at the last moment (they had nice pictures on them that Jill thought would be fine for brightening up the cabin) and back we went to the gangway in triumphal procession. The quartermaster was presented with his cinnammon rolls, and we returned to *Salmo* once again in a haze of goodnights.

Quite suddenly, and well before we were ready for it, we found that only two days remained until Christmas, so Jill dragged me ashore to do some shopping. The ostensible aim of the operation was to decorate the boat, but other ideas soon sprouted from this root. " What we want," said Jill, " is a really ENORMOUS Chinese lantern." The first three shops that we visited didn't offer anything that she considered enormous enough, but at the fourth we found something that looked like one of the pioneers of the ballooning era, and we soon agreed that in spite of its colossal price it would clearly be an economy to buy it, because it would last for years and years and be terribly useful at home when we finally bought ourselves a house. We could hang it in one of the downstairs windows, Jill explained, and it would be much more original than a Christmas Tree. As an afterthought she added that we could always have a Christmas Tree as well, if we thought we wanted one.

Having bought the lantern we decided that the boat would look so gay that really there would be no other course open to us but to have a party on Christmas morning, so we went on and bought ten litres of white wine and ten litres of red wine to act as a good firm party base on which we could build later.

That, of course, led us straight on to Christmas presents, and I learned by a strange coincidence that yes, as a matter of fact, Jill's eye HAD been caught by something that she'd rather like, a length of simply HEAVENLY French print in the window of one of the shops. We visited the shop and came practically skipping out of it again with a dress length of the print in a brown-paper parcel. A hundred yards down the road we had to stop to make sure that it looked just as exciting out of the shop as it did inside it, and it did, so we went to a Chinese tailor where Jill drew pictures on the back of a cigarette-packet of what the dress was to look like. A tape-measure was run over her and she was told that if she came back at five o'clock next evening the dress would be ready. Jill was almost transported with delight. " Oh, I'll be able to wear it for the party," she kept on telling me, and then a thought struck her : " What would YOU like ? " she asked. " Christmas presents are much more difficult for you. You never seem to want anything."

" I should like an umbrella," I told her.

" What on earth do you mean, you'd like an umbrella ! You CAN'T have an umbrella. What would you use it for ? And besides," she added, irrelevently, " you don't wear any shoes. Of course you don't want an umbrella."

I did want one, I explained to her. In Hong Kong, I went on loftily, EVERYONE had them. Most people had two or three, so that wherever they were when it started raining they could be fairly sure of having one to hand. It was too hot to wear a coat, I told her, and too wet if you didn't, so that an umbrella was the obvious answer.

Jill didn't seem to be at all convinced by my arguments, but finally, very reluctantly, she did buy me one, a large black one. (And very soon it became one of our most important pieces of shipboard equipment. We took it with us everywhere, shoes or no shoes, on bicycles or on foot, and it saved us a terrific amount of wetting.)

On Christmas Eve we collected Jill's dress from the tailor and then, mounting our bicycles, we pedalled out along the coast road for a small private celebration party. There was a full moon that night, and as it hung, round and yellow as a cheese, over the black mountain-tops, the palms threw great blotches and bars of shadow across the road. On our left we could hear the murmur of the breakers on the reef, and from all round about came the drone, the rustle, and the chirp of the night insects. We had no lights on our machines, so our progress was erratic, and every now and then we had to fling ourselves out of the saddles and scramble into the ditch as cars came swishing along the road from behind, zigging like errant snipe at the carefree whim of the driver.

The last part of our journey was down a sandy side-track that led towards the beach, where stood the hotel for which we were heading. It was difficult to control the bicycles in the soft sand, and two or three times we succeeded in falling off before we finally sighted the lights we were looking for in a little clearing amongst the palms. We dusted ourselves off as best we could, and then pushed through the door of the hotel into a huge airy room built of pandanus thatch. There was a bar at one end, a dance floor, and several rows of tables. A stir went through the staff on our entrance. The waitresses readjusted the flowers in their hair, a chef retired briskly through a swing-door, and the barman and assistant barman broke off their conversation and began to polish glasses expectantly. We were the only guests.

The meal was brought to us on a verandah overlooking the beach. The moon lit up the waves as they tumbled lazily onto the sand. Two fishermen with torches worked on the reef as we ate, and the winking lights moved slowly up and down, drawing our eyes seaward, drifting our minds from the present to the past. We began to think of other Christmases and other places. " Do you remember last year ? " Jill asked, " up at St Sauveur in Canada.

How all the houses had Christmas trees standing outside
. . . and the little church, all made of logs where we had
our Christmas service."

Back flew our minds, farther and farther yet, to Christmases before we had met each other : Christmases in
England, Christmases at sea, hot Christmases and cold
ones. We talked and talked, reminiscing happily until
the voice of the wine-waiter interrupted our thoughts and
jumped us both back to the present once again. " Liqueur
with your coffee, M'sieur, Madame ? Cognac ? Benedic-
tine ? Cointreau ? "

We chose brandy and then wandered down over the
sand until we found a fallen palm-trunk to sit on, where
we spent nearly an hour talking quietly to each other and
soaking up the peace and the pleasantness of the deserted
beach.

Before we left we cut a branch from an ironwood tree
to take back on board for the masthead. It was the
nearest approach to a Christmas Tree that Tahiti could
offer, and at Christmas time all good ships have Christmas
trees at the masthead. But we hadn't counted on the
temperament of our bicycles or the roughness of the path
that led to the road. " Oh, come on," said Jill, as I
toppled off for the third time, " I'll take it. I didn't
have as much of that wine as you did."

She mounted her bicycle and began scooting along with
one foot, " Just wait till I've got going," she panted, " and
then hand me the branch. That's where you went wrong.
You never got going properly first."

She scooted faster and faster until I had to run in order
to keep up with her. " Right," she shouted. " Now,"
and grabbed the branch from my hands like a standard-
bearer seizing the colours from a stricken comrade. There
was a rapidly recurring ' stinka, stinka, stinka, stinka '
noise as a frond of ironwood nuzzled against her front
spokes, and then CRASH !

Pushing my own bicycle I came up to view the wreckage.

" It's all right," said a small voice from the ditch, " I don't think anything's broken. Not even the bicycle." We walked for the rest of the way until we reached the road, and then very very gingerly mounted once again and returned without further incident to where our huge red lantern beamed a welcome from its place on the backstay.

There was no English church on the island, so as soon as we had well and truly secured our branch aloft, we went down to the cabin and sat in the yellow lamplight reading aloud the Christmas story.

' . . . And there were in the same country shepherds abiding in the field, keeping watch over their flock by night. . . . '

As we finished reading, a clock outside struck midnight. " Happy Christmas," we said to each other and then, both in the same breath, " I wonder where we'll be NEXT Christmas."

THE BEACH AT TAHITI

ALONGSIDE AT PAPEETE

" You didn't come here in that thing, did you ? "

CHAPTER SEVENTEEN

NEW YEAR AND NEW PLANS

THE New Year came in to the rhythm of drums and guitars at the Bar Leah, which is one of the smaller and lower of the Papeete joints. It was a stirring rhythm, and so it should have been, for Jill and I were the drummers ; Tonk, tonk, tonka, tonka, tonk went our hands ; the guitars beside us twanged and tinkled, and the dancers swayed and stamped on the floor in front of us. The band was an ever-changing affair. As individual members grew tired or thirsty they handed their instruments to dancers or drinkers who would leave the floor and take a turn on the side-lines. We seemed to be the only ones incapable of being entrusted with guitars, and always it was the drums that were offered when our turn came.

We had started the evening respectably enough by having a very classy dinner in *Pandora* with Joe and Freddie and their respective partners, but somehow at Quinn's, our first port of call thereafter, we had drifted apart. Quinn's is the principal Papeete dive and is a large and ramshackle building with a horse-shoe bar, a dance floor, and dimly lit booths and tables round its perimeter. It had started to do business soon after breakfast on the morning of New Year's Eve, and the more stalwart and persistent of its patrons were already falling asleep where they stood or sat by the time we arrived.

At the door we had run into a milling throng, and it had taken some minutes of persistent burrowing before we could reach the bar and order beer. Our immediate neighbours, we noticed, were two bejewelled French ladies in low-cut gowns of white satin, and a gigantic Tahitian, six foot five and broad in proportion, who was propped against a pillar with a beatific expression and tightly-closed eyes.

Two old ladies thrust wreaths upon us as soon as we emerged from the thickest part of the mob, and the sweet smell of the blooms is one of my principal memories of the evening. We watched the crowds, we danced, we drank our beer, and drifted like the rest from one bar to another. All the bar fronts had been ingeniously expanded by intricately-woven pandanus screens, which not only doubled the capacity of each one, but also added a pleasingly festive touch. Everyone on the island was in Papeete that night, but though there were terrific crowds and a simply staggering intake of alcohol, we never met any unpleasantness all night. Twice Jill danced with newly resurrected figures who, moments before they took the floor, had been sleeping peacefully. But neither, as soon as he reached the floor, had lost his instinct for rhythm and music. "They're the most TERRIFIC dancers," said Jill, each time, as she was politely escorted back to my side again. " Why can't YOU swing your hips like that ? "

And all that I could answer was that my hips weren't made that way.

At intervals during the evening, like wandering stars, we crossed the orbits of others we knew. Freddie, after our initial parting, loomed ponderously up two or three times, resplendent in a white dinner-jacket, treading stately measures. Joe, with a rhythm as wild as the islanders' own, kept flashing into view, and many more from the waterfront and the administration appeared and then vanished again. We would greet each in turn as we met, pause for a moment or two, and then drift apart again until finally, when the stars were dimming overhead and the masts and rigging of the yachts and schooners showed grey instead of black, we returned on board to find our paper lantern still glowing redly, and the last of its candles guttering.

True to our resolve, as soon as we'd slept off our New Year's arrears of sleep we began to work in earnest, instead of just playing at working. There were far too many distractions in Papeete we decided, so we slipped out of the harbour very early one morning and skirted down the coast beyond the reef until we reached Papeare. The pass is narrow, and we flew in through it with our hearts as usual in our mouths until the roaring fury of the broken water was well astern. It was late evening by then, and on the wings of the dying breeze we nosed our way into a perfect anchorage no more than a boat's length from the beach. Ashore was one of the most beautiful stretches of garden in Tahiti, a boat-house set amongst palm-trees, and a disused bungalow whose bathroom had been thrown open to us. As we sat in the infinite peace of this deserted hideaway to have our first supper, we blessed Freddie a thousand times for the introductions which had opened its doors to us.

Our first job was to re-varnish the mast and check every wire and shackle of the rigging to see that they were still strong and unrusted. It was a laborious job, but one that we never scamped because of the peace of mind which it brought at sea in bad weather.

As soon as the mast was finished we turned our attention to the hull. We couldn't dry out completely, for there is no more than a foot of rise and fall to the tide at Tahiti, so we did as the buccaneers used to do. We rigged tackles from the masthead to the foot of a palm-tree and hauled and hauled until *Salmo* lay on her side on the steep sand-bank, for all the world like a stranded whale, and then we attacked her with scrubbers, scrapers and finally sandpaper.

The days were hot at this time of year, and by midday every day (for we started work at six in the morning) we would be exhausted. We usually bathed then and rowed

the Prout over to the home of Bonnie, a New Zealander,
who had just got rid of a nudist visitor. " He was such
a DULL man," she told us, " and SO inconsiderate about
parking his car. He nearly ruined my lawn by driving
over it."

Bonnie loved her garden and kept it looking beautiful
with shaven grass and beds ablaze with flowers. We often
used to sit in the shade during the afternoon and try to
catch up with long-neglected correspondence while Bonnie
weeded or cut the grass in the background. ' Weekend '
magazine in far-off Canada were wanting another article
from us, and all our Christmas letters had still to be
answered.

After a week at Papeare *Salmo* began to look something
like a yacht again and less like a floating junk-shop. We
had finished work on her bottom and were well on with
the topsides when Jill suddenly sat down on the sand one
morning with the world all grey and spinning round
about her.

" I think," we said, " that we'd better visit a doctor."

The bus to Papeete rattled and banged along the road,
filled to overflowing with villagers taking fruit and vegetables to the market. At intervals, on the way, it would
stop when the driver saw a palm-branch laid just so on
the roadside, and the horn would blow until a leaping
figure rose from the ground rubbing his eyes and clambered
on board. Two guitars struck up a tune, and while everyone sang, Jill and I, the only white faces in a sea of brown,
tried to sort out our ideas and adjust our minds. " Well,
we'll know soon," we thought, " one way or the other."

In both our minds a sort of turmoil raged. We were
longing for a family, but at the same time we had been
thinking for so long that we would sail right round the world
that the idea was hard to get rid of. Each of us had made
little mental pictures of arriving back in England ; we
had even decided that Lymington would be our first port

of call : families would be there to welcome us and we
would have achieved (for what it was worth) what we
had set out to achieve. That was one side of the picture.
On the other was a big unknown. If this WAS to be a
child, where would we go to ? What would we do with
Salmo ? What would happen about agreements with
' Weekend ' magazine ? And yet the very word 'child'
was a thrilling one : Our own child. Us parents. Could
we hope for that ? Did we ?

We just didn't know, and the bus banged and rattled
remorselessly on ; the guitars played ; and we sat in our
seats playing mental patball with an never-ending round
of ' ifs ' and ' buts ' and ' perhapses.'

" Allow me to congratulate you, *m'sieur*," said the
doctor, ushering Jill out of the consulting room. " You
can expect the birth to take place in early September."

At least he didn't say that. He said it in French, but
that was what he meant.

September. It was now nearly the end of January.
Because we wanted our first child to be born in England
we should have to do some quick thinking. Quick moving
too. There were innumerable snags to be overcome :
but the first one, and the most important, the doctor
might be able to help with.

" *M'sieur*," I began, in creaking schoolboy French,
" *croyez-vous qu'il serait possible pour madame faire un
grand voyage dans un tout petit bateau à voile ?* " The
voyage, I added, would be six or eight weeks in longness.

The doctor seemed taken aback, so we judged that this
was not among the questions he reckoned on being asked
by prospective parents. He thought for a while and
then put his finger on the nub of the problem by saying :

" To where would you sail then, in this small boat ? "

And we found ourselves completely floored. For, after
all, where on earth would we sail to ? The choice was a

wide one, and we had already considered such diverse possibilities as Auckland, Sydney, Hawaii and Los Angeles.

" We don't know yet," we replied rather feebly, feeling it was most unfair to be invited to tie ourselves down to mere navigational detail before we had even had a chance to become used to the idea of parenthood.

" Well, all I can say to you then," said the doctor doubtfully, " is that madame MIGHT make such a voyage. But it would surely be wiser for her to travel in the steamship."

That's what we'd thought he would say, and in the circumstances it wasn't much help. For one thing there was a three-month waiting-list for passages in the steamship, and we had neither the money nor the inclination to sit in Tahiti all that time.

We asked a few further questions, and the doctor must have realised that madame was in a ' to-hell-with-steamships ' frame of mind ; for he soon relaxed his professional air, shook us both warmly by the hand and, as he ushered us into the blinding midday glare of Papeete, adjured Jill to be very sure to eat much fish, " Preferably," he added, rather wistfully, " lagoon fish."

That night after supper we pulled out our much smeared (and only) chart of the Pacific and decided to procrastinate no longer but to agree once and for all where to make for. The trouble is, with Tahiti, that it is more or less bang in the middle of the South Pacific, and whichever edge you choose as a target is roughly three thousand miles distant.

" I suppose," I said, " that we should really go to Auckland. It's the closest at about two thousand three hundred miles, but we'd probably get a better price for *Salmo* if we went on to Sydney. After all, it's not very much farther."

" Oh, I hate talking of selling her," Jill replied. " Poor *Salmo*. It doesn't seem fair after all she's done for us.

Do you suppose that whoever buys her will like her as
much as we do ? ''

" Don't quite see how they could," I answered. " Not
till they get to know her, anyway. But what else can
we do ? After all, it's going to be the money we get from
her that's going to buy our tickets home."

" Yes ; I know it is," she said gloomily ; but then a
thought struck her and she went on more cheerfully
" But if we went to Hawaii we'd probably get lots more
for her even than at Sydney, wouldn't we ? They say
that everyone in Hawaii is a millionaire, and besides the
passage home will be cheaper, at least it ought to be.
That's the worst of Australia ; it's one of the few places
in the world that are farther from England than Tahiti is."

" Well, if you come to that," I went on, following her
train of thought, " Los Angeles is even nearer England
than Hawaii is, and by all accounts it's probably the best
market of any for selling a boat in."

The seed was sown and very soon took root. All sorts
of motives prompted us. To go to Australia and stop
would have been a fizzle out to our voyage, we somehow
felt. California, though, was a different kettle of fish
altogether. '. . . Oh we knoo we shouldn't do it but
before we hardly knoo it . . .' Los Angeles had been settled
upon in our minds. Not only was it almost twice as far
away as Auckland but it was also dead to windward, and
Salmo, like any small sailing boat, slams and bangs and
bounces into a head sea in a way she never does with the
wind more free. And somehow the goal seemed all the
more attractive for being a bit difficult to achieve.

" Oh, that'll be terrific," said Jill. " Won't it be splendid
when we arrive ! We'll sell our film to the Hollywood
television tycoons and they'll fairly smother us in dollars.
Oh, I bet they do."

We hadn't actually had any of our film developed yet.
Reel upon reel of it had been shot and posted back to

England for processing, and never a foot of it had we so far seen. Often we became thoroughly depressed about it, thinking of all the money we were spending on film and never being sure whether the heat might be melting it, the exposures haywire, or any one of a hundred and one other things wrong. But now that we'd decided to go to California all this was forgotten. Life had suddenly become very, very, good and very exciting.

The first person we told of our change of plan was Freddie. He was quite horrified and drew me to one side. " But, my dear chap," he said, " you must be absolutely out of your mind. Honestly, old boy, you just don't know what you'll be up against. Why I mean to say . . . well, pregnant women, they're really quite extraordinary. Quite extraordinary. Take my tip. Don't do it."

We convinced him, at last, that things were not as black as he painted them. For after all, we explained, there were always the Marquesas. We intended to make them a sort of staging post. If all had gone well thus far, we'd go on. If not, we'd come back.

Freddie cheered up immediately, congratulated us warmly, and invited us to supper, for he was bursting to tell us about his goat. The cook's nephew had given him half a goat the week before apparently, and he had been injecting it with brandy with a hypodermic every day since ; and tonight, he declared proudly, it was ripe at last, absolutely perfect.

We accepted at once. We'd never tasted brandied goat before and felt that it was an experience that shouldn't be missed. Besides, we'd been feeling shy before making our announcement and were glad to have got it over.

Salmo with two anchors out and lines festooned to various useful palm-trees was safe enough at Papeare, so we decided to spend our last night in Tahiti, ashore with Freddie. It turned out to be just as well that we weren't worried about *Salmo* ; for during the afternoon it began to rain, gently at first and then harder and harder and harder. The wireless issued a hurricane warning.

The sky grew dark as pitch and we had to put the lights on a full hour before sunset. This was no mere shower, so we abandoned our original plan of going out to do some last-minute shopping and sat instead reading old copies of the ' Sunday Times ' from the consulate collection. The wind whined eerily, and the rain, which had become a deluge, lashed and splashed as it hit the sodden ground. The paths in the garden ran like rivers and the heavy canvas screens that sheltered the verandah clattered and clashed despite all our attempts to lash them firmly in place.

" The blasted Foreign Office," said Freddie savagely, as we dragged the enormous dining-room table to one side of the room. " They WON'T let me mend the roof. It's this perpetual economy campaign of theirs. They're even thinking of shutting the consulate altogether, and until they've made up their minds they won't give me a penny, not a single penny for repairs. And now look at it."

We looked. The sight was impressive ; for the largest of the holes in the roof seemed to have been directly over the table and it was as if a tap had been turned on. The cook, a wizened old crone by the name of Virginie, brought in a large zinc bath and placed it on the floor to catch the worst of the torrent, cackling to herself. " *Eh, aiee, c'est le toit. C'est le toit.*"

In due course we had our supper, the verandah screens still banging and clattering furiously and the rain hissing and roaring outside among the palms. Beside us the zinc bath tinkle, tinkle, tinkled as it filled. But the goat was delicious. There were no fresh vegetables to go with it, for the island was in the throes of a shortage ; instead we ate lentils. Even our last meal ashore, we reflected, was not providing Jill with an overabundance of the vitamins which the doctor had invited her to collect. Altogether it was a strange farewell, but then it would hardly have been Tahiti if it had been otherwise.

By morning the disturbance was past and the whole island steamed as the bus took us back to our anchorage. By some oversight we had no beer with us and all our bus-mates considered this a most disturbing state of affairs. Everyone else had lots. Our immediate neighbour, a big brawny six-foot Tahitian, nudged Jill, politely wiped the neck of the bottle on his *pareu*, and handed the bottle to her, including me in the offer with a wave of his arm.

Tahitian buses, I think, are the friendliest I have ever travelled on. They invariably carry several guitar players and everyone sings for all he is worth. Luggage is carried on the roof, with two small boys perched on top to load and unload it as required, and fish are slung in lines from bars at the back. Why everyone who travels on buses in Tahiti has to carry fish with him, I'm not sure but apparently it is more or less *de rigueur*. The same applies to beer, and the whole atmosphere is one of carnival. Now that we'd adjusted our minds slightly we were in more of a mood to appreciate all this than we had been on our first bus.

At length we arrived in Papeare. The two small boys flung down our bundles and the bus rattled away through the palm-groves ; the last we saw of it were the festoons of fish flapping as they jolted, and the crown of bananas that encircled the luggage on the roof.

It was only the work of a few moments to change from our shore-going clothes and stow such shopping as we had been able to do before visiting Freddie. The lines were untangled from the palm-trunks, the anchors weighed, and the sails set. " At last," we said, " here goes."

Salmo heeled to the breeze as she headed for the pass, overtaking a huge canoe with four men on board, perched on a seine net, paddling out on a fishing expedition. The water inside the lagoon was green, but beyond the wide white wall of surf that marked the reef everything was a deep pure blue. It was nearly low water and we could see the top of the reef breaking the surface in the troughs of the waves. The overnight disturbance had thrown up a heavy swell and each wave swept in, in a torrent of white foam that roared over the coral, leaving a white mist of spindrift behind it that trailed in silver threads against the blue sky. The pass was only three hundred yards wide, and as we lifted high on the crest of each succeeding monster we could see the reef stretch unbroken on either hand, our own little blue pathway the only fragment of unbroken water in a long, long ribbon of raging foam. The roaring filled our ears. It is a frightening sound, and we both heaved an inward sigh of relief as we left it behind and turned our bows north-eastwards.

Gradually the palms, the beaches of black sand, the houses, and the hillsides astern merged into a greenish blur; by evening all that we could see of the land was the blue-black silhouette of saw-toothed mountains. Around us stretched the sea : miles and miles and miles of sea, unbroken to the horizon ahead and far beyond it.

We should have felt calm, unhurried and at peace with the world, for it was a lovely evening. But we didn't . we just felt sick. "At least," I reflected, as an invisible hand squeezed and squeezed again at my innermost digestive tracts, "I should take comfort from this situation. For after all we are both sick. It is therefore more probably that it is seasickness than morning sickness which is to blame." We knew that seasickness passed off in time. Of morning sickness we had no experience.

The diagnosis was correct. Our agony only lasted its usual time and the ordered routine of life at sea soon settled down upon us. But progress was miserably slow. We had expected a beam wind and a steady beam wind at that ; for were we not in the south-east trade-wind belt, as marked on our chart ? Instead of that, day after day, all that we encountered were calms and foolish little head winds, the legacy we presumed of the near hurricane of our last night ashore.

I had intended to steer a more or less direct course for the Marquesas, but we found ourselves pushed farther and farther to starboard of our intended route. One evening we met an island, and the next day another, and began to have doubts about the wisdom of relying exclusively upon our one and only chart.

" Which way do we go round this darned island ? " Jill had asked me when we sighted the second one (the first had been safely away to starboard) and I had gone down to the chart to find out, though without much confidence in the outcome.

" Well," I had replied guardedly, " can you see either of its edges ? If you can, then go round that way."

" All I can see at the moment," said Jill, " is five palm-trees sticking up out of the sea. Oh, no. There's another one, that makes six. Don't you know where we are ? What island is it ? "

" It doesn't actually give it a name," I said after pro-longed study. " It's just a sort of dot, and besides, there's a good deal of marmalade on the chart round here. I told you not to spread the bread on the chart-table. Any-way I don't think it matters much, it can't be more than about ten miles long. Either side will do."

Needless to say we chose the wrong side and promptly ran into more islands—Tuomotus (or as the early navigators cheerfully called them, ' The Dangerous Archipelago ')—before we drew clear once more. They're fidgety little brutes ; even from the masthead you can't see much more than palm-trees growing out of the water, but like all these coral atolls they have reefs. The reefs, though unpleasant to run into, do have their advantages how-ever ; for the water is deep right up to their edges and the breaking surf even on the lee side makes such a roar that, except in very unusual conditions, one is unlikely to hit them without warning.

In due course we sighted Uopo Island, the first of the Marquesa group, dawdled past it for three mortal days and at last, after twenty days (we had reckoned on ten) flung our anchor over the side in Taiohai Bay in Nukuhiva. We had a bunch of letters on board for Bob the Trader, one of the dwindling number of old-timers left in the islands, so we set off ashore to deliver them.

" These damn flies," said Jill, dancing up and down and slapping herself as we walked along the sandy track that skirted the bay ; " aren't they biting YOU at all ? Oh ! Ooo ! Oow ! " She doesn't take kindly to insects. Or to suffering in silence either.

Bob, when we found him, was nearly as bad as she was. " Aye ; it's these no-no flies," he said. " They're the curse of the Marquesas. Never known them as bad as they are this year, though." His forty years in the Pacific had left his Liverpool accent completely intact. Dressed in shorts and a blue-and-white striped pyjama jacket he was a patriarchal figure as he sat at the little table on the verandah in front of his store, a typewriter idle beneath his fingers. The schooner was due from Papeete next day, but he didn't seem at all anxious to get on with the paper-work that its arrival would entail.

" Number Two, Pacific Road, is my address here," he said. " The Angermeyers at Academy Bay in the Galapagos are Number One. All the yachts go there first and on to me afterwards. Regular as clockwork. There was one in last week who'd done that. He brought me a sack of potatoes from Academy Bay that I'd ordered four months ago from a yacht going the other way. Best potatoes in the Pacific they grow there. But, as I was saying : terribly conservative yachts are about the routes they follow. You're the first one for a long, long time who's doing something a bit different. Here. Have some

of the Flit, ma'am. Those dam' no-no's seem to be bothering you again."

Bob's store stands fifty yards back from the water's
edge at the very head of Taiohai Bay. Sitting on the
verandah we looked down the long fjord-like bay to
Uopo Island, twenty miles away, bristling up from the
water in tall, impossible crags and towers like a stylised
fairy castle. The colours are superb at all times, but the
sunrises, Bob told us, are sometimes unbelievable. He'd
looked for a situation like this for years, he said, before
he finally picked this particular spot to build his house.
We found it easy to believe him.

Bob was most hospitable, but he had very few fresh
provisions to offer us. Mostly, he said, the fruit and
vegetables of the island were grown in Taipeevai, the next
valley to the northward. If we planned to stock up before
sailing, why didn't we go on there for a day or two ?
" Besides," he said, " there's a young American archæolo-
gist and his wife staying there now. Name of Suggs "—
he called it Soogs—" they'd be pleased to have a bit of
company."

We'd been reading Herman Melville on the way up to
the Marquesas, so we knew all about Taipee Valley and
thought that this seemed to be a good suggestion.

The Soogses (we never could stop ourselves calling them
that) lodged with a Marquesan family three miles up the
river. We paddled the dinghy up the first mile and a
half and then walked the rest of the way through palm-
groves. Most of the villagers hereabouts had horses, and
probably because of the impending arrival of the schooner,
terrific quantities of copra were on the move, slung in
sacks on the horses' backs. The quantities were terrific
by Polynesian standards, but as Bob and everyone else
assured us, any other race could produce ten times as
much with the facilities at hand. The islanders' philosophy
however, very sensibly dictates that if you earn enough

money to buy tinned meat, cigarettes and beer, then there's no point in making any more. Better to sit and gossip, or bathe, or make an odd flower garland or two to wear on your hat. The present surge of activity Bob attributed to a craze for motor-scooters which had suddenly hit the island. One had appeared a few months back and at once everybody else wanted to own one.

Mrs Soogs, when we found her, was looking slightly harassed and obviously wasn't expecting visitors. She was dressed in a *pareu* and could just be seen, in the very middle of their bedroom, entirely surrounded by a sort of zareba of cardboard boxes. She was packing, she said. Some of the boxes contained clothes, some of them stone artifacts and shells, but most were full of bones. Her husband, she explained, had been concentrating mainly on graves. It all sounded rather ghoulish.

Apart from the more ordinary difficulties to which archæology seems to be prone, such as no-no flies and ham-fisted diggers, the Soogses were suffering from visa and money trouble. They had come out intending to spend three months in the Marquesas, and thanks to the scarcity of passages had already been there for six. Now their visas had expired and the New York Museum for which they worked was having difficulty in getting more money out to them. To crown all, said poor Mrs Soogs, that very morning they had been told that they had to leave by tomorrow's schooner. "And just LOOK at all the stuff we've got to take with us !" she wailed, " and now Bob's just found ANOTHER big grave. He's out there digging at it now and he'll probably be back with another dozen boxfuls."

In this she did Bob less than justice. It seemed that he, too, had spent a harassing morning. Instead of being out digging as his wife had thought, he'd been having another set-to with the Papeete visa authorities by way of the wireless-office. His first words on arrival home

were, " Relax, honey, we're not to go on this schooner
after all." We later heard that they didn't get away for
yet another three months.

We bought two hens in Taipeevai to provide fresh meat
(and with any luck an egg or two) on our journey. I
had given them to Jill to carry down to the dinghy upon
our final embarkation, pleading that I was lame. (As a
matter of fact I was, having misguidedly gone for a walk
in bare feet to the very top of one of the passes that led
out of Taipeevai ; my theory that my feet had out-
toughened those of the Polynesians proved to be mistaken.)
I had also told her (though this is in dispute) to make
sure that the hens' legs were properly tied. Jill reached
the dinghy and plonked the hens into it, then turned
her back on them to see how I was getting on with the
remainder of the load which we had somehow accumulated.
With a squawk, one of the hens leaped up, scrambled out
of the dinghy, and raced like a wing three-quarter for a
large bush well up the beach. " Look out ! " I yelled.
" Oh I TOLD you to see that its legs were tied together.
Oh, for goodness' sake CATCH the darned thing."

" Oh, you DIDN'T," wailed Jill. " Oh, I thought that
you'd tied them," and she dived in pursuit.

Behind the bush the hen had chosen lay impenetrable
prickles and safety. But the thought of fresh meat fading
out of her life untasted spurred Jill almost to a frenzy.
The hen, with a triumphant cackle, covered the last six
feet without touching the ground ; but so did Jill, and
she disappeared head first into the bush, her legs waving
and jerking spasmodically. There were muffled cursings
and cacklings and finally Jill came out of eclipse, triumphantly clutching her victim once again. " I got it," she
announced proudly.

Afterwards the hens settled down well to life on board.
We fed them every morning on rice and bananas in their
hutch on top of the cabin, and grew quite fond of them.

Los Angeles : Great Lumps of Coral

They never did lay any eggs, but they tasted quite delicious. Perhaps it was the bananas.

Four days out, Jill became overcome with a sort of Kanga complex and decided to count everything on board, with the idea of finding out whether we had enough food to last the voyage, though what we would have done if we hadn't remained unspecified. " We've got twenty-seven tins of meat," she announced at the end of it all, consulting a grubby little bit of paper, " and four of kipper and those two of sauerkraut that you insisted on buying, but what on earth you did it for I never COULD understand ; neither of us likes it ; and two big ones, of de-hydrated cod and. . . . Oh, well, it looks as though it should be about enough. How many days do you think this leg is going to take ? "

The same question had been running through my mind for some time, but somehow we'd never quite got round to working out exactly what route we'd have to follow and what winds we'd be likely to encounter. This seemed to be as good a moment as any to do so ; better than most, in fact ; for that very morning I had found that we had gone far enough north for me to be able to plot our position on the very bottom edge of the North Pacific chart instead of at the top edge of the South Pacific one. For the first time, therefore, Los Angeles and *Salmo* lay on the same bit of paper. I doodled with dividers, drawing bold pencil scribbles to indicate the course I hoped we would be able to make if the trade winds behaved as advertised, and found that with luck we'd be able to go more or less due north as soon as we encountered the north-east trades, sail straight through them and then go about on to the port tack and head for Los Angeles.

" Two weeks," I muttered, " till we meet the trades ; seventeen days or thereabouts to get through them ; ten on the port tack. . . . Well, taken all in all, say probably forty days or a little bit more. We've been out four already so that leaves about another forty. Call it forty from today," I finally suggested.

" But you keep on saying forty," said Jill, " I thought it was going to be forty from Tahiti. And then I thought that if it wasn't, it was going to be forty from the Marquesas and now you say it's going to be forty from today. It's all very difficult. We probably won't have enough food in that case."

" Oh, well," I said rather guiltily, " we'll manage all right. I probably SHOULD have worked it all out before. I always USED to do it before we set out for anywhere."

A thought struck me. " How much have we to drink on board ? I'd hate to run out of *that* half-way."

Jill knew I was talking of six o'clock drink, not water. We both knew we had plenty of that. Our six o'clock habit, however, had become very precious to us. It was one of the day's most important milestones.

We had, we discovered, half a gallon of Bob's *vin ordinaire* (very), two bottles of whisky, and one of brandy. I therefore divided up our proposed course into four equal chunks, crossed by heavy dotted lines spread a couple of hundred miles on either side in case we didn't follow the intended track, and with great ceremony we marked these lines : ' Penultimate Whisky,' ' Brandy ' and finally ' Ultimate Whisky.' We would not allow ourselves to open a bottle, we swore, until we had crossed the appropriate line. Thus, we hoped, if we had to go six o'clockless at all, we should do so in little patches throughout the trip and not have a long sad vista of it to look forward to at the end as we might otherwise have to do.

On the twenty-third day, much to our surprise, the paraffin ran out. Or rather it showed signs of doing so. When I went to fill the ready-use tank from the bulk tank nothing more than a dribble came out.

We tried to think back and remember when we'd filled it last, and came to the conclusion that it must have been soon after Christmas. We had each thought the other had put in another fill since then. This was rather disturbing ; for we had been using paraffin at the rate of nearly a quart a day and had grown very smug about the splendour of the cooking, our weekly bread-bakes, our toast for breakfast and our curry suppers.

By draining the cabin-lamps and the heater which lay neglected and rusting in the fo'c'sle, and by wringing the last dribble from the tank, we collected half a gallon and decided that we should light the stove only once a day from now on. Life seemed very bleak all of a sudden. The twenty-odd days still to go seemed to stretch themselves into an æon.

The most economical way to use the stove, we decided, would be to fill the pressure-cooker as full as we could conveniently manage, with rice or some other bulky food like spaghetti, every time the stove was lit, cook it, and then wade through the rather depressing contents at successive meals until the performance had to be repeated.

" This is perfectly beastly," said Jill, spooning a dank skein of spaghetti into her mouth at breakfast the next morning. " If it were even warm it wouldn't be quite so foul. But like it is—cold. Ugh."

I tried to be stoical about it, but cold spaghetti for meal after meal calls for very high quality stoicism. We began to rack our brains for palliatives.

Methylated spirits was the answer. We had, we discovered, more than a gallon of that and began to experiment with ways of using it. The best turned out to be to fill the cabin lamps with spirit, remove the glass chimneys and shield the flames from draught by putting the lamps into a biscuit tin. A saucepan could then be put on top and heated. It was a somewhat laboured process, and entailed squatting on the deck and nursing the biscuit-tin and saucepan between the knees to prevent *Salmo* from throwing the whole contrivance endways, but it was an

enormous improvement.   We now ate our rice and spaghetti warm, and even on occasions when we felt reckless,
made a sauce to put over the top of it.

The flour too was giving trouble.   It must have been a
bit of a job lot when we bought it, for creepy-crawlies
began to appear within a week of purchase.   Now, after
six weeks, the big glass sweet-jar in which it lived looked
like a museum exhibit :   ' The Life Cycle of the Flour
Beetle.'   Our hunger was such, however, that we dared
not throw the stuff overboard :   it was, after all, more or
less edible.   We had no sieve on board, but we still had
the petticoat from the dress that Jill bought in New
York ;   the one we had used as a langouste trap in the
Galapagos.   So we tore up the mangled remains and used
them for removing flour-bugs ;   every time we needed to
use flour we sieved it through two thicknesses of petticoat
and dumped the wriggling catch over the stern, cursing
the Chinese shopkeeper from whom we'd bought the consignment every time we did so.

Fortunately the actual process of sailing *Salmo* was
extremely easy.   For nine-tenths of the time she sailed
herself, and only on two nights in all the forty-six that
the voyage finally took us did we have to keep night
watches.   One of these two nights was during our crossing
of the Doldrums.   We had had very light winds all the
preceding day, but the evening looked threatening.   All
round the horizon giant thunderheads piled themselves
up like great black drifts of smoke ;   lightning flashed
continuously, and there was a hot, menacing feel in the air.

Salmo slipped through the water, riding over the oily
swell, her bow-wave whispering and big bubbles of silver-
blue phosphorescence trailing out astern.   Every now and
then the wind fell so light that the sails shook, and as
I sat at the tiller I could hear the shackles on the sheets
flap against the rigging with dry clacking noises.   The
lightning grew closer and brighter and great peals of

thunder followed. The stars were gradually blotted out but still no wind came. It was all rather uncanny.

The change from calm to violence was very abrupt. One moment we lay inert and lifeless, rolling to the swell, and the next there was a whistle of wind, *Salmo* heeled far over, and the whispering of her bow-wave changed to a strong surging swish. I took the Genoa jib off and rolled down a couple of reefs on the mainsail and no sooner had I done so than the rain arrived. It hissed and pelted down, but as it came, so the wind freed, and I was able to let *Salmo* rush on through the darkness without shortening sail further. As abruptly as the squall started, so it stopped. The wind backed, fell away, and then died altogether and we were left rolling and rocking idly ; stars came out, and I was able to see another squall forming up behind the first. Our period of idleness was only a short one.

Seven different squalls hit us that night and the next day, all with dangerously strong winds that ruined our record for unbroken sleep. We had grown very lazy we found, after so many nights of idleness.

Slowly, slowly, eighty miles a day, we worked our way northward, passing in turn our ' Penultimate Whisky ' and our ' Brandy ' lines. Each day we marked with a cross our noon position as estimated by dead reckoning, and once a week we checked it by taking a sight.

Jill was wonderfully well, and it was only the cooking that she found too much for her. Each time she tried she would be overcome with seasickness, so we decided that the effort wasn't worth the making. Instead, she began to make herself a maternity dress to wear on arrival. ". . . Well, if I don't, I won't have a THING to wear."

Still the days ticked on, each one very like the last : sunlit days and, more and more as time drew on, slightly hungry ones. We began to dream of food and spent hours discussing it. "What I'd really like," Jill once said,

" would be a HUGE leg of lamb, with roast potatoes and brussels sprouts and mint sauce and after that fruit salad and lots and lots of cream . . . whipped." Our mouths watered and we ploughed on through our dehydrated cod and cabbage. On Sunday mornings for breakfast we had tinned kippers.

Once we caught a fish on the line which we always trailed astern—a tunny—and it was delicious, but very soon afterwards we had to stop fishing altogether because of the albatrosses. These infuriating creatures seem to swarm in the North Pacific, and the particular brand with which we were afflicted were even more gormless than albatrosses usually are. Which is saying quite a lot, for all albatrosses seem to be half-witted. No sooner would they see us putting the fishing-line out than down they'd swoop at it in a clumsy sort of dive and grab the spinner in their beaks where the hook would catch them. The first time it happened I dashed on deck as soon as I heard the reel go screeching out, much elated at the thought of fish, only to see a great flapping bird being dragged along the top of the water, with two of its mates, greatly perturbed about things, hovering over its head. Slowly I reeled in, grabbed the creature by the scruff of the neck and unhooked it. Then I threw it into the air and off it sailed, making two graceful circuits of the boat before doing exactly the same again. We soon grew bored with this and hauled in the line. We were hungry, but not hungry enough to eat albatrosses.

At last we crossed the ' Ultimate Whisky ' line, which left us with eight hundred and fifty miles to go. Almost immediately the wind shifted. With great delight, after five solid weeks on the starboard tack, we went about. There was a coat of barnacles all down the port side above the level of the anti-fouling paint, and the galley, for a change, leaned towards us instead of away. It took a day or two to get used to, but we were both jubilant.

It's a great event when, going to windward, you are at last able to head directly for your destination instead of merely towards it.

We were getting nearly to the end of our methylated spirits by this time, and the last of the paraffin had been poured into the Primus. How many more ' brew-ups ' could we manage with it, we wondered : six perhaps ?

With the freeing of the wind our speed increased. Seven hundred miles to go, six hundred . . . and then, for about the forty-ninth time, we split the Genoa. This time it was worse than usual ; the rent went right across and we had no light canvas left for patching. Jill kindly volunteered one of her skirts. " After all, it doesn't fit now, anyway." So our staid tan sail, after six hours' solid stitching, developed a gay white cotton stripe across it, enlivened by the signs of the zodiac in blue.

Three hundred miles to go. We felt we were practically there, and to confirm our optimism we saw a ship, the first we'd seen since leaving Tahiti. She was a long way off, but it was a memorable occasion. Our speed had increased greatly, and we dared to hope we'd perhaps make port in two days and a bit. I was taking sights every day now and had begun to wonder, as usual, whether the chronometer had kept it's rate properly. If it hadn't then we might have a day more or a day less at sea, depending on whether it had gone faster or slower than our estimate.

One hundred miles to go and the wind grew really boisterous. It was then that we ran into shallow water, shallow by comparison only, and the motion grew horribly violent. I sat at the helm for hours on end glorying in the speed but slightly apprehensive at the same time. We swooped and surged and curvetted on our way, and every now and then buried our nose in an unusually steep wave. In the normal course of events we should have reefed, but neither of us was in the mood.

" When do you think we'll see land ? " Jill asked.

" Sometime about midnight, I expect," I told her. " We go in between two islands about then, and both of them have lighthouses. If we don't see one we should certainly see the other."

" Oh, boy ; oh, boy ! Then with any luck we'll get in tomorrow. About midday. And we'll go ashore and have a bath and a really enormous meal. I wonder if we'll be able to get roast lamb."

We found that we'd enough whisky left for one largish drink apiece, or two smallish ones, and unanimously decided to make it one largish one. It was while we were having it that my nerve broke. " We'll really have to heave-to for a while," I said, " it'd be silly to go and carry away the mast now, and we're quite likely to if we go on like this much longer."

We hove-to. It was really rough now, but the temptation to go on had been strong.

For supper we had rice with curry powder in it. The last tin of meat had been eaten the day before. The methylated spirit was finished and the Primus was on its last sniff of paraffin. " Oh I DO hope we get in tomorrow," said Jill.

As darkness fell the wind lessened. We got under way once more and I peered eagerly round as the first watch wore on, looking for some sign of a lighthouse. Nothing was to be seen. I turned over to Jill at midnight and asked her to wake me as soon as she saw something. In my bunk I kept wondering and wondering whether the chronometer was right . . . why hadn't we seen a light ? Why ? Why ? Why ?

Four o'clock came and still nothing was in sight. " But I think it's a bit foggy," said Jill ; " perhaps we've gone past the island."

" Perhaps," I replied ; " but even if we passed one of them we should surely have seen the other. The gap between them is only about twelve miles."

The wind failed altogether. *Salmo* lay motionless in absolutely calm water. There seemed to be no point in staying on deck any longer, so I too went below to sleep. ' How long is this all going to last ? ' was my final thought before dropping off completely. The Pilot-book told us that on this coast fogs and calms were both very frequent at this time of year ; it was not an encouraging outlook.

Breakfast was a gloomy meal of cold curried rice. There was still no wind, and visibility was less than a mile. " Oh, well. If we don't get in today, then perhaps we'll manage to get in tomorrow," said Jill. " Oh, I DO hope we do."

A small breeze whiffled over the water just before mid-day and set us on our way once more. Simultaneously the haze partly cleared and allowed me to take a sight, which showed us to be where I thought we should be. . . . " Funny," I mused, " I suppose we COULD have gone between those two islands without seeing them. Well, if we did there's another that should show up fairly soon now, it's called Catalina Island."

The mist on the starboard bow shredded away as the sun sucked it up ; the base of the fog-bank took on a slightly solid look, and within moments we were able to identify it as Catalina. Almost immediately afterwards the same thing happened astern ; two islands appeared and we saw that we HAD come in between them. We danced a sort of jig together. After all this time it seemed almost too good to be true. *Salmo* had made her last landfall under our ownership, forty-six days out. And Jill, though hungry, was fighting fit.

CHAPTER EIGHTEEN

As we passed the northern tip of Catalina Island, our spinnaker set and pulling like a horse, an astonishing sight met our eyes, used as they were to seeing only our own two sails at the centre of an empty saucer of ocean. Streaming out from every cove and bay of the island's eastern shore were never-ending streams of yachts, each stream converging slightly until they merged into a mile-wide river of sails that vanished into the mist ahead.

It was, we suddenly realised, a Sunday, and all these hundreds of boats must belong to Los Angelans returning to their week's work.

We hoisted the U.S. flag to the starboard crosstree and proudly stuck the cleanest of our Blue Ensigns on the ensign staff, and our excitement mounted every moment as we closed in towards the fleet. All our hunger and worry were totally forgotten, and we chatted and laughed and felt as pleased with ourselves as we had when we'd found Pitcairn. Long before it was time to do so, and when the land was still only a grey and formless blur, we went down to the now gleaming cabin (for Jill, to ward off the gloom of the morning's calm, had spring-cleaned it to within an inch of its life) and changed into respectable clothes ; washed ourselves in unrationed bowls of fresh water and generally titivated. Jill's powder-compact, gold when the voyage had started, was now a greenish pewter shade, but she plied it none the less, determined that her nose should not shine for its first trip ashore for seven weeks. Another point was interesting her too. " Now,

does this skirt I made look all right ? " she kept asking.
" Are you SURE it doesn't look too home-made ? I've got
to wear it anyway because it's the only one that fits now.
But is the hem all right . . . not too wavy ? "

Quite truthfully I was able to assure her that it was a
thoroughly professional-looking job, and she sat down like
a lady to take the tiller on the home straight. A big
ocean racer, beautifully varnished, came sweeping past us,
her gleaming sails putting our poor tired mainsail to shame,
and we could see the crew eying us with interest, wondering quite obviously at our ensign and at the line of barnacles
that disfigured our cream topsides. Scrub as we would
we hadn't been able to remove the weal they had made.

The breakwater loomed up through the mist, with a
lighthouse on the end of it, and we began to wonder
what we should do once we were past it. We had no
chart of Los Angeles, and no idea what would appear
beyond the breakwater. And an awful thought struck
us. Would we, perhaps, have to anchor in some off-lying
quarantine anchorage until Monday morning ? No baths,
no food, no going ashore ?

This gloomy idea was momentarily banished by the
bustle of having to take off the spinnaker, but it returned
with renewed force when we found ourselves inside the
harbour. The river of boats had split up into little streams
once more, and each stream was headed for a different
part of the huge bay that the breakwater enclosed. We
had no idea which stream to follow, so blundered on in
the wake of our next ahead and hoped for the best.
There seemed to be more cranes and warehouses and tall
buildings in the direction he had chosen than in any other
direction, so we supposed that one of the buildings might
turn out to be a harbour office.

As we came closer and closer to the land, one building
in particular caught our eye. It had a flagstaff on top,
with a few balls and shapes dangling from it, as harbour

offices tend to have the world over. There was also a wooden jetty sticking out from the foot of it with a greenhouse affair at it's head, so we sailed as close as we dared and hove to.

Behind the glass windows we could see heads, a row of heads, so I shouted up asking where we could get inward clearance. One of the heads leaned out of the greenhouse with a loudspeaker and asked where we had come from.

" Tahiti," we shouted in chorus.

" You HAVE ? " said the head and disappeared again.

In a moment it reappeared and we realised that it was a most helpful and co-operative head. " You see that small pontoon across the way there ? " it said, pointing across the channel from where we lay ; " well, that's the Quarantine Station. You just go alongside there and there'll be a doctor waiting for you and I'll just ring up the Immigration Office right now. Good luck to you."

He waved in a friendly manner and off we shot across the channel. " Oh we WILL get baths. We WILL get supper. O I KNOW we will," Jill crooned to herself.

It hardly took five minutes to reach the quarantine jetty, but by the time we dropped our sails and slid along-side, the doctor was already waiting to take our lines.

" How long have you been away from land ? " he asked.

" Forty-seven days," we replied.

" Feeling pretty fit ? " said the doctor.

" Fine," we replied, " thank you."

" Well, I guess you can't be bringing much in the way of infection ashore then," said the doctor. " It's Sunday and my wife says things are always a bit of a mess Sundays, but if you would like to come over and have a bath and some supper she'd be proud to have you do so. The Immigration say they'll take care of you tomorrow morn-ing. If they came down to clear you right now you'd have to pay overtime, but if you'll wait right here till tomorrow morning they're quite agreeable."

It was almost too much. After all our awful visions of lying at anchor waiting for a quarantine launch and not being able to go ashore, this wonderful and friendly reception fairly took our breath away. In a sort of daze we followed the doctor up to his house, clutching our washing implements and our shoes, and feeling the land rolling gently beneath our feet. *Salmo*, when we looked back at her from the doorway, looked very small all of a sudden, and we both felt a clutch at our tummies as we realised that this would be one of the last times that we ever WOULD look back at her.

Two days later, at breakfast time, the mail arrived, and amongst other things came a huge parcel containing our film—all twenty-eight reels of it—and we grew madly excited.

" Oh give it to me, oh give it to me ; I want to open it," said Jill, grabbing it and slashing at the paper,the string, and the sealing wax with a rather buttery knife. The box burst open and a cascade of yellow boxes came slithering down onto the table.

" Oh, I wonder if they've come out. Oh, how can we look at them ? We MUST borrow a projector. Oh I can't bear it," she said, pawing at them, half opening the boxes and then deciding not to in case she put butter on the film.

At that moment a voice blared out over the loudspeaker system : " Mr HAMILTON, please, yacht *Salmo*. Telephone."

We had moved by this time from the Quarantine station where we had spent a blissful first evening, wallowing in boiling water and stuffing ourselves with supper, to a little harbour within a harbour called Henry's Yacht Station. Now instead of being the only yacht in the world (as we had often felt ourselves to be) we were just one rather small and grubby little boat amongst hundreds of other very glamorous ones. There were showers and telephones on the pontoons; we had the use of a refrigerator, and there was a swimming-pool and a restaurant and a barbecue pit at the head of the pontoon gangway. We had become part of a community and a very kindhearted and helpful community it was.

I clambered onto the pontoon and unhooked the telephone from its little box. "Hamilton speaking," I said.

It was a woman at the other end, very gushing, very golden voiced: "Oh is that Mr Hamilton. Oh good morning, Mr Hamilton. I represent the Jack Douglas Adventure Film Corporation, Mr Hamilton. Do I hear that you may have some movies that would be of interest to us for our programmes?"

I pricked up my ears immediately and asked who or what the Jack Douglas Adventure Film Corporation might be when it was at home.

"Oh, but, Mr HAMILTON," said the voice, deeply shocked, "we're the JACK DOUGLAS show. We do all the best adventure billings. We do ' Seven League Boots,' we do ' I Search for Adventure,' we do ' Bold Journey '; why, EVERYONE knows the Jack Douglas programmes."

"Are you," I said, inspired by a flash of genius, "anything to do with television?"

"Yes. But that's just what I've been saying, Mr Hamilton. We do ' Seven League Boots,' we do ' I Search for Adventure,' we do ' Bold Journey,' we do . . ."

"Yes," I said hastily, "yes, I think we've got just exactly what you're looking for. Shall I come up and see you?"

We fixed a date and I returned triumphantly to Jill. "We've got a date with a television tycoon who lives in Sunset Boulevard, Hollywood, California," I said. "Tomorrow. At eleven o'clock in the morning."

"Hooray," she shouted, "hooray-ooray-ooray. I KNEW

we'd meet a television tycoon sooner or later. I wonder what he'll be like."

" I wonder what the film'll be like," I countered rather gloomily, though I didn't feel gloomy, and we leaped ashore and cantered down the pontoon to go and tell all the neighbouring boats that we'd got a date in Hollywood and to find out who and what Jack Douglas was.

There were always little groups of people moving about on the pontoons, and we were so full of ourselves that we never noticed a family party approaching until they accosted us: " Why hullo, Jill ; hullo, Peter, we've come down to find you. How are you ? "

It was the Hathaways, the owners of the *Seafarer*, who'd towed us through the Panama Canal. The children were all with them, much bigger now than we remembered them (for the Panama Canal passage, incredible though it was to think of, was nearly a year behind us) and everyone began talking at once : " How did you get on ? " " Did you sell your film ? " " How was Pitcairn ? " " Where are the Hancocks ? "

The mystery of Jack Douglas was quickly explained. The Hathaways had sold the film that THEY had made to him. They had seen in the newspapers that we had come in (" Say, Jill, did you really have to patch the Genoa with your skirt or was that just a newspaper story ? ") and remembered that we too had been making a film. They'd got in touch with Jack Douglas, hence our telephone call. " And be sure," they told us, " that he gives you the full price if he buys it. Twelve hundred dollars : that's what we got."

" Oh boy, Oh boy, Oh boy, Oh boy," we began thinking to ourselves. " Twelve hundred dollars. Twelve HUNDRED," and we had so often been reduced to regarding twelve dollars as a fortune.

The thought of all this money went so much to our heads that we spent a terrible night dreaming that the film was a ghastly failure and that none of it had come out.

Very promptly at eleven the next morning, after a perfectly hellish journey on what we had now learned to call ' public transportation,' we presented ourselves at a delicately blue-painted door marked ' Jack Douglas Enterprises Inc.'

We were ushered inside and were greeted by a very soignée woman, the owner of my telephone voice. " Now good morning, Mr and Mrs Hamilton. Now may I have your movie, please, just so's we can give it a run through before Mr Douglas sees it ? "

I produced the battered ship's attaché-case from under my chair and tipped the twenty-eight reels in their boxes out onto the top of her immaculate desk. She looked as though I was pouring snakes onto her lap. With memories of the Toronto studio in our minds, we knew just what was going to come next.

" Why ! You mean to say you've not even EDITED all this. Not even JOINED IT TOGETHER ? "

" Oh, no," said Jill, chattily, " we've not even seen it yet. It only arrived from England yesterday."

" You've not even SEEN IT ? " said the woman, giving me an extremely dirty look. " Why, Mr Hamilton, I thought you said . . . well, I guess you'll just have to get it all onto two reels now," and she ushered us out into a bare sort of passage where there was a viewing bench standing against one wall. She waved at this, " There's all you'll need there. Reels, cement, everything," and then she swirled back into the office and shut the door with a decisive click.

We looked at each other : " Do you have any idea at all how to splice these things together? " said Jill, " because I haven't."

" No, none at all," I replied, " I did once read about it in a book, but I can't remember what it said. I hadn't the heart to ask our girl friend because she seemed so upset."

"Yes," said Jill, "she did seem upset, didn't she."

At this moment a man in shirt-sleeves shot into the passage with a pile of films in his arms. Saw us. Stopped dead and then said, "Aw hell, you using this machine? O.K.," and started backing out again.

"Oh, excuse me," we said, waving helplessly at our pile of reels, "but we've got to splice all these together. Do you think you could show us how to do it?"

"Show you how to do it?" he said, much surprised. "Yeh, I suppose so," and then, realising from our accents that we must be strangers, he suddenly became friendly, dumped his pile of film in a corner, and settled down on the bench to give a running commentary: "Now you put the end of the film in like this, see and clamp it with this gimmick here . . . say, where do you folks come from anyway? . . . then you scrape off the emulsion like this . . . why I bet you're the first that've been in this office for years that have had to be shown how to JOINT a film . . . then you take the cement and dab it on like this, eh? . . . How many reels you got? Twenty-eight! Huh, why boy, that's going to take you quite some time. Yeh, quite some time . . . and there you are, see? The joint's made. Got it?"

"Yes, thank you very much," we said. "Yes, I think we've got it."

It certainly did take quite some time. Clamp, scrape, cut, glue, press, and then again, clamp, scrape, cut, glue and press. The office staff went out to lunch and left us locked inside alone, cutting, pressing and glueing.

At last we got the whole job finished and went back into the office where our hostess had once more recovered her poise. In our hands we bore, instead of twenty-eight little reels, two great big ones, and we were ushered back to our chairs again, and a slinky dove-grey projector was produced from a box and the first of our reels put onto it. The curtains were drawn and a white square of light flashed onto the wall in front of us.

" Seven, six, five, four, three, two, one," went the white square rather unexpectedly, as the leader ran through the machine . . . blackness for a while—and then *Salmo* suddenly leapt onto the wall, her tan sails barely drawing, as we saw ourselves leaving Montreal and slipping beneath the Jacques Cartier bridge, just as we had done on that morning that now seemed so long ago.

It was all wonderfully thrilling, that first sight of our film. We frightened ourselves once more with the sight of the long white icefloes, laughed at the sea-lions on the sand at Barrington Island, and watched in silence as the gale sequence off Rapa made *Salmo's* mast twist and turn anew on the white office wall while the great Southern Ocean rollers came bursting up from astern of her. Bits of the film, of course, were terribly disappointing. One whole reel seemed to have melted, and many of the shots seemed silly and meaningless, but in amongst it all were bits that we knew were good.

But what would Jack Douglas think of it ? That was the question. It was fun for us, we knew. But then we were biased. Our audience had remained silent throughout the showing ; only the sea-lions seemed to have entertained her. We didn't know what she thought.

She took the two reels under her arm and left the room. We sat rather nervously on our chairs trying to pretend we didn't care whether the film was accepted or not, and wondered what sort of impression it had made on professional eyes.

" Will you step up this way, please, Mrs Hamilton, Mr Hamilton ? Mr Douglas would like to see you now."

We went up to the next floor in a lift, a door swung open and we were ushered into the presence. Mr Douglas, quite obviously, was a keen film-goer and knew exactly what a Hollywood executive's office ought to look like. His looked exactly like it, for it had rows of Oscars standing on ledges and a carpet with a pile like a hayfield. Douglas himself was sitting behind a desk that was nearly as large as a billiard table, in a complicated sort of dentist's chair that allowed him to put his legs on the desk with the minimum trouble. That's where they were when we came in and he was speaking on the telephone. " No. Tell them we can't take it. How much did you say ? Half a million ? No. No. What ? Warner Brothers DID ? You don't say. . . ."

We wondered if the telephone was connected to anyone or was just for our benefit. He waved to us, flashed Jill a photogenic smile, laid down the first telephone and picked up another one. " Harry. Call me back later. I don't want to be disturbed right now. No. Not for another half-hour. No. Not for anyone. They'll all have to wait." He laid that receiver down, too, and greeted us with great cordiality. " Why, delighted to make your acquaintance, Mrs Hamilton, ma'am. Mr Hamilton. Now sit right down, Mrs Hamilton. Quite comfortable ? Good. Now can we just run through this movie of yours and perhaps you can give a little commentary ? Fine. Fine."

And we settled down for Round two, the novelty of sailing down the St Lawrence, meeting ice, and going through New York harbour wearing a little thinner this time. We left the ice, we met a whale, and finally reached New York again : " and here we are going down the East River with Manhattan in the background. In a boat without an engine . . ."

" Say," said Mr Douglas, " isn't that the United Nations building there ? "

" Yes," I said, " it is. Now, without an engine in a boat it's . . ."

" Why, Janet," he switched off the machine and turned

to his faithful lieutenant, " we could make a good comment about that. That'd be right popular."

" Why yes, Mr Douglas. Yes, it would."

He turned back to me. " Now I think in your commentary, Mr Hamilton, you should make a little MORE of the United Nations building. Any little thing would do, something like : ' Now, we in Britain have heard of the United Nations and we think it was mighty generous of the United States of America to have donated the ground on which their headquarters has been erected. And I'm sure that if United States had NOT donated the ground, then we in Britain would have been proud to have done so.' "

" Why yes, Mr Douglas," said Janet. " Yes, I think that's JUST the sort of comment that could very well be made there."

I was a little more doubtful, and murmured something about " not quite sure that I think it's very appropriate," but no one paid any attention. The show went on.

We were spared having to do more than one of the reels. The first, as a sample, was apparently adequate, so we sat down to talk turkey.

" Why, I reckon that's fine. Just fine," said Douglas. " We'll draw up the contract right away." He picked up one of the telephones and asked Sadie to come through.

Sadie came through, or rather she poked her nose round the door as if she expected someone to grab it and drag her round the room. " Yes, Mr Douglas ; you rang, Mr Douglas ? "

" Yes, Sadie. Just take the Hamiltons' particulars, here, and make out the usual contract for them. It's for ' Bold Journey ' and also for ' I Search for Adventure.' "

" Yes, Mr Douglas. How much shall I make the contract out for, Mr Douglas ? "

A cloud passed across Mr Douglas's godlike brow and

he said rather impatiently, " We'll give the Hamiltons top price, Sadie ; top price."

" Er, yes, Mr Douglas," said Sadie uncertainly, and hesitated for a moment, " Er . . . what IS top price, Mr Douglas ? "

" Twelve hundred," he almost shouted at her, and off shot Sadie, determined to go while the going was good, and we heard the rattle of her typewriter floating gently in from the next door office as she wrote up our contracts. We'd never signed contracts before and it made us feel frightfully important.

That was the beginning of a couple of weeks of darned hard work. Every morning, sometimes with Jill, but more often alone, I used to closet myself with a professional editor in one of the Hollywood studio workshops while we snipped out bits of film here and snipped out bits there to reduce an hour and three-quarters' worth of material into a coherent twenty-five minutes. All round us sat other editors snipping and reeling and synchronising sound-tracks, and the room was a bedlam . . . but it was interesting to see the professional touch, and learn how to take two apparently unconnected shots, join them together and find that they made a little story . . . even though it wasn't necessarily the story we had intended when we took them.

One thing that was missing was interior shots. We hadn't been able to take them because we had no lighting equipment, so we arranged for one of Jack Douglas's entourage to come down with some lights, borrow our camera, and take them for us.

The man appeared one morning while we were still eating breakfast, with a list in his hand of what he had been told to produce, and we waded through the sequences with great stoicism, even to the lengths of eating interminable hanks of uncooked spaghetti, with cold tomato sauce (to give it a good colour) poured over it. On top

of a large breakfast, this was suffering in the cause of art
in a very big way.

" Now, there's just one more shot I'd like to take,"
said the man, an earnest youth with spectacles, " and
that's one that we'd work in at the very beginning of the
movie : of you, Mr Hamilton, carrying your bride on
board, over the threshold as it were. . . ."

Jill by this time had achieved a distinctly portly silhouette and was wearing the latest thing in maternity
wear, so we both burst out laughing and suggested that
if he did that the film should be called ' Maidens, Beware.'

The young man blushed deeply and said no, he guessed
that that shot might not be very suitable after all, because
' Bold Journey ' was a very PARTICULAR programme. They
never even associated themselves with cigarettes or alcohol
advertising. . . .

We woke up very early indeed on our last day but one
in California, and paddled along the pontoon in pyjamas
to have showers. Three big packing-cases stood with their
lids off, encumbering our passage. They were marked in
large black letters ' Cyanide Gas. VERY DANGEROUS '
and we had scrounged them to receive all our belongings
for shipment back to England. Salmo had been sold,
and we were living on board by sufferance only, and bottled
up inside us was a turmoil of emotions : excitement, sad-
ness and (on Jill's part particularly) an ' OH-we'll-never-
be-ready ' sort of feeling, each taking it in turn to take
control.

After our showers we ate boiled eggs and drank coffee,
washed up (still in the pressure-cooker) for the last time,
and started to pack.

" We'll do the books first," said Jill, and began to
hand them out to me. Most of the covers were stained
with salt water from the splashes that had hit them when
they had been read in the cockpit, and their faded backs,

blue, red, green and brown, recalled all the peaceful sunny days which had been spent in their company rippling over the great blue distances. . . . Shakespeare, ' Other Men's Flowers,' Winnie The Poo, ' Birds of the Ocean ' . . . all were very much read, very much liked. I laid them in their cyanide crate and more books came out and more, and more—Flecker, Kipling, Steinbeck, Conrad —all were crated, and the cabin, our familiar homely cabin, began to look bare and unlived-in.

" What about the cutlery ? " said Jill. " We can take that with us, can't we ? "

" No, of course we can't," I said, " it goes with the boat. You'll be wanting to take the sails back with you next."

" Oh, I HATE parting with it all," she said. " How about the pressure-cooker ? Oh, I MUST take the pressure-cooker. Surely they won't want that ? Oh, I MUST take it home."

And so it went on. Item by item came out. Clothes, bedding, chronometer (we left the sextant so that the new owner could learn to navigate), ensigns, registration certificate, cameras, were laid away and the lids were nailed onto two of the crates.

Time was running out. Our television interview was nearly on us so we had to stop . . . ten o'clock sharp was what we had been told to prepare for. Our faces were running with sweat, so we dived back into the shower again, taking the opportunity to shove all the crates well out of the picture, for *Salmo* was to star in the interview, and we wanted her to look lived in and not as if she was no longer ours.

The camera-men were the first to arrive. They swept up in a big white Plymouth and began to assemble their equipment while we watched in wonder their open-toed shoes, their shirts besprinkled with palm-trees and bathing belles, and one whose cap was of the tartan of the Clan Cameron.

While they opened their tripods, mounted their cameras and ran out their cables, we were taken in hand by a little old Austrian in a black suit and with a bootlace fastening to his monogrammed shirt. He sat us beneath a striped umbrella beside the barbecue pit and plied his brushes, his paints and his unguents.

Stage directors, sound-men, clapper-operators, a continuity girl in a Tyrolean hat, and our golden-voiced friend Janet turned up, and an air of expectation pervaded the scene . . . we were like an orchestra awaiting the arrival of the conductor. The sun blazed down, the U.S. flag at *Salmo's* crosstrees stirred very faintly as a zephyr breath plucked at it, but the ensign hung limp at its staff, and I felt beads of sweat gathering along my spine ; everyone began to glance furtively at his watch and we saw the time was one minute to ten o'clock.

A melodious toot came from the car-park entrance and a Cadillac swept over the gravel ; the door opened and out stepped Mr Jack Douglas in light-grey trousers and an immaculate white shirt. A dresser followed him with his jacket on a coathanger, and I found myself murmuring snatches of the ' Jackdaw of Rheims ' . . . ' a nice little boy held a nice cake of soap, worthy of washing the hands of the Pope. . . .'

Jill and I were arranged upon the cabin top in graceful attitudes while Jack Douglas, still coatless, practised holding onto the shrouds in a nautical manner in order to talk to us.

" How's this for angle ? " he called to the tartan-hatted camera-man.

" Mr Douglas is never photographed in profile," murmured the stage director in our ear, " always three-quarter face or full face."

" Quite so," we murmured back. " Quite so."

" O.K. for angle, Mr Douglas. O.K. for lighting."

A microphone was passed round from hand to hand

and we all spoke into it in turn. Adjustments were made and then it was " O.K. for sound."

Mr Douglas's jacket was reverently taken off its coat-hanger and off we went.

" Well, ladies and gentlemen, here we are again to welcome to Los Angeles charming Jill Hamilton and her seafaring husband Peter, who have just completed their BOLD JOURNEY (we could practically hear the roll of drums that would be dubbed in in the workshop).

" Now, good morning, Jill and Peter Hamilton, may I come on board your staunch little craft ? "

" Good morning, Mr Douglas," we said in unison.

" Cut ! " yelled everyone else, also in unison.

" Now, for goodness' sake. Don't you do the reserved Britisher stuff here. Everyone's friendly round these parts. It's not ' Good morning, Mr Douglas,' it's ' Good morning, Jack.' "

We started off again. The cameras ground round, we ' Good morning, Jack-ed ' and the show went on, medium shot, long shot, and close up, the continuity girl dragooning everyone into their right positions for all the re-takes : " Now for this one, Mrs Hamilton, your legs were crossed and your right hand was resting on your knee. No. Not quite like that, a little lower, that's just right. . . ."

The interview safely over at last, we went back to the Hollywood studio to show the film. We had seen it so often by this time that we knew it almost by heart : down the St Lawrence, ice, New York, the Galapagos Islands. We only had to shut our eyes and we could practically see the film playing, we'd seen so much of it in the cutting-room. We were beginning to hate the darned film. Out rolled our commentary, taking it in turn, nudging each other when it was time to change over, trying not to sound nervous, trying not to let any ' ers ' get into what we were saying.

Tahiti flashed onto the screen, Jill was doing this bit :

" It was at Tahiti that we had to make a change in our plans.   Instead of going on westward as we had intended, we had to turn north-east and aim for the United States."

The scene on the monitor changed from Tahiti to some views of porpoises, a sunset or two, and finally the break-water at Los Angeles.   I took over here : " At last, after forty-seven days at sea, we sighted land . . . sailed through the calm water of the harbour, and finally, after all our voyaging, we leave *Salmo* lying peacefully moored. . . ."   The picture faded.   The studio lights came on, and a general air of relief and relaxed tension swept over everyone.

It was our last ordeal.   Back on board we nailed the lid over the remaining crate, packed our suitcases and walked from the pontoon.

Salmo still lay moored in the placid water of the yacht station, but now it was the U.S. Flag which drooped from her ensign staff, and her new owner would come down early in the morning to take possession of her.

But we, by that time, were half the world away, roaring over the Atlantic in an air-liner.

APPENDIX

SOME RANDOM THOUGHTS ON LONG CRUISES

JILL says that I am didactic, overbearing and generally insufferable when goaded to talk about boats, and also that I suffer from the illusion that no one else knows anything about them. What follows, she says, is all good enough stuff in its way, but the tone of patronage is appalling. I will therefore recommend that anyone who is in any way a sailor should skip it, lest he grow infuriated.

The most difficult part of a cruise is certainly the start of it. Revolutions are always painful, and it needs a little private revolution within yourself before you can jump out of one way of life and take to a boat and find the whole world lying at your feet, waiting to be visited.

And then there is the decision to be made about companions. More cruises come to grief from ill-assorted crews than from any other reason. During our own cruise we met very many boats—far more than I have been able to talk about. Some were happy and enjoying themselves ; some were grimly determined to keep going because it was difficult to turn back (but it was a joyless existence) and others again had given up, their dreams shattered.

There seems to be a lot of truth in the maxim ' If you want a good crew, then you should marry her.' But if that solution doesn't offer, then a single-handed voyage may well be the best answer.

It is only after you have decided upon your crew that you should decide about your boat. And the best boat for the purpose is almost certainly the best boat you can afford, so long as the money is spent on the boat herself and not upon embellishments. For the more you have in a boat, then the more there is that can go wrong with her. If, for example, you decide to take no engine, then you need no holes in the hull that may one day leak : furthermore, if you take no engine, you don't have to carry petrol, and you don't have to carry tools and spare parts to keep the engine running. And if you don't carry a wireless, then you don't have to have a generating-set. Batteries, too, are hard to come by in far-off places. And if you don't have a wireless, then you don't have to listen to weather forecasts, so you have no reason to grow depressed and worried before a gale arrives. No gale arrives so suddenly that a small boat does not have time to take every necessary measure in ample time.

And remember, when thinking of gales and the measures you will adopt to make yourself comfortable and safe while they are raging, that much more of your life will be spent in finer weather. So don't choose a boat which can only sail and be comfortable in a gale. And remember that when you hear a man boast that his boat is a wonderful seaboat, that what he really means is almost certainly ' It takes a gale to make my boat sail.' For all well-built and well-designed boats are wonderful seaboats. But some of them will get you to your destination faster than others. And the fun of sailing is far more in the arriving than in the sailing itself, so why spend more of your time at sea than you have to ?

And always remember that the sea has the last word. If you argue with the sea and try to be clever and snatch a few extra miles from a favourable gale (and who doesn't), sooner or later (and probably sooner) you will regret it, for the force of a wave that comes over a boat and not under it is very frightening. So you should always try to make the waves stay where they belong, which is beneath you. And remember that an orange-box is a very fragile sort of boat ; yet an orange-box will remain undamaged in the roughest sea BECAUSE IT ALWAYS GIVES WAY TO IT.

And remember that the strength of your rigging is the strength of the weakest bit of it—which may well be a shackle or a bottle-screw, or a length of stainless steel wire that has been curved too tightly round a thimble (though it may still look perfect). And that the only way to be certain that shackles and wires are in good condition is to look at them . . . even if they are at the masthead. Though it's very heroic to bring your boat in safely after she has been dismasted or half-wrecked, it is far more pleasant when she hasn't. And considerably less expensive.

Which brings us to money—another very frequent cause for abandoned cruises. For even in far-off places you still must eat, and so must the inhabitants of those places, so you must not expect them to come racing to greet you with presents or to refit your boat without accepting payment. And if they do, then surely, for your own self-respect, must you not give them back something, even if the return gift is much delayed ?

A reasonable figure to calculate on, for the expenses of two people and a small boat, is £50 per month, though that does not leave much over for frivolities. And though, perhaps, writing about your experiences may seem to be the simplest way of providing those £50 each month, you must remember that editors too have a living to make ; and they have a wide choice of contributors ; for at any one time there are probably nearly twenty small boats engaged in trundling their way around the world.

But money may be made in other ways than writing. In far-off places for instance, a knowledge of medicine, or of dentistry or of boatbuilding or metalwork are all in high demand. But you must have the tools of your trade in your possession, for they do not grow on palm-trees.

And though it is painful for a Briton to acknowledge the

fact, dollars are far more useful than pounds, so you should
do your best to arrange things accordingly.

Food is only as good as the cook allows it to be. So
before you set sail, make sure that you can cook. And
that if there are two of you then that both of you can
cook. For why should one person always do it ? Tinned
food is expensive and not always particularly convenient
or palatable. So take as much that is fresh as possible.
And you can salt things, and you can use dehydrated
things, and you can bake bread and scones and such.

When calculating the length of your voyagings allow
100 miles a day, or if you are single-handed and without
a means of making the boat steer herself, then cut it down
to seventy-five miles a day. And remember that water
caught in the sails or on deck is fine for washing in, but
perfectly beastly to drink. So take lots of fresh water
because it makes life so much pleasanter. And half a
gallon a day per person is ' lots.' And towards the end
of the trip, when you find you have more left than you
thought you had, then you can use it for washing and
similar luxuries.

Don't forget to buy paraffin before you sail, or food
either, for that matter.

And don't ever be put off from going where you want
to go. Nine times out of ten the person who advises
against it knows nothing about the facts of the case. And
even if he does, it's worth trying to confirm them.

Navigation is said to be the art of taking a ship in
safety from one point on the earth's surface to another.
The operative phrase is ' In Safety.' How you decide to
do it really doesn't matter, though as a general rule you
must know all the accepted rules before you decide to
disregard them. And if you do disregard them and come
to grief as a result, then you have only yourself to thank.
You need not overburden yourself with charts. But remember that if you are in waters which are to you un-

charted, then you must be cautious. And that though you may waste a few hours by heaving to to wait for daylight or a break in a fog, you may waste a few months if you hit a rock. And ships are more easily wrecked in harbour than they are at sea. For anchors drag ; or anchor chains part, or the wash from passers-by may throw you against a wall or you may be rammed.

And do not set too great a store on lifeboats and life-rafts and lifelines and lifebelts. Try instead to avoid having to need them. It is easier to fall overboard on a calm day through carelessness than ever it is when it is rough. For when it is rough it is instinctive to take pre-cautions. And if you are single-handed then you're far more likely to come to grief by slipping on a wet deck and breaking an arm or a leg than you are being run down by a passing liner while you sleep . . . or of hitting an iceberg, or of any of the other much publicised hazards of the deep. Yet people don't worry about falling down, so why should they worry and take expensive and over-elaborate precautions about collision ? But perhaps the best precaution against collision that can be taken very often isn't—that is to choose a route where no other ships are likely to go.

But having said all this I remember the best advice that was ever given to me, which was ' Take a dinner jacket.'